Elisa Kriza

ALEXANDER SOLZHENITSYN: COLD WAR ICON, GULAG AUTHOR, RUSSIAN NATIONALIST?

A Study of the Western Reception of his Literary Writings, Historical Interpretations, and Political Ideas

With a foreword by Andrei Rogatchevski

ibidem-Verlag
Stuttgart

Bibliographic information published by the Deutsche Nationalbibliothek
Die Deutsche Nationalbibliothek lists this publication in the Deutsche Nationalbibliografie; detailed bibliographic data are available in the Internet at http://dnb.d-nb.de.

Bibliografische Information der Deutschen Nationalbibliothek
Die Deutsche Nationalbibliothek verzeichnet diese Publikation in der Deutschen Nationalbibliografie; detaillierte bibliografische Daten sind im Internet über http://dnb.d-nb.de abrufbar.

Cover picture: "Solzhenitsyn in February" © Elisa Kriza, 2014. Indian ink and watercolor on paper.

ISSN: 1614-3515

ISBN-13 Paperback edition: 978-3-8382-0689-9

ISBN-13 Hardcover edition: 978-3-8382-0690-5

Printed in the United States of America

Soviet and Post-Soviet Politics and Society (SPPS)

ISSN 1614-3515

Soviet and Post-Soviet Politics and Society (SPPS)

ISSN 1614-3515

Founded in 2004 and refereed since 2007, SPPS makes available affordable English-, German-, and Russian-language studies on the history of the countries of the former Soviet bloc from the late Tsarist period to today. It publishes between 5 and 20 volumes per year and focuses on issues in transitions to and from democracy such as economic crisis, identity formation, civil society development, and constitutional reform in CEE and the NIS. SPPS also aims to highlight so far understudied themes in East European studies such as right-wing radicalism, religious life, higher education, or human rights protection. The authors and titles of all previously published volumes are listed at the end of this book. For a full description of the series and reviews of its books, see www.ibidem-verlag.de/red/spps.

Editorial correspondence & manuscripts should be sent to: Dr. Andreas Umland, DAAD, German Embassy, vul. Bohdana Khmelnitskoho 25, UA-01901 Kyiv, Ukraine. e-mail: umland@stanfordalumni.org

Business correspondence & review copy requests should be sent to: ***ibidem*** Press, Leuschnerstr. 40, 30457 Hannover, Germany; tel.: +49 511 2622200; fax: +49 511 2622201; spps@ibidem.eu.

Authors, reviewers, referees, and editors for (as well as all other persons sympathetic to) SPPS are invited to join its networks at www.facebook.com/group.php?gid=52638198614 www.linkedin.com/groups?about=&gid=103012 www.xing.com/net/spps-ibidem-verlag/

Recent Volumes

122 *Michael Moser*
Language Policy and the Discourse on Languages in Ukraine under President Viktor Yanukovych (25 February 2010–28 October 2012)
ISBN 978-3-8382-0497-0 (Paperback edition)
ISBN 978-3-8382-0507-6 (Hardcover edition)

123 *Nicole Krome*
Russischer Netzwerkkapitalismus
Restrukturierungsprozesse in der Russischen Föderation am Beispiel des Luftfahrtunternehmens "Aviastar"
Mit einem Vorwort von Petra Stykow
ISBN 978-3-8382-0534-2

124 *David R. Marples*
'Our Glorious Past'
Lukashenka's Belarus and the Great Patriotic War
ISBN 978-3-8382-0574-8 (Paperback edition)
ISBN 978-3-8382-0675-2 (Hardcover edition)

125 *Ulf Walther*
Russlands "neuer Adel"
Die Macht des Geheimdienstes von Gorbatschow bis Putin
Mit einem Vorwort von Hans-Georg Wieck
ISBN 978-3-8382-0584-7

126 *Simon Geissbühler (Hrsg.)*
Kiew – Revolution 3.0
Der Euromaidan 2013/14 und die Zukunftsperspektiven der Ukraine
ISBN 978-3-8382-0581-6 (Paperback edition)
ISBN 978-3-8382-0681-3 (Hardcover edition)

127 *Andrey Makarychev*
Russia and the EU in a Multipolar World
Discourses, Identities, Norms
ISBN 978-3-8382-0529-8

128 *Roland Scharff*
Kasachstan als postsowjetischer Wohlfahrtsstaat
Die Transformation des sozialen Schutzsystems
Mit einem Vorwort von Joachim Ahrens
ISBN 978-3-8382-0622-6

129 *Katja Grupp*
Bild Lücke Deutschland
Kaliningrader Studierende sprechen über Deutschland
Mit einem Vorwort von Martin Schulz
ISBN 978-3-8382-0552-6

130 *Konstantin Sheiko, Stephen Brown*
History as Therapy
Alternative History and Nationalist Imaginings in Russia, 1991-2014
ISBN 978-3-8382-0565-6

In loving memory of my grandfather, Teodoro García (1921-2013)

Contents

Foreword

A SALAMANDER IN PERMAFROST?

Without Solzhenitsyn the world would hardly have been the same—but does the changing world still need him? As Elisa Kriza's book demonstrates, the answer often depends on where and who you are and which part of the author's legacy you prefer to focus on.

In Russia, Solzhenitsyn's works defeated the Soviet ban, have (re-)entered the school curriculum and are being staged and televised. His *Dictionary of Linguistic Expansion* (1990)—a quixotic attempt to save underused Russian vocabulary from oblivion—has recently gone into a third edition. The Customs Union of Belarus, Kazakhstan, and Russia, in operation since 2010, can be seen as a partial implementation of Solzhenitsyn's 1990 manifesto *Rebuilding Russia*, which advocated fostering ties between Russia, Belarus, and Ukraine; and suggestively noted the share of Southern Siberia and the Ural Mountains in what Kazakhstan consists of. His film scripts about a Soviet car mechanic (*The Parasite*, 1968) and the Kengir uprising (*Tanks Know the Truth*, 1959) are perhaps the only substantial pieces that remain unwanted, possibly because of their high production costs.

As far as the West is concerned, with communism in retreat, Solzhenitsyn is no longer a household name as one of the doctrine's most iconic detractors and victims. The general decline of the readership in our increasingly visual age is probably affecting Solzhenitsyn more than other authors, because the average length of his books appears prohibitive even to those appreciably intrigued by his controversial (or maybe misunderstood) views on Nazism, homosexuality, Western democracy, and the role of Jews in Russian history (all of which are discussed in Kriza's study). Anybody who has read Solzhenitsyn's unfinished *Red Wheel* epic, about World War I and the Russian Revolutions of 1917—in its entirety, in ten volumes, up to 800 pages each—may well deserve a monument.

Of Solzhenitsyn's relatively shorter fiction, his 1962 novella about Soviet labour camp experience in the early 1950s, *One Day in the Life of Ivan Denisovich* (his arguably best known and most impactful title), is frequently perceived to be of purely historical significance, while his novel *Cancer Ward*

(1967) is likely to gain following among cancer patients and their friends and relatives, given that the number of cancer cases across the globe, now at approximately 14 million annually, is expected to rise twofold over the next two decades. Solzhenitsyn's memoirs about his life in the West, *The Grain and the Millstones* (1998-2003; a sequel to the 1975 USSR-based *The Oak and the Calf*), are bound to cause quite a stir when they are translated into English—but they have not yet appeared as a separate edition even in Russia, although more than ten years have passed since the last instalment in their serialization (the delay may have been caused by some potentially litigious content).

According to Kriza, Western academia may have a role to play in helping Solzhenitsyn retain some form of public interest beyond Russia, especially if his reception is regularly mediated by recourse to various literary theories (as opposed to judgements dictated largely by political stances and affiliations). All in all, it is not easy to speculate if Solzhenitsyn's Western reputation as a credible artist-cum-prophet would rebound any time soon, or, to use his own image from the preface to *The Gulag Archipelago*, his ideas would stay well preserved, like a salamander in permafrost, hoping to impress distant future generations. Meanwhile, in 2012, as a testimony to Solzhenitsyn's lasting relevance, the Council of Paris voted (against the objections from the Left) to name a city square in his honour. This may or may not be an encouraging sign.

Andrei Rogatchevski
Professor of Russian Literature and Culture
University of Tromsø, Norway

Acknowledgements

This book is based on the doctoral research I conducted as a fellow at Aarhus University. First of all, I would like to thank the Faculty of Arts for the generous stipend that made this project possible. I am deeply grateful to my supervisor Karen-Margrethe Simonsen of the Section of Comparative Literature for her valuable advice and her helpful comments on my text. I also thank my co-supervisor Henrik Kaare Nielsen, and the members of my PhD defence committee—Svend Erik Larsen, Galin Tihanov, and Anja Tippner—for their insightful observations on my thesis. I would like to express my gratitude to Andreas Umland, the editor of this series, and *ibidem*-Verlag for the opportunity to publish in a series I have long been a fan of. I thank Andrei Rogatchevski for his detailed reading of my manuscript and for kindly contributing the foreword of this book. I would also like to thank Victoria Gosling, my proof-reader, for her good work. I am very grateful to my husband, Thomas, for his unwavering support and encouragement (not only) while I worked on this project.

Aleksandr Solzhenitsyn, Russian writer and Nobel prize winner, looks out from a train, in Vladivostok, summer 1994, before departing on a journey across Russia.

Photo by Mikhail Evstafiev.

1. Introduction

1.1 The Goal and the Scope of the Study

In this book I analyze the reception of the Russian writer Alexander Solzhenitsyn in three Western countries: the US, the UK, and the Federal Republic of Germany. My goal is not a quantitative study of Solzhenitsyn's reception in its entirety but a qualitative analysis under specific perspectives. I investigate the role of the historical and political context in Solzhenitsyn's reception and its effect on the canonization of his works. Furthermore, I propose new critical readings of his work from a contemporary viewpoint.

The end of 2013 marked exactly forty years since a Russian émigré publisher in Paris printed the first edition of Solzhenitsyn's *The Gulag Archipelago*. The apex of Solzhenitsyn's world fame is now a few decades behind us. What makes a study of his reception relevant today?

Studying the reception of this author is relevant both in a particular sense and more generally. First of all, the results of this study have broader significance because the process of Solzhenitsyn's international canonization is associated with his status both as a victim of state violence and as a dissident—and this is not unique to the Soviet case. Identifying different canonization mechanisms operating in his reception will give insight into the influence of political, humanitarian, and/or ethical criteria in the assessment of literature under similar circumstances.

Furthermore, Solzhenitsyn is a Nobel Prize winner, and he is an author often described as one of the most significant writers of the 20th century. He has a vast international reception which has received scant attention, making a new and updated study necessary. It is therefore relevant to study the reception of one of the Cold War's most iconic authors in itself.

Out of the hundreds of dissident writers in Russian history I have chosen to focus on Solzhenitsyn because political dissent has been more central to his reception than it was in the case of other politically troubled authors, such as Alexander Pushkin, or Joseph Brodsky. In my book, I will explore why this aspect of Solzhenitsyn's work is so central, and why his reception seems much more ample than that of similarly politicized writers such as Andrey Sinyavsky.

Solzhenitsyn belonged to the generation of dissidents who enjoyed a period of cultural freedom during the Khrushchev era (1953-1964), only to be persecuted in the more restrictive environment under Brezhnev (1964-1982). In 1974, he was forced into emigration like many other dissidents. For twenty years he belonged to the Russian Diaspora and émigré culture. Widespread Western interest in the Soviet dissident movement of the late 60s and 70s welcomed him and gave his work an international platform. Because of both foreign interest in dissidents, and his forced exile in the West, Solzhenitsyn became an international object of research and journalism. A foreign gaze focused upon Solzhenitsyn and his work is bound to offer different perspectives than a Russian observation would. In this book I analyze what it was that sparked special interest in the author, but also delve into possible misunderstandings and misrepresentations relating to him. I also take a look at Solzhenitsyn's place among émigrés and the type of conflicts that arose from his peculiar position.

The time scope of this study will begin with Solzhenitsyn's first work, which was published in 1962, and end shortly after 2008, the year of the author's death. This will allow a contrastive analysis of his reception both before and well after the end of the Cold War. The temporal distance from the crest of Solzhenitsyn's Western reception makes both a diachronic as well as a synchronic approach more accessible. The fact that Solzhenitsyn passed away and that the corpus of his work is now complete makes it feasible to follow the ups and downs of his reception within the context of his entire oeuvre.

As opposed to earlier reception studies of Solzhenitsyn's work, I not only analyze his reception but also examine aspects of his work it relates to. Solzhenitsyn's texts have a characteristic ambiguity in genre and authorial voice that had an often neglected impact on their reception. As I will show in this book, this is central to the interpretation of his reception. The parallel presentation of reception and the problematization of key aspects in Solzhenitsyn's oeuvre will allow me to map the various ways this author has been read, but also ways he has not been read. Areas of emphasis and neglect are both very telling with regard to the workings of Western criticism.

In my study, I will update the discussion on Solzhenitsyn by drawing on recent developments in three areas of study: witness literature, politics and aesthetics, and the role of literature in historiography and memory culture.

The structure of this book will reflect these three areas. This is a new and modern approach to the topic that will contribute to contemporary theoretical debates on a general level.

Two core chapters—chapters two and three—build the body of my reception analysis. Chapter two is defined by the theme of witness literature,[1] and starts with an analysis of the genre and style of Solzhenitsyn's prison camp-related works *One Day in the Life of Ivan Denisovich*, *First Circle*, and *The Gulag Archipelago*. These three works are worthy of special attention for two reasons. The most obvious one is that these are Solzhenitsyn's most influential books. Additionally, it is because of their subject matter—the prison camp experience—that close attention needs to be paid to their genre and authorial voice. Because Solzhenitsyn was a survivor of the Soviet prison camps, the reception of the connection between fact and fiction in these works is particularly complex. I therefore begin this chapter with an introduction of the style and genre of these three works, and discuss the authorial voice in them. This is a key foundation for later discussions of different forms of reception. I then elaborate upon the relationship between the authorial voice used in these works and their genre, and reflect on the way this can be integrated into theoretical ponderings about witness literature and camp literature. Many scholars who have written about these works emphasize their character as testimonial texts and theoreticians of witness literature and camp literature consider them to belong to these genres. In section 2.2 I will bring these two—very similar—genres into a dialogue about Solzhenitsyn's work and its reception. In this way, I will clarify if these works can be best understood as witness literature, if the theoretical foundations of these forms of literature are adequate to analyze the complexity of the works they refer to and I will adumbrate how camp literature and witness literature differ from each other. I thus acknowledge one of the most salient features of Solzhenitsyn's reception—the emphasis on his status as a witness of the Soviet camps—and contrast different understandings of what this implies. Solzhenitsyn was not the first author to touch on the subject of the Soviet prison camps, but he became the most well-known author to do so. What

1 The term witness literature was coined by Elie Wiesel in the 1970s to define testimonial texts describing the ordeal of Shoah survivors. By now, the term is used for many other types of literary testimony as well.

arguments were used to mark out his testimony as better, or as more important than that of other former victims of repression in the USSR? What made his texts stand out in the perception of Western critics? Section 2.3 looks into these questions.

The interaction between aesthetics and politics in Solzhenitsyn's reception define the outline of chapter three. The central question is, what are the main types of political readings of Solzhenitsyn's work, and how do they relate to his work? As some of Solzhenitsyn's texts were relevant to diverse debates I do not build the chapter around his texts, but around the common denominator of these debates. The framework of the chapter takes into account the socio-political particularities of each of the countries of my study and their divergent readings of Solzhenitsyn's work.

Having achieved fame at the peak of the Cold War, Solzhenitsyn's work stood in the midst of political debates until the collapse of the Soviet Union. His first text was published weeks after the Cuban Missile Crisis in 1962, and he was sent into exile while détente and *Ostpolitik* were leading the headlines. The rise of conservative and neo-conservative movements in the 1970s and 80s is a further aspect that affected Solzhenitsyn's reception. Yet, how central were directly political arguments in the appraisal of Solzhenitsyn's work? How far did his influence in political discourse go? How did this change after 1991? The most prominent of the political readings of Solzhenitsyn's work is anti-communism. I begin my chapter by scrutinizing his reception in anti-communist debates in the Cold War and its aftermath in section 3.2. Less encompassing, but more controversial topics follow. Section 3.3 introduces the phenomenon of revisionism in Solzhenitsyn's work and looks at examples of these quantitatively vast—yet marginal—readings. Solzhenitsyn's nationalism as well as his portrayal of World War II and Jews have long been the cause of unease among some liberal readers, but have made the author a standard reference for extremist groups and right-wing scholars. However, because much of this reception takes place outside academia and mainstream media, it has not been the most influential. This explains the short space dedicated to this subject. Lastly, in section 3.4, I discuss readings of Solzhenitsyn that focus on the role of Christianity in politics and society. Several Christian scholars have written numerous books inspired by Solzhenitsyn's Christian thought. Although this ideological perspective remains peripheral, it is an area in which Solzhenitsyn continues to be avidly read and written about.

In this extensive chapter I show dominant political perspectives emphasized in Solzhenitsyn's reception, and also sketch some of the topics that are commonly relevant in literary criticism but have been neglected in this particular case. In doing so, I propose possible causes for this selectivity.

In the fourth chapter, I will discuss the role of history in Solzhenitsyn's work and reception. Most of Solzhenitsyn's works present historical topics in an innovative and/or peculiar manner, and they have influenced the way scholars write about Russian/Soviet history in the past. For those readers not familiar with historiography of Russia in the West, it may come as a surprise that works like Solzhenitsyn's novels, novellas, and life-writing have been used as factual sources by different historians. At relevant moments in this book, I discuss the consequences of reading Solzhenitsyn as a factual source. In this chapter, I sum up the problems related with historiographical readings of his work, and propose a constructive way of dealing with history in Solzhenitsyn's oeuvre by redefining it as a form of memory culture. I will explore this subject while taking into account new developments in the study of historiography, and recent changes in source criticism. Furthermore, this chapter elevates the analysis to a meta-level by appraising the role of Solzhenitsyn's work and his persona as a part of memory culture in East and West. By drawing from the findings of modern memory theorists, I contrast the meanings attached to Solzhenitsyn in the countries of my analysis and in Russia, and how these have evolved in the last decades. I also argue for the benefits of analyzing the dissident within the methodological framework of memory studies.

The core sources in my project are reviews, articles, and books written about Solzhenitsyn's works. I focus on the reception of scholars and prominent publicists in the UK, US, and the Federal Republic of Germany. Confining my attention to scholarly and publicistic reception allows me to make meaningful conclusions about influential forms of reception, the development of literary criticism, and the appraisal of literary works in aesthetic and/or political terms as expressed in this paradigmatic case. Although I do include certain controversial scholars and authors, I have decided to exclude authors from the extreme edges of the political spectrum.[2] Because of their peripheral nature their inclusion would skew the results of my research.

Solzhenitsyn's reception is vast, thus creating the need to set boundaries in its study. I have decided to focus on three influential Western countries:[3] the United States, the Federal Republic of Germany, and the United Kingdom. All three countries had a dynamic relationship with the Soviet Union that affected the way they related to its dissidents. At the same time, these countries have held a lively tradition of cultural exchange with Russia and of studying its literature in specialized institutes and departments in many of their universities. During the Cold War, the US represented the polar opposite to the USSR and it was therefore compelling to include this country in my reception study: no other place embodied anti-communism more vividly than the US and no other dissident represented anti-communism more famously than Alexander Solzhenitsyn. The US was also the country that hosted Solzhenitsyn for nearly twenty years. In the US, Solzhenitsyn continued writing and publishing, and he made important public appearances, such as his famous *Harvard Address* (1978).

As Solzhenitsyn's obituaries in the US and Britain show, he is remembered as someone who brought the gulag to the world's attention. My choice of including the Federal Republic of Germany was based in part on the fact that the knowledge of the gulag there was not new by the time that Solzhenitsyn was writing about this subject. Hence, including a country in my study where this topic did not have the same novelty effect adds more nuance to my research. Furthermore, Solzhenitsyn's entire oeuvre was translated into German, including books that have remained unpublished in English. The availability of a wider variety of his works in German has also led to a more diverse form of reception, which is interesting in its own right. The effects of the Cold War in Germany awakened a special interest in Solzhenitsyn in the Federal Republic: his claims about what went on behind the Iron Curtain were of particular concern to a divided country. Solzhenitsyn's relationship to US and German intellectuals remained strong throughout the years. This

---

2 For example, I exclude convicted Holocaust denier David Irving's texts on Solzhenitsyn.

3 Throughout this study, the term "West" refers to the countries in Europe and America that did not belong to the communist bloc during the Cold War.

influenced the continuing public interest in Solzhenitsyn in the US and West Germany.

In the United Kingdom, Solzhenitsyn was part of discussions about communism and how Britain was to relate to the USSR. The scholarly and intellectual relationships between the US and the UK are at times so close that some of the scholars who wrote about and promoted the knowledge of Solzhenitsyn's work moved from one country to the other, making an inclusion of the UK in my study indispensable. At the same time, the inclusion of Britain prevents a possibly misleading pattern from arising that would be caused by the juxtaposition of merely the US and German reception. Similarities and differences in reception are not easily explained as "European" or "American" peculiarities, but are rooted in both the historical and cultural environment in which they develop as well as the political circumstances and diplomatic ties these countries had with each other.

A further country lurks in the background of this study, and that is, of course, Russia (i.e. the USSR). Very often Solzhenitsyn's Western reception reflects the way he is read (or not) in his own country, but above all, the rejection or acceptance of the author by his government had a considerable influence on his early readership. The exceptional conditions under which Russian literature developed in the 20th century complicate the question of how and why an author was read. In my study, I introduce a glimpse of Solzhenitsyn's Russian reception when it relates to that of the countries I discuss. The examination of convergences and divergences of Solzhenitsyn's reception in East and West can allow local priorities to percolate. I do not study all of Solzhenitsyn's reception in Russia because of its highly desultory character: Solzhenitsyn was only published in the USSR in the early sixties, late eighties and early nineties. Soviet reception did not develop freely or in parallel to the Western one.

I generally quote from the English or German translations of Solzhenitsyn's work because, in most cases, these are the decisive versions for his reception. Additionally, I discuss any salient discrepancies between the Russian original and its translations. In this book, I do not discuss translation as a form of reception except for a couple of instances in which the actual translation is relevant to my study—due to its singular effect upon the non-Russian reader. The types of reception texts I analyze are those that helped create, or maintain a certain image of the author and his work and in this case the role of translation is relevant in only few, very particular moments.

In a nutshell, these are some of the questions at the core of this book: How did Solzhenitsyn's reception in the West evolve and how has it changed since the end of the Cold War? Does his work have a mere ethical or political relevance? Why have aesthetic aspects of his work been neglected by literary critics? Was his work of international relevance only as long as the Soviet Union had a somewhat unified camp of foes interested in anti-Communist literature? How does Solzhenitsyn's work relate to history and how has this been interpreted? What place does he have in culture—and world literature—today?

1.2 Review of Research Literature on the Subject

There are few previous studies of Alexander Solzhenitsyn's Western reception, and even fewer that are comparative. In addition to the following specific studies of Solzhenitsyn's reception, in this book I will also refer to articles or book sections that thematize this subject in some way, and discuss their findings.

Birgit Meyer and Robert Conquest have written on this author's reception in the media in West Germany and in the UK, respectively.[4] John Dunlop has written on Solzhenitsyn's reception in the US in general, and Edward E. Ericson, on his Western reception.[5] Friedhelm Boll and Stephane Sirot recently published an article on Solzhenitsyn's reception among French and

4 Birgit Meyer. *Die sowjetische Dissidenten-Bewegung in der bundesdeutschen Presse*. Frankfurt/ New York: Campus Verlag, 1981. Birgit Meyer. "Solzhenitsyn in the West German Press since 1974." *Solzhenitsyn in Exile: Critical Essays and Documentary Materials*. Eds. John B. Dunlop, Richard S. Haugh, and Michael Nicholson. Stanford: Hoover Institution, 1985. 56-79; Robert Conquest. "Solzhenitsyn in the British Media." *Solzhenitsyn in Exile: Critical Essays and Documentary Materials*. Eds. John B. Dunlop, Richard S. Haugh, and Michael Nicholson. Stanford: Hoover Institution, 1985. 3-23.

5 John B. Dunlop. "Solzhenitsyn's Reception in the United States." *Solzhenitsyn in Exile: Critical Essays and Documentary Materials*. Eds. John B. Dunlop, Richard S. Haugh, and Michael Nicholson. Stanford: Hoover Institution, 1985. 24-55. Edward E. Ericson. "Solzhenitsyn's Western Reception since 1991." *Transactions of the Association of Russian-American Scholars* 29 (1998): 183-213.

German intellectuals in the 1970s.[6] Furthermore, Solzhenitsyn has been included in Birgit Meyer and Sonja Hauschild's respective studies on the reception of Soviet dissidents in Germany—as well as France in Hauschild's case.[7] The scope, the focus and the approach of all these studies have been very diverse. All of these scholars have been confronted with a gargantuan task, which they could not tackle in all its complexity within the limited frame of an article or book section. Some authors decided to concentrate on one type of reception, or a smaller time frame. A couple of studies of Solzhenitsyn's reception simply contain an overview of the reception of one work or speech, but lack, of course, more general results.[8] Unfortunately, none of these earlier studies had a framework that allowed for a deeper look into the historical and social context of the reception or into the type of work that was receiving it. At times, this has resulted in generalizations that reflect these restraints and perhaps mirror the political constraints of Cold War scholarship. Three studies by Conquest, Dunlop and Meyer (1985) were all published in the same anthology of articles on Solzhenitsyn, and all share the view that détente and *Ostpolitik* were central to the author's appreciation in the West. They also give rise to a false impression that Solzhenitsyn was under siege in East and West due to his controversial views. Edward Ericson shares the sympathy with the Russian dissident that these three authors express in their articles, but this unfortunately affects the way they all write about others' reception, for example by repeatedly describing criticism as "attacks" or "misrepresentations". For instance, Conquest writes about some

---

6 Friedhelm Boll and Stephane Sirot. "Deutsche und französische Intellektuelle und der Fall Solschenizyn." *Deutschland - Frankreich - Rußland Begegnungen und Konfrontationen.* Ed. Ilja Mieck. Munich: Oldenbourg, 2000. 321-344.

7 Meyer, 1981; Sonja Hauschild. "Propheten oder Störenfriede? Sowjetische Dissidenten in der Bundesrepublik Deutschland und Frankreich und ihre Rezeption bei den Intellektuellen (1974—1977)." *Digitale Osteuropa-Bibliothek: Reihe Geschichte* 13 (2006). (http://epub.ub.uni-muenchen.de/1359/1/ hauschild-dissidenten.pdf) (as of 15 December 2013). In her Master's thesis, Hauschild analyzes French-German cooperation by looking into intellectuals' reception of Soviet dissidents.

8 Cf.: Robert Porter. *Solzhenitsyn's One Day in the Life of Ivan Denisovich.* Bristol: Bristol Classics Press, 1997; Ronald Berman, ed. *Solzhenitsyn at Harvard: the Address, Twelve Early Responses, and Six Later Reflections.* 2nd ed. Washington: Ethics and Public Policy Center, 1980.

British commentators' claim that Solzhenitsyn's tone is authoritarian as follows:

> This view of his "authoritarianism" merged into attacks on his supposed hostility to democracy, together with his supposed predilection for Tsardom. This is, of course, a complete misrepresentation of Solzhenitsyn's position.[9]

Conquest ends his article by comparing Solzhenitsyn with a doctor who has come to warn us that a cholera outbreak is spreading—cholera being his choice of a metaphor for communism—and compelling his readers not to choose denial or wrongful criticism but rather accept Solzhenitsyn's message.[10] This example underlines the import of examining Solzhenitsyn's work while discussing his reception, and the need for a new, less polemic approach. The effects of widespread worries and fears in the Cold War are evident in this case, and they are a reminder of the advantages that I enjoy by working in dramatically changed conditions. Today, the political overtone of previous studies becomes apparent and can be re-evaluated. Newer readings and approaches can contribute to the identification of past misjudgements and an assessment of their consequences. However, I do not wish to dismiss the relevance of these previous studies. They made an important contribution to scholarship by raising questions about the role of dissidents in a politically delicate environment. I can build upon their experience and reflect on this topic from a different historical context.

1.3 Theoretical and Methodological Background of the Project

This book is a reception history of Solzhenitsyn's work in three different countries. Hans Robert Jauss and Gunter Grimm's reception theories build the theoretical backbone of this study.[11] Despite the fact that these theories have been around for a few decades, they have key elements that render them adequate to approach the topic of this book.

In his reception theory, Jauss underlines the importance of the historical location of both the work and its reader. Although Jauss' ponderings were

---

9 Conquest, 1985, p. 11.

10 Conquest, 1985, p. 22-23.

11 Hans Robert Jauss. *Literaturgeschichte als Provokation der Literaturwissenschaft.* 2nd ed. Konstanz: Universitätsverlag, 1969. Gunter Grimm. *Rezeptionsgeschichte: Grundlegung einer Theorie mit Analysen und Bibliographie.* 691 Vol. Munich: Wilhelm Fink, 1977.

made in the disciplinary realm of literary history, there are several concepts that are useful for my work as well. A reader's experience of reading a literary text is affected by his previous knowledge of other works. Reception develops within a "horizon of expectations" that can be reconstructed by the literary historian.[12] Three aspects are key for a reconstruction of the "horizon of expectations" of the reader, and these are: a) the genre of the work, b) the text's relationship to earlier works, c) the contrast between fiction and reality: the reader's juxtaposition of his literary expectation and his life experience.[13] Understanding the horizon of expectations is helpful in evaluating a work's importance in literary history. But, as I will show, these three factors are also valuable in the analysis of the changing impact a work can have. Some works become trendsetters, but over time it is difficult to see them as the innovative works that they once were. Therefore, when I look at Solzhenitsyn's work and his reception, I take into account the expectations that existed at first publishing and how these developed over time. I will therefore weave the analysis of his reception into the literary-historical context within which it took place.

Gunter Grimm points out that the horizon of expectations is not sufficient for the study of reception, and adds that beyond the literary expectations, other aspects of the historical context of the reader and extra textual elements have a considerable effect on reception.[14] At the same time, he warns that a reconstruction of the historical context of the reader always retains a certain hypothetical character. In my study, the importance of the historical context is salient: if it were not for the history of state violence of the 20th century, Solzhenitsyn's work and his reception would have been very different. As I base my study on written reception, I can delineate the various reminiscences that Solzhenitsyn's work evoked in his readers. I choose prominent moments of Solzhenitsyn's reception for such a synchronic analysis. The publication of *Ivan Denisovich* and *Gulag*—two of his most influential works—but also the time of his expulsion from the USSR, the publication of the re-written version of *August 1914*, his return to Russia in 1994 and his death in 2008 were

12 Jauss, 1969, p. 173-177.
13 Jauss, 1969, p. 177.
14 Grimm, 1977, p. 66-68. Further aspects will be discussed in section 3.1.

some of the key moments that occasioned a heightened amount of attention being focused on this writer's oeuvre.

When analyzing reception texts, I use Grimm's central question which is: "why does who read what and how?"[15] I read the reviews, articles, or books on Solzhenitsyn's works under this premise. To be sure, there will always be some aspects of this question which remain obscured, but generally, there is enough material to derive an answer to this question and be able to work from there. By exploring the reasons that Solzhenitsyn was read and considered to be a relevant author, I can chart the priorities his readers had: was he read primarily as a political author, or for the beauty of his language? Were his works read as entertainment, as historical works, as witness accounts? Who read and wrote about him?

As opposed to previous reception studies which define groups of readers *a priori* by their affiliation—for example: the "liberal media" or "conservative journalists"—I focus on the reception texts as such and appraise the type of narrative they share. As Grimm has pointed out, the reception-analyst must decide if he approaches his topic through the subject, or through a group or class.[16] In my case, I compare individual readings and present resulting salient trends. This approach has the advantage of avoiding ideological pigeonholes and reflecting a complex reality in which some authors may belong to different groups depending on the issue at hand: an author of a reception text might be anti-communist when it comes to the Soviet Union, but leftist when it comes to his local political priorities in the West. Furthermore, I benefit from Roger Chartier and Stanley Fish's notion of "communities of interpretation".[17] The community of interpretation is created by the environment in which readers are confronted with a particular work.

15 Grimm, 1977, p. 61.

16 Grimm, 1977, p. 62. „Der Analytiker muss sich grundsätzlich entscheiden, ob er mit seiner Analyse am rezipierenden Subjekt oder an der Klasse als umgreifende Formation ansetzt. Da die Konkretisationen jeweils Produkte von Individuen sind, empfiehlt sich methodologisch der Zugang über das Subjekt." "The analyst must decide categorically, if his analysis will encompass the receptive subject or the class as a larger group. As concretizations are always the product of individuals, a methodological approach through the subject is advisable." (My translation.)

17 Roger Chartier and Guglielmo Cavallo. "Einleitung." *Die Welt des Lesens von der Schriftrolle zum Bildschirm.* Eds. Roger Chartier and Guglielmo Cavallo. Frankfurt Main: Campus-Verlag, 1999. p. 13-17.

Their interpretation reflects their context to a considerable extent. This calls for a contextualization of reception: a reader in the US had a different type of reading experience and expectations than one in West Germany. This becomes more poignant in certain cases, especially when one literary text was available in a country many years before another, or when a book was not translated at all into a certain language, as is the case with some of Solzhenitsyn's books.

The context of Solzhenitsyn's readership has changed over the years, as have its points of reference, and its interpretation of his works. As a reception history, this study combs through several decades of reception and pinpoints important areas of reception and types of reception while taking this context into account.

I do not seek to add new perspectives on reception theory in this book. These theoreticians provide the main framework and the point of departure for my analysis. However, there is an important point in which I depart from Jauss and Grimm's theories. Contrary to the task of a standard reception analyst, I complement my study with an analysis of relevant parts of Solzhenitsyn's works. This is necessary for two reasons. Firstly, Solzhenitsyn's texts are often a complex amalgamation of genres and styles. The variety of interpretations and their implications can only become clear if I explain what they refer to. Earlier reception studies followed the classic paradigm of avoiding the discussion of Solzhenitsyn's texts. However, their criticism of certain readings made it clear that they had a concrete expectation of how these books should be read. In sketching my own analysis, I explore why the same book can be read in many different ways while clarifying what my own reading is. Secondly, the importance of doing this goes beyond the avoidance of opaqueness or lack of clarity. As I will show, Solzhenitsyn's work has suffered what recent critics termed "critical exile".[18] In this book, I argue that his work is interesting from a contemporary theoretical point of view.

---

18 William H. Thornton. "A Post-Modern Solzhenitsyn?" *Comparative Literature and Culture* 1.3 (1999); Lisa Ryoko Wakamiya. *Locating Exiled Writers in Contemporary Russian Literature*. Basingstoke: Palgrave Macmillan, 2009. p. 70.

Many developments in literary theory do not occur in Solzhenitsyn's reception. Psychoanalytic readings of Solzhenitsyn are scarce.[19] Feminist and gender studies are yet to thoroughly analyze his work.[20] There is only one post-colonial reading of one of his novels.[21] In my study, I explore the possibility of different factors that influenced which types of readings of Solzhenitsyn were seen as adequate and which were relegated to the background or fully neglected. As I will show, the environment in which Solzhenitsyn's reception developed was strongly polarized and intolerant of ambivalence or ambiguousness. Newer theoretical approaches to his work might have resulted in less black and white readings, which would have broken with an established pattern. In a recent book about the development of Slavic studies in the US, historian David Engerman describes the relative theoretical and methodological isolation that Russianists in the US worked in.[22] This appears to be a paradox, considering the important contributions early US Russianists—such as Roman Jakobson and Victor Erlich—made to literary theory in general. But it is true that Russianists had to work under entirely different circumstances as, say, their colleagues in English departments. The *a priori* politicization of literature due to Soviet censorship mechanisms and the problems of accessibility of certain texts were bound to create a peculiar research environment.

In the 1960s and 70s—parallel to the apogee of Solzhenitsyn's reception—new developments in literary criticism proliferated. Anti-colonialist, civil rights and women's rights movements in the UK, US and West Germany influenced scholarship and resulted in new understandings of literature and culture. The purely aesthetic analysis of literature was called into question and feminist, Marxist, post-structuralist, and post-colonial interpretations offered a reassessment of established canons. The new readings by Terry Eagleton, the Frankfurt School, and proponents of gender studies triggered innovative

---

19 One rare example: Daniel Rancour-Laferriere. "Solzhenitsyn and the Jews: A Psychoanalytic View." *Soviet Jewish Affairs* 15.3 (1985): 29-54.

20 He is mentioned in passing in: Barbara Heldt. "Gender." *The Cambridge Companion to the Classic Russian Novel*. Eds. Malcolm V. Jones and Robin Feuer Miller. Cambridge: Cambridge University Press, 1998. 251-270.

21 In: Ewa M. Thompson. *Imperial Knowledge: Russian Literature and Colonialism*. 99 Vol. Westport, Conn.: Greenwood Press, 2000.

22 David C. Engerman. *Know Your Enemy: The Rise and Fall of America's Soviet Experts*. Oxford; New York: Oxford University Press, 2009. p. 150-152.

approaches to literature, which are unfortunately widely ignored in the reception of Alexander Solzhenitsyn. When I present the ideological readings of Solzhenitsyn's work, I will not delve into these developments because they are not mirrored in his reception (although I deliberate on the consequences of this neglect). When defining the ideological aspect of Solzhenitsyn's work I draw from Eagleton's work on ideology, and discuss readers' confusion about the presence of ideology in Solzhenitsyn's texts. I also benefit from György Lukács' and Katerina Clark's understanding of the political literary mode of Socialist Realism and discuss the challenges that Solzhenitsyn's proximity to this literary mode causes to many of his readers. In chapter four of this book, I apply the methodology of German memory studies experts Aleida Assmann and Astrid Erll in analyzing the interaction of political interests with historical interpretations and literary texts. Assmann and Erll's experience in studying the polemical memory culture surrounding Germany's troubled past is helpful in understanding the similar complexity of Western memory of Soviet history.

In my study, I argue that reading Solzhenitsyn's work in the 21st century demands new approaches and new interpretations. For example, I sketch the importance of re-interpreting his image of women and homosexuals and of evaluating his literary treatment of minorities according to contemporary theories. I point out why Solzhenitsyn is relevant enough that he should be drawn back from his "critical exile", but I do encourage a view of the author and his work which is significantly more differentiated and perhaps less homogenous than past interpretations. In this process, invariably, Solzhenitsyn's image risks losing some of its iconic features, while gaining authenticity.

2. Solzhenitsyn as a Writer and a Witness

> There is no doubt, though, that his witness as a writer has already earned itself an enduring place in the Russian literature of this century.[23]

Alexander Solzhenitsyn (1918-2008) was educated as a mathematician and worked initially as a teacher. He wrote books in his free time and his first break into publishing was in late 1962. Himself a former inmate, Solzhenitsyn's first printed work was a story about everyday life in a Soviet prison camp. It was published in the most prestigious Soviet literary journal and hit the shelves just weeks after the Cuban Missile Crisis. Solzhenitsyn's literary debut made him world famous and turned this and later works into international best-sellers.

Solzhenitsyn's reception as a writer begins with his prison-camp literature. In this chapter I will take the topic of the prison camp experience as the foundation for my analysis of a part of his reception in the US, UK, and West Germany. I begin the chapter by introducing Solzhenitsyn's three main camp-related works and analyzing their style and genre. This will provide the necessary basis for understanding how the reception relates to these works and how it is linked to debates concerning witness literature and camp literature. The theme of certain works by Solzhenitsyn implies that they can belong to these forms of literature, and I will discuss what theoretical advantages and challenges this categorization brings. What role does Solzhenitsyn's witness status play in the reception of his camp-related texts? What kind of expectations did his readers have, and what did they see in these works?

2.1 The Style and Genre of Solzhenitsyn's camp-related Literature

Alexander Solzhenitsyn wrote three prominent works that deal directly with the Soviet prison camp system: *One Day in the Life of Ivan Denisovich* (1962), *The First Circle* (1968), and *The Gulag Archipelago* (1973-1975).[24]

---

23 Richard Freeborn. "Russian Literary Attitudes from Pushkin to Solzhenitsyn." *Russian Literary Attitudes from Pushkin to Solzhenitsyn.* Eds. Richard Freeborn, Georgette Donchin, and Nicholas J. Anning. London: Macmillan, 1976. p. 16.

24 Due to its limited reception, I do not include his much lesser known play *Olen' i Shalashovka* (1969, translated as: *The Love-Girl and the Innocent* or *The Greenhorn and the Camp-whore*).

These three works vary widely in a number of different ways—length, style, authorial voice—and they relate to their subject matter diversely. Solzhenitsyn presents these works as belonging to certain genres. For example, he defines his first work as a povest,[25] a Russian genre that denotes a short novel with a plot focusing on one main character. *The First Circle* is described by its author as a polyphonic novel, as it constantly changes its point of view. Solzhenitsyn's much longer work *The Gulag Archipelago* (1973-5) bears the intriguing subtitle "an experiment in literary investigation" and has a very versatile structure.

Hans Robert Jauss points out that among the factors which predispose readers towards a text are its assigned genre, its topic, and its relation to other similar works.[26] As I will show, debates within the reception of Solzhenitsyn's camp-related literature have often revolved around the genre-definition of these works, the authorial voice in them, the topic, and their relation to Soviet literature of their time. All these questions are closely related and all affected the way the work was later canonized. But what made these issues both so relevant *and* so contentious?

The apparent simplicity of defining the genre of a work hides an unexpected depth and complexity in the case of Solzhenitsyn's oeuvre. Even the genres of his two first camp-related works—which at least seem to have a more standard genre definition—have been disputed since their publication. Not only is there a disagreement over the definition of what type of literary work they are, sometimes the real issue is if they are literature at all. Because of their subject matter—life in Soviet prison camps—some scholars consider these books to be history rather than literature; other readers disagree completely and see them as fictional literature that can and should be weighed in aesthetic terms.

---

25 In the Soviet journal where *Ivan Denisovich* first appeared, the work is subtitled "povest'". This genre definition was kept in the version printed by the YMCA Press in Paris, which Solzhenitsyn had described as the "final" and canonical version of the work. (Cf.: Gary Kern. "Solženicyn's Self-Censorship: The Canonical Text of Odin den' Ivana Denisoviča." *The Slavic and East European Journal* 20.4 (1976). p. 422, 425.)

26 Jauss, 1969, p. 173.

Not only does the topic complicate the categorization of Solzhenitsyn's camp literature: the fact that *he* is a survivor of the Soviet prison camp system sparks speculation about autobiographical aspects of his work. The role played by the author's autobiographical experiences in his books affect their genre definition. Hence, some readers may wonder if *First Circle* and *Ivan Denisovich* are memoirs. Indeed, it would be easier to see the autobiographically inspired *Ivan Denisovich* and *First Circle* as memoirs, if there was clarity as to the relationship between the point of view and the author in these works. But there is great confusion as to whose the authorial voice is in these works—and this issue becomes even more challenging when it comes to *The Gulag Archipelago*.

As will later become clear, one possible understanding of Solzhenitsyn's camp-related literature is to define it as witness literature. In order to discuss how this term might or might not apply and the issues connected with it, it will be necessary to begin by discussing other difficulties connected with the categorization of these works' genre. For example, the possible adherence to Socialist Realism of these works needs to be clarified as a step in the quest to define how the content of the books relates to reality, realism, and ideology. Are they spontaneous testimonies or carefully crafted literary works? Many scholars and reviewers perceived *Ivan Denisovich* as a unique and innovative work; however, others were more sceptical: they saw it as just another Socialist Realist novella with a "new" topic. In the following section, I will look at the roots of this disagreement.

One Day in the Life of Ivan Denisovich

One Day in the Life of Ivan Denisovich is a povest, a short novel, often described in English as a novella. It narrates the life of one prison camp inmate in the Soviet Union over one winter day in 1951. It starts with a wake up call, and ends predictably with lights out. Ivan Denisovich Shukhov, the central character, is a peasant turned soldier who was accused of having become a Nazi spy after having being taken prisoner by the Germans in World War II. Most of the story is narrated by a different voice than that of Ivan. That the point of view is not that of the protagonist becomes clear by the following: he refers to Ivan in the third person, knows things that Ivan does not, and does not possess the same dialect as Ivan.[27] At times, however, the narrator informs us of Ivan's thoughts in his language without necessarily pointing it out explicitly, in the form of represented discourse (*erlebte Rede*, *style indirect libre*) which in the Russian context is called *skaz*.[28] For example, Ivan, at the end of the workday, remembers that he had had back pain in the morning and intended to go to the doctor. Now he ponders about whether to go:

> He'd manage it if he skipped his supper. But now somehow his back wasn't aching. And his temperature wouldn't be high enough. A waste of time. He'd pull through without the benefit of the doctor. The only cure those docs know is to put you in your grave.[29]

This example shows how the two different narrative voices—the omniscient narrator and the *skaz*—flow into one another. Both of these voices have their own purpose: the omniscient narrator describes external aspects, such as actions and situations; the *skaz* voice expresses the opinions and the emotional state of the protagonist.[30] Vladimir Rus identifies the narrator as an educated person—because of his language—who is so familiar with camp life that he is most likely living inside a camp himself.[31] Thus, Rus claims, one could justifiably think that the narrator is the voice of the author. External

---

27 For example, Ivan did not know that the "medical assistant" in the camp infirmary was in reality a student of literature, whom the camp doctor had advised to redefine his profession in order to be allowed to work in the infirmary, where he could continue writing poetry. Alexander Solzhenitsyn. *One Day in the Life of Ivan Denisovich.* Tran. Ralph Parker. 1st ed. New York: Dutton, 1963. p. 30.

28 Occasionally, reviewers of *Ivan Denisovich* have termed this voice not *skaz*, but *nesobstvenno-priamaia rech'* a Russian term translated as "quasi-direct discourse" which is an equivalent to *erlebte Rede* or *style indirect libre*. The term *skaz* evokes stronger associations with the 19th century literary tradition, as it was a popular device at the time. Vladimir Rus writes that both *skaz* and *nesobstvenno-priamaia rech'* have identical signals. Vladimir Rus. "One Day in the Life of Ivan Denisovich: A Point of View Analysis." *Canadian Slavonic Papers* 13.2/3 (1971). p. 170. (On the Russian terminology of narrated discourse, cf.: Rachel May. *The Translator in the Text: on reading Russian literature in English.* Evanston: Northwestern University Press, 1994. p. 89-91.)

29 Only very high body temperature would justify a day off work. Solzhenitsyn, 1963, p. 137.

30 In certain scenes, however, it is unclear if the emotions expressed in the *skaz* voice are those of Ivan or of other prisoners. Cf. Georg Witte. *Appell, Spiel, Ritual Textpraktiken in der russischen Literatur der sechziger bis achtziger Jahre.* Wiesbaden: Harrassowitz, 1989. p. 18-19.

31 Rus, 1971, p. 173.

knowledge of Solzhenitsyn's experience and opinions further confuses the separation between the narrator and the author. For example, the historian Robert Conquest interprets Ivan's voice and experience as that of Solzhenitsyn when he uses *Ivan Denisovich* as a source for his history of the Stalinist purges.

> Solzhenitsyn deals [in Ivan Denisovich], indeed, with a later period in camp history than that of the purges; a time, moreover, when the death rate had been radically reduced. If I have quoted largely from *his* experience it is because it remains one of the most vivid, and at the same time is scarcely open to a charge of misrepresentation. [32]

Conquest admits that the description in *Ivan Denisovich* is of another era than the one he is describing, but by identifying Ivan with Solzhenitsyn he feels confident of the genuineness of the representation of camp life. However, there is no "I" in the narration or any *explicit* reference that would in fact identify the narrator with the author.

In contrast, the literary critic Robert L. Jackson sees Ivan as an independent character, and identifies another character in the novel as Solzhenitsyn's alter ego.[33] The "old man" whom Ivan Denisovich watches silently at the canteen—a rigid, bitter man—fits Jackson's image of Solzhenitsyn as a harsh and acrimonious person.[34] Jackson underlines the difference between Solzhenitsyn the author and Ivan Denisovich:

> The reader, of course, has no difficulty sensing Solzhenitsyn's pain and bitterness in this work; he does not mistake the curiously well-adjusted [Ivan Denisovich] Shukhov for the author [.][35]

Jackson compares the tone of *Ivan Denisovich*, in particular the character of Ivan, with the authorial voice of *The Gulag Archipelago*. He notes that in *Ivan Denisovich*, Solzhenitsyn's voice was hidden, but it was nonetheless "visible on the horizon."[36] Ivan was a humble, well adjusted, and down-to-earth

---

32 My italics. Robert Conquest. *The Great Terror: Stalin's Purge of the Thirties.* London: Macmillan, 1969. p. 567.

33 Robert Louis Jackson. "The Mask of Solzhenitsyn: Ivan Denisovich." *One Day in the Life of Ivan Denisovich: a Critical Companion.* Ed. Alexis Klimoff. Evanston: Northwestern University Press, 1997. p. 51.

34 Alexander Solzhenitsyn. "Odin Den' Ivana Denisovicha, Povest'." *Novii Mir.* 11 (1962). p. 63-64.

35 Jackson, 1997, p. 43.

36 Jackson, 1997, p. 52.

peasant. Solzhenitsyn's "real voice"—revealed in *Gulag*—is a loud and bitter one.

In *Ivan Denisovich* language and tone are the most important means by which different points of view are marked. Nevertheless, the nuances of this distinction get slightly lost in translation, especially in the English translation by Max Hayward and Ronald Hingley, as some scholars have pointed out.[37] The earliest German translation is a translation of Hayward and Hingley's English version. Fortunately, enough remains clear in all English translations and the German for the reader to become aware of the change in perspective.

The language of the Russian original differs from the English and German mostly in its local color, the inclusion of profanity, and the occasional archaic term. For example, the Ukrainians in the novella have an identifiable accent and Ivan speaks in archaisms and broken words intended to indicate his provincial origin—both these nuances get lost in translation. Some of the sayings in the book, such as "A man who is warm cannot understand the one who is cold" are old sayings taken from Vladimir Dahl's dictionary of 19th century colloquial language.[38] The linguistic complexity of these sayings is ironed out in the more prosaic English and German versions. When it comes to obscene language, different translators had different approaches. In Robert Parker's English translation, four-letter-words are either not translated or merely suggested (e.g. "f...k"). His language is described as too civilized by Irina Shapiro, who analyzed early English translations of this work.[39] Max Hayward and Ronald Hingely gave their English translation a more colloquial tone,[40] but they remained cautious when it came to obscenity. In the German version from Gerda Kurz and Siglinde Summerer, obscenities are toned down as it is Hayward's English version they use as a source text. A poignant example of the watering down of the language is when Ivan says in Russian:

---

37 May, 1994, p. 94; Klimoff agrees in: Alexis Klimoff. "The Sober Eye: Ivan Denisovich and the Peasant Perspective." *One Day in the Life of Ivan Denisovich: a Critical Companion.* Evanston: Northwestern University Press, 1997. p. 11-12.

38 Porter, 1997, p. 90.

39 Irina H. Shapiro. "Review: [Untitled]." *Slavic Review* 22.2 (1963). p. 377.

40 Shapiro, p. 376-7.

"A tebe khren v rot!" which means: "may a dick be shoved in your mouth!" and is translated into German as: "Das wär' ja wie ein Tritt in den Arsch!"[41]

Among Western scholars of Russian literature, the language of *Ivan Denisovich* is often praised as one of the highlights of the work. Marc Slonim sees the language as part of the work's literary merit, but admits that it must be a nightmare for translators.[42] Other scholars saw Solzhenitsyn's language as adding to the work's impression of authenticity since they saw it as a more sincere form of realism. Geoffrey Hosking interprets Solzhenitsyn's language as genuine as opposed to the "fake" sounding language of the Soviet intelligentsia often used in literature.[43] In his view, it strengthens the works adherence to realism. Marc Slonim's praise is similar:

> The realistic crudeness of the language is skilfully mitigated by the rhythm and tone of the narrative. Its masterfully controlled racy language which recalls that of Remizov, its rich texture and its ring of authenticity, which was such a relief after the false pathos of most Soviet fiction, show an artistic maturity quite surprising in a newcomer.[44]

According to Nicholas Anning, the vividness of the language and the choice of protagonist imbued Solzhenitsyn with the moral status he attained.[45] Because of its language, Ludmila Koehler eulogized the novella as a return to the "real" Russian literary tradition[46] and contrasts Solzhenitsyn's *Ivan Denisovich* with other Soviet literature:

> Literature was regimented into a mouthpiece of party-line propaganda and became one of the mass production tools of Soviet "soul engineering." In contrast to this Solzhenitsyn's masterpiece marks a return to the great tradition of the nineteenth century.[47]

---

41 This translates as: "It would be like a kick in the ass!" (Page 67 of the Russian version, and 131 of the German). The word "khren" (lit. horseradish), which is a vulgar term for penis in Russian, is used very generously throughout the text.

42 Marc Slonim. "The Challenge was the Need to Stay Alive." The New York Times 7 April 1963: BR4, 34.

43 Geoffrey A. Hosking. "The Russian Peasant Rediscovered: 'Village Prose' of the 1960s." *Slavic Review* 32.4 (1973). p. 712.

44 Slonim, 1969, p. 334-335.

45 Nicholas J. Anning. "Solzhenitsyn." *Russian Literary Attitudes from Pushkin to Solzhenitsyn.* Ed. Richard Freeborn. London: Macmillan, 1976. p. 125; 128.

46 Ludmila Koehler. "Alexander Solzhenitsyn and Russian Literary Tradition." *Russian Review* 26.2 (1967). p. 177.

47 Koehler, 1967, p. 176.

Koehler places Solzhenitsyn in this old tradition because he uses what she sees as peasant and prison-camp slang, and because he recurs to old sayings and words from Vladimir Dahl's dictionary, thus sounding a lot like the 19th century author Nikolai Leskov.[48] This raises the question, which Koehler does not address, of the inconsistency between presenting allegedly contemporary peasant and camp slang while using Dahl's and Leskov's archaic language: after all, Leskov and Dahl's language might only have been contemporary during their lifetime. Geoffrey Hosking describes *Ivan Denisovich*'s language as simultaneously new and old—new in Soviet literature and old because it is reminiscent of 19th century speech.[49] Paradoxically, Hosking also places *Ivan Denisovich* in the tradition of "Village Prose", a strand of Soviet literature that focused on the life of peasants without embellishment.

David Stewart Hull assesses the novella as aesthetically unremarkable and lacking experimentation beyond its language:

> It belongs in that category of works which include the official anti-Stalin film *Clear Skies*, which it superficially resembles in its choice of protagonist. *Ivan Denisovich* contains little, however, of stylistic interest to distinguish it from the usual run of socialist-realist fiction, no experimentation of any kind save in the constant use of very vulgar language.[50]

The seemingly contradictory claims that Solzhenitsyn's language is new and old—an example of literary trends of the 19th or perhaps the 20th century—can be explained by the fact that language in Russia was particularly politicized in the Soviet era. Since the foundation of the Soviet Union, purity of language was a priority—but there was no consensus over what that was. Over the years, prominent authors, politicians, and linguists fought over what proper Russian should be. Purity and closeness to linguistic "reality" were an aim when Lenin ordered the redaction of a dictionary that was to replace Dahl's in 1920.[51] Lenin regarded Dahl's dictionary as outdated and too regional. The new dictionary was to reflect both modern reality and classical

48 Koehler, 1967, p. 181-183.

49 Hosking, 1973, p. 711-712.

50 David Stewart Hull. "[Untitled]." *Russian Review* 22.3 (1963). p. 337.

51 Michael S. Gorham. "Mastering the Perverse: State Building and Language 'Purification' in Early Soviet Russia." *Slavic Review* 59.1 (2000). p. 134.

language as written in the classics of Russian literature.[52] Years later, the "Village Prose" literary movement defended the use of provincial dialects in literature from the 1950s onwards. Solzhenitsyn had his own views as to what proper Russian was, and he became one of the most radical language "purists" of the second half of the 20th century.[53] Solzhenitsyn's efforts began in his fiction and reached their zenith in the dictionary he published in 1990.[54] Michael Gorham describes Solzhenitsyn's linguistic mission thus:

> The idea [...] is that once actively reinstated into the literary language, these words, almost regardless of how they are used, will help rescue that language (and its speakers) from its current impoverished state.[55]

Solzhenitsyn's vision of Russian consisted of cleansing "foreign" elements such as barbarisms or words with Latin roots and replacing them with words with Slavic roots which he either took from 19th century lexica or invented himself.[56] He placed his language in opposition to what he saw as the alien sounding language of the Soviets and the use of foreign terms by ordinary Russians. By doing so, he was aligning himself with those who saw purity of the mother tongue as a nationalist priority.[57] Ultimately, his language can be seen as new—because it was not currently in use, but also old—because most of it was a re-introduction of old terms. He belonged to the Soviet tradition of striving for linguistic purity, but offered his own atavistic vision of what this should be.

Solzhenitsyn's attitude to language and his linguistic choices in *Ivan Denisovich* raise serious doubts about how genuinely they portrayed the spoken Russian of the time. According to Miriam Dobson's study of Soviet readers' response to *Ivan Denisovich*, readers did not only express

---

52 Gorham, 2000, "Mastering", p. 134.

53 Michael S. Gorham. "Natsiia ili Snikerizatsiia? Identity and Perversion in the Language Debates of Late- and Post-Soviet Russia." *Russian Review* 59.4 (2000): p. 625.

54 Alexander Solzhenitsyn. *Russkii slovar' iazikovogo rasshireniia*. Moscow: Nauka, 1990.

55 Gorham, 2000, "Natsiia", p. 625.

56 Gorham, 2000, "Natsiia", p. 625-6.

57 Gorham, 2000, "Natsiia", p. 626-7. Gorham explains the connection between the search for language purity and nationalism: "Only a nation actively respectful of both the purity and fate of its language can hope to revive its strength and spirit, a concern which must manifest itself in a society-wide struggle against blind servitude to foreign and foul tongues." (p. 627).

discomfort with the profanity, but also criticized the language as far from genuine.[58] When looking at the unusual, archaic words and sayings used in *Ivan Denisovich*, it is not easy to believe that peasants spoke like this in the middle of the 20th century. From today's point of view it is difficult to render how genuine the language was, without recurring to sociolinguistic studies which in the Soviet case are not necessarily reliable. Nevertheless there is no doubt that an effect is achieved by the language used. For one thing, it marks Ivan as a simple rural person, but it also makes him sound *different*. In this sense, Ivan stands out rather as Solzhenitsyn's imagined peasant than as a "real" person, in fact, strengthening an impression of fictionality and not realism in the text. The same can be said about the intellectuals in the book, who seem ridiculously disconnected from reality.[59]

As much as some Western critics may have understood the difference between the language in *Ivan Denisovich* and the language of earlier Socialist Realist novels as an expression of authenticity, this does not necessarily mean that it was authentic in the sense that it was the language used by people similar to the imaginary peasant Ivan Denisovich. A Western reader's interpretation of Ivan's language depends on the version he reads—as translators do not necessarily render the nuances of Ivan's speech, and the Russian version might seem foreign and unusual, but it is after all a foreign tongue. An exact representation of linguistic reality does not appear to be a requirement for the perceived authenticity of *Ivan Denisovich*'s diegesis. The ideological motivation for Ivan's language is generally not problematized by Russian-reading critics in the West, as it has been mostly seen as a mere turning away from what is seen as Soviet literary traditions. Moreover, Western critics seem to ignore the diverse reactions that Russian readers' might have when reading Ivan's obscene language. For Russian readers, the "strangeness" of Ivan's language will always pose more of a challenge in its interpretation: is a "peasant" who speaks in 100 year old terms peppered with profanity a credible character for a witness-bearing text or not? Dobson's study shows how numerous Russian readers who were gulag survivors could

---

58 Miriam Dobson. "Contesting the Paradigms of De-Stalinization: Readers' Responses to 'One Day in the Life of Ivan Denisovich'." *Slavic Review* 64.3 (2005): p. 589-590.

59 This is especially the case with the prisoner Tsezar, who is rarely aware of what happens around him.

not identify with this protagonist and rejected him because they—as former victims—did not want to be considered as vulgar as he is, and/or because they didn't think his imprisonment was wholly undeserved.[60] From a theoretical point of view, Ivan's status as an uncouth, foul-mouthed, and uneducated peasant is not a hindrance to his role as protagonist in a work of witness literature. As it is, this apparently obscene peasant is an effective challenge to an intellectual or elitist reader who is confronted with the question of the worth of a human's lost years in unjust imprisonment *even if* this person is not deemed a particularly indispensable member of society.

To sum up, the language of *Ivan Denisovich* in Russian reflects both Solzhenitsyn's linguistic abilities and his ideological preferences but these are not mirrored in the early translations in the US, UK, and Germany. Hence, the language of these translations is less controversial, and easier to understand, thus helping the reader focus on the plot of the story and its details.

Ivan Denisovich is a very carefully crafted work, and its form, style, and language can be interpreted as belonging to different traditions. One of them is witness literature, as will be discussed in section 2.2. But a question that always comes up is if it is Socialist Realist or not. According to Katerina Clark, *Ivan Denisovich* adheres—with few exceptions—to most of the conventions of Socialist Realism of the 1960s.[61] This work's relationship to contemporary Russian works was important in shaping its readers' "horizon of expectations", and because Socialist Realism was so dominant at the time it is necessary to look at how far it influenced *Ivan Denisovich*.

In 1934 Socialist Realism became the official style dictated as binding for Soviet writers. From that point in time, political restraints became an integral part of Soviet literature. In general, political loyalty had precedence over aesthetic refinement in Socialist Realism. Although political requirements changed often, a degree of aesthetic homogeneity was achieved by certain formal literary conventions. It lacked, however, a stringent set of rules, which is why it evolved over time. There is a marked difference between the works

---

60 Some readers assumed he was a petty criminal or swindler. Cf.: Dobson, 2005, p. 583ff.

61 Katerina Clark. "Russian Epic Novels of the Soviet Period." *The Cambridge Companion to Twentieth-century Russian Literature.* Eds. Evgenij Dobrenko and Marina Balina. Cambridge: Cambridge University Press, 2011. 135-151.

written in the 1930s and 40s and later works still written under Stalinism. The greatest shift, however, took place after Stalin's death in 1953. As a long-term result of Khrushchev's liberalization policy known as the "Thaw", Socialist Realism evolved so greatly and gave room to such a large diversity of works that Ronald Hingley wrote:

> We may say if we wish that Socialist Realism has been tacitly abandoned; or we may choose to express the same idea in different form by saying that the doctrine has come to be applied more flexibly.[62]

To say that Socialist Realism was abandoned in the Khrushchev era seems too rash, as its main aesthetic parameters continued to be applied.

Several literary conventions serve as a common platform for Socialist Realist fiction. For instance, the plot takes place in a single location, which acts as a microcosm of Soviet life. This is the case in *Ivan Denisovich*, which does not go far beyond the boundaries of the prison camp. As other Socialist Realist novels, *Ivan Denisovich* has a linear narrative, with a hard working hero, and some lazy, or evil anti-heroes.[63]

Furthermore, Socialist Realism calls for the work to be *narodnyi*, an adjective derived from the Russian term *narod* which means people. The *narodnyi* quality of a literary work was twofold; its subject was to reflect the life of ordinary people and the work itself was to be comprehensible to ordinary people.[64] This implied that the work had to be written in a language accessible to the majority of the Soviet people, most of which had learned to read and write only after the October Revolution. In the High Stalinist era (1930s-40s), Socialist Realist literature was expected to avoid obscene language, and slang[65]—a development which made its language appear antiseptic and unnatural. This changed slowly after Stalin's death, and at an increasing pace during the 1960s and 70s. Solzhenitsyn's *Ivan Denisovich*

---

62 Ronald Hingley. *Russian Writers and Soviet Society: 1917-1978.* London: Weidenfeld and Nicolson, 1979. p. 204.

63 For example: the Moldavian who falls asleep next to the oven, Fetiukov with his parasitic behavior, and Der, who is cruel and addicted to power.

64 Hosking, 1980, p. 3.

65 "Though Socialist Realists were indeed expected to use simple language comprehensible to the common man, they were not permitted full latitude to incorporate the common man's language, in so far as it consisted of slang, obscenities and the equivalent of 'four-letter-words'–to which the Russian *hoi polloi* are no less given than are those outside the Soviet orbit." Hingley, 1979, p. 202.

was part of the post-Stalinist trend in Soviet literature to break away from a homogenized Russian and use colloquial or regional terms.

Ivan Denisovich is *narodnyi* in both ways. Ivan is quite an ordinary man, a peasant turned soldier—like millions of other Soviet citizens of his generation—and like many other of his fellow citizens he was falsely accused and sent to a prison camp. Moreover, the predominantly undemanding literary devices in the work contribute to its accessibility, which is—perhaps paradoxically—obstructed by colloquial and archaic terms in the original Russian. Foreign translations' language is mostly contemporary and unremarkable. It is possible that the translators of *Ivan Denisovich* have in fact contributed to the universality of the work by simplifying its language.

An additional key feature of Socialist Realism is its partisan character, that is, its adherence to the ideals of the Communist Party and its current goals. For example, during the early stages of Soviet industrialization, many Socialist Realist novels portrayed the goals and resulting challenges of this policy. *Ivan Denisovich,* which was written and published in the early 1960s, conforms to the then contemporary goal of the CPSU to confront the excessive use of state violence during the Stalin era. Party Chairman Khrushchev announced in a speech that the publication of *Ivan Denisovich* and other camp-related works was part of the de-Stalinization process that began with the 20th Party Congress and that it was simultaneously part of a campaign to democratize Soviet life.[66]

The Marxist theoretician György Lukács categorizes this work as a new form of Socialist Realism that marks the vanguard of a Marxist renaissance by confronting the past.[67] Lukács believes that socialist art had been negatively affected by the strict political constraints under Stalin, and that the way to progress within Marxism was through an honest depiction of the past.[68] For him, Solzhenitsyn's *Ivan Denisovich* is part of this trend. He praises the fact that Solzhenitsyn poses important questions about life in prison camps—about survival and human dignity—which Lukács believes later works in the

---

66 Seymour Topping. "Easing of Curbs on Soviet Literature is Attributed to Order by Khrushchev." The New York Times 29 November 1962: 4.

67 Georg Lukács. *Solschenizyn.* 28 Vol. Neuwied und Berlin: Luchterhand, 1970. p. 20.

68 Lukács, 1970, p. 9-10.

USSR should respond to.[69] The absence of an ideological sermon is a salient trait of this work which will be discussed in part 2.2 of this chapter. However, it must be pointed out that, as I will later show, some of the ideological undertones of the work do seem to defend several concrete positions of the CPSU.[70]

Another aspect in which *Ivan Denisovich* reflects the changes in Socialist Realism of the post-Stalin era is the way that Moscow is portrayed. According to the Socialist Realism expert Katerina Clark, the meaning of Moscow as a topos changed radically in Socialist Realism after the death of Stalin.[71] As it was the Soviets who chose Moscow as their capital after the October Revolution, this city came to represent the values of the new state. During the Stalinist era, Moscow was usually portrayed in a positive manner as a place that combines justice and innovation; Muscovites were modern and progressive people. Nevertheless, after the emergence of the "Youth Novel"—a current of Soviet literature that began in the Khrushchev era—an inversion of meaning took place. Instead of being the place that set a positive example, Moscow now "functions as the 'false' place, polluted by bureaucracy, careerism, insincerity, and other such 'Stalinist' ills".[72] Now, humble people far from Moscow represented positive values. Although, *Ivan Denisovich* does not belong to the current of the "Youth Novel", this juxtaposition of Moscow and Muscovites and the humble inhabitants of far away takes place in the interaction between Ivan and some Muscovite camp inmates. This is a recurrent theme throughout the novel that peaks at different stages. The negative topos of Moscow and its inhabitants does not only align *Ivan Denisovich* to current trends in Socialist Realism, but it is also reflects Solzhenitsyn's own opinions.

In *Ivan Denisovich*, Muscovites are marked as distant and alien to the Russian people. All Muscovites in this text are secondary characters; however, Tsezar is the most important among them because of his closeness to Ivan and the frequency of their interaction. Tsezar is described as follows:

---

69 Lukács, 1970, p. 11, 13, 20.

70 For example its continuing critical stance on artistic formalism, and its criticism of Muscovite intellectuals.

71 Katerina Clark. *The Soviet Novel: History as Ritual.* Chicago: University of Chicago Press, 1981.

72 Clark, 1981, p. 227.

"Tsezar was a hotch-potch of nationalities: Greek, Jew, Gypsy—you couldn't make out which."[73] The otherness of Tsezar and his fellow Muscovites is also symbolized by comments on their language.

> Those Muscovites can smell one another at a distance, like dogs: they sniff and sniff when they meet, in a way of their own. They jabber so fast too, each trying to out-talk the other. When they're jabbering away like that you hear practically no Russian: they might be talking Latvian or Rumanian.[74]

These outlandish Muscovites, Tsezar and Pyotr Mikhailych, are not by chance members of the intelligentsia. There are several hints in the text that seem to confirm the ideologically charged portrayal of the members of the intelligentsia in *Ivan Denisovich*. The most telling scene takes place in the office of the camp. Tsezar, a filmmaker who has a job at the office, is talking to another prisoner, identified as "X 123", during lunch break:

> 'If one is to be objective one must acknowledge that Eisenstein was a genius. *Ivan the Terrible*, isn't that a work of a genius? The dance of the masked oprichniki! The scene in the cathedral!'
>
> 'Ham,' said X 123 angrily, arresting his spoon before his lips. 'It's all so arty there's no art left in it. Spice and poppy-seed instead of everyday bread and butter. And then, that vile political idea-the justification of personal tyranny. A mockery of the memory of three generations of Russian intelligentsia.'
>
> He ate as if his lips were made of wood. The kasha would do him no good.
>
> 'But what other interpretation would have been allowed?'
>
> 'Allowed? Ugh! Then don't call him a genius! Call him an arse-licker, obeying a vile dog's order. Geniuses don't adjust their interpretations to suit the taste of tyrants!'
>
> 'Hm, hm!' Shukhov cleared his throat. He hadn't the nerve to interrupt such a learned conversation. But there wasn't any sense in standing there, either.
>
> Tsezar swung round and held out his hand for the bowl, not even looking at Shukhov, as though the kasha had materialised out of thin air.
>
> 'But listen,' he resumed, 'art isn't a matter of what but of how.'
>
> X 123 struck the table angrily with the edge of his hand.
>
> 'To bloody hell with your 'how' if it doesn't arouse any good feelings in me.'[75]

This conversation immediately catches the reader's attention because it is a clear anachronism. The film Tsezar is discussing with X 123 was not

---

73 Solzhenitsyn, 1963, p. 38.
74 Solzhenitsyn, 1963, p. 150-151.
75 Solzhenitsyn, 1963, p. 94-95.

premiered until 1958, ten years after director Sergei Eisenstein's death. Eisenstein shot *Ivan the Terrible part II* during World War II, but Soviet censors forbade it during post-production in 1946.[76] On September 4, 1946 the Central Committee of the CPSU attacked Eisenstein's film because it allegedly portrayed the *oprichniki* as "degenerates", who were "similar to the Ku Klux Klan" and Ivan the Terrible as "a man of no will and weak character."[77] The film premiered in 1958 as part of the de-Stalinization process. The conversation is therefore anachronistic in several ways: firstly, the conversation is supposed to take place in 1951, so the characters could not have seen the film. Secondly, the "only allowed interpretation" of the movie until then was not that it was a "justification of personal tyranny". Even disregarding official criticism, and looking at the movie itself, it is difficult to see it as a justification of tyranny: The scene of the dance of the *oprichniki* is part of a sequence that includes the scene of Ivan the Terrible tricking his own mentally handicapped cousin into his death in the cathedral. The almost demonic scene in which Ivan leads the *oprichniki* into the cathedral wearing black hooded cloaks is indeed reminiscent of the Ku Klux Klan. Eisenstein, a member of the Jewish Anti-Fascist Committee, is unlikely to have meant such a visual allusion to be a positive one.[78] However, the criticism expressed in *Ivan Denisovich* seems to point towards Eisenstein more than to the film itself. Eisenstein symbolizes a Soviet intellectual who is at once refined in his art—and therefore "formalist"—but somehow subservient to politics. Here, Solzhenitsyn is combining typically Soviet objects of scorn with his own, more dissident opinions.

Abraham Rothberg found this scene "technically awkward" because he rendered it unlikely that a peasant would remember or take note of so many details from such a debate about a film.[79] He therefore comes to this conclusion:

---

76 Jay Leyda. "Two-Thirds of a Trilogy." *Film Quarterly* 12.3 (1959): 16-22.

77 Leyda, 1959, p. 21.

78 Arno Lustiger. *Rotbuch: Stalin und die Juden: die tragische Geschichte des Jüdischen Antifaschistischen Komitees und der sowjetischen Juden*. Berlin: Aufbau-Verlag, 1998. p. 39.

79 Abraham Rothberg. *Aleksandr Solzhenitsyn: The Major Novels.* Ithaca: Cornell University Press, 1971. p. 39.

> Anyone reading those words of X 123 who has also read Solzhenitsyn's letters and his speeches to the Writers' Union knows that this is the novelist speaking in his own voice, speaking not only with a rigorous artistic criterion that refuses to rule out personal and political morality, but also with contempt for all those artists who helped to justify Stalin's tyranny and contribute to the 'cult of personality'.[80]

Ian Christie places the comments made by X 123 in a Russian dissident tradition of ignoring all of Eisenstein's humiliations and suffering under Soviet censorship in favor of bashing him as Stalin's toady because of the canonical status attained by some of his movies.[81] Indeed, comparing *Ivan Denisovich* with Solzhenitsyn's other works, there seems to be more than just antipathy towards Eisenstein at work in this scene—although another one of his films is discussed negatively in the text.[82] Tsezar's constant absent-mindedness, his tendency to argue about aesthetic experience for itself instead of content, and his privileged status in the camp are the embodiment of what Solzhenitsyn describes in his essay *Obrazovanshchina* as the new, shameful intelligentsia of the Soviet capital cities.[83] The capital as the home of morally objectionable and false people as a new Socialist Realist topos is combined with Solzhenitsyn's own ideological priorities. As X 123, Solzhenitsyn alleges that the new intelligentsia is different to the intelligentsia *under the old regime*. According to Solzhenitsyn, the focus of the new intelligentsia is to secure its own material well-being; and he accuses it of loyally serving the state in order to "establish our common prison."[84] Solzhenitsyn argues that instead of education, strength of the soul, and the acceptance of the religious foundations of morality should determine the intelligentsia.[85] By these criteria,

---

80 Rothberg, 1971, p. 40.

81 Ian Christie. "Introduction." *Eisenstein Rediscovered.* Eds. Ian Christie and Richard Taylor. London: Routledge, 1993. p. 20-21.

82 Gary Kern, who studied all different versions of *Ivan Denisovich*, writes that the version that Solzhenitsyn called the "canonical" one expands the conversation about Eisenstein's *Battleship Potemkin* (1925) criticizing his portrayal of marine officers. Kern, 1976, p. 429.

83 This term, which is derived from the Russian word for education, is used by Solzhenitsyn to define a group of people whose claim to belonging to the intelligentsia is based solely on their education. The term was translated "The Smatterers" in English and "Intelligenzler" in German.

84 Alexander Solschenizyn. "Intelligenzler." *Stimmen aus dem Untergrund. Zur geistigen Situation in der UdSSR.* Ed. Alexander Solschenizyn. Darmstadt: Luchterhand, 1975. p. 243.

85 Solschenizyn, 1975, p. 252, 265.

Ivan Denisovich has better chances of counting himself among the intelligentsia than Tsezar. Solzhenitsyn claims that the real intelligentsia should live in opposition to the state and "reject the lie", even if it means raising one's own children on dry bread.[86] The parallels with X 123's rejection of the "spice and poppy-seed" *in lieu* of "everyday bread and butter" stand out.

Solzhenitsyn's anti-intellectualism, which seems directed at the Soviet establishment, merges with a rejection of "formalism" akin to official Soviet cultural policy. X 123's preference for content that elates instead of "arty" forms, and the depiction of Tsezar's ponderings as escapism are reminiscent of Anatoly Lunacharsky's attacks on formalism in the 1920s that were revived in the post-Stalin era.[87]

Additionally, the conversation between Tsezar and X 123 is an instance in which what appears to be the opinion of the author breaks through a text that otherwise appears as a very controlled narrative of everyday life in a Soviet prison camp. This scene in *Ivan Denisovich* gives insight not necessarily into Solzhenitsyn's memories of life in a prison camp, but rather into opinions that seem very similar to his own.

Although *Ivan Denisovich* is inspired by the author's own experience in a prison camp and presents some of his views, it is not a memoir. It is very meticulously crafted, and is fully void of the spontaneity of other testimonial texts on the prison camp experience. The author's categorization of *Ivan Denisovich* as a povest, while true in a formal way, had hardly an impact on its reception. The exceptionality of the topic blurred its relationship with Socialist Realism among its Western readers. It is indeed the topic of life in a prison camp in the USSR that made the strongest impact, and this will be will be further studied in part 2.3.

The First Circle

The First Circle, Solzhenitsyn's next camp-related work, was not published in the Soviet Union. For a few years it stalled in the editorial phase, until it became known it had been printed in the West in 1968. This angered the

---

86 Solschenizyn, 1975, p. 245, 269.

87 Cf.: Victor Erlich. *Russischer Formalismus.* Munich: Suhrkamp, 1973.

Soviet Writers Union considerably and the publication of the novel in Russia was not to take place until decades later.

First Circle is at first glance a conventional novel.[88] It lacks an introduction from the author noting that he had very similar experiences to those described in the book. This information is nonetheless supplied in its marketing; this is mentioned on the cover or back of the book, and in reviews written about it. For example, Helen Muchnic writes in *Russian Review*:

> [Solzhenitsyn] himself has endured what he has written, has looked on tragedy with his realist's eyes and has not distorted his grim knowledge to fit the formula of any predetermined solution.[89]

First Circle is set in a *sharashka*—an institution for intellectual forced labor. The novel presents us with a microcosm rooted in a prison environment, as in the case of *Ivan Denisovich*. Similarly, the time span of the novel is very short—just a few days at the end of December—but flashbacks reach further back in time. Although the heroes of the novel—Gleb Nerzhin and Innokenty Volodin—are members of the intelligentsia, they are men who reject the alleged philistine corruption of the Soviet bourgeoisie. They are idealistic men who develop certain ascetic qualities in order to achieve higher goals. Nerzhin's experience is analogous to Solzhenitsyn's in many different aspects, and both Nerzhin's and Volodin's opinions correlate with opinions the author expressed in other texts. Hence, the novel does have strong autobiographical references, despite its careful assembly and its purely fictional elements.

It is almost impossible to analyze *First Circle* and its structure without mentioning the parallels between this text and the motifs and style of Socialist Realist novels of its time. Therefore it will be essential to begin by looking at the novel from this perspective.

The hero common to Socialist Realism became more individualized during the 1960s and 70s.[90] This process is apparent in the differences between *Ivan Denisovich* and *First Circle*. In the section on *Ivan Denisovich* I have

---

88 In this chapter, I base my discussion on the first version of the book; the second (longer) version wasn't published in English until 2009.

89 Helen Muchnic. "Solzhenitsyn's 'The First Circle'." *Russian Review* 29.2 (1970). p. 166.

90 Witte, 1989, p. 10-13.

already discussed how the author endeavors to single the titular character out of the crowd by using represented discourse (*skaz*) and telling us *his* thoughts in *his* language. Ivan is represented as an individual with a unique personality, an impression strengthened by his wide range of emotions including anger and disappointment. In *First Circle*, individualization of the characters goes a step further—although the heroes and villains remain to a certain degree stereotypical. The author endeavors to imbue each character with a specific personality and individuality. He achieves this mostly by using the literary device of polyphony.

Although polyphony in literature can be used to present different but equally valid points of view, in Socialist Realist literature of the 1960s and 70s polyphony was used to present different points of view within a consensus of values.[91] In *The First Circle* the narrator presents the point of view of different characters, depending on their centrality in certain scenes and/or chapters. As Gary Kern points out, the whole structure of the novel is shaped like a pyramid leading up to the chapters in which Stalin is the main actor, and then moving away from him.[92] As the point of view changes according to this almost mathematical structure, Kern proposes the following plausible interpretation of the authorial voice of the novel:

> Since the thread of the narrative passes from character to character in a manner incomprehensible to any one character, it is obvious that an omniscient author is recording the fates of diverse people. And by presenting each character within the context of a problem and revealing his thoughts through interior monologues or omniscient appraisals, the author orchestrates a composition of shifting perspectives on the society at large.[93]

Points of view may change, but their credibility and depth vary. Here or there, the unnamed narrator adds a detail which shows his partiality. At times, it seems to be the result of the narrator's worldview that some of the characters in this longer work are somewhat clichéd. For example, Robin Blackburn describes the Marxists in the novel as too "unconvincing and wooden".[94] This is the case, for example, in the characterization of Lev Rubin, one of the inmates of the *sharashka*.

---

91 Witte, 1989, p. 28.
92 Gary Kern. "Solzhenitsyn's Portrait of Stalin." *Slavic Review* 33.1 (1974). p. 5.
93 Kern, 1974, p. 2-3.
94 Robin Blackburn. "The First Circle." *New Left Review* I.63 (1970). p. 60.

Throughout the book, ideological and political questions are discussed in confrontations between Gleb Nerzhin—Solzhenitsyn's apparent alter ego—and Lev Rubin the "Jewish Communist"[95]—a character allegedly based on Lev Kopelev. In what seems a rather affected portrayal of a Communist, Rubin staunchly defends, in a conversation with Nerzhin, the idea that Stalin is wise, and in fact the smartest man in the country:

> 'He's the Robespierre and the Napoleon of our revolution rolled into one. He sees far beyond what we can possibly see.'
>
> 'Better to trust your own eyes. Listen, when I was still only a kid I started to read his books after I'd read Lenin's, and I just could not get through them.[...] Everything Stalin says is crude and stupid-he always misses the most important point.'
>
> 'You made this discovery when you were still a kid?'
>
> 'When I was in the last year at school. You don't believe me? Neither did my interrogator...But I'm driven crazy by his oracular style-and the condescending way he has of laying down the law. He really seems to believe that he's the cleverest man in the country—'
>
> 'But he is!'[96]

Nerzhin's argument that he had fathomed Stalin's "stupidity" and crudeness from his texts as a teenager, adds to the hyperbolism of the scene.

In a later scene, a certain bias in the narrative voice becomes more apparent. Lev Rubin is assigned to identify the voice of a man on a tape, in order to facilitate his arrest. The narrator describes to us how Rubin feels, and how he looks:

> [Rubin's] greatest fear was that he might not be allowed to go on working with the tape. His own career having long ceased to concern him, Rubin lived only for the higher cause of humanity. Even before he had heard the tape he already felt strongly involved in it.
>
> [...] Rubin stared into the coloured fabric which covered the loud-speaker, as though it might reveal the enemy's face. When Rubin stared so intently his face looked drawn and cruel: no one could expect any mercy from a man with a face like that.[97]

There is an ironic undertone in the description of Rubin's inner life—a prisoner who wants to work in order to put more people in prison, seeing this

---

95 Solzhenitsyn, 1968, p. 15.
96 Solzhenitsyn, 1968, p. 40-41.
97 Solzhenitsyn, 1968, p. 195.

as a service to a higher cause of humanity. The identification of the voice on the tape is central to the novel's plot. The novel begins with the recorded phone call, and it climaxes with the identification and arrest of the caller. As the caller is one of the novel's heroes (Innokenty Volodin), his identification is a negative deed. The narrator's depiction of Rubin's face strengthens the distance from the character that breaks his neutrality.

Of all the characters of *First Circle* which seem overly stereotypical, Stalin stands out the most. His depiction has been interpreted as satire due to its closeness to caricature.[98] In the novel, Stalin is often described as animal-like:

> Stalin was terrible because he never listened to excuses. He never even accused you; the only sign was a malignant gleam from his yellow, tigerish eyes and a slight puckering of his lower eyelids.[99]

Hyperbolism[100] and sarcasm[101] are further devices used to emphasize Stalin's absurdity or stupidity. His awkwardness is emphasized in the Russian original text in that Stalin speaks *and* thinks with a thick accent. The author's decision to turn to ridicule instead of focusing on describing the deeds of Stalin as an evil-doer marks a certain distance both to a form of relativist polyphony and—as we shall see—to the genre of witness literature. Kern describes a common impression of readers when confronting this portrait of Stalin:

> Many readers of *The First Circle* regard the portrait of Stalin as a crude caricature. The satire is so bitter, the authorial comments so sarcastic, that one feels the author vents his personal rancour and loses control of his craft.[102]

Kern is able to argue that—despite all the sarcasm and caricature—this is not due to lack of control; indeed, the text is produced with punctilious care. In the

---

98 Karen Ryan analyzes Solzhenitsyn's Stalin as satire in: Karen L. Ryan. *Stalin in Russian Satire, 1917-1991*. Madison: University of Wisconsin Press, 2009.

99 Solzhenitsyn, 1968, p. 105. He is also described as having claw-like hands (p. 120), or looking like an owl (p. 107) or a raven (p. 113).

100 "Just as King Midas turned everything he touched into gold, so Stalin's touch turned everything into mediocrity." Solzhenitsyn, 1968, p. 110.

101 For example, after a pathetic description of how Stalin had not even trusted his own mother, the narrator tells us that the only man he had ever trusted in life was Hitler. And that "Every peasant woman in every market-place in Russia had prophesied the war day in and day out. Only Stalin remained unperturbed. He had trusted Hitler..." Solzhenitsyn, 1968, p. 109.

102 Kern, 1974, p. 2.

four chapters dealing with Stalin, who at the time is thinking back on his life in the aftermath of his recent birthday, four different narrative voices can be identified. There is an omniscient narrator, Stalin's interior monologue, an ironic version of Stalin's interior monologue, and direct quotations (with quotation marks) of his alleged thoughts and his writings.[103] Through these different narrative voices, Solzhenitsyn tries to awaken the readers' disgust towards Stalin. This shows how polyphony is not only used to individualize the novel's characters, but also to present certain values and opinions.

Beyond the mere use of polyphony as a trend of Socialist Realism of the time, some of the characters of *First Circle* and the values expressed are very similar to those in other Socialist Realist novels—including High Stalinist novels. Katerina Clark and Evgenii Dobrenko argue that most Socialist Realist novels were politicized *Bildungsromane*.[104] The plot centered on the learning process in which the hero achieves a "greater harmony both within himself and in relation to his society."[105] An important motif in High Stalinist novels is sacrifice. Both Innokenty Volodin and Gleb Nerzhin sacrifice something (their freedom and/or certain comforts) in order to achieve inner harmony and a feeling of having done the right thing in society. Volodin risks his diplomatic posting by calling an old friend and warning him that he is about to fall into a trap set by the KGB. Nerzhin decides not to continue working in the more comfortable setting of the *sharashka*, in projects that force him to collaborate in the arrests of others, and is moved to a hard-labor camp. Because their sacrifice also has to do with their attitude towards imprisonment and the suffering incurred by them there, it also relates to Solzhenitsyn's controversial views on suffering as a political prisoner. This is a topic that will be discussed later on in this chapter. However, it is important to note that this motif was central to Bolshevik mythology and Socialist Realism in the 1930s and 40s.

---

103 Kern, 1974, p. 5-6.

104 Evgenij Dobrenko. "Socialist Realism." *The Cambridge Companion to Twentieth-Century Russian Literature.* Eds. Evgenij Dobrenko and Marina Balina. Cambridge: Cambridge University Press, 2011. p. 104-105; Clark, 1981, p. 16-17.

105 Clark, 1981, p. 17.

Furthermore, *The First Circle* shows a strong similarity to the High Stalinist novel in its portrayals of villains both in the way that it presents them (the in-depth portrayal of their inner life, their double-facedness, the satirical elements), but mainly through the type of values that they represent. Enemies in this novel are historical figures such as Stalin, or the Minister for State Security Viktor Abakumov. It is clear that by making Stalin the villain of a novel otherwise similar to Stalinist novels, Solzhenitsyn is confronting the assessment of these earlier novels on their own terms. Other villains are fictional characters, most of whom are members of the Moscow elite and some of whom have a merely secondary role. Among the fictional villains, Innokenty Volodin's wife "Dottie" stands out. In general, women play a subordinate role in the novel. And it is quite salient that all of them are only objects that are easily abandoned or renounced by men. Rothberg notes with bewilderment a "curious detachment" to the author's estimation of them.[106]

> They seem somehow less important to men than political or moral commitments, less meaningful than work or war, reflection or dispute; their company seems less fulfilling than male comradeship.[107]

Despite their concomitant role, women correspond with the typical female characters of Socialist Realist novels as described by Clark.[108] Women's roles in such novels were either to help the hero, or to tempt him.[109] Among them are women such as Nadezhda ("Nadya"), Gleb Nerzhin's "absent wife" who only meets him once during the novel but is faithful and supportive, and "Dottie", Volodin's wicked wife. "Dottie's" birth name is Datoma (an acronym for "daughter of the toiling masses"). Her Westernized nickname symbolizes her high social standing. She is the daughter of a major-general and is married to Volodin, a diplomat. "Dottie" fits well into the stereotype of the woman as "witch and temptress" that Clark describes.[110] This type of woman represents "petit-bourgeois individualistic values" and/or belongs to "the wrong social class"; her role is to try to seduce the hero, a trial the hero must pass in order to achieve his goal of becoming a better man.[111] Although

106 Rothberg, 1971, p. 107.
107 Rothberg, 1971, p. 107.
108 Clark, 1981, p. 183-185.
109 Clark, 1981, p. 183-185.
110 Clark, 1981, p. 185.
111 Clark, 1981, p. 185.

"Dottie" and Volodin are married to each other, they are estranged. He feels increasingly repulsed by her neophilia, her greed, her growing assertiveness, and her bourgeois lifestyle.[112] Most of all, he deplores her unfaithfulness at home while he was in Rome, (having an affair himself).[113] Volodin decides that he does not want to continue living like "Dottie" and the other members of the Soviet elite he has contact with. However, "Dottie" is depicted as a clever temptress who lures him into her bedroom; Volodin feels lost when he realizes that he has fallen into "her trap".[114] In the end, he ultimately rejects her and decides to "do the right thing" even if he puts her in danger. The anti-values she represents, and the way she is sensualised,[115] fits into the Socialist Realist image both of the villain and the witch.

In general, the interaction between Volodin and his wife would be a picture perfect criticism of what was denounced in the post-Stalin era as an excessively bourgeois lifestyle by the Soviet elite—were it not for one detail. In Volodin's consciousness-gaining process, he shows admiration for the pre-revolutionary bourgeoisie—even if their lifestyle was outwardly the same as that he criticizes—but he feels that they had inner values.[116] This is inconsistent with the otherwise paradigmatic search for higher consciousness, sacrifice, and redemption that marks the whole plot—and might have its explanation in the author's pro-Tsarist outlook. The fact that Nerzhin and Volodin achieve the ideal state of consciousness through imprisonment is controversial and will be discussed in the next section. Above all else, it is in this question that the author's private views can be recognized—but only to those who know his other works. Hence, this ethically questionable view, common in many of Solzhenitsyn's works, that prison is a

---

112 Solzhenitsyn, 1968, p. 343ff.

113 "She didn't even bother to deny that she had been unfaithful but, with unanswerable feminine logic, put the blame on Innokenty—why had he left her on her own?" Volodin believes his own affair "did not count", which is why he can be angry at his wife; and that "as a man, he could never forgive what had happened." Solzhenitsyn, 1968, p. 349; 409. The fact that female infidelity is demonized and male infidelity is depicted as a matter of course in the novel is perhaps part of its general anti-feminist slant.

114 Solzhenitsyn, 1968, p. 408-9.

115 She is described as shallow and depraved (p. 408) and as wearing sensually arousing clothing (p. 409).

116 Solzhenitsyn, 1968, p. 436-7.

school for moral and spiritual improvement will be discussed in the context of the analysis of his work's reception as witness literature.

Even though many aspects of *First Circle* give it a striking resemblance to Socialist Realist novels, categorizing it as one is controvertible. Deming Brown argues that it is a satire of the Socialist Realist mode that "attacks Stalinist literary whoredom".[117] Hingley agrees and quotes Solzhenitsyn's claim that Socialist Realism is "a vow to abstain from truth."[118] In a lighter tone, Wolfgang Kasack understands the novel not as a sample of Socialist Realism, but as an "Auseinandersetzung" with this literary mode.[119] Klaus Städtke interprets *First Circle* as a revival of 19th century literature for the same reasons as Clark considers it Socialist Realist.[120] However, as Clark points out, even dissident writers often co-opted the language and motifs of Socialist Realism to express their criticism.[121] From a merely formal point of view, the resemblance of *First Circle* to other—contemporary—Socialist Realist novels need not be seen as a political statement, but an aesthetic one.

As opposed to *Ivan Denisovich*, the horizon of expectations surrounding *First Circle* was less strongly molded by the paradigm of witness accounts. The striking alignment of *First Circle* with the conventions of Socialist Realist novels—including a variety of classic villains and heroes—underline its capacity as a conventional work of literary art. A further factor that strengthened the image of the work as literature rather than testimony was that Solzhenitsyn revised the work several times. He even mentioned in interviews that he wasn't sure that his preferred version was the one

117 Deming Brown. "Cancer Ward and The First Circle." *Slavic Review* 28.2 (1969). p. 312.

118 Hingley, 1979, p. 203.

119 Kasack, 1973, p. 200.

120 Klaus Städtke. "Zwischenzeit. Anmerkung zu Solženicyns Roman *Der Erste Kreis der Hölle.*" *Eine Andere Welt? Kultur und Politik in Osteuropa 1945 bis heute: Festschrift für Wolfgang Eichwede.* Eds. Wolfgang Eichwede, et al. Stuttgart: ibidem-Verlag, 2007. 97-105.

121 "Yet when they [the critics] produced fiction containing critiques of Stalinism, they often used the ready-made code or system of signs of the Socialist Realist tradition. Inevitably, the system of signs was modified as a result; some epithets, for instance, changed their value import from positive to negative. Nevertheless, the changes came from within the tradition the writers were opposing." Clark, 1981, p. 13.

translated into foreign languages.[122] Because his alterations consisted mainly in changes to the plot to add dramatic effect, this seemed to suggest that the novel was a literary work to be perfected instead of a testimony that was largely based on memory.[123] In part 2.3, I will discuss elements of its content that also undermine an interpretation of this work as a form of testimony.

The Gulag Archipelago

The question of genre is an entirely different one in the case of *The Gulag Archipelago, 1918-1956: an experiment in literary investigation*, Solzhenitsyn's most voluminous work on the labor camp experience. Soon after its publication, Slavicist Harold Swayze wrote:

> The subtitle of Solzhenitsyn's book should warn the reader that this is no ordinary memoir, historical study, or political analysis, and it points to the difficulty of defining the work in terms of genre.[124]

This work, which was published in 1973 when Solzhenitsyn was already a Nobel laureate, was much publicized as the history of the Soviet prison camp system from the point of view of one of its victims.[125] Rufus Mathewson described it in 1975 as "the documented historical record" of the Soviet prison camps.[126] Until today, it is at times characterized as a work of historical scholarship: for example, political scientist Siegfried Jenkner described it as *the* classical definitive work on the history of the camps in his annotated bibliography on gulag literature.[127] The book is introduced by a first person

---

122 For instance in an interview with *The New York Times*: Hedrick Smith. "Solzhenitsyn Puts Back Parts of Self-Censored Works." The New York Times 4 December 1974: 32.

123 *Ivan Denisovich* was likewise altered; however, the changes were minimal and were not publicized in the same way (Cf. Kern, 1976).

124 Harold Swayze. "Review: [Untitled]." *Slavic Review* 34.4 (1975): p. 825.

125 In *The New York Times* and in *Der Spiegel*, for instance, it was presented as a report on the history of the prison camp system in the USSR, cf.: Stephen F. Cohen. "The Gulag Archipelago." The New York Times June 16 1974: 1; N.N. "Bereit, den Tod auf mich zu nehmen." Der Spiegel 7 Januar 1974: 46-51.

126 Rufus Mathewson. *The Positive Hero in Russian Literature*. 2nd ed. Stanford: Stanford University Press, 1975. p. 280.

127 Siegfried Jenkner. *Erinnerungen politische Haeftlinge an den GULAG: Eine kommentierte Bibliografie.* 2nd ed. Dresden: MEMORIAL, 2005. p. 5; Anne Applebaum similarly refers to this book as an "oral history of the camps" in her own history of the gulag: Anne Applebaum. *Gulag: A History.* New York: Anchor Books, 2004. p. xix.

narrator who claims to give an account of his own experience in a prison camp, and that of 227 other people, *and* to expose the real history of the prison camps in the USSR. A note at the beginning of the work points out that all the events described are facts and nothing in it is fictitious:

> In this book there are no fictitious persons, nor fictitious events. People and places are named with their own names. If they are identified by initials instead of names, it is for personal considerations. If they are not named at all, it is only because human memory has failed to preserve their names. But it all took place just as it is here described.[128]

Paradoxically, he also claims not to be "so bold as to try to write the history of the Archipelago"[129], and then warns that the evidence of these facts might be destroyed, thus placing the reader under pressure to trust the writer fully, because uncertainty might never be solved by verification.[130] These introductory remarks indeed add to the confusion about the genre of the book.

The goal of the book is multifarious and complex. Next to the explicit aim of telling the true story of the Soviet prison camp system, the author also dedicates the book to the memory of those who have died in Soviet prison camps.[131] Outside this work, Solzhenitsyn claims to have published it in the hope that tens of millions of people would read it and it would contribute to the downfall of the USSR.[132]

The Gulag Archipelago consists of seven parts, each divided into several chapters. The narrative frame of the book is the process of getting arrested and all that follows. Solzhenitsyn weaves together tales of what he presents as his own experience, and the alleged experience of other people in the

---

128 Aleksandr Solzhenitsyn. *The Gulag Archipelago, 1918-1956. An Experiment in Literary Investigation.* Tran. Thomas P. Whitney. 1 Vol. New York: Harper & Row, 1974. p. vi.

129 Solzhenitsyn, 1974, vol. 1, p. x.

130 Solzhenitsyn, 1974, vol. 1, p. x.

131 In an unnumbered page directly after the title page he dedicates this book to "those who did not live to tell it", and asks for forgiveness that he did not "see it all, remember it all, and divine it all." Solzhenitsyn, 1974, vol. 1.

132 In one of his memoirs, he describes his thoughts in the early seventies: "I want *everyone* to read it! Just so long as it makes its impact, just so long as it smashes into the Soviet monster! Let tens of millions read it in the West - and there is nothing more I want from it!" Alexander Solzhenitsyn. *Invisible Allies.* Trans. Alexis Klimoff and Michael Nicholson. Washington, D.C.: Counterpoint, 1995. p. 210.

process of becoming a political prisoner and being sent to the gulag. In between, he adds his rendering of what he sees as the history of the prison camp system of the Soviet Union, and other ponderings on life and history in general.

In part, the authorial voice in *Gulag* can be understood as Solzhenitsyn's own, because that is the way he frames his account in his foreword; he later identifies himself as Solzhenitsyn and as the author of *Ivan Denisovich*, he speaks in first person singular of "his" arrest,[133] and the opinions and experiences related in it are consistent with those he has otherwise made public as his own. However, the narrative voice in *Gulag* is not homogenous—Solzhenitsyn is not only a first-person narrator, at times he is an omniscient narrator who tells us of what other people thought, what they said, and how they behaved without ever informing us of how he knows this. In other instances, Solzhenitsyn sustains imaginary dialogues with certain readers, for example when he imagines his communist readers' reaction to his book. He spares no sarcasm in portraying what he wants his audience to think would be the comments and arguments of this group of readers:

> But I hear an angry roar of voices. The *comrades*' patience has run out! They will slam my book shut, toss it away, spit on it:
>
> 'In the last analysis, this is brazen impudence! It's slander! Where is he looking for genuine political? Whom is he writing about? About some priests, technocrats, sniveling schoolboys...? The real political are us! Us, the unshakable! Us, the orthodox, crystal clear people.' (And Orwell called them the *Goodthinkers*,) Us, who even in the camps stayed faithful to the very end to the one-and-only-true...[134]

What should the reader make of this complex work? It might be easy to point out the authorial voice when Solzhenitsyn speaks of his own experience, but what about the voice of the 227 that are allegedly represented in his book? The definition of the genre of this work affects the way scholars have answered this question. Some take it literally, and they trust that Solzhenitsyn faithfully remembered these stories, but others don't.

---

133 "Across the sheer gap separating *me* from those left behind, the gap created by the heavy-falling word 'arrest,' across that quarantine line not even a sound dared penetrate, came the unthinkable, magic words of the brigade commander: '*Solzhenitsyn*. Come back here.'" Solzhenitsyn, 1974, vol. 1, p. 19. (Italics mine).

134 Alexander Solzhenitsyn. *The Gulag Archipelago, 1918-1956: an experiment in literary investigation.* Tran. Thomas P. Whitney. 2 Vol. London: Collins & Harvill, 1975. p. 322f.

In one of his works on Soviet literature, Geoffrey Hosking describes *Gulag* as a hybrid work of art that includes history, and personal—subjective—elements.[135] He interprets Solzhenitsyn's soliloquies and dialogues as reflecting what he sees as one of the roles of the Russian writer—that of a prophet and social commentator, whereas the historical narrative of the book reflects Solzhenitsyn's role as a chronicler.[136] Hosking's trust in Solzhenitsyn's accuracy is perhaps evident in the fact that in his history of Russia *Rulers and Victims* he quotes Solzhenitsyn's *Gulag* as evidence of strong ethnic solidarity between certain people groups, and the alleged lack of it among Russians.[137]

J. Arch Getty appreciates Solzhenitsyn's literary achievement as follows: "He artfully weaves thousands of personal horror stories into a captivating piece of subjective literature that brilliantly portrays the personal, psychological effects of being repressed."[138] But he warns that, from a methodological point of view, *Gulag* is not adequate as a historical source of facts; instead, he places it in the genre of émigré literature: "his book is thus the most brilliant example of a genre based on rumor, hearsay and personal impression."[139] According to Getty, if seen as a work of literature, the *Gulag*'s imprecision with facts is not a serious problem.

Because of the immense pathos with which the book is written, the strong political conclusions it offers, and the unlikeliness that any man could remember so many life stories by heart, *Gulag* does not comply with generally accepted standards of historiographical objectivity. It is nevertheless not a conventional essay, with its mammoth size, and it goes way beyond the scope of an ordinary memoir. It seems as if each scholar who wrote about this book had to decide for him/herself what genre it belongs to. But, as I will explore in my next chapters, there are indeed certain

---

135 Geoffrey A. Hosking. *Beyond Socialist Realism: Soviet Fiction since Ivan Denisovich.* New York: Holmes & Meier, 1980. p. 116-122.

136 Hosking, 1980, p. 116, 122.

137 Geoffrey A. Hosking. *Rulers and Victims: the Russians in the Soviet Union.* Cambridge, Mass.: Harvard University Press, 2006. p. 128, 221.

138 J. Arch Getty. *The Origins of the Great Purges: The Soviet Communist Party Reconsidered, 1933-1938.* Cambridge: Cambridge Universtity Press, 1987. p. 219.

139 Getty, 1987, p. 219.

theoretical frameworks that can help us gain a better understanding of Solzhenitsyn's work and its reception.

Factual inaccuracy is one reason why *Gulag* can be seen as fiction, not as historiography, but the ideological tendentiousness behind the factual inaccuracy further complicates the question of its genre within literature.[140] Overall, in *The Gulag Archipelago* Solzhenitsyn expresses his worldview more directly than in all his previous works. Deviation from facts serves concrete political aims. His complex political position is not only proclaimed loudly though his many exclamation marks, italics, and capital letters, but also with hyperbole, exaggeration, and use of stereotypes. For instance, when he describes Tsarist political prisons as allowing prisoners to read, hold lectures, tend gardens, and to verbally abuse prison wardens he creates a radical contrast with the image of Soviet prison camps he describes.[141] As political repression under the tsars was far from the picnic he depicts,[142] this literary device undermines Solzhenitsyn's claim that he writes the factual truth.[143]

The problematic use of hyperbolic comparison is even more poignant when he favourably compares the Nazis with the Soviet interrogators. In one occasion he begins by mentioning a few examples of tsarist leniency towards political prisoners, and then goes on to tell a story of a Soviet woman who was allegedly in a Nazi camp. Her husband, who was allegedly in the same camp, had fled, and she was interrogated but refused to speak. Solzhenitsyn writes:

> For a reader with a bitter Gulag past it's a model of inefficient interrogation: Yuliya did not die under torture, and she was not driven insane. A month later, she was simply released-still very much alive and kicking.[144]

It is highly unlikely that Nazis would have released the *imprisoned* wife of an escaped prisoner, instead of killing her. Assuming that such a thing happened, she would not have been released *in* Germany, as she was likely

---

140 In section 3.2 I discuss how an ideology can use different methods to convey its message, as is the case in *Gulag*.

141 Solzhenitsyn, 1974, vol. 1, p. 456-457.

142 Hard labor in a camp, execution, exile abroad, and exile to Siberia were all methods of political repression during the old regime. Richard Pipes describes how even mere suspicion of political crime could become a cause for exile (p. 299). Richard Pipes. *Russia under the Old Regime.* 1st ed. London; Penguin Books, 1979.

143 He makes this claim in the preface of the work, (see quote earlier in this section).

144 Solzhenitsyn, 1974, vol. 1, p. 133.

a slave laborer, as other captured Soviet citizens were.[145] There is nothing paradigmatic in this tale, but Solzhenitsyn later gives another—similar—example, in order to directly compare the Nazis with the Soviets. It is the case of a Russian émigré named Divnich, a Christian preacher, who was allegedly a prisoner of the Nazi secret police, who had accused him of "Communist activities among Russian workers in Germany."[146] Later the Soviet secret police accuses him of "having ties to the international bourgeoisie". Solzhenitsyn writes:

> He was tortured by both, but the Gestapo was nonetheless trying to get at the truth, and when the accusation did not hold up, Divnich was released. The MGB wasn't interested in the truth and had no intention of letting anyone out of its grip once he was arrested.[147]

Divnich's story seems implausible because simply by being a Russian according to Nazi ideology he was an *Untermensch* and would not have been released—except as a collaborator.[148] However, Solzhenitsyn seems to suggest that there is a general truth to the fact that he was released, for his conclusions are a generalization. Solzhenitsyn implies with his examples that the Gestapo, as opposed to the Soviet secret service, was humane in its interrogations and was interested in knowing the truth. If taken literally, one could hardly defend him from the accusation that he is a revisionist writer. Historian Jay Bergman interprets Nazi comparisons in the texts of dissidents as mere metaphors.[149] Nevertheless, the claim that torture for its own sake was common in the USSR is not generally found in gulag literature, as Leona Toker points out: "Gulag narratives contain little evidence of torture for the

---

145 Cf.: Mark Spoerer and Jochen Fleischhacker. "Forced Laborers in Nazi Germany: Categories, Numbers, and Survivors." *The Journal of Interdisciplinary History* 33.2 (2002): 169-204; John Connelly. "Nazis and Slavs: From Racial Theory to Racist Practice." *Central European History* 32.1 (1999): 1-33.

146 Solzhenitsyn, 1974, vol. 1, p. 145. The term "workers" for slave laborers is very euphemistic.

147 Solzhenitsyn, 1974, vol. 1, p. 145. (MGB was a forerunner of the KGB, the Soviet secret service).

148 Nazi racial ideology regarding Slavs was not as stringent as towards Jews. Nazis allowed certain Slavs to live in "freedom" as long as they were useful to their purposes, i.e. they collaborated with their goals in some way. Cf. Spoerer, 2002; Connelly, 1999.

149 Jay Bergman. "Soviet Dissidents on the Holocaust, Hitler and Nazism: A Study of the Preservation of Historical Memory." *The Slavonic and East European Review* 70.3 (1992): 477-504.

sake of torture, as at the hand of the Nazis."[150] However one chooses to deal with Solzhenitsyn's claims, one cannot interpret *The Gulag Archipelago* as history in a factual sense without having to confront these issues at some point. Seen as literature, determining Solzhenitsyn's bending of historical facts as mere poetic licence leaves the thorough political coherence of his diegesis insufficiently explained. What did the author intend to achieve by dealing with history in such an inventive manner? There is a tension between the lofty goal of keeping alive the memory of the dead, on the one hand, and belittling others' suffering by making unfounded allegations about the oppression they experienced, on the other.

The horizon of expectations of the readers of *Gulag* was influenced by its description as the true history of the prison camp system in the USSR. The additional information that Solzhenitsyn was a Nobel Prize winner, and later that he had been thrown out of his country for publishing this book, added to the readers' impression that this was a trustworthy source of information that the Soviet authorities wanted to conceal. The witness status of the author, which is so central to the work's legitimacy, strengthens this relationship of trust between the Western reader and the author. This all creates an ethical tension when the political claims of the work are taken into account. This tension is, as I will explain in the next section, a result of the types of expectations brought forth by what is or seems to be witness literature.

The political implications of Solzhenitsyn's allegations in *Gulag* and a possible political interpretation of *Gulag* will be explored in chapter three of this book.

150 Leona Toker. *Return from the Archipelago: Narratives of Gulag Survivors.* Bloomington: Indiana University Press, 2000. p. 88.

2.2 The Experience behind the Text: Camp Literature and Witness Literature

It is *he*, Solzhenitsyn, the man remembering with sobriety and perhaps too much control, who emerges most vividly from the book [*One Day in the Life of Ivan Denisovich*].

-Irving Howe[151]

Solzhenitsyn's literary work springs directly from his own experience in all its principal ingredients and is at its most powerful when the autobiographical impulse is central to it.

-Richard Freeborn[152]

One Day in the Life of Ivan Denisovich was published in the Soviet Union in November of 1962, and its publication was soon reported in all major newspapers in the countries of my study.[153] In the Soviet Union, the editor of the Soviet literary journal where *Ivan* appeared, Alexander Tvardovsky, added a note alluding to the author's experience.[154] From the very first print onwards, every mention of this short novel included the indication that the author wrote out of his own experience in a prison camp. Through these perennial extra-textual allusions, an immediate and indelible connection was made between the story of a prison camp inmate named Ivan Denisovich Shukhov and the author of the story. Some of the questions about the authorial voice in *Ivan Denisovich* have already been discussed in the past section. What I will now explore is the possibility of reading this text as witness literature. According to Horace Engdahl, the content of witness literature refers to acts of torture, and/or great injustice.[155] A literary work can be defined as witness literature because of the link between its content and the experience of its author.[156] In fact, Engdahl writes that "the effect of such a book depends on the reader's conviction that the author is an authentic

151 Irving Howe. "Predicaments of Soviet Writing." The New Republic 11 May 1963. p. 19.
152 Freeborn, 1976, p. 15.
153 For example: Nicholas Daniloff. "Red Reveals Torture in Stalin Prison Camps." The Washington Post 22 November 1962: B5. More examples will follow.
154 Alexander Tvardovsky. "Vmesto Predisloviia." *Novyi Mir.*11 (1962): 8-9.
155 Horace Engdahl. "Philomela's Tongue." *Witness Literature: Proceedings of the Nobel Centennial Symposium.* Ed. Horace Engdahl. Singapore: World Scientific Publishing Co Pte Ltd, 2002. p. 3.
156 Engdahl, 2002, p. 2-3.

witness."[157] The main proposition in this section is that the reception of *Ivan Denisovich* is highly dependant on the fact that it had been written by a former inmate. The reception of Solzhenitsyn's further works that refer to his experience as a prisoner—*First Circle*, and *The Gulag Archipelago*—are likewise very sensitive to the factor of the author's experience. Interestingly, this is less so in the case of his semi-autobiographical *Matryona's Home*, which barely alludes to prison camp life. Although his memoir *The Oak and the Calf* did draw considerable attention upon its publication in 1975, in literary histories it is rarely mentioned as one of his great achievements as opposed to his camp-related books which always are.[158] Later memoirs such as *Invisible Allies* (1995) received positive reviews but barely drew the attention of scholars—not to mention the public at large. This strengthens my impression that it is not autobiographical allusion as such that renders certain works by Solzhenitsyn particularly attractive to scholars and the public at large, but his actual role as a witness author. But do Solzhenitsyn's camp-related novels fit into the paradigm of witness literature, or not?

At this stage it is important to point out that contrary to major trends in literary criticism of the late 20th century, scholars who write about Solzhenitsyn rarely disassociate the author from the work. The interpretation and appreciation of his work is based on who the author is and what he experienced as a prisoner. This at times translates into negligence of literary analysis in favor of details about the author's life. It is thus no wonder that Elisabeth Markstein and Felix Ingold write the following in the introduction to their volume on Solzhenitsyn:

---

157 Engdahl, 2002, p. 7.

158 Literary histories of Russian or Soviet literature always mention Solzhenitsyn's camp literature, yet this book is hardly noticed. For example, Dobrenko and Balina's and Vinitsky and Wachtel's books don't mention it at all, and Lauer names it in a parenthesis as a source about Solzhenitsyn's publishing struggles. Evgenij Dobrenko and Marina Balina, eds. *The Cambridge Companion to Twentieth-century Russian Literature.* Cambridge: Cambridge University Press, 2011. Andrew Wachtel and Ilya Vinitsky. *Russian Literature.* Cambridge England; Malden, MA: Polity, 2009. Reinhard Lauer. *Geschichte der russischen Literatur.* Munich: C.H. Beck, 2000.

> Es wurde mit dem vorliegenden Band der Versuch unternommen, dem Schriftsteller Solschenizyn gerecht zu werden. Die Akzentsetzung mag überflüssig, gewollt paradox erscheinen. Aber es ist in der Tat erstaunlich wenig Literaturkritisches zum Verständnis Alexander Solschenizyns beigetragen worden, und viel Außerliterarisches—angesammelt in zahlreichen Dossiers zum »Fall Solschenizyn«—überdeckt und verdunkelt bisweilen die Gestalt des Autors, der einmal vor Jahren sagte, der einzige Weg vom Schriftsteller zum Leser führe über das Buch.[159]

Even their very book, entitled *Über Solschenizyn*, contains documents about Solzhenitsyn's life and some critical articles rely on extra-literary information in their assessment of his work.[160] In another context, Barbara Bode writes about Solzhenitsyn in Soviet literature and describes the feeling of both readers and critics that "so little is known" about who Solzhenitsyn is, despite the overwhelming amount of information that was in fact available from the start.

> Die Journalisten schrieben Lobeshymnen auf Solshenizyn [sic], die Leser verschlangen seine Erzählung und erörterten sie endlos, die Sensation erreichte in Rußland und in der übrigen Welt ihren Höhepunkt, aber auf die Frage, wer eigentlich dieser neue Autor, was das für ein Mensch sei, der da plötzlich in einer Woge russischen Ruhmes aufgestiegen war, auf diese Frage wußte niemand etwas Vernünftiges zu antworten.[161]

---

159 Elisabeth Markstein and Felix Philipp Ingold, eds. *Über Solschenizyn Aufsätze, Berichte, Materialien.* Darmstadt: Luchterhand, 1973. p. 7. "In this volume the attempt was made to do the author Solzhenitsyn justice. The emphasis may seem superfluous, and seem intentionally paradox. But there is a surprisingly small amount of literary criticism that has made a contribution to the understanding of Alexander Solzhenitsyn, and a lot of non-literary works, often gathered in dossiers about the 'Solzhenitsyn case'. This veils and obscures the form of the author, who once said that the only way from the writer to the reader goes through the book." (My translation.)

160 One example is: Wolfgang Kasack. "Die epische und dramatische Struktur im Werk Solschenizyns." *Über Solschenizyn Aufsätze, Berichte, Materialien.* Eds. Elisabeth Markstein and Felix P. Ingold. Darmstadt: Luchterhand, 1973. 184-202.

161 Barbara Bode. "Die Diskussion um Solshenizyn als Zentrum der Auseinandersetzungen in der Sowjetliteratur." *Osteuropa* 10 (1965). p. 682. "Jounalists wrote hymns of praise about Solzhenitsyn, readers devoured his novella and debated about it without end. The sensation reached its climax in Russia and the world and yet no one could give a reasonable answer to the question of who this new author—who suddenly rode the crest of Russian fame—actually is, what type of person he is." (My translation.)

Even Solzhenitsyn's own attitude towards the press has been a zigzag between rejection, and attention seeking. As an artist, Solzhenitsyn drew on his experience as a persecuted Soviet citizen and claimed it gave him a certain authority to teach the world through his works.[162]

Solzhenitsyn's camp-related literature is difficult to categorize because of its topic in combination with the fact that he is a survivor of the Soviet labor camp system. One way of understanding it is by placing it on one bench together with Shoah literature and to treat it as a form of witness literature. There are indeed reasons why this categorization may seem sound, but there are also weighty reasons why this is not as simple as it may initially seem.

There are many definitions of witness literature. Most—albeit not all—of these definitions agree on two aspects: the writer is a witness to some form of human-inflicted suffering and the content of his texts refers to this. There is broad disagreement when it comes to the question of the genre of the text—must the text be a straightforward autobiography, or are fictionalized texts acceptable? How factual does the author need to remain? Further conflict arises when it comes to the question of intention: is the author merely informing the reader of what he witnessed, or does he have an ideological agenda?

Horace Engdahl has a very narrow definition of what constitutes witness literature. For him, such literature results from the author's desire to give voice to the silenced and preserve the memory of their names.[163] He includes both Shoah literature and literature about Soviet camps in his definition of witness literature: for Engdahl both Elie Wiesel and Alexander Solzhenitsyn are witness authors. However, in Engdahl's theoretical definition, witness literature must be free of an ideological or pedagogical agenda: "One cannot be a debater and a witness to truth at the same time."[164] Engdahl sees the intention of explanation as alien to witness literature: this is rather the duty of the historian.[165] A similar view on witness literature is held by Avishai Margalit. Margalit—whose term for the author of witness literature is "moral

162 Alexander Solzhenitsyn. *Nobel Lecture* (1970); Alexander Solzhenitsyn. "Interview with Two Western Correspondents." *Index on Censorship* 2.31 (1973): 31-45.

163 Engdahl, 2002, p. 4.

164 Engdahl, 2002, p. 8.

165 Engdahl, 2002, p. 10.

witness"—believes that such a witness should abstain from causal or functional accounts of the evil witnessed.[166] He draws a line between a moral witness and a political witness. The former speaks only of what he or she witnessed, the latter can also speak for others, and use testimony as argument for a specific cause.[167] The intention of the moral witness is mere testimony, "no matter what the instrumental consequences of it are going to be."[168] Léon van Schooneveldt argues that Margalit's concept of moral witness is too abstract, as most witnesses do have programmatic goals in their witness bearing—an argument that I will test against Solzhenitsyn's example.[169]

Another important point in Margalit's definition is that a moral witness can only provide testimony on what he or she *personally* witnessed, and not base this testimony on hearsay.[170] Regarding the experience the witness refers to, Margalit writes that it can be any type of evil that inflicts suffering—such as political persecution or genocide—and the act of witnessing must involve personal risk.[171] The risk may refer to danger that the author goes through as a victim, or the personal risk he takes to bear witness against all odds. However, Margalit differentiates between the martyr who welcomes death, and the witness who does all he or she can to survive and to testify.

The terms "witness literature" and "moral witness" have both been used by Engdahl and Margalit to refer to literature about political persecution and/or camp imprisonment in the Soviet Union among other types of suffering. But over a decade before them, contentious discussions about the nature of "camp literature"—referring to socialist prison camps—had taken place within the area of Slavic studies.[172] As this debate illustrates some forms of

166 Avishai Margalit. *The Ethics of Memory.* Cambridge, Mass.: Harvard University Press, 2002.
167 Margalit, 2002, p. 165-7.
168 Margalit, 2002, p. 167.
169 Léon van Schooneveldt. "The Moral Witness in the Field of Cultural Remembrance." *Literature and Memory: Theoretical Paradigms - Genres - Functions.* Eds. Ansgar Nünning and Marion Gymnich. Tübingen: Francke Verlag, 2006. 235-247.
170 Margalit, 2002, p. 163.
171 Margalit, 2002, p. 148-150.
172 This debate took place in the English-speaking realm. In German, the term *Lagerliteratur* has long been used to refer to both Nazi and Soviet camp literature.

perception and definition of Solzhenitsyn's work, it is necessary to have a look at the arguments.

On the pages of *Slavic Review*, a leading journal of Slavic Studies in the US, controversy ensued after the interdisciplinary researcher Oskar Gruenwald published an article on camp literature.[173] He begins his article by defining camp literature as a genre, and not "merely a sigh of wronged souls."[174] Notwithstanding his disdain for politically neutral witness literature, and its exclusion from his definition of the genre of camp literature, Gruenwald's definition of camp literature is very broad: it includes not only works about the camp experience, but also books which could lead their authors to camp imprisonment. Nevertheless, Gruenwald also requires a concrete *ethical* content in camp literature: "The essence of any camp and prison literature is not that it deals only with prisons and camp, but, rather, that it treats universal themes of freedom and basic human rights."[175] Gruenwald writes that Solzhenitsyn "immortalized Soviet camp literature", but because literature has a universal nature, certain types of literature—like camp literature—can arise in different geographical locations. Furthermore, Gruenwald, who writes about camp literature in Yugoslavia, has a very concrete notion about the political effects of camp literature:

> Camp and prison literature thus promises to develop into a major catalyst in the current process of liberalization, democratization, and humanization in both politics and culture in contemporary Yugoslavia.[176]

Gruenwald's definition of camp literature includes a desire for a form of political fallout as a result of its publication. This may be a contradiction to Engdahl and Margalit's central vision of the witness writer as a-political, and non-didactical, but it is more in line with the expressed wishes of witness authors themselves. Not only Solzhenitsyn, but also other, earlier witness authors have expressed a longing that political change or some form of action follows the publication of their work. Elie Wiesel convincingly wrote of the painful disappointment many Holocaust survivors—who lived waiting for a

---

173 Oskar Gruenwald. "Yugoslav Camp Literature: Rediscovering the Ghost of a Nation's Past- Present-Future." *Slavic Review* 46.3/4 (1987): 513-528.

174 Gruenwald, 1987, p. 513.

175 Oskar Gruenwald. "Response: Camp Literature: Archetype for Dissent." *Slavic Review* 48.2 (1989): 280-283.

176 Gruenwald, 1987, p. 513.

chance to tell the world what they had experienced—felt when they realized that the world had remained largely indifferent, despite the fact that it had known all along of what was being done to the Jewish people in Europe during World War II.[177] Wiesel himself had hoped to have a positive effect on society with his testimony, and was saddened at the ongoing revisionist resistance to the truth.[178]

Anthropologist Robert Hayden[179] and Slavicist Matt F. Oja[180] challenged Gruenwald's definition of camp literature in later articles in *Slavic Review*. Hayden argued that literature about the camps published in communist countries should not count towards it because it was openly published and it rarely fulfilled Gruenwald's stated requirement of promoting liberty and human rights. Moreover, Hayden contested the role of camp literature in leading to democratization because a) most of it was printed abroad and had little effect upon local communist governments, and b) dissident camp literature at times promoted ethnic strife.[181] The main disagreement between Hayden and Gruenwald might actually stem from the difference in their definition of what freedom and human rights mean, rather than from their expectations of what camp literature is to achieve. In an earlier article on Solzhenitsyn's worldview, Gruenwald explains how all of Solzhenitsyn's works demonstrate his rejection of the Enlightenment and his idea that a Christian authoritarian government would be desirable for Russia.[182] Despite this illiberal ideological stance, Gruenwald sees Solzhenitsyn as the paradigm of a camp writer. This might be because he agrees with Solzhenitsyn's criticism that communist countries have cut off too many liberties, but that the West has offered too many.[183] When Gruenwald places his hopes for "liberalization" in camp literature, the desired outcome might be an entirely different one to which other scholars—

---

177 Elie Wiesel. "Art and Culture after the Holocaust." Cross Currents 26.3 (1976): 258-69.

178 Wiesel, 1976, p. 258-261.

179 Robert M. Hayden. "Using a Microscope to Scan the Horizon." *Slavic Review* 48.2 (1989): 275-279.

180 Matt F. Oja. "Toward a Definition of Camp Literature." *Slavic Review* 48.2 (1989): 272-4.

181 Hayden, 1989, p. 278.

182 Oskar Gruenwald. "The Essential Solzhenitsyn: The Political Nexus or the Russian Connection." *Thought* 55.217 (1980): 137-52.

183 Gruenwald, 1980, p. 150-1.

such as Hayden—might have in mind. This illustrates how, even when many scholars agree that witness literature is linked to ethical, political, and even moral values, this does not mean they agree on what these values are.

Matt Oja's disagreement with Gruenwald refers to literary aspects of his definition. Oja claims that there are no epistemological benefits in calling camp literature a genre. He rather suggested seeing it as a "thematic strand running through world literature."[184] Oja argues that the camp experience includes not only the gulag or Nazi concentration camps, but can also refer to Chinese prison camps or neo-fascist prison camps in Latin America: the essence of the camp experience is one of extreme repression exercised by the state on the individual.[185] A universal definition of camp literature would facilitate a cross-cultural comparative framework, and would allow us to gain a "universal insight into the nature of the [camp] experience and its influence on whatever individuals it touches."[186]

Oja's emphasis on the universality of the prison camp as a topic of literature is very much in agreement with the definitions of witness literature offered by Engdahl, and Margalit, but also Leona Toker's work on camp literature. Toker sees camp literature not as part of a national literary tradition, but a universal one, although she does draw the line between Shoah literature and camp literature.[187] Toker sees a fundamental difference between the persecution of an *entire* people group that was destined to be killed in an industrial manner, and the arbitrary—albeit cruel and inhumane—persecution of individuals in communist countries.[188]

As Toker points out, the differences between Shoah literature and communist prison camp literature are mainly a result of the different type of victims and the type of experience they describe. These differences create disparity in the content of the texts. The Nazi policy of extermination against European Jews had no parallel within its own system towards any other group and there was no analogue policy by the Soviet government against any group within or

---

184 Oja, 1989, p. 274.
185 Oja, 1989, p. 273.
186 Oja, 1989, p. 274.
187 Leona Toker. "Toward a Poetics of Documentary Prose—from the Perspective of Gulag Testimonies." *Poetics Today* 18.2 (1997): 187-222.
188 Toker, 2000.

outside its territory. Historian John Connelly writes about the Nazis' policies towards Jews:

> Unlike policies toward the Slavs, or toward any other identifiable human group, policies toward the Jews were an end in themselves. Read backward, the final solution to the 'Jewish question' appears as the logical culmination of an essential ideological predisposition, whereas policies toward Slavs appear as constant improvisation, in which opportunity and ideology shaped one another.[189]

Nazi extermination camps had the explicit goal of annihilating their inmates. Nazi work camps were used to kill inmates through labor; however, inmates were treated with protean harshness according to the assigned "racial" origin of the inmate or his or her ideology.[190]

The Soviet Union had a complex system of prison camps, which—despite all its severity—was based on the ideological goal of re-educating the inmates for future re-integration to society.[191] There was a great difference between prison camp and exile, and there were marked differences between prison camps themselves. The most brutal camps were the "special camps", where inmates had to wear a number on their uniform, and sleep in locked barracks; the most lenient were corrective labor colonies where convicts were not necessarily confined and could learn a profession.[192] There was a high mortality rate in Soviet prison camps in general, but there was also a high rate of release.[193] As a rule, the behavior of the inmate influenced his or her

---

189 Connelly, 1999, p. 33. For further sources, cf.: Saul Friedländer. *Die Jahre der Vernichtung: das Dritte Reich und die Juden: zweiter Band 1939-1945.* Munich: C. H. Beck, 2006; Steven A. Barnes. *Death and Redemption: the Gulag and the shaping of Soviet society.* Princeton: Princeton University Press, 2011. p. 20-26; Hiroaki Kuromiya. "Review Article: Communism and Terror." *Journal of Contemporary History* 36.1 (2001): 191-201.

190 Indeed, Slavic peoples were treated worse than Western European inmates, and Jews were treated worse than all others. The difference between Slavic peoples (e.g. Poles, Czechs, Russians, etc.) was adapted according to contingent ideological and economical demands. Cf. Spoerer, 2002; Connelly, 1999.

191 Barnes, 2011, p. 14-18.

192 Barnes, 2011, 20-21; 25-26. Applebaum, 2004, p. 467.

193 There was an average release rate from camps of about 20-40% every year. The death rate changed radically from year to year and between different camps. The highest death rate and highest release numbers took place at the same time between 1941-44 due to the lack of food supplies during the war and the liberal policy of release respectively. Barnes, 2011, p. 10, 113; Amir Weiner. "Nature, Nurture, and Memory in a Socialist Utopia: Delineating the Soviet Socio-Ethnic

release, or the amelioration of his or her conditions.[194] As a general rule, prisoners of the Soviet prison camp system were categorized according to the perceived danger they posed to the state and the people.[195] Nevertheless, there were several instances in which groups of people were collectively punished for several reasons—mostly due to alleged disloyalty. These cases involved forced internal exile, and only rarely imprisonment.[196] Once in exile, the "special settlers"—as they were euphemistically called—were confronted with widely varying conditions because regulations depended on their particular case. Generally, families were allowed to stay together in exile; however, while the children of exiled kulaks were free to move away from the place of exile once they came of age, the children of exiled Chechens could not move back to Chechnya until the amnesty to all Chechens in 1956.[197] The conditions of the places of exile were generally very harsh, and there was a high death rate among exiles.

These initial differences mean that, although Jewish survivors of the Nazi camps might have had a very similar experience one to the other, victims of the Soviet repression system had a very different experience from each other. Authors of Shoah literature are often of Jewish origin but citizens of a wide variety of nations; Soviet prison camp survivors were generally Soviet citizens—except for the thousands of foreign POWs from World War II. Victims of the Nazi work camps were either foreigners or people tagged as foreigners working as slaves for the Germans; the majority of survivors of Soviet camps were socialized in the Soviet Union and many understood their work at the forced labor camp as a contribution to their own society.[198]

Body in the Age of Socialism." *The American Historical Review* 104.4 (1999). p. 1132.

194 Barnes, 2011, p. 84.

195 Barnes, 2011, p. 124.

196 Barnes, 2011, pp. 94-97; 143-153.

197 Barnes, 2011, p. 153. Michael Kaznelson. "Remembering the Soviet State: Kulak Children and Dekulakisation." *Europe-Asia Studies* 59.7 (2007): p. 1173-6. Surprisingly, from 1938 onwards kulak children were even granted passports, a right that not even regular peasants possessed at the time. Weiner, 1999, p. 1132.

198 Barnes, 2011, p. 16.

Shoah literature developed after the Nazis were defeated, Soviet camp literature was written while these camps still existed. The Nazis never condemned their camps. The Soviet government rebuked the excessive use of state violence—at least to a certain extent—in Khrushchev's speeches at the 20th and 22nd Party Congresses of the Communist Party of the USSR. In the 1960s and 80s, the Soviet state funded the publication of articles, literary works, and films criticizing the inhumanity of the camps.[199] Throughout the years, it issued a large number of amnesties and rehabilitation decrees for those wronged. All these details have an important effect on the literature describing the prison camp experience. Shoah literature can be integrated into the national literature of the place of origin of the author and has thus both a national and international scale; Soviet camp literature was written mostly in Russian—but frequently published exclusively abroad until the 1960s and 80s. Although authors of Shoah literature and Soviet camp literature likewise express the need to preserve the memory of what happened, Soviet authors were confronted with a more ambiguous situation, as the system that repressed them continued to operate in some way. This meant that until 1991 concrete political motives and political activism played a more crucial role in Soviet camp literature than in Shoah literature, where more general humanistic goals were at stake. This is not to say that Shoah literature never has a political or ideological leaning; however, the tendency is to warn against genocide *per se* and not so much to offer concrete political programs. Moreover, the unprecedented violence against the Jewish people in the 1940s created certain challenges from a literary point of view: it is difficult to find metaphors or analogies that do not relativize what had happened;[200] the experience also defies the limits of realism in literature.[201] Michael Hofmann describes the problem as follows:

---

199 Solzhenitsyn's camp literature was published by state publishers in the 60s and 80s, as were other texts with a similarly critical stance. Regarding film, the most prominent example is the full-length documentary criticizing the Solovky labor camp by Marina Goldovskaya, *Vlast' Solovetskaia: Svidetel'stva i Dokumenty* (Moscow: Mosfilm, 1988).

200 Michael Hofmann. *Literaturgeschichte der Shoah.* Münster: Aschendorff, 2003. p. 14-15.

201 Phyllis Lassner. "Life Writing and the Holocaust." *The Cambridge companion to the literature of World War II.* Ed. Marina MacKay. Cambridge: Cambridge University Press, 2009. p. 184.

> Wer die Grauen und das Unwahrscheinliche der Realität des Völkermordes darstellen will, muss um der Annäherung an die Realität willen einen konventionellen Realismus entsagen[.][202]

Literature is often shaped by meaning, but authors of Shoah literature face a particular quagmire finding meaning in what happened.[203] According to Toker, the authors of gulag literature display a different attitude: although most former inmates recognize the injustice of the Soviet penal system, they at times interpret this experience as a form of school for the soul.[204] In fact, some convicts even sought additional suffering—such as fasting—in order to further "purify" their souls.[205] This position is not uncontroversial because this view can be seen as a justification or relativization of the suffering incurred to prisoners, and it will be discussed in detail later on in this chapter. In their testimonies, gulag survivors often exhibit pride in the work they did during their internment at labor camps, probably as a result of a shared understanding of the redemptive power of labor by the authorities and the convicts.[206] A third major difference in content between Shoah literature and gulag literature is that the latter often reverts to the metaphors and topoi of conventional prison literature.[207]

The main similarities between Shoah literature and literature describing the gulag experience are: the definition of the genre by its content—a practice that has its theoretical downsides—and the dependency of the authority and credibility of the text on the author's biography.[208] When it comes to Shoah literature there is a greater tendency towards scepticism regarding fiction;[209] whereas in the case of gulag literature the use of fiction is less controversial,

---

202 Hofmann, 2003, p. 32. "Whoever wants to depict the cruelty and improbability of the genocide needs to renounce conventional realism for the sake of proximity to reality." (My translation.)

203 Hofmann, 2003, p. 20; Andrea Reiter. *Narrating the Holocaust.* Tran. Patrick Camiller. London: Continuum International Publishing Group, Limited, 2005. pp. 59-60; 217-219; 223.

204 Toker, 2000, p. 94-97.

205 Toker, 2000, p. 97.

206 Barnes, 2011, p. 16, 98.

207 Cf.: Martha Grace Duncan. "'Cradled on the Sea' Positive Images of Prison and Theories of Punishment." *California Law Review* 76.6 (1988): 1201-47; Martha Grace Duncan. *Romantic Outlaws, Beloved Prisons: the unconscious meanings of crime and punishment.* New York: New York University Press, 1996.

208 Sue Vice. *Holocaust Fiction.* London: Routledge, 2000. p. 4.

209 Vice, 2000, p. 4-7.

but at the same time its veracity tends to be more easily taken for granted.[210] The third similarity is the ethical drive in writing the text: the author writes for a specific ethical purpose, be it to testify and keep alive the memory of the dead, or to help avoid further genocide, etc. As we shall see in Solzhenitsyn's case, authors of testimonial literature rarely understand their texts as conventional literature.

In sum, there are theoretical challenges that thwart Oja's suggested creation of a universal definition of camp literature. Experiences in prison camps in the 20th century are too diverse to be seen as a universal thematic strand in world literature. On the other hand, the similarities of traumatic experiences involving arbitrary captivity and forced labor are compelling.

2.3 The Reception of Solzhenitsyn's Camp Literature

In this section I will analyze Solzhenitsyn's reception in light of his role as a witness, and relate this to the theoretical ponderings on witness literature, Shoah literature, and camp literature presented in the previous section. This will allow a clearer understanding of the shaping of Solzhenitsyn's authority as a writer, and the canonization of his work; at the same time it will present an opportunity to evaluate the plausibility of the theoretical premises of witness or camp literature. There are three key issues at stake in the reception of literature about prison camp experience: a) authenticity, b) authority, and c) intention. All three are closely related to each other, and they underline the difference from literature about other topics.

According to theoreticians of witness literature, authenticity derives from the fact that the author is a genuine witness of what he writes about.[211] In her book about Shoah fiction, Sue Vice points out that the "lack of perceived authenticity and consequent suspicion of authorial motives" leads to a negative critical appraisal of this type of literature.[212] In the case of literature relating to the communist camp experience, Matt Oja argues that both fiction

---

210 Cf. Oja, 1989, p. 274. This point will be studied in detail at a later point in this study.

211 "The discovery that an allegedly authentic testimony is a fiction or a plagiarism immediately robs it of its power. However, misrepresented facts in a testimony to some extent remain unimportant. A witness is allowed to err, but the writer may not pretend to be a witness." Engdahl, 2002, p. 7.

212 Vice, 2000, p. 160-161.

and non-fiction are equally legitimate in claiming the theme of prison camp.[213] He also points to a common problem in the reception of the surge of prison camp literature that started in the 1960s, which is the temptation of treating fiction as history:

> It is a theme that often demands an exceptionally strong emotional and sympathetic response from the reader and can earn works that deal with it a level of attention or influence they might not otherwise merit on purely artistic grounds. The theme bears a special, though very complex and treacherous, relation to historical truth and so presents the historian with an often irresistible temptation to treat as historical sources works in which it predominates.[214]

Oja's uneasiness about the challenge historians face when confronted with literature about the camp experience is a reflection of a general attitude towards Soviet prison camp literature that came about in the last decades of the Cold War. For many years, it was commonplace for camp literature—be it in the form of memoirs or novels—to be used as a factual source for histories of life in the Soviet Union. This tendency eventually evolved into a long-running controversy regarding source criticism that will be discussed in chapter four of this book. The bone of contention was whether camp fiction should be trusted for historical details, or just as an expression of individual experience. Nonetheless, it is important to bear in mind that—as opposed to Shoah fiction—Soviet prison camp fiction did not awaken mistrust or suspicion as a rule: its authenticity was derived primarily from the author's experience and not from the fictionality of the text. For example, Victor Erlich writes that the salient quality of Solzhenitsyn's fiction is its "relentless veracity."[215] The fact that *Ivan Denisovich*, *Cancer Ward* and *First Circle* are fictional accounts relating to the experiences of prison camp life and surviving cancer treatment does not qualify Erlich's positive appraisal of them, or his view that in these books Solzhenitsyn is speaking the truth about these experiences *because* he went through similar travails.[216] Erlich also states that Solzhenitsyn's camp novels are successful in their goal to bear witness:

---

213 Oja, 1989, p. 274.
214 Oja, 1989, p. 274.
215 Erlich, 1973, "Writer", p. 26.
216 Erlich, 1973, "Writer", p. 18, 20.

"In his fiction the speechless have found a voice; the dispossessed a home."[217]

The choice of fiction in the case of *Ivan Denisovich* had a recurrent positive effect. Kasack describes the fictionality of the diegesis in *Ivan Denisovich* as a literary device that seeks to represent the typicality of a single day in an ordinary prison camp.[218] According to Kasack, by thus describing everyday reality in the prison camp, Solzhenitsyn is obeying a moral obligation to tell the truth.[219] Victor Zorza also understands the choice of describing one fictitious day in prison camp as an effective way of speaking out about the general state of affairs in the Soviet Union.[220] Zorza writes:

> [Solzhenitsyn] reduces the national experience to the personal experience of one man, and the many years of torment to one perfectly ordinary day. The beastliness of the prison guards elicits from the writer no more condemnation than the beastliness of the whole prison-camp system, or indeed of the larger political or social system that made it possible.[221]

Solzhenitsyn's choice of writing a text focusing on a peasant—someone with a different level of education and background than himself—was a further fictitious element in *Ivan Denisovich* that was widely commented on. Here, the perception of the aptness of the choice of protagonist and the way he was portrayed are mixed.

Max Hayward praises Solzhenitsyn for writing from the perspective of a simple peasant "who has neither the language nor the 'ratiocinative powers' to 'rationalize' his situation."[222] Hayward continues:

> He belongs to a totally different world from that of the intellectuals who can still derive some solace from conversation, from the feeling of still belonging to a larger intellectual world outside.[223]

Andrew Wachtel also praises the choice of a peasant as the central character of this prison camp story, precisely because the peasant does not "rationalize" his situation.[224]

---

217 Erlich, 1973, "Writer", p. 27.
218 Kasack, 1973, p. 185.
219 Kasack, 1973, p. 186.
220 Victor Zorza. "Story of the Stalinist Terror." The Guardian 31 January 1963: 8.
221 Zorza, 1963, p. 8.
222 Max Hayward. "Solzhenitsyn's Place in Contemporary Soviet Literature." *Slavic Review* 23.3 (1964). p. 435.
223 Hayward, 1964, p. 435.

Elie Wiesel writes that a child's testimony of the Shoah is purer than that of adults because their words "become experience".[225] This seems to be the way many critics see Ivan: a man as simple as a child, who cannot rationalize his experience. The text itself contributes to this interpretation, for instance, when Ivan thinks about his village and recalls fantastic stories about how the village men are becoming rich by doing stencil paintings of carpets on bed linens—even flying across the Soviet Union to do their work.[226] But he is not a child; there are certain scenes in the book that reveal more mature intellectual dilemmas, such as when he talks to his bunk neighbor Alyosha and tells him that, as opposed to him, he is not in prison for his faith, but "because we weren't ready in 'forty-one".[227] He was accused of spying because he had been a captive of the Germans, but he has come to the conclusion that it wasn't that his accusers really believed that he was a spy but that they used him as a scapegoat for their own lack of preparation and the catastrophic consequences this had. In this sense, the point of view of a simple peasant does not exclude intellectual rationalizations, although these might differ from those of an intellectual. Ivan is no simpleton; however, so little of Ivan's thoughts and reasoning are betrayed in the text that he at times comes across as child-like and even boorish. Wolfgang Kissel wrote about Ivan's language:

> Vor allem aber gelang es Solženicyn, für die Lagesprache ein literarisches Äquivalent zu schaffen, das dem Leser einen exakten Eindruck von der Verrohung der Lagerinsassen vermittelte.[228]

Despite Kissel's claim that the language gives an impression of the brutalization of the prison camp inmates, he affirms that Solzhenitsyn's

---

224 Wachtel, 2009, p. 246.

225 Wiesel, 1976, p. 266.

226 Solzhenitsyn, 1963, p. 50-51.

227 Solzhenitsyn, 1963, p. 187.

228 Wolfgang Kissel. "Samizdat als kulturelles Gedächtnis: Terror und GULag in der russischen Erinnerungsliteratur der Sechziger Jahre." *Samizdat – Alternative Kultur in Zentral- und Osteuropa; Die 60er bis 80er Jahre.* Ed. Wolfgang Eichwede. Bremen: Edition Temmen, 2000. p. 96. "Solzhenitsyn was especially successful in finding a literary equivalent for camp language, thus conveying an exact impression of the brutalization of camp inmates to the reader." (My translation.)

novella shows that the inmates preserve their dignity throughout their ordeal.[229]

A view completely opposed to this is held by the former prison camp inmate Aleksandr Gudzenko who criticized *Ivan Denisovich* claiming that it depicts victims as "half-animal and half-human".[230] Gudzenko affirms that prison camp inmates were able to keep their dignity, as opposed to what he saw in *Ivan Denisovich.* Gudzenko's opinion was originally printed in the newspaper *Kazakhstanskaia Pravda*—a paper that underwent severe censorship—so there is room for doubt regarding the frankness of his opinion. However, his views are confirmed by the results of historian Miriam Dobson's archival research of Soviet readers' responses to the novella.[231] There seems to be an opposite perception of Ivan: on the one hand, a positive view among many Western critics who see him as refreshingly simple and unpretentious, and a negative appraisal of him by many Russian readers.

Overall, when it comes to the choice of a peasant as the protagonist of a testimonial text, I disagree with those who see a lack of rationalizing as a stylistic strength. Keeping a text strictly focused on the experience of everyday life is certainly valuable, and in cases of non-fiction it might even have a court-room value. There is no doubt that the richness in details about the camp and life in it gives the text a sense of credibility.[232] Nevertheless, as Margalit points out, one of the differences between a chronicler and a witness is that the witness speaks of how it feels to be subjected to suffering; he can tell what it was like to go through it, without even needing to describe the details of the horrors suffered.[233] Letting us know more about Ivan's inner life, through *skaz* or conversation, might have made Ivan's experience more universally accessible, despite his rural origin and archaic language.[234] Had

---

229 Kissel, 2000, p. 96.

230 N.N. "Special to the New York Times: Russian Defends Labor-Camp Life." The New York Times 13 October 1963: 5. All references to Gudzenko relate to this article.

231 Dobson, 2005, p. 580-600.

232 Both Victor Erlich and Kathryn Feuer allude to this quality: "Post-Stalin Trends in Russian Literature." *Slavic Review* 23.3 (1964): p. 410; Kathryn Feuer. ed. *Solzhenitsyn: A Collection of Critical Essays*. Englewood Cliffs, N. J.: Prentice-Hall, 1976. p. 17.

233 Margalit, 2002, p. 162-168.

234 In this sense, I agree with György Lukács praise of Tolstoy's ability to convey the intellectual life of his characters in conversations he describes as follows: „[S]ie

Solzhenitsyn allowed himself this type of depth, it would certainly have enriched this work without diminishing its authenticity.

Authority in witness literature often results from the perception of authenticity. Erlich writes about Solzhenitsyn:

> [W]hile the import of Solzhenitsyn's fiction clearly transcends its immediate setting, much of his authority and persuasiveness derives from his immersion in Soviet reality, his unerring sense of the characteristically, if not always uniquely, Soviet institutional patterns, of the characteristically, if not always uniquely, Russian modes of repression and protest, of depravity and integrity.[235]

Solzhenitsyn's experience in prison camps and life in the Soviet Union was part of what imbued him with authority to write about these issues. However, other political, ethical, and aesthetic factors played a role in establishing his authority as an author of the camp theme.

Books about life in communist prison camps had been published outside the USSR since 1919 and were mostly witnesses' accounts. In the early sixties, several critical depictions of the camps were officially published in the USSR, some even before Solzhenitsyn's.[236] But why did *Ivan Denisovich* have more of an impact than these others?

Some scholars, like Alexis Klimoff and Marc Slonim, see the publication of Solzhenitsyn's work as sensational because of the combination of a) the topic (prison camp life) with, b) the author's experience (as a former victim) and c) Khrushchev's political intervention in its publication. Klimoff writes:

> Let it be stated right at the start: the appearance of Aleksandr Solzhenitsyn's *One Day in the Life of Ivan Denisovich* in a Moscow journal in 1962 was an event that cannot be measured by literary standards alone. The publication became an instant political sensation, one greatly intensified by the knowledge that the work had

---

erheben sich aber so steil zu einer großen dramatischen Höhe, dass die äußeren Umstände der Umgebung in die Gespräche selbst nur sehr wenig hineinspielen können." György Lukács. *Der russische Realismus in der Weltliteratur*. Berlin: Aufbau, 1952. p. 210. "They soar so steeply into great dramatic heights that outer circumstances can play but a small part in the conversation." (My translation.)

235 Erlich, 1973, "Writer", p. 18.

236 One example is Georgy Shelest's short story "A Nugget" published in *Izvestiia* in one of the issues celebrating the anniversary of the October Revolution in early November 1962.

> received the personal imprimatur of Nikita Khrushchev, the head of the Soviet Communist Party at the time.[237]

Van Schooneveldt insightfully notes that the question of who is accepted as a moral witness has more to do with the cultural practices of authority than with the purity of the testimony.[238] This is an important clue to understanding why Khrushchev's authorization of Solzhenitsyn's testimony has been of such a radical importance in the subsequent reception of his work. By leaking the process of approval, Khrushchev was legitimizing Solzhenitsyn's words and protecting him from possible repercussions through local organs of the KGB. But in the West, this also had an important effect. As Irving Howe suggested, the embrace of *Ivan Denisovich* in the West may well have occurred because it could conveniently be used by both communists and non-communists in their rhetorical fights.[239] Communists could point to Khrushchev's decision as a sign of liberalization and change—after all, this publication happened *because* and not despite of him. Non-communists, on the other hand, could point to the *content* of Solzhenitsyn's novella to condemn Soviet crimes against their own population.

Solzhenitsyn had dreamt of winning the Nobel Prize for literature even before any of his work was published; this is how he describes his feelings towards the publication of *Ivan Denisovich* all over the world in one of his memoirs:

> *Ivan Denisovich*, which was seized on all over the world as a Khrushchevite political sensation, and nothing more (it had been mauled into English in Moscow by the pot boiling parasite R. Parker and matters have not improved since), had not brought me much closer to the Nobel Prize.[240]

As we now know, *Ivan Denisovich* did bring the author closer to the Nobel Prize, but his impression that its publication was perceived as a political gambit is to a certain extent correct. As it is, it actually helped to legitimize his work and, luckily for him as a writer, this perception did not preclude a serious analysis of his work.

The publication might have been a political act, but the work itself was appreciated by Slonim for aesthetic reasons:

---

237 Klimoff, 1997, p. 3.
238 Schooneveldt, 2006, p. 237-8.
239 Howe, 1963, p. 19.
240 Solzhenitsyn, 1980, p. 292-3.

> *One Day* is not only a political sensation, its publication being authorized by Khrushchev after the intervention of Tvardovsky. It also has great literary merit because of the unity of its 'point of view,' in the Jamesian sense, and in its stylistic originality. The realistic crudeness of the language is skilfully mitigated by the rhythm and tone of the narrative.[241]

The question of *Ivan Denisovich*'s aesthetic value is quite a controversial one. Most of the earliest reports and reviews of the book focus on the content, and the fact of its publication in the USSR. Critics are divided about the aesthetic value of the work. For example, Howe and Magner write that it is not a literary masterpiece, in spite of its political importance.[242] In other cases, there is a mixture of aesthetic and political commentary, which is not only multifarious—many texts are in fact extremely ambivalent.

Not only Khrushchev's authorization and its publication within the USSR, but also certain qualities in the text of *Ivan Denisovich* influenced its acceptance as a special or even "first" type of literary document coming from the Soviet Union. Kasack characterizes *Ivan Denisovich* as the first honest depiction of a camp in Soviet literature.[243] He likens this text to Nadezhda Mandelshtam's *The Century of Wolves*, in which she writes that the only motivation to survive the camp was the perception of a duty to bear witness of what went on there.[244] Kasack claims that by writing *Ivan Denisovich*: "Solschenizyn lebt diese Verpflichtung."[245]

Dariusz Tolczyk has a similar view. He points out that some of the other Soviet accounts of the camps that had been published before *Ivan Denisovich* displayed even more shocking scenes than Solzhenitsyn's book. Nonetheless, Tolczyk writes:

> The constant readiness [...] [of other authors] to dismiss the moral challenges presented by the camps per se by means of facile ideological statements produced a situation where camp experience did not seem to have enough significance to unsettle the protagonists seriously, to say nothing of transforming them. These

---

241 Slonim, 1969, p. 333.
242 Howe, 1963, p. 19; Magner, 1963, p. 418-9.
243 Kasack, 1983, p. 22.
244 Kasack, 1973, p. 186.
245 Kasack, 1973, p. 186. "Solzhenitsyn abides by this commitment." (My translation.)

> writers thus failed to uncover the sources of human behavior that could be revealed in this traumatic test of the limits of humanity.[246]

Kasack and Tolczyk underline that the fact that Solzhenitsyn was a witness was not enough for *Ivan Denisovich* to be perceived as unique. There was a certain moral quality to his text that made it stand out in their eyes. In a compendium of gulag memoirs she edited, historian Anne Applebaum describes *Ivan Denisovich* as the "only authentic piece of Gulag literature" printed in the USSR before the 1980s.[247] However, her book's tendency to derive authenticity from the ability to recognize the "evilness" of Soviet communism has recently been questioned.[248] Perhaps this is a good example of how political arguments sometimes become leading criteria in scholarly understandings of authenticity in literature. How far this has come in Solzhenitsyn's reception in general is a question that will be scrutinized in the next chapter, but as will be shown, this was common in the reception of most of his works.

The fact that Solzhenitsyn achieved fame with a work on the camps affected his further reception in the sense that it had a special testimonial quality that critics appreciated more than Solzhenitsyn's historical novels or analysis. This is evident, for example, in Kasack's treatment of Solzhenitsyn's prose. He acknowledges a superior quality in Solzhenitsyn's works that are related to his suffering, and expresses his astonishment at Solzhenitsyn's expressed goal as a writer:

> Angesichts der vorher geschriebenen Werke mit der großen Anklage gegen die Unfreiheit des Menschen im kommunistischen System, bei denen die dichterische Kraft aus dem persönlichen Leid erwachsen zu sein scheint, erstaunt es, dass Solschenizyn nun sagt, er habe in der Darstellung dieses historischen Themas [der Zeit zwischen 1914-1917] stets »den Hauptsinn seines Lebens« gesehen.[249]

246 Tolczyk, Dariusz "Who is Ivan Denisovich? Ethical Challenge and Narrative Ambiguity in Solzhenitsyn's Text." *One Day in the Life of Ivan Denisovich: a Critical Companion*. Ed. Alexis Klimoff. Evanston: Northwestern University Press. 1997. pp. 70-84.

247 Applebaum, 2011, "Gulag Voices", p. xi and again in p. 126.

248 Dobson, 2012, p. 739.

249 Kasack, 1973, p. 193. (The specification in square brackets was added by me.) "In contrast with his earlier works with their great indictment against people's lack of freedom in the communist system—in which the poetic strength appeared to grow out of personal suffering—it is surprising that Solzhenitsyn now says he has always

Kasack's contention at Solzhenitsyn's own ranking of the importance of his works might strike one as petty—or even absurd—if he had claimed that Lev Tolstoy's work was most valuable when it reflected his own experience as an aristocrat. But in the case of Solzhenitsyn, this disappointment possesses a certain plausibility which is very likely the result of an implicit perception of the significance of testimonial literature. Klaus Mehnert wrote in 1975 that the parts of *Gulag* that did not refer to Solzhenitsyn's own experience seemed like "Fremdkörper" in this work.[250] For his readers, Solzhenitsyn will hardly have written anything more powerful and impressive than his works on his experience in the gulag. The intensity of such an experience, which is similar to other forms of extreme suffering, can have repercussions that are not quite comparable with that of a conventional novel. Elie Wiesel polemically wrote:

> A novel about Treblinka is either not a novel or not about Treblinka; a novel about Treblinka is about blasphemy—is blasphemy. For Treblinka means death—absolute death—of a language and of the imagination.[251]

For Wiesel, personal testimonies of the Shoah have a much stronger impact than fiction ever will.[252] This radical scepticism of fiction is not common when it comes to the Soviet prison camp topic, but there are differences in appreciation of fictional works dealing with this subject. In the case of *Ivan Denisovich* the reception analyzed does not point to a negative impact due to its fictionality. It is generally understood as a form of summary of Soviet prison camp life, and in this sense fully justified in its form. However, in the case of *First Circle* it is less clear why it did not call forth the same tidal wave of reception Solzhenitsyn's other camp-related works did.

It is an interesting question if *First Circle*'s strong adherence to the conventions of the novel is one of the reasons why it had a lesser impact. Toker, who defines *First Circle* as a semi-documentary novel, points out that Solzhenitsyn's "transposition" of plot lines, the changed names of the characters, and the fact that he later changed important scenes to strengthen their dramatic effect draws a parallel with conventional novels, and not to

---

seen the depiction of this historical topic [the time span between 1914-1917] as the 'main purpose of his life'." (My translation.)

250 Mehnert, 1975, p. 524. This translates as "a foreign object".

251 Wiesel, 1976, p. 260.

252 Wiesel, 1976, p. 261.

documentary prose.[253] In 1974, Gary Kern suggested that *First Circle* can be appreciated for aesthetic qualities in the West and its political message in the East.[254] According to Kern, in the East, its informational value concerning Stalinism is of heightened social and political relevance.

In practice, the reception of *First Circle* was ambivalent regarding its testimonial, its aesthetic, and political quality. As I will later discuss, it may be that some of its ideological premises undermined the witness-bearing aspect of the work. All this notwithstanding, it does not mean that *First Circle* was not acknowledged by Western critics.

Both Erlich and Kasack appreciated the inclusion of so many members of different social groups in this novel, because it rendered a picture of the totality of fear in Soviet life.[255] But they perceived it as essentially different to *Ivan Denisovich*, a work which Erlich sees as obvious proof of the kind of writer Solzhenitsyn is, namely a witness.[256]

Max Hayward describes the difference between *Ivan Denisovich* and *First Circle* as the latter being "much longer, more ambitious and less sharply focused" than the former.[257] On the aesthetic side, the length of the novel and lack of focus worked against *First Circle*, but these formal aspects had repercussions on the content, too. According to Hayward, the greatness of *Ivan Denisovich* lies in the simplicity which endows it with universality: by reducing the story to the essential description of an unexceptional day in labor camp it becomes independent of time and place.[258] Hayward thus sees Solzhenitsyn's first book as describing a universally known "feeling of being trapped and doomed to a hopelessly monotonous and meaningless existence".[259] In contrast, the plot and protagonist of *First Circle* are closer to Solzhenitsyn's own persona, its achievement being a detailed description of life in the late Stalin era.[260] For him, the quality and authority of Solzhenitsyn's work was not a result of how exactly he describes his experience, but how

---

253 Toker, 1997, p. 199, 203.
254 Kern, 1974, p. 1-22.
255 Erlich, 1973, "Writer"; Kasack, 1973, p. 187.
256 Erlich, 1973, "Writer", p. 16.
257 Hayward, 1977, p. 204.
258 Hayward, 1977, p. 203.
259 Hayward, 1964, p. 436; He expresses a similar thought in: Hayward, 1977, p. 203.
260 Hayward, 1977, p. 204.

well the anti-exploitation message gets through. He meets this type of work with a combination of aesthetic and political expectations. But his expectations, in turn, reveal an important aspect of his appraisal and therin lies the possible universality of the text. *First Circle* is so linked to a specific time and person that it loses the universality and timelessness of *Ivan Denisovich*.

Helen Muchnic, who claims that the detail in the descriptions of *First Circle* confirm its authenticity, finds more than just a contingent criticism of Stalinism in *First Circle*:

> And even without knowing that Solzhenitsyn's work is largely autobiographic, one could not doubt its authenticity, so minute are his details of prison life from the moment of arrest, through searches and interrogations, to the daily routine of labor camps and city jails, and the rare, heartbreaking encounters with the outside world, so graphically recorded, so tangibly present in the unemphatic tone of habitual 'true experience.' But his theme is deeper and wider than the pitiful and terrible theme of physical suffering. It is the theme of man's spiritual fate, the death and survival of qualities and ideas, the degradation, preservation, and endurance of the human mind and will.[261]

For Muchnic, this novel goes beyond life in a prison camp: it is about "man's spiritual fate." She identifies Solzhenitsyn as belonging to "the tradition of Russian nineteenth century Realists" for his description of good and evil, and his disapproval of materialism.[262] A type of ethical or ideological content marks Muchnic's appreciation of *First Circle.* Although this spiritual aspect of *First Circle* might initially seem to question its historical contingency, the changing relationship of society towards religion may nonetheless dampen the resonance of the book's spiritual message in the long run.

But not every author saw historical contingency as a disadvantage. Edward Crankshaw regards both *Ivan Denisovich* and *First Circle* to be literary masterpieces.[263] He reflects upon the adequacy of the novel as a medium to portray the subject of 20th century state violence, and comes to the conclusion that *First Circle* is successful in tackling this topic. Despite its weak beginning, the novel is effective in expressing its central truth about the

---

261 Muchnic, 1970, p. 162.
262 Muchnic, 1970, p. 165-6.
263 Edward Crankshaw. "A Masterpiece from Russia: Review of *First Circle*." The Observer 10 November 1968: 26. All Crankshaw references stem from this source.

complete domination of the Kremlin and the Lubyanka prison (as a symbol of the KGB) over the lives of Soviet citizens. For Crankshaw, the relevance of the novel at the time it was written is enough to justify its literary greatness.

Perceived authenticity, Khrushchev's sanction of *Ivan Denisovich,* ethical and aesthetic qualities of Solzhenitsyn's camp fiction, and the Nobel Prize all influenced the establishment of Solzhenitsyn's authority as an author of gulag literature. One important question that remains to be solved is this: what was the intention of Solzhenitsyn's gulag literature? How does this confirm or undermine the theoretical definitions of witness literature as ideologically neutral and camp literature as necessarily dissident?

Nicholas Anning writes that Solzhenitsyn's authority grew at the same time that the political aspect of his work increased.[264] It is true that with time, Solzhenitsyn became more cunning. Solzhenitsyn describes how—very much as he expected—winning the Nobel Prize gave him the authority he felt he needed in order to deliver the political and moral message he longed to share with the world.[265]

At its very core, the interpretation of *Ivan Denisovich* as primarily a political sensation seems to be linked to a widespread hope for political change as a result of its publication. This unrealistic presumption becomes more plausible when one considers that witness literature calls forth completely different expectations than other literary works (on other topics) do. Such works are expected to produce ethical, humanistic, and at times even political effects.

Solzhenitsyn himself stated that he wrote in the hope that his work would bring change to his country by "restoring" its past.[266] Alexander Tvardovsky's foreword to *Ivan Denisovich* already sets out to frame this short novel as a step in the process of de-Stalinization and as part of an effort to avoid such forms of repression from happening again.[267] Barbara Bode recognized three main elements in the early Soviet reception of *Ivan Denisovich*: 1. the desire for the whole truth about the past to be revealed, 2. the demand for guarantees against the return to the past, 3. hope for a better future.[268] This

264 Anning, 1976, p. 127.
265 Solzhenitsyn, 1980, p. 292ff.
266 As quoted in Klimoff, 1997, p. 7.
267 Tvardovsky, 1962, p. 8.
268 Bode, 1965, p. 681.

exemplifies how close Soviet and Western ideas about camp literature once were, but also that, at least from the 1960s onwards, political and humanist hopes were very much invested in this type of literature.

Ivan Denisovich seems to have been written and perceived as breaking the silence about life in prison camps. It was published as a part of a political program, but few other works from this era are as memorable. Paradoxically, the vagueness of its political content might have been a central factor in creating long lasting interest in the text by allowing for more diverse interpretations. The political goal of *The Gulag Archipelago*—which has been briefly mentioned above—was to contribute to the demise of the Soviet Empire. Its reception has thus been more polarized when it comes to the ideological claims in the book, but more positive when it comes to the personal testimonial aspects of the text. *First Circle* is more complex to decipher: its condemnation of the Soviet government is not as acerbic as in *Gulag*, and its testimonial value is more ambivalent than *Ivan Denisovich*. In *First Circle*, Innokenty Volodin makes the impassionate claim that a good writer's duty is to teach and to guide.[269] But what exactly Solzhenitsyn aims to teach us in *First Circle* is an interesting question, the investigation of which might give insight into the ambivalent critical attention it has received.

Geoffrey Hosking writes that the message of *First Circle* is coherent with Solzhenitsyn's *Ivan Denisovich* and *Gulag*.[270] Hosking sees a Christian worldview seeping through these works that includes a certain attitude towards prison and freedom: it is in prison and not in freedom that people achieve spiritual freedom,[271] and "learn the true nature of happiness".[272] Helen Muchnic describes in her review of *First Circle* how the prisoner Gleb Nerzhin prefers prison over life outside, because it is in prison where he can meditate freely and learn about life.[273] Robin Blackburn, on the other hand, has an entirely different reading of Solzhenitsyn when it comes to the happiness of prison. He sees the description of the diegesis and Volodin and

269 Solzhenitsyn, 1968, p. 361.
270 Hosking, 1980, p. 102-22.
271 Hosking, 1980, p. 103.
272 Hosking, 1980, p. 105.
273 Muchnic, 1970, p. 162-3.

Nerzhin's attitude as a contradiction and interprets this as the intention of the author.[274] He writes:

> Solzhenitsyn shows us the numberless ways in which this blissful isolation is fictitious: the consequences for themselves and their families of the prisoners' acute deprivation of everyday social intercourse; the corrosive presence of the informers; the dilemmas in confronting the subtler techniques of repression; and, above all, the yawning abyss of the labour camps awaiting them, should they refuse to co-operate.[275]

Deming Brown writes that every time the protagonists make a morally correct decision their conditions in prison worsen as a result of the evilness of the Soviet system—and not out of irony.[276] Brown does point out that *First Circle* is about *spiritual* freedom; however, he interprets this novel "of course [as] a protest against physical bondage".[277] Although Brown does not hide his impression that the Soviet Union and life in its prison camps are appalling, he believes that prison made Solzhenitsyn a better writer than Gorky because of the authority and wisdom he acquired there:

> Deprivation of physical freedom, paradoxically, has contributed greatly to his strength and wisdom as a writer. His knowledge of 'the people'—the product of his years of imprisonment, exile, and hospitalization—enables him to write of them with a dispassionate authority unexcelled by such a celebrated plebeian as Gorky.[278]

The ambivalence in the reception of Solzhenitsyn's image of prison is a result of the ideological complexity of his text, and influenced by the worldview of the reader. In order to understand the contradiction between interpretations of the authorial intention in this issue, it is necessary to take a closer look at what Solzhenitsyn wrote.

The concept of prison as a special place for spiritual growth is expressed in different ways in Solzhenitsyn's work. A recurring topos is eating in prison as a spiritual act that strongly differs from the experience of eating in freedom. This motif is already hinted at in *Ivan Denisovich*, and in *The First Circle* it is repeated and complemented by an ascetic outlook.

---

274 Blackburn, 1970, p. 59.
275 Blackburn, 1970, p. 59.
276 Brown, 1969, p. 307.
277 Brown, 1969, p. 313.
278 Brown, 1969, p. 313.

In a conversation between two prisoners (Lev Rubin and Gleb Nerzhin), one of them—Nerzhin—gives Rubin a speech about how life in prison has taught him the meaning of life and happiness. He then describes how eating porridge in prison is like “Holy Communion”. He continues:

> You quivered from the exquisite feeling you got from those sodden little grains and the muddy slops in which they floated. And you went on living like that, with virtually nothing to sustain you, for six months, or for twelve. Can you compare that with the way people wolf down steaks?[279]

Later on, another prisoner—a diplomat named Innokenty Volodin—experiences an epiphany on his first night in jail. Volodin had lived a life of privilege and luxury, attending fancy dinners, wearing fine Western clothing.[280] Once in prison, he experiences great pleasure in feeling the warmth of his own body when he is stripped naked for searching.[281] The morning after his arrest, he drinks his tea “with relish” and “gulped it down with a shiver of pleasure”.[282] The narrator explains how this first night of prison taught him more about life than everything he had experienced previously.[283] He had learned how to obey without thinking, and he had finally understood that Epicurus' teachings—which he had recently read—were useless.[284] The author links the simplicity of prison food and the asceticism of life there with spiritual growth. This is not only obvious in the characterization of the novel's hero Nerzhin who claims “Thank God for prison!”[285] and who allegedly only achieves happiness in captivity,[286] but also in other (minor) characters such as Professor Chelnov. Chelnov goes as far as to believe that “only prisoners were sure of having immortal souls, whereas a man living in the vain bustle of the world outside might well not have one.”[287] As Abraham Rothberg has insightfully noted, throughout the entire novel a certain “moral hierarchy” that establishes those who have suffered the most above others is

---

279 Solzhenitsyn, 1968, p. 38.
280 Solzhenitsyn, 1968, p. 344-351.
281 Solzhenitsyn, 1968, p. 534.
282 Solzhenitsyn, 1968, p. 555.
283 Solzhenitsyn, 1968, p. 555.
284 Solzhenitsyn, 1968, pp. 536, 547-8, 555.
285 Solzhenitsyn, 1968, p. 38.
286 Solzhenitsyn, 1968, p. 37-8, 87.
287 Solzhenitsyn, 1968, p. 171.

discernible.[288] Rothberg understands this as a form of elitism. The literary representation of imprisonment as a form of ordination that improves individuals raises ethical questions irreconcilable with the purpose of witness literature: should human beings be sent to prison to be transformed into better people? This opposes the very thought of bearing witness so that such suffering will not be repeated.

However, it seems that the concept of prison as school is close to Solzhenitsyn's heart, as it is also recurrent in *Gulag*. There, Solzhenitsyn writes from a personal point of view:

> All the writers who wrote about prison but who did not themselves serve time there considered it their duty to express sympathy for prisoners and curse prison. I... have served enough time there. I nourished my soul there, and I say without hesitation:
>
> "*Bless you prison*, for having been in my life!"[289]

Toker, a specialist in gulag literature, writes that Solzhenitsyn's attitude towards prison camp cannot be generalized: some former gulag inmates see this experience as having robbed them not only of years of life, but of their physical and mental health.[290] She interprets Solzhenitsyn and like-minded former prisoners' positive view of prison as a "school" as a result of their dislike for their younger selves or their view that they had certain "sins" to atone.[291] Martha Duncan analyzes Solzhenitsyn in her study of positive topoi in prison literature—most of which is written by former criminals.[292] She sees these images—of prison as a place of refuge, of peace and quiet, or as a school, or a place where special friendships are forged—as psychological reactions which compensate for convicts' wasted years.[293]

Edward E. Ericson writes that the prison camp experience had positive effects on Solzhenitsyn, because it gave him rich literary material, and it also led to his development of a Christian worldview.[294] Considering the cruelty of life in the camps, this view strikes one as inhumane, but Ericson speaks from the perspective of a Christian who defines *Gulag* as a martyrologue; for him

288 Rothberg, 1971, p. 114-5.
289 Solzhenitsyn, 1975, vol.1, p. 617.
290 Toker, 2000, p. 79, 198-9.
291 Toker, 2000, p. 199.
292 Duncan, 1988.
293 Duncan, 1988, p. 1236.
294 Ericson, 2006, p. 215.

the camp experience is part of Christian martyrdom.[295] He considers Solzhenitsyn's description of life in camps to be written from a Christian perspective that is unfathomable for unbelievers, and sparks criticism from them.[296] Oskar Gruenwald similarly sustains that criticism of Solzhenitsyn is founded on the disparity between his Christian faith and his critics' lack thereof:

> In sum, Solzhenitsyn's prophetic vision strikes one as radically out of step with the trends of secular age ringing with the Nietzschean exclamation that God is dead. How can an age without God understand a believer?[297]

This brings us back to the question of the intention and the universality of camp literature and of Solzhenitsyn's work in particular. Gruenwald claims that camp literature—and Solzhenitsyn's work specifically—has a universal, ethical, and political purpose. But he also contextualizes it in a Christian worldview that he claims many modern thinkers cannot grasp. However, it is well possible for a reader to understand this view, even if he or she does not agree with this Christian evaluation of imprisonment. Nevertheless, it is quite possible that the portrayal of prison as creating happiness and enlightenment in *First Circle* might have negatively affected its testimonial value, both in the traditional sense of witness literature and in the politicized view of gulag literature as catalyst of political change. Indeed, if the gulag was ideologically buttressed by the idea of re-educating its inmates, a depiction of prison as school was no attack on its foundations.

When it comes to the intention of *The Gulag Archipelago*, Solzhenitsyn's aims are much more fundamentally state-opposed. From a political point of view, *Gulag* is a general indictment against communism as such, and the Soviet state in particular. But because the experience of political repression, torture, and forced labor has taken place in so many countries, and in so many different eras, there are some conventional elements that can be found in Solzhenitsyn's work—even if his ideological interpretations may be overstretched or even flawed. The feelings of pain, helplessness, and despair described in them have a universal nature—even for those who have never been through such an ordeal. Controversially, however, an all-embracing

---

295 Ericson, 1980, p. 157-8.
296 Ericson, 1980, p. 3, 149, 214, 215
297 Gruenwald, 1980, p. 138.

solidarity for the victims of state violence is missing in *Gulag*. Witness literature consists of texts that give testimony of a type of violence, and this creates the expectation that the author would condemn similar violence to other people under the same or similar circumstances. But this is not the case in *Gulag,* and this also affects the related goal of preserving the victim's memory, which is both common to witness literature and Solzhenitsyn's expressed aim. If *The Gulag Archipelago* was to become a cornerstone of the *Aufarbeitung* of Stalinism, one would expect certain equality in the condemnation of victims' ordeal. However, Solzhenitsyn appears unable to sympathize with some of Stalin's victims, as the case of Nikolai Bukharin poignantly illustrates.

Nikolai Bukharin was a revolutionary who had experienced both prison and exile during the Tsarist era. After participating in the October Revolution, he became part of the state elite. He opposed some of Stalin's key policies, including the instalment of Socialist Realism as a binding mode of artistic expression, and the forced collectivization of agriculture.[298] Bukharin was arrested in 1937; he was tried at a show trial and executed in 1938. At the time of the trial, his alleged confession, known as the *Last Plea*, was publicized. At the time Solzhenitsyn wrote the *Gulag*, information about what Bukharin experienced in captivity was rare, as most of his texts written in prison were still under lock and key. Unlike many other victims of the Stalinist purges, Bukharin was not rehabilitated during the Thaw. In 1974, Leonard Schapiro writes:

> To rehabilitate Bukharin, to permit, in other words, the open discussion and study of his works and his career, would be to remove the very foundations on which Brezhnev's police state rests, just as much as Stalin's did—arbitrariness, illegality, terror, albeit much reduced in extent, suppression of freedom of discussion even of Marxist theory, party control of literature and scholarship (again reduced in extent as compared with Stalin, but real nevertheless), and a morbid fear of economic incentives. The rehabilitation of Bukharin may come—who can tell? If it ever does it

---

298 Anthony Kemp-Welch, ed. *The Ideas of Nikolai Bukharin.* Oxford: Clarendon Press, 1992. p. 2-3; V. P. Danilov. "Bukharin and the Countryside." *The Ideas of Nikolai Bukharin.* Ed. Anthony Kemp-Welch. Oxford: Clarendon Press, 1992. 69-81. p. 73-74.

> will be a sure sign that real and substantial changes have taken place in the essential nature of the Soviet system of rule.[299]

In *Gulag*, Solzhenitsyn discusses Bukharin's trial over several pages. His depiction includes dialogues, historical allusions, and "psychological" analysis. Solzhenitsyn describes Bukharin as a cruel, lazy, self-absorbed man who is exposed as an absolute sycophant and weakling when he is persecuted.[300] Solzhenitsyn did not have access to Bukharin's prison documents, but his willingness to assume the worse and believe official publications about what happened to Bukharin—despite his expressed knowledge of the unreliability of the Soviet press, and stenographic records regarding the show trials[301]—shows Solzhenitsyn's own bias. He writes:

> But the inaccuracies of the stenographic record do not change or lighten the picture. Dumfounded, the world watched three plays in a row, three wide-ranging and expensive dramatic productions in which the powerful leaders of the fearless Communist Party, who had turned the entire world upside down and terrified it, now marched forth like doleful, obedient goats and bleated out everything they had been ordered to, vomited all over themselves, cringingly abased themselves and their convictions, and confessed to crimes they could not in any wise have committed.
>
> This was unprecedented in remembered history. It was particularly astonishing in contrast with the recent Leipzig trial of Dimitrov. Dimitrov had answered the Nazi judges like a roaring lion, and, immediately afterward, his comrades in Moscow, members of the same unyielding cohort which had made the whole world tremble—and the greatest of them at that, those who had been called the 'Leninist guard'—came before the judges drenched in their own urine.[302]

Solzhenitsyn now takes the position that no matter how inaccurate the records, the picture is not improved. The members of the communist elite who became victims of the Great Purge behaved shamefully when it was "their turn on the dock". By using the topoi of obedience, vomit, self-abasement, and later urine, Solzhenitsyn awakens disgust towards the

---

299 Leonard Schapiro. "Bukharin's Way." The New York Review of Books 7 February 1974.

300 Solzhenitsyn, 1974, vol. 1, p. 408-12.

301 "Let us make one qualification, though not a big one; the published stenographic records did not coincide completely with what was said at the trials. One writer who received an entrance pass—they were given out only to selected individuals—took running notes and subsequently discovered the differences." Solzhenitsyn, 1974, vol.1, p. 408.

302 Solzhenitsyn, 1974, vol. 1, p. 408-409.

victims. At the same time he reveals a patronizing attitude towards these victims by choosing topoi that are reminiscent of helpless toddlers, who cannot contain their bodily fluids and who react with fear and obedience to their parents. By portraying these victims as disgusting, incontinent toadies he undermines his own stated goal of restoring the memory of the victims of communism; by ridiculing them he is emulating the Soviet press of the 1930s.

A further problematic aspect of his argument is the contrast with Dimitrov's trial in Nazi Germany. The magnitude of this comparison becomes clear later on, as this does not remain the only one in this passage. But already at this point it becomes clear that he is only superficially comparing the victims of Stalinist and Nazi trials. He sizes up Dimitrov's courageous speech in court with the shameful performance of his comrades in the Soviet Union—although they were allegedly greater and better than him and were among those who had "made the whole world tremble". Dimitrov was a close follower of Stalin at the time, and it would therefore seem puzzling why he comes out better in this juxtaposition than his Russian peers at the show trials. Solzhenitsyn repeatedly suggests that the victims of the show trials behaved in a cowardly manner because they were unprepared for the hardship they experienced. He does this by belittling their previous prison experience:

> The Party leaders who were the defendants in the trials of 1936 to 1938 had, in their revolutionary pasts, known short, easy imprisonment, short periods in exile, and had never even had a whiff of hard labor. Bukharin had many petty arrests on his record, but they amounted to nothing. Apparently, he was never imprisoned anywhere for a whole year at a time, and he had just a wee bit of exile on Onega.[303]

The fundament of his argument is that the revolutionaries' experience of persecution outside or before the Soviet Union amounted to nothing, no matter what it was like. Of those who were condemned to hard labor he writes: "but even they had never in their lives experienced a genuinely merciless interrogation (because such a thing did not exist at all in Tsarist Russia). And these others, the Bolshevik defendants at the treason trials, had never known either interrogation or real prison terms."[304] He contrasts this with Soviet citizens' regular experience:

---

303 Solzhentisyn, 1974, vol. 1, p. 410.
304 Solzhentisyn, 1974, vol. 1, p. 409.

> Kamanev, despite long years of propaganda work and travel to all the cities of Russia, spent only two years of prison and one and a half years in exile. In our time, even sixteen-year-old kids got five right off. [...] In comparison with the ordinary natives of our Archipelago they were callow youths; they didn't know what prison was like.[305]

He claims that the revolutionaries in Tsarist prisons—and Dimitrov—had it easy without offering any hard evidence. He even goes so far as to describe how Trotsky would have acted if he had been caught in a show trial, by the same reasoning.[306] Not only is the speculative nature of his argument problematic, it displays a high level of callousness to write off other people's prison experience and their oppression as not amounting to anything. It is also a type of attitude that he himself expressly rejects when used towards non-communist victims of communism.

His "explanation" that the victims of the show trials were chosen for their weakness is likewise ethically questionable:

> They put on trial the most compliant. A selection was made after all.
>
> The men selected were drawn from a lower order, but, on the other hand, the moustached Producer knew each of them very well. He also knew that on the whole they were weaklings, and he knew, one by one, the particular weakness of each.[307]

He then goes on to describe his version of the story of Bukharin's persecution, beginning by claiming that there was a choice if one was to become a victim of the show trials—the choice being suicide when the persecution began.[308] But Bukharin chose to live. Solzhenitsyn depicts Bukharin's attitude at the moment when his fall had already began as follows:

---

305 Solzhentisyn, 1974, vol. 1, p. 410.

306 "(There is no basis for assuming that if Trotsky had fallen into those jaws, he would have conducted himself with any less self-abasement, or that his resistance would have proved stronger than theirs. He had no occasion to prove it. He, too, had known only easy imprisonment, no serious interrogations, and a mere two years of exile in Ust-Kut. The terror Trotsky inspired as Chairman of the Revolutionary Military Council was something he acquired very cheaply, and does not at all demonstrate any true strength of character or courage. Those who have condemned many others to be shot often wilt at the prospect of their own death. The two kinds of toughness are not connected.)" Solzhenitsyn, 1974, vol. 1, p. 410.

307 Solzhenitsyn, 1974, vol.1, 412.

308 "The most farsighted and determined of those who were doomed did not allow themselves to be arrested. They committed suicide first (Skrypnik, Tomsky, Gamarnik). It was the ones who wanted to live who allowed themselves to be arrested." Solzhenitsyn, 1974, vol. 1, p. 411.

> And all during these months he wrote endless letters: 'Dear Koba! Dear Koba! Dear Koba!' And he got no reply.
>
> He was still trying to establish friendly contact with Stalin!
>
> And *Dear Koba*, squinting, was already staging rehearsals. For many long years Koba had been holding tryouts for various roles, he knew that *Bukharchik* would play his part beautifully.[309]

Solzhenitsyn's readiness to ridicule one of the most prominent victims of Stalinist arbitrariness and injustice is irreconcilable with his goal of preserving the memory of the dead. If the rehabilitation of Bukharin was considered a litmus test of the willingness of the Soviet Union to deal with its past, Solzhenitsyn's *Gulag* was not an attempt to achieve this general goal. His criticism and ridiculing of this show trial and its victims displays an ideological bias that will be discussed in detail in chapter three. The reason why I have dwelled on this example at this stage is because it illustrates in the clearest way possible how Solzhenitsyn differentiates between victims in the *Gulag*: just as some of them enjoy his sympathy with all his rhetoric energy, other victims suffer from his contempt—with all the fire and brimstone he is capable of.

The example of Solzhenitsyn's treatment of Bukharin exhibits the subjective dimension of texts written by witnesses. Witnesses are fallible, emotional, and idiosyncratic human beings who do not necessarily wish to restrain their personal views when writing their testimonies or commenting on repression in their own countries. Perhaps it is us, as readers, who would gain from adjusting our expectations of these texts.

---

309 Solzhenitsyn, 1974, vol. 1, p. 413. Koba is Stalin's nickname.

2.4 Chapter Conclusion

The reception of Solzhenitsyn's main camp-related works shows that he is largely perceived as a witness. The type of expectations brought forth by these works is akin to those of witness literature: the description of the author's own suffering, to speak the truth about injustice, to commemorate others who died, etc. However, the ambiguity of these works' genre and their multi-layered ethical and political message pose challenges to the reader and the theoretician.

Witness literature is mainly associated with Shoah literature, and camp literature is strongly linked with the prison camp experience in communist prison camps. In this chapter I have delineated the convergences and divergences between witness literature/Shoah literature and camp literature. The disparity in the type of experience and the time of the publishing of the texts are the most obvious differences: German concentration camps interned people from all over Europe as part of their policy of extermination and/or enslavement of certain peoples; Shoah literature became available after the Germans had been defeated. Communist prison camp literature developed while communist states still existed, and—occasionally—it was promoted by these states themselves. It is therefore not surprising that the ethical focus of Shoah literature tends to lean towards a general humanistic message of "never again" and camp literature has a strongly contingent message referring to (then) current policies. For a long time, the contingency of camp literature and the urgency of its message had a centripetal effect that drew criticism to the central questions of authenticity and overall veracity.

Paradoxically, the initial official sanctioning of Solzhenitsyn's work made it the sensation it became—and the repression he later suffered strengthened his relevance in the West. There may have been byzantine political interests involved in publishing *Ivan Denisovich*, but it certainly was one of the more radical steps in confronting the Stalinist past taken during the Khrushchev Era and this turned the work into world news. Solzhenitsyn's persecution under Brezhnev also took place under the keen gaze of the Western press. Solzhenitsyn was perceived as suffering for telling the truth in his texts. This often shifted the attention of critics from the text to the author, making constant associations of the author's experience with his descriptions of the camp experience. Solzhenitsyn's ongoing persecution in the Soviet Union affected more in-depth aesthetic or historical analyses of these texts.

Nowadays, the immediate relevance of camp literature in raising awareness about Soviet prison camps is gone, and it is possible to see it in the context of other works relating to the prison experience as such, or the experience of extreme injustice regardless of geographical and political constraints. I agree with David Galloway and Leona Toker that it is due time to analyze Solzhenitsyn's and other authors' camp literature without the constraints of Cold War fears.[310]

The paradigm of witness literature helps us understand the role of the author's biography in the reception of Solzhenitsyn's camp literature. However, there are differences between his works that make a nuanced use of this approach necessary.

Despite the fact that it is a work of fiction, the work with the strongest adherence to the theoretical framework of witness literature is *Ivan Denisovich* owing to its diluted ideological imprinting, its richness in detail, and its low-key tone. It possesses a universality that enhances its accessibility to a wide variety of readers and will likely secure its reception by future generations.

The First Circle, on the other hand, has deviated far enough from the realm of personal testimony to be seen as witness literature in its narrowest sense. Its fictionalization and plot structure are much more elaborate than *Ivan*. *First Circle* is an allegory of the first circle of hell, and the whole novel is built as a spiral leading through several realms and characters all the way to Stalin. But it is not only the aesthetic complexity that has hindered its wider appraisal as a witness bearing text. Hayden White describes how Primo Levi's *Se questo è un uomo* (1947) is emplotted like Dante's *Divina Commedia*.[311] Similar to Solzhenitsyn, Levi writes as a witness who desires that the truth about what happened becomes known. By plotting his work like a fictional work, Levi is breaking with a factual understanding of his text, but White explains that this does not diminish its value.[312] His subjectivity underlines the horror of what he experienced and the use of Dante's plot calls into question the "myths of

310 Toker, 1997; David J. Galloway. "Polemical Allusions in Russian Gulag Prose." *The Slavic and East European Journal* 51.3 (2007): 535-552. p. 537.

311 Hayden White. "Figural Realism in Witness Literature." *Parallax* 10.1 (2004): 113-24.

312 White, 2004, p. 117-119.

divine justice" which became irrelevant for Shoah victims.[313] White adds that Levi's work is a compelling and effective piece of witness literature because it shows "what it felt like" to have gone through such an ordeal.[314] Solzhenitsyn's *First Circle* is, in contrast, built around the idea of suffering as a redeeming force. However, the Christian virtues of martyrdom and asceticism seem to be appreciated by only a small portion of his critics. Although several critics managed to focus on the merely anti-communist aspects of the work, perhaps it is for this spiritual slant that this work has received less attention than Solzhenitsyn's two other major camp texts. If the aim of witness literature is understood as a condemnation of the prison camp experience, a work underlining the camps' spiritual "benefits" can hardly count as such.

Beyond *First Circle*, and perusing Solzhenitsyn's other works, it is evident that in his view, the camp experience had a spiritual purpose: it had a purifying effect for some prisoners, and it served as a righteous or at least justified form of punishment for certain people groups.[315]

Despite their differences, Solzhenitsyn's three camp-related works all seem to divert from the theoretical expectation of witness literature as a politically neutral form of testimony. The simple detailed description of life in a prison camp was done with a political purpose—and it was understood this way by contemporary Soviet and Western critics as well. But the work which is most defined by its political rhetoric and force is *The Gulag Archipelago*.

The Gulag Archipelago as a form of political witness contains both factual as well as literary elements, and—most importantly—a strong ideological background. This cannot be ignored and must be problematized, as I will later on. The fact that a good deal of the content in *Gulag* is based on hearsay and speculation undermines its status—and authority—as witness literature.

The axiomatic ideological proclivity of *The Gulag Archipelago* is the main reason why I propose to define it as a work of political witness literature, rather than witness literature as such. Margalit defines the political witness as one with a concrete political agenda in mind, and who also takes it upon himself to speak for others. I think that this describes *Gulag*, and, as I will

313 White, 2004, p. 118.
314 White, 2004, p. 123.
315 For example: Solzhenitsyn, 1975, vol. 2, p. 322-352.

demonstrate in the next chapter, *Gulag* has been read primarily as a politically relevant work.

In *Gulag*, as I have argued, controversial aspects of Solzhenitsyn's worldview come out into the open, with his entire rhetorical prowess. This is the case in his relativization of political oppression under the tsars, or the euphemistic description of Nazi crimes. Not only is this disrespectful towards the victims of Tsarist Russia and Nazi Germany, such relativizations have repeatedly been co-opted in political arguments, some of which have far from humanistic goals in mind.[316]

As the political reception of *Gulag* will illustrate in the next chapter, Solzhenitsyn's political stance had a mutual interaction with his reception. And because Solzhenitsyn was anti-communist but had originally been legitimized by the Soviet authorities as a genuine witness of communist crimes, his testimony was seen as useful and significant. A key factor that legitimized Solzhenitsyn's claims was the fact that he was a witness. He had been in the camps, and doubting what he said during the Cold War was not easy without being accused of being a communist.[317]

Although this conclusion may seem overly critical of the parameters of witness literature, I do believe that using this term as a description of certain types of text can be very fruitful. However—at least in the case of gulag literature—theoretical adjustments are necessary. For one thing, theoreticians of witness literature have to keep in mind the possible incompatibility of their theoretical and ethical parameters with the ethical and artistic goals of the author. Most theoreticians of witness literature expect the witness—who is usually a victim of violence—to describe what he or she experienced with the

---

316 Thus, the claim that Stalin was Hitler's teacher in *Gulag* (Solzhenitsyn, 1974, vol. 1, p. 399) was used by certain scholars in order to legitimize their own views—for example by German historians Joachim Fest and Ernst Nolte. Fest and Nolte both use *The Gulag Archipelago* to "prove" that the Germans had not been the first to commit genocide, that they had learned it from the USSR. In the case of Nolte, this is later used to suggest that Nazi attacks on the Jews and the Soviet Union were somehow justified. This type of conclusion is very far from the ethical and humanistic goals normally expected from witness literature. Joachim Fest. "Das Beispiel Solschenizyn." Frankfurter Allgemeine Zeitung 9 January 1974: 1; Ernst Nolte. "Vergangenheit, die nicht vergehen will." Frankfurter Allgemeine Zeitung 6 June 1986: 25.

317 Cf.: Martin Malia. "Review: A War on Two Fronts: Solzhenitsyn and *The Gulag Archipelago*." *Russian Review* 36.1 (1977): 46-63; Meyer, 1985, p. 56-79.

sole purpose of testifying about it. However, victims of severe forms of violence often report having difficulties speaking about these experiences unless it is to help avoid such things repeating themselves, or if it helps keep alive the memory of those who were not lucky enough to survive. Already at this early stage there is a discrepancy which points to a further problem: who would read a testimony of a horrible act of violence just for the sake of reading it? What would be the purpose of it? It is not hard to imagine that many readers of descriptions of violence are not motivated by disapproval of the violence in question but simply succumbing to morbid curiosity.[318] Both neutrality and political bias in witness literature do not guarantee a specific ethical position. By claiming that a witness is a moral exemplar when he or she does not have a political intention might seem very lofty at first glance, but it may also be a way of avoiding the difficult questions of what type of content we are actually looking for.

How to deal with Solzhenitsyn's ideology and his political ideas will be a crucial issue in the following chapter, which is dedicated to the analysis of the interplay between aesthetics and politics in Solzhenitsyn's work and his reception. Ideological and political considerations are present in all of Solzhenitsyn's work—in some cases more obviously than in others. I will look into the role that political aspects played in his reception and canonization in Russian literature (from the point of view of Western scholars). Moreover, the results of the next chapter will respond to some of the questions that have remained unanswered in this one. Such as, why political partisanship can fundamentally change the nature of witness literature—in one direction or another—, and how political arguments affect the universality of a literary work.

---

318 The literary critic Alvin Rosenfeld pinpoints this problem in the case of the Shoah, in: Alvin H. Rosenfeld. *The End of the Holocaust.* Bloomington: Indiana University Press, 2011. p. 15.

3. Solzhenitsyn's Oeuvre between Aesthetics and Politics

The previous chapter was structured around the prison camp theme in three of Solzhenitsyn's major works. My analysis was based on a specific reading of his work which aligns it with witness literature. But in the case of Solzhenitsyn's camp literature, it became clear that politics is often referred to in its reception. The political aspects of his reception will be the focus of this chapter.

Ever since Alexander Solzhenitsyn published his first text, the relationship between aesthetics and politics in his work has been central to his reception. Certainly, writing anti-communist literature during the Cold War meant a political interpretation was inevitable. However, its aesthetic quality has not been entirely ignored. In this chapter I will discuss Solzhenitsyn's reception as it reflects the interaction of aesthetics and politics in his work and offer an analysis as to what contributed to these readings: why was he read in specific political ways?

Solzhenitsyn's politicized reception has undergone stark changes throughout his career. His forced exile severed him from direct cultural interaction in his country, and his eventual voluntary isolation in the US created distance between him and his readers. But, more than anything, it was the collapse of the Soviet Union that affected his relevance in the West: he had for so long been identified as a foe of the USSR that the dismembering of this state and the seemingly final de-legitimization of its ideology confronted his readers with the question of not only of how to read Solzhenitsyn, but why. In this chapter I will show how certain political readings of his work went beyond anti-communism. This chapter will end with a comparative summary, in which I will consider in which ways Solzhenitsyn's reception contributes to the debate about the relationship between aesthetics and politics in literary criticism.

Because of the overlapping references to different works in politicized reception texts, I will divide this chapter not according to specific works by Solzhenitsyn, but along the topics of political readings. This means that this chapter will be divided by the ideological premises that dominated debates about certain works by the dissident. Anti-communism is surely the most prominent ideological trend both in Solzhenitsyn's work and his reception, as will become clear in the first section of this chapter (3.2). Solzhenitsyn's claims about World War II, Nazism, and what he sees as the role of Jews in communism have drawn the attention of scholars with revisionist tendencies. In section 3.3, I will examine their readings of Solzhenitsyn's works, and how these correlate with the content of Solzhenitsyn's texts. Do some of his texts contain revisionist ideas, or if not, how did these interpretations come about? What did non-revisionist scholars write about these same texts? The last ideological issue to be discussed in this chapter is the role of (political) Christianity in Solzhenitsyn's work and reception (3.4). Although this has played a lesser role in his reception, it has been one of the most long-lasting ideological aspects in Solzhenitsyn's reception to this day.

In order to comprehend the relationship between these politicized forms of reception and Solzhenitsyn's work, it is compulsory to become acquainted with the texts that triggered such a response. Consequently, I will scrutinize aspects of the works by the Russian dissident which have obtained a more politicized reception, and examine their relation to the reception. This will include studying the types of reader guidance (*Leserlenkung*) that Solzhenitsyn practiced and how his reception reacted to these strategies.

3.1 Introduction to Methods and Contextualization

Hans Robert Jauss, Gunter Grimm, and other reception theorists point out the relevance of understanding the historical context in which reception takes place. Because the historical environment in which Solzhenitsyn's work was written, published, and read was highly politicized, it is particularly important to take it into account in this study. As the Sovietologist Leopold Labedz highlights, even the consideration of what political literature is depends on its context:

> As the Pasternak affair had already demonstrated, the definition of what is political is quite different in the Soviet Union from what it is elsewhere. In the Soviet Union, a refusal to submit to political dictates of the Party on aesthetic or ethical grounds is in itself termed 'political'.[319]

319 Leopold Labedz. "Introduction." *Solzhenitsyn: a Documentary Record.* New York: Harper & Row, 1971. p. xvii.

In order to determine what a political reading of a text is, it is necessary to look both at the text, the environment of its publication, and the context of the reader who writes about it. Literary theorists Grimm and Toker have both emphasized the relevance of the social and political context of both the writer and the reader. Grimm warns that a text can be interpreted completely differently from how the author intended, depending on the ideological and social background of the reader: the disguised criticism of an authoritarian state might be so well camouflaged that hardly anyone "gets" the message.[320] On the other hand, if an ironic tale is read by a person to whom this genre is foreign, it might lead to a literal interpretation that misses the point of the irony. Toker argues that Soviet authors were well aware of the type of censorship common in their country; therefore, texts that were written in the hope of being published locally were written with different audiences in mind.[321] Firstly, authors thought of their so-called "hurdle audience". These were the readers involved in the selection process of publication: editors, censors, KGB assessors, etc. Authors developed different strategies to overcome this hurdle audience, in order to write for their "target audience."[322] The target audience of many dissident writers consisted of educated readers who possessed a critical stance towards the government, but the exact target audience depended on the particular author and text. Toker recognizes that beside the hurdle and target audiences, there was a "general audience" which authors could not necessarily plan on acquiring. Among the general audience are readers of translations and future editions that the author might not have predicted, as well as everyone else. Because there have been very few moments in Russian history in which literature—or even society—has been allowed to develop freely, the consideration of different types of audiences is crucial in understanding Russian literature and its reception.

Solzhenitsyn admittedly wrote for different audiences. He wrote books he hoped to publish in the USSR; he edited them or even rewrote them if he knew they were to be printed abroad. But he also wrote texts little affected by

---

320 Grimm, 1977, p. 247-251.

321 Leona Toker. "Target Audience, Hurdle Audience, and the General Reader: Varlam Shalamov's Art of Testimony." *Poetics Today* 26.2 (2005): 281-303. Toker's categories were very helpful in understanding my sources, even if I do not use her terminology throughout this text.

322 Toker, 2005, p. 282.

self-censorship, with hardly any hope of legal circulation locally: how he went about making these decisions was determined by the contemporary political and cultural environment he was in. The goals he pursued with his works became radicalized as his new-found freedom was jeopardized: if *One Day in the Life of Ivan Denisovich* can be seen as an attempt to bring change to the Soviet Union, *The Gulag Archipelago* was described by the author as an attempt to bring it down.

Constant changes marked the condition of freedom and security for writers throughout the Soviet era. From full freedom to a great amount of repression, from solid economic support from the state to great financial insecurity, the experience of writers in the Soviet Union was everything but uniform or homogenous. Because of these and other changes in the outer framework of writers' experience, Soviet literature developed in different ways, at different times. Solzhenitsyn was directly affected by the extent to which political issues and decisions influenced Soviet literary life. From 1962 to 1969 he was a member of the Soviet Writers' Union, and this meant that he was entitled not only to royalties but also to other privileges beyond the reach of the common Soviet citizen. Geoffrey Hosking describes the situation as follows:

> The Union offered its members security, material resources, privileges and access to publication on a scale undreamt of by all but the most successful writers in capitalist societies.[323]

Solzhenitsyn was one among the many Soviet writers who experienced initial support from the state and then decided to defy the regime with their pen. He was a member of the "Thaw" generation of writers who had experienced both freedom and repression: with the help of the Soviet establishment he was able to break into publishing and become known as an author. Solzhenitsyn often spoke of himself as a one-man-gang, but he was not alone in his fight against the Soviet Union. Like many dissidents, he too was expelled not only from the Writers' Union (1969), but also from his country (1974). Unlike many other dissidents, Solzhenitsyn was awarded the Nobel Prize for Literature after his expulsion from the Writers' Union. This prize enhanced his status on the world stage and among the liberal Soviet intelligentsia. However, ideological differences among Soviet dissidents also meant that solidarity went hand in hand with sharp criticism. Solzhenitsyn's views about his

323 Hosking, 1980, p. 7.

country's past and his visions for its future clashed with those of other dissidents whom he often publicly affronted in his own work. In his essays, he acerbically denounces émigrés and dissidents he disagrees with in his bid to influence US foreign policy. A look into the volatile relationships between writers and the state and among the writers themselves will help place some of Solzhenitsyn's scathing rhetoric into perspective. Solzhenitsyn's interaction with the dissident and later the émigré scenes of Russian culture influenced his choice of topics, genres, and also the texts he referred to in his work.

Another reason why knowing the author's historical context is important in understanding his reception is that the political awareness of his readers was raised in relation to his work when he began experiencing artistic repression. This strengthened his image not only as a nonconformist writer but also as an icon of defiance towards the state.

To understand the reception of an author and his work, it is not only necessary to study the primary sources (the texts by his readers, and the author's work), and the historical and political environment of these texts (including that of the reception-texts), but also the literary cultures in which this all took place. There are at least two distinct levels to this question: the context of the writer and the context of the authors of the reception-texts. Therefore, it will be necessary to contextualize Solzhenitsyn's work within the Soviet literary milieu in order to understand the genre they belong to, and their intertextuality, both of which mold the horizon of expectations for his readers.

Defining the genre of Solzhenitsyn's work is not only a question of aesthetics, since the result has political repercussions. Both the political motivation and the content of his works make it imperative to look beyond the formal in order to understand what genre they belong to. Solzhenitsyn claims, for instance, that *The Gulag Archipelago* is not ideological, but rather the anti-ideological rendering of the true history of Soviet prison camps. However, the goals pursued in this work are admittedly political. From the point of view of reception, interpreting this work as history is very much a political decision, as the work does not adhere to the minimum requirements of historiography and contains claims with serious political consequences. The same can be said about Solzhenitsyn's late work *Two Hundred Years Together* about Russian-Jewish relations over two centuries. Interpreting Solzhenitsyn's politically charged works as literature does not necessarily simplify the question. The presence of politics in literature—regardless of what type of politics—can be evaluated in many different ways. For example, some literary critics see this as an "unnatural" phenomenon that was brought about in Russian literature by the political constraints of censorship, as I will later show. Other critics see it as an integral part of literature. Views about politics in literature have changed a great deal since the appearance of Solzhenitsyn's first work in 1962, and they have never been incontrovertible.

The types of reception-texts that I will analyze in this chapter represent different types of readers. Some of these texts are reviews that represent what Gunter Grimm calls "mediating-reception".[324] These texts are written with the goal of expressing and disseminating a specific opinion about a literary work. Some of these texts are written by literary scholars, others are written by political scientists or journalists. In some cases, they are written by people closer to the production process, such as editors and translators of Solzhenitsyn's works. These types of mediating texts will represent the main part of my material. Another form of reception-text I will include in this chapter is that of literary histories. In reception analysis, the literary historian can be seen as a "reader with an explanatory function."[325] I take this last group into account in order to convey the importance given to Solzhenitsyn in histories of Russian literature in the West. What do literary historians think about the relevance of his work? What type of relevance was it: social, artistic, political? Is he worth mentioning, or reading? What aspects of his work are praised or criticized? Another form of reception text I will take into account to a much lesser extent is Solzhenitsyn's own comments on his works. These will hopefully help fathom the attitude he had towards his own work, and his priorities.

Scholars of many different disciplines read and write about Solzhenitsyn in vastly different ways. Disciplinary boundaries are stretched to the limit in the reception of this Russian dissident, but dividing the analysis of his reception along the lines of scholarly disciplines would only further complicate the matter. For instance, political scientist Daniel J. Mahoney writes about Solzhenitsyn's work both in the form of literary reviews and as analyses of political thought. In order to achieve as much clarity as possible this chapter

324 Grimm, 1977, p. 75-77.
325 Grimm, 1977, p. 77.

will be divided by the ideological issues in the reception, and not the discipline of the author.

Ideology has been very important in Solzhenitsyn's reception in many ways. One of the most obvious manners in which ideology made itself visible in Solzhenitsyn's reception can be seen in how scholars link his work with current political questions. Another was the way that the authors of these reception texts related to other authors who had written about Solzhenitsyn: it is not unusual to find quite a bit of mud-slinging in this context. These aspects will have to be analyzed in their specific historical and social environments.

By the end of the chapter, a problematization of the politics of Solzhenitsyn's works as reflected in his reception should become clear: What are the questions that need to be answered in order to assess Solzhenitsyn's work, how have they been addressed or ignored in the past? What has led to a certain reading of his works, how did the context of their origin and the context of their reception affect these readings?

3.2 Anti-communism: Solzhenitsyn at the Heart of the Cold War

The Cold War lasted several decades in the post-war era and ended in 1991 when the Soviet Union was dismantled. The period that is referred to in this subchapter begins in the late 1960s when Solzhenitsyn was no longer considered a part of the liberalization of his state but its opponent.[326] This includes Soviet rule under Party Chairmen Leonid Brezhnev (1964-1982), Yuri Andropov (1982-84), Konstantin Chernenko (1984-5), and Mikhail Gorbachev (1985-1991). It was a time of great change in the Soviet Union, and a time when Western political attitudes towards the USSR were constantly challenged.

Soviet nuclear weapons, its military and ideological expansionism, and internal human rights abuses were some of the key issues that worried the West during the Cold War. Although these problems were not static, Western

---

326 My definition is based on the way he was treated by the state. His self-image as a dissident developed later. It wasn't until August 1973 that Solzhenitsyn openly identified himself with other dissidents. Before that, his communication with the media and the state focused on his personal struggles with the Soviet literary bureaucracy. Cf.. Abraham Brumberg. "Dissent in Russia." *Foreign Affairs* 52.4 (1974). p. 792.

thinkers, scholars, and politicians tried to fathom the nature of the Soviet Union and its troubles when discussing the way the West should relate to the USSR. Indeed, adherents of the left and the right disagreed on the provenance of repression in the Soviet Union. Did this stem from communism as an ideology, or not? The Western left's confrontation with this question was very multifaceted. Although many Western leftists admitted that the Soviet Union had severe difficulties in respecting human life and the sovereignty of foreign nations, they did not necessarily see communist or socialist ideology as the origin of these problems: some thinkers believed "socialism with a human face" was possible; others sought for a "Third Way", etc.[327] However, anti-communism as a form of criticism of the state of affairs in the USSR was not at all foreign to Western leftist movements, as I will show. For members of the right—as a general rule—communist ideology was at the root of the problem. With some exceptions, anti-communism based on this premise was an ideology which was largely embedded in conservative, neo-conservative, and right-wing movements during this period.

Anti-communism is a set of ideologies that has survived communist states. I work with Terry Eagleton's definition of ideology as "a body of meanings and values encoding certain interests relevant to social power." [328] Ideologies are "typically a mixture of analytic and descriptive statements on the one hand, and moral and technical prescriptions on the other."[329] An ideology can use different strategies to convey its message, including means such as rationalizations, justifications, unifications, universalizations, and naturalizations.[330] Despite its longevity and protean forms, anti-communism can be seen as a set of ideologies because of the way it has been pursued by its followers.[331] I acknowledge that during the Cold War the term ideology was sometimes used in a depreciative sense. In fact, Solzhenitsyn and some of his supporters used this term in such a way. However, in this book I use

327 Cf.: Geoff Eley. *Forging Democracy: The History of the Left in Europe, 1850-2000.* New York: Oxford University Press, Incorporated, 2002. p. 416. Van Gosse. *Rethinking the New Left: An Interpretative History.* New York: Palgrave Macmillan, 2005. p. 26.

328 Terry Eagleton. *Ideology: an Introduction.* London: Verso, 2007. p. 45.

329 Eagleton, 2007, p. 48.

330 Eagleton, 2007, p. 45; 50ff.

331 Cf.: Wolfgang Wippermann. *Heilige Hetzjagd eine Ideologiegeschichte des Antikommunismus.* 1st ed. Berlin: Rotbuch-Verlag, 2012.

ideology as a descriptive and not as a pejorative term. As I will demonstrate, at times Solzhenitsyn's thought also had the features and function of an ideology in Eagleton's sense.

As such, anti-communism has affected not only politics, but also culture and academic scholarship.[332] During certain periods of the Cold War, political considerations were even a part of the selection process of students and professors in universities in the West.[333] In discussions about Soviet art and literature, political premises have been part of scholarly arguments just as in policy debates. This is not to say that all scholarship is ideological, or that ideologically tainted reviews of Solzhenitsyn's work are necessarily the result of a programmatic political goal on the author's part. Nevertheless, in order to assess the relevance of Solzhenitsyn's work and to understand its importance during the Cold War it is compulsory to find out how and why ideology played a prominent part in his reception.

Solzhenitsyn's Reception during the Cold War

Solzhenitsyn's early works—his autobiographically inspired novellas and novels—have an ambivalent relationship to politics. The works he either published or planned to publish in the USSR were mostly written in such a way that the political tone was adapted to overcome a hurdle audience.

The first longer book Solzhenitsyn released in the West, which he had not previously tried to print in his country, was the novel *August 1914*,[334] part of

---

332 For example, Stephen Cohen describes the anti-communist post-war consensus in Soviet studies in the US, in: Stephen F. Cohen. *Rethinking the Soviet Experience: Politics and History since 1917.* New York: Oxford University Press, 1986.

333 Political restrictions and/or support in academia changed over the years, and manifested itself in different ways within each of the countries of my study, c.f.: David C. Engerman. "The Ironies of the Iron Curtain: The Cold War and the Rise of Russian Studies in the United States." *Cahiers du Monde russe* 45.3/4 (2004): 465-96; Michael F. Hopkins. "Teaching and Research on the Cold War in the United Kingdom." *Cold War History* 8.2 (2008): 241-58; Helmut König. "Ostforschung - Bilanz und Ausblick." *Osteuropa*.8-9 (1975): 786-814.

334 Solzhenitsyn has given contradictory information regarding his publishing plans for this novel: in an interview with the *New York Times* in 1972 he claims to have offered this novel in a letter to several Soviet publishing companies which never responded. In a memoir, he writes that he wrote *August 1914* on the assumption that it would be considered as explosive as *Gulag* and therefore had kept it hidden in the USSR. It is likely that he wrote it without a hurdle audience in mind, but might have claimed to have offered it to print in his country in order to counter a suspicion

his series *The Red Wheel* about the prelude to the Russian Revolution. This book came out in 1972 in Russian, in two editions in English, and in German. The central topic of this colossal novel is the Battle of Tannenberg during World War I, and it includes thoughts on intellectual life in Tsarist Russia.

For the first time, Solzhenitsyn diverts from the autobiographically inspired novel and presents his readers with his interpretation of pre-revolutionary history. Solzhenitsyn believed this work to be politically as explosive as the yet unpublished *Gulag Archipelago*, due to the negative opinion of Lenin he expresses in it.[335] Solzhenitsyn posited that Russia had taken a wrong turn in October 1917 that led to the political repression he experienced. For him, writing about the Revolution and the years leading up to it had a strong connection with his work on the prison camps.[336] This linking of events was less obvious to his readers.

August 1914 was Solzhenitsyn's first explicitly anti-communist novel, and part of a long-term project to undermine the authority of the communist movement. Solzhenitsyn's view of the relevance of *August 1914* and the rest of the *Red Wheel* series is not shared by the bulk of his Western reception.[337] In contrast, the work that can be seen as the foundational document of Solzhenitsyn's anti-communist reception is *The Gulag Archipelago*, originally published in the West in late 1973. But why did Western scholars and reviewers see this book as so much more relevant than other works by the Russian author?

In September of 1973, Solzhenitsyn made the sensational announcement that a person hiding a manuscript of his work *The Gulag Archipelago* had committed suicide after the KGB seized the book.[338] The author described

---

of having sent it to the West as part of a subversive plan. Cf.: Hedrick Smith. "Solzhenitsyn Tells of Struggle to Write despite Soviet Pressures." The New York Times 3 April 1972: 1, 10. Solzhenitsyn, 1995, p. 184

335 Solzhenitsyn, 1995, p. 184.

336 He asserts this in several interviews including: Hilton Kramer. "A Talk with Solzhenitsyn." The New York Times 11 May 1980: 3.

337 "Solzhenitsyn almost exclusively used the word *glavnyi* (most important, principal) to describe the status he accords *The Red Wheel* among his works." Wakamiya, 2009, p. 73. I will discuss Western perspectives on this work in a later section of this book.

338 N.N. "Special to the New York Times: Solzhenitsyn Links a Suicide to His Work." The New York Times 7 September 1973: 3.

this work to the *New York Times* as a "'multivolume research work about Soviet prison camps that contains only true facts, places, and the names of more than 200 persons still alive.'"[339] He expressed fear that the security service would use this material to repress the people who had provided him with testimonies for his work.

The first volume of *Gulag* came out in Paris in December 1973; translations in various languages were published within days. *The New York Times,* the London *Observer*, and *Der Spiegel* were some of the Western news sources which published several excerpts of the book upon its release. Parallel to this, reports of Solzhenitsyn's revelations and his fate remained in the headlines for months.

Different countries reacted differently to the publication of *Gulag*, however, in all three countries of my study, it was perceived as a historical event.

Solzhenitsyn in Brandt's Germany

The most attention Solzhenitsyn ever received in West Germany was in the months preceding and following the publication of *Gulag*. This was for various reasons, some of which were directly connected to Solzhenitsyn and this particular work; others were the result of the concrete historical phase Germany was going through.

Since 1969, the relationship between the Federal Republic and the Soviet Union and Poland had changed radically. Until the Moscow Treaty and later the Warsaw Treaty were signed in 1970, West Germany had not officially recognized the 1945 borders between the two Germanys and that of their Eastern neighbors. Irredentist Germans had therefore continued to hope that they would one day regain Silesia, the former Königsberg (now Kaliningrad), and other territories currently ruled by other countries. This changed dramatically when the Social Democrat Chancellor Willy Brandt decided to launch his *Ostpolitik*—a German rapprochement with the East that included the recognition of the status quo and negotiations to avoid armed conflict between the two Germanys.

---

339 Cf. previous footnote, and again quoted in: Theodore Shabad. "Life is too closely Imitating Art." The New York Times 9 September 1973: 206.

Ostpolitik was opposed mostly by conservative politicians and scholars because some of them considered the proposed treaties to be a form of capitulation *vis à vis* the communist East: they either disputed the borders as such, or the legitimacy of communist rule in these territories. Other critics objected against easing relations with countries with such a poor human rights record. Conservative arguments opposing *Ostpolitik* could even amalgamate concern for Soviet dissidents with irredentist demands. It is therefore not surprising that in an early study on Solzhenitsyn's reception Birgit Meyer claimed:

> [T]he history of Solzhenitsyn's reception in the West German press from 1974 to 1979 is simultaneously a history of the domestic political tensions and controversies arising from the Federal Republic's *Ostpolitik*.[340]

Conservative interest in Solzhenitsyn pre-dated the publication of *Gulag*, but it definitely intensified directly after. The fact that Solzhenitsyn was sent into exile in February 1974 and shipped directly to Frankfurt Main was another reason why the German press as a whole was particularly zealous to report about the dissident. During this time, even the simple fact that Solzhenitsyn mentioned he liked snow was enough to reach the news.[341] But how much attention was paid to *The Gulag Archipelago* in this media frenzy?

The topic of the Soviet prison camp experience was better known in West Germany than in the other countries of my study. During Stalin's purges of the 1930s, some German communists had been sent to camps, and later on, thousands of Nazi soldiers and officers became prisoners of war in Soviet prison camps. A number of those Germans who survived and later moved to the Federal Republic published their memoirs. Germans' horizon of expectations of camp-related literature was decidedly different than that of US or British readers. Solzhenitsyn's broad-ranging allegations about the different waves of repression that took place in his country had previously been assimilated in West Germany. Scholars and intellectuals who wrote about *Gulag* thus focused less on the most apparent details of repression, and more on the question of the relationship between communism and state violence, and on issues dealing with the German past.

---

340 Meyer, 1985, p. 56.

341 D.W. "Solschenizyn über Norwegen: wundervoll viel Schnee." Die Welt 25 February 1974: 3.

Early reviews of *Gulag* in prominent journals and papers had the status of mediating-reception: they prepared the general public for what promised to be a best-selling book. In many ways, these early texts were formative for the way Solzhenitsyn was remembered decades later.

The influential historian and publicist Joachim Fest wrote one of the earliest German reviews of *Gulag*. In his review of *Gulag,* Fest writes that the difference between this and previous works on the subject is the acerbity of the tone and Solzhenitsyn's goal of requital against the Soviet state as a whole. For Fest, the decisive aspect of *Gulag* is the claim that from October 1917 onwards, there was a rupture between morality and the revolution. According to Fest, this assertion is extraordinary because followers of the October Revolution had hitherto believed that morality and revolution became one in 1917. But now, the Soviet citizen Solzhenitsyn was claiming exactly the opposite. Fest believes that the significance of this work is enormous:

> Vielleicht wird Alexander Solschenizyns „Archipel GULag" einmal zu den Markierungspunkten zählen, die den Verfallsprozeß der kommunistischen Idee anzeigen.[342]

State terror in the USSR is thus no longer considered a "mistake" or an "exception" but rather the norm. Fest emphasizes that this is not all new,[343] but he nevertheless believes that this book will have a different type of impact. Fest, who was a conservative, immediately recognized the anti-communist potential of *Gulag*: so, how did left-leaning Germans see it?

Members of the German Communist Party (DKP) were obliged to follow the Party line of the CPSU, and thus to repeat the official Soviet assessment of *Gulag*. In this sense, they did not enjoy the freedom of speech that their own country warranted them. Furthermore, the DKP had been re-established only in 1968 and had no significant influence on German politics, as their candidates never won a mandate. Therefore, it is more fruitful to look at what

---

342 Fest, 1974. "Perhaps some day Alexander Solzhenitsyn's 'Gulag Archipelago' will count among the marks that point to the process of the decline of communism." (My translation.)

343 The only aspect of Gulag he sees as innovative is the openness with which Solzhenitsyn claims that Hitler's persecution of the Jews was just a repetition of what Stalin had done before him. This topic will be discussed later on in this chapter.

other left-wing, and left-leaning German scholars and intellectuals wrote about *Gulag*.

Rudolf Augstein, the editor in chief of *Der Spiegel*, decided to buy the rights to print parts of *Gulag* in the magazine's pages as soon as it was available in German. The partial serialization of the work took place over several months and included parts of the first and second volumes. A leading article presents the work as an effort to overcome the Soviet Union's violent past.[344] It also claims that Solzhenitsyn plans to bring about 250 thousand Soviet officials to court, an artificial number calculated as an analogue to an alleged number of Nazis brought to court in the Federal Republic.[345]

In his own review of the book, Augstein introduces it as more than just *Aufarbeitung* of the past or a call to reform communism.[346] Augstein notes that the information in *Gulag* is not new, and adds that, being the minority in the country, the *Bolsheviki*[347] could not have prevailed over the majority in any other way but terror. Nevertheless, he emphasizes the importance of the text and adds that there is "no way around it".

Similarly to Fest, Augstein describes *Gulag* as an "Abrechnung" with the Soviet regime. This German term has several connotations including "list of transgressions", "revenge", and "punishment". It does not preclude the text from having a goal beyond that of listing the wrongs of the state. Augstein fathoms Solzhenitsyn's intention with this book, and is dissatisfied with the Russian author's call for Soviet leaders' spiritual repentance—doubting this could bring much practical change to the Soviet state. For Augstein, it is open to debate if this approach will foster or hinder liberalization in the USSR. Augstein nonetheless respects Solzhenitsyn's moral approach, and softens his own criticism by claiming that he does not possess the moral authority to patronize him.

---

344 N.N. 1974, "Bereit". p. 46-51.

345 Solzhenitsyn claims that 86,000 Nazis had been convicted in the FRG, a number that the *Spiegel* repeats (the actual number was less than 10% that amount). Solzhenitsyn calculates what percentage of the West German population this was, and thus comes up with the number of 250,000 for the Soviet Union.

346 Rudolf Augstein. "Solschenizyn oder die Ehre Gottes." Der Spiegel 7 January 1974: 4-5.

347 The Russian word "Bolsheviki" means "majority", but as a political movement they were initially a minority in Russia.

In his first article on *Gulag*, Augstein is very cautious in his criticism of the text, and he focuses very much on what Solzhenitsyn is saying and what effect it could have. One of the points Augstein disagrees with is Solzhenitsyn's deriding of Nikolai Bukharin for "not having had his own standpoint"—Augstein argues that having a standpoint would not have saved him from death. The German criticizes Solzhenitsyn for his arrogant attitude towards Bukharin, and his suggestion that what had happened to the old revolutionary would not have happened to him. Augstein's early criticism of Solzhenitsyn is therefore focused on the way the author portrays certain victims of repression, and his speculation on how things could have been under different circumstances.

In his second article on *Gulag*,[348] Augstein becomes more absorbed in his own arguments against Solzhenitsyn's claims about the revolution. Augstein contests the absoluteness with which Solzhenitsyn rejects the October Revolution as being the worst case scenario in 1917. Augstein does not express admiration for the way things turned out, but he points out that when the Tsar abdicated in early 1917—during a world war—things were bound to go awry. Russia's territorial integrity was in danger, and its lack of industrialization made it very vulnerable. In this sense, Augstein's review of *Gulag* develops into an essay of its own, a plea not to look back and speculate how things could have turned out—but to focus on lessons for the future.

Augstein's articles on *Gulag* are of relevance not only because he was a leading publicist at the time, but also because of the way his dealing with *Gulag* was later criticized. Shortly thereafter, the journalist and Eastern Europe expert Carl Gustav Ströhm writes an angry article in which he describes Augstein's reviews as follows:

> Wenn Rudolf Augstein im 'Spiegel' Solschenizyn als einen gewissermassen lebensfernen Skribenten darzustellen suchte, so zeugt das ebenso von tiefer Ignoranz wie auch von einer gewissen Unverfrorenheit: denn Solschenizyn ist mit seinem Buch der politischen Wirklichkeit viel näher als der neurasthenische ,Spiegel'-Herausgeber, dem – ebenso wie anderen Linken und Linksliberalen im

---

348 Rudolf Augstein, "Ein Betriebsunfall Namens Stalin." Der Spiegel 11 Februar 1974: 89-91.

> Westen – dieser Solschenizyn höchst peinlich ist, weil er nämlich die vorgefaßten Meinungen durcheinanderbringt.[349]

Ströhm claims that "lefties" are too aware of the moral authority of the dissident and therefore do not dare insult him directly as a "reactionary" or "conservative"; so, he claims, they try to "relativize" Solzhenitsyn. He accuses Augstein of wondering whether *Gulag* is helping the process of détente—which Augstein did not—and claims that this is an example of how truth had now become functionalized and adapted to individual comfort. Ströhm then goes on to criticize other named and unnamed "leftist" critics. He dedicates a third of his article to a confrontation with those leftists who "defend" Solzhenitsyn as a fellow communist. He sees this as an attempt to neutralize the Russian dissident.

For Ströhm, Solzhenitsyn's achievement lies in his ability to "hold the mirror of self-recognition" up to his government and the rest of the world.[350] He describes Solzhenitsyn as a master of the Russian language, unparalleled since Tolstoy; and as a courageous political moralist. He places Solzhenitsyn in the category of Russian historians who claim the October Revolution was not a revolution but a coup d'état. Ströhm points out that Solzhenitsyn could not be a communist because he treated even communist *victims* of the purges with scepticism and contempt: he quotes the following claim by Solzhenitsyn that their deaths may have been necessary in order to show the uselessness of their ideology, and that these victims had once been perpetrators themselves:

> And all the big Bolsheviks, who now wear martyrs' halos, managed to be the executioners of other Bolsheviks (not even taking into account how *all of them* in the first place had been the executioners of non-Communists). Perhaps 1937 was *needed* in order to show how little their whole ideology was worth—that *ideology* of which they boasted so enthusiastically, turning Russia upside down, destroying its

---

349 Carl Gustav Ströhm. "Im Visier der Deutschen Linken: Solschenizyn." Deutschland Magazin February, March 1974: 42-3. The *Deutschland Magazin* was a widely read conservative journal that ceased publication in 2002; it was published by the controversial "Deutschland Stiftung". "When Augstein in 'Spiegel' attempts to present Solzhenitsyn as a literary hack who is somehow disconnected from reality, it is evidence both of deep ignorance and of a certain brazenness because Solzhenitsyn is closer to political reality than the neurasthenic editor of 'Spiegel', to whom Solzhenitsyn is highly embarrising—just like to other leftists and liberal-leftists in the West—because he confuses ready-made opinions."

350 Ströhm, 1974, p. 42.

> foundations, trampling everything it held sacred underfoot, that Russia where *they themselves* had never been threatened by *such* retribution.[351] The victims of the Bolsheviks from 1918 to 1946 never conducted themselves so despicably as the leading Bolsheviks when the lightning struck them. If you study in detail the whole history of the arrests and trials of 1936 to 1938, the principal revulsion you feel is not against Stalin and his accomplices, but against the humiliatingly repulsive defendants—nausea at their spiritual baseness after their former pride and implacability.[352]

Ströhm closes his argument by citing that Solzhenitsyn's attitude towards communism is clear enough in his conclusion that ideology is the cause of all the "mass murder" of the 20th century, and adds: "Vielleicht wäre es gut, wenn unsere ideologieversessenen Linken sich gerade diese Botschaft des großen russischen Schriftstellers zu Herzen nehmen würden."[353]

Ströhm, a prominent conservative of the time, considers anti-communism so central to Solzhenitsyn's *Gulag* that any attempt by leftists to either instrumentalize this work or to associate themselves with the author, amounts to an attack on the work and its writer. He recognizes leftists' mistake in counting the dissident among them. However, he does not confront Augstein's question regarding Solzhenitsyn's contempt towards communist victims. Augstein was uncomfortable with the complacency with which Solzhenitsyn ridiculed Bukharin, his argument being that another person—even Solzhenitsyn—could well have met Bukharin's fate. If repression was as arbitrary and overwhelming as Solzhenitsyn describes it in *Gulag*, is it fair to mock any of its victims? By responding to this criticism with yet another example of Solzhenitsyn's scorn towards communist victims, Ströhm is avoiding a confrontation with this complex ethical question.

In 1985, Birgit Meyer wrote a study of Solzhenitsyn's reception in the mid-70s in which she likewise criticizes Rudolf Augstein's articles on *Gulag* and accuses him of calling Solzhenitsyn a "moralizing bourgeois intellectual".[354] I did not find record of Augstein using these words in the article referred to, but her perception of Augstein's criticism as such is an interesting example of

351 Ströhm quotes this passage word for word until this point and summarizes the rest.

352 Solzhenitsyn, 1974, vol. 1, p. 129-130. The emphasis is Solzhenitsyn's.

353 Ströhm, 1974, p. 43. He uses the term ideology pejoratively. "Perhaps it would be good if our ideology-crazed leftists would take to heart particularly this message from the great Russian writer." (My translation.)

354 Meyer, 1985, p. 66.

how easy it was to understand minor objections to *Gulag* as something more serious during the Cold War.

Perhaps no other article on *Gulag* exemplifies the polarity and difficulty of dealing with this book more than Slavicist Wolfgang Kasack's article *Missglückter Kritik an Solschenizyns ‚Archipel GULAG'.*[355] Kasack refers to another professor's criticism of the language of *Gulag* as boorish and counters that it is inappropriate to criticize the language of what he called the first report of the Soviet prison camp system. As a further counterargument, he adds that language has always been the cause of great recognition[356] among Solzhenitsyn's Russian readers. He points out that the whole world had expressed admiration for Solzhenitsyn, who is allegedly the first to write a text about the prison camps. Kasack continues by claiming that the language of *Gulag* is just as good as that of his earlier prose, but that because it is a documentary text, critics must approach it differently. Kasack's complicated logic that it is both wrong to criticize the language of a book about the camps but that—incidentally—the language is what causes admiration among his readers, can seem confusing, but it may be the result of an insecurity in dealing with a book on such a controversial subject during a time of political tension. Perhaps Kasack considered a discussion on language superficial and insulting when the subject was the torture and execution of millions, but at the same time did not want to hide the fact that he did indeed admire the language used. What the original critic was probably referring to when he described the language as boorish, was Solzhenitsyn's stylization of his language as a form of peasant language peppered with the slang and rudeness of prison jargon.[357]

The timing of the publication of *Gulag*—shortly before Solzhenitsyn's expulsion from the USSR and during some of the most significant rapprochement talks between West Germany and the East—prompted a

355 Published in 1975, and re-printed in the following collection of essays: Wolfgang Kasack. *Die russische Schriftsteller-Emigration im 20. Jahrhundert Beiträge zur Geschichte, den Autoren und ihren Werken.* 62 Vol. Munich: Sagner, 1996. p. 280-1. The title translates as: "Failed criticism of Solzhenitsyn's 'Gulag Archipelago'".

356 His words are "höchste Anerkennung."

357 Elisabeth Markstein, the translator of *Gulag* into German, describes this odd sounding language in her article: Anna Peturnig. "Einige Gedanken zur Übersetzungsarbeit an Solschenizyns Archipel GULAG." *Osteuropa* 3 (1975): 151-61. (She wrote this article under her pseudonym.)

strong emotional response towards the author and his work. The political content and the tone of the work heightened a sense of urgency and divisiveness. In general, conservative and right-wing scholars and intellectuals in Germany tended to portray their support towards Solzhenitsyn as a united front. Meyer rightly points out how the enthusiasm with which conservatives embraced Solzhenitsyn caused great confusion and awkwardness for leftist thinkers who sympathized with the Russian but loathed the company of their conservative countrymen.[358]

The feuilleton-editor-in-chief of *Die Welt*, Günter Zehm, described the situation as follows:

> Alexander Solschenizyns ‚Archipel GULag' ist ein in vielerlei Hinsicht folgenreiches Buch. Unter den linken deutschen Schriftstellern etwa wirkt es zur Zeit wie Scheidewasser. Die Frage ‚Für oder gegen Archipel GULag?' macht ehemalige Freunde zu erbitterten Gegnern, wirft Schützengräbern auf, in die man sich grollend zurückzieht, um aus der Deckung heraus den anderen mit Meinungsfeuer zu überziehen.[359]

Zehm singles out Heinrich Böll and Günter Grass as two left-wing writers who decided to break with other German writers who criticized or attacked Solzhenitsyn. Zehm points out that their attitude has brought practical help to the dissidents, but on the "other side of the coin" he criticizes Böll and Grass for their "moralistic" attitude. He writes:

> [Die andere Seite] zeigt uns zwei Schriftsteller, deren Ton oft herrisch und anmaßend klingt, so, als wüssten nur sie allein, was wahr oder nicht wahr, gerecht oder ungerecht ist, als dürften nur sie entscheiden, wer sich zu welchem Zeitpunkt und unter welchen Bedingungen für wen oder gegen wen einzusetzen habe. Hier wird das moralische Konto, über das ein engagierter Schriftsteller verfügen kann, eindeutig überzogen. Die temperamentvolle, warmherzige persönliche Stellungnahme verwandelt sich in eine Kanzelabkündigung.[360]

---

358 Meyer, 1985, p. 67

359 Günter Zehm. "Was nach der Brautnacht kommt: Die Diskussion um Solschenizyn spaltet Deutschlands Literaten." Die Welt 6 February 1974: 4. "Alexander Solzhenitsyn's 'Gulag Archipelago' is a momentous book in many ways. Among leftist German writers it currently has the effect of *aqua fortis*. The question: 'for or against Gulag Archipelago?' turns former friends into bitter enemies. It opens up trenches into which one can resentfully turn back in order to overrun the others with opinion-ammunition from a position of safety." (My translation.)

360 Zehm, 1974, p. 4. "[The other side] shows us two writers, who often sound despotic and overbearing, as if only they knew what is true and what isn't, what is just and

Zehm emphasizes that only in countries without freedom may writers take the position of a "counter-government". Zehm finishes his article in the hope that German writers may learn the lessons of *Gulag* which he sees as two simple truths: that freedom can be as important as bread and that the path that Russia took in 1917 was the wrong one. Here it becomes clear that Zehm does have certain expectations about what the political beliefs of local writers should be, and a specific understanding of what *Gulag* is all about. According to Meyer, the dismissal of Böll and Grass's solidarity towards the dissidents in *Die Welt* was part of an effort to discredit these writers as a threat to political freedom.[361]

Heinrich Böll was personally acquainted with Solzhenitsyn and gave him refuge during his first days in the West. Politically, one may say that he was a liberal leftist, and he openly supported Brandt's *Ostpolitik.*[362] Böll struggles to extract the book from the left-right political mud-slinging in a lengthy review of *Gulag.*[363] The structure of his review reveals his topical orientation towards Soviet criticism of the work: the Soviet press reviled what they saw as Solzhenitsyn's ridiculing of certain victims of state violence; praise of the so-called Russian Liberation Army which fought side-by-side with the Nazis against the USSR during World War II, and his belittling of Nazi crimes.[364] Böll discusses these delicate issues and then adds what he believes the Soviet Union should have noted but did not: the deadly consequences of any ideology.[365] He also adds that this book is a monument to all victims of repression in the USSR, and that Solzhenitsyn gives the victims back their dignity. Böll considers this to be a special work because of its richness in detail and facts, and also because of the way it is written:

---

what is not, as if they alone could decide when and under which circumstances one must or must not support whom. The moral account of the engaged writer is obviously overdrawn in this case. The passionate, warm personal statement becomes a sermon." (My translation.)

361 Meyer, 1985, p. 62.

362 Heinrich Böll. "Heinrich Böll Interview: 'Es ist Zeit, öffentlich energisch zu werden'." Der Spiegel 16 July 1973: 100-1.

363 Heinrich Böll. "Die Himmlische Bitterkeit des Alexander Solschenizyns." Frankfurter Allgemeine Zeitung 9 February 1974.

364 As these latter subjects belong to another type of political debate, I will analyze them independently in section 3.3.

365 He uses the term "ideology" in a pejorative way. Böll, 1974.

> Das Einmalige des Buches liegt denn auch in der Komposition, der Intonation und der Instrumentierung. In der Auswahl von allgemeiner Darstellung der Entwicklung sowjetischer Gesetzgebung, Rechtsprechung und Strafvollzug und den zu jedem Stadium dieser Entwicklung ausgewählten, dokumentierten Details, die, da sie zum größten Teil wiedergegeben, nicht in falscher Mündlichkeit zitiert werden, stilistische Meisterwerke sind, auch in ihrer Kürze.[366]

Böll emphasizes that despite the explosive material, the author's craft is what makes it work. In this sense, he considers Solzhenitsyn's *Gulag* a masterpiece from an aesthetic point of view but also a politically relevant work. Böll did not consider that ideological aspects of *Gulag* contradicted his own beliefs. As other left-leaning intellectuals and scholars, he looked for the common ground in *Gulag* and valued solidarity towards Solzhenitsyn above the need to criticize more controversial aspects of his work. The poet and critic Horst Bienek, himself a former Soviet prison camp victim, took a similar stance. In his review of *Gulag*, Bienek claims that he was unable to find a hint of anti-communism in the text.[367] Bienek criticizes Moscow for calling those who praise *Gulag* "anti-communists" or "cold warriors", but he also feels sorry for Solzhenitsyn because he is lauded in the "Springer Press"—the publications of the famously conservative Axel Springer.[368]

Axel Springer, the German media mogul, had set certain political goals for his publishing company. Two were of particular importance during the Cold War: anti-Sovietism and the fostering of a feeling of German national unity.[369] This latter goal of strengthening the feeling that Germans behind the Iron Curtain were part of the same people was linked to Springer's unwillingness to recognize the German Democratic Republic. In this sense, *Ostpolitik* was very much contrary to his own media policy. In the 1970s, he developed a personal friendship with Solzhenitsyn, printed several of his works, and

---

366 Böll, 1974. "The uniqueness of the book is likewise based on its composition, intonation, and instrumentation. On the choice of a general presentation of the development of Soviet legislation, jurisprudence, and the penal system and the documentary details chosen for each of the phases of this development, which are—even in their brevity—stylistic masterworks because they depict and are not quoted in false orality." (My translation. Böll's wording.)

367 Horst Bienek. "Blutige Farce." Die Zeit 25 January 1974.

368 The "Springer Press" includes newspapers such as *Die Welt*, and the book publisher *Ullstein*.

369 Jochen Staadt; Tobias Voigt; Stefan Wolle. *Feindbild Springer*. Göttingen: Vandenhoeck & Ruprecht, 2009. p. 235.

quoted him when arguing against *Ostpolitik*.[370] Other authors who were published in his papers followed this line of argument, so that it became common for articles on Solzhenitsyn to develop into criticism of German policy.[371] Most of the time, conservative authors did not focus on one of Solzhenitsyn's works, but quoted several of his works or speeches, and used these texts in their own arguments.[372]

As time went by, the German leftist discussion about *Gulag* started to focus less on the work, and more on how to deal with Solzhenitsyn's growing popularity among conservatives and right-wingers.

Journalist Ulrich Rosenbaum wrote both about *Gulag* and Solzhenitsyn in *Vorwärts*, the organ of the Social Democratic Party.[373] Rosenbaum describes the publication of *Gulag* as the most critical moment for Western leftist parties since the Soviet invasion of Czechoslovakia in 1968. Even though Rosenbaum points out that there is "nothing new" in the revelations made in *Gulag*, he considers it an important work because of its literary qualities but especially because of the circumstances surrounding its publication. In his article, Rosenbaum criticizes Western communists who attack Solzhenitsyn and *Gulag* in the strongest terms. Rosenbaum explains that as socialism means different things to different people, it is important to show no solidarity with Soviet communism. Rosenbaum addresses the "problem" of Solzhenitsyn's conservative admirers. He considers their attitude toward him that of abuse (Missbrauch) and asks his social-democratic readers not to judge Solzhenitsyn because of the way he is applauded by the right. Although

---

370 He printed several of Solzhenitsyn's works and essays including: *Ivan Denisovich* (1963); and *Warnung: die tödliche Gefahr des Kommunismus* (1980). He quoted Solzhenitsyn's anti-Detente claims in his "Christmas Greetings to Friends and Supporters" in 1974 and 1975, cf. Axel Springer Verlag Unternehmensarchiv (ASV UA) Kontinent-Mappe: 2.4.

371 For example: Dieter Cycon. "Der Dichter in der Schlinge." Die Welt 11 February 1974: 4; Walter Günzel. "Die bösen Friedensstörer." Die Welt 1 January 1974: 4; Walter Günzel. "Zittern vor leerem Schrecken: Warum einige Linke Solschenizyn vor 'falschen Freunden' warnen." Die Welt 18 February 1974: 4; Cf.: Meyer, 1985, p. 59ff.

372 A good example is: Hans Graf Huyn. *Weder Frieden noch Freiheit: Bilanz der Ostpolitik in Dokumenten.* Informationen über die DDR. No. 6. Bonn: CDU-Bundesgeschäftsstelle, 1974.

373 Ulrich Rosenbaum. "Ist der Wurm nun aus dem Apfel Gefallen?" Vorwärts 21 February 1974: 3.

Rosenbaum does recognize that *Gulag* contains certain problematic claims about the Nazis, he dismisses this as a misunderstanding. He does not consider the connection between what Solzhenitsyn writes and the affinity of the Western right to be one of ideological compatibility. Rosenbaum's hope is that, once Solzhenitsyn has settled down in the West, he will be able to choose who he really wants to be associated with.

Other representatives of the Left, including the *New Left* leader Rudi Dutschke considered it an obligation to clarify their position towards Solzhenitsyn and his newest work. Dutschke edited a collection of essays about Solzhenitsyn and the Western Left.[374] In this book, there are both calls for unconditional solidarity with the author,[375] but also political criticism of *Gulag*. For instance, Ernest Mandel writes in detail why *Gulag* can be seen as a work representing a reactionary ideology.[376] Mandel appreciates many aspects of *Gulag* including its thoroughness in describing all the different kinds of people who suffered repression during the first decades of Soviet history. However, he claims that Solzhenitsyn's tendency to go only half-way into certain subjects is not a mistake, but most likely an ideological choice. For instance, Mandel wonders how Solzhenitsyn comes to the conclusion that repression is a result of ideology as such and is so passionate and accurate in showing how state violence was ideologically justified in the USSR, but he does not dedicate a moment to the way religion and patriotism as ideologies have likewise served as justification for the deaths of millions over the centuries. He suspects this may be a result of Solzhenitsyn's sympathy towards Christianity, but that his way of dealing with this problem in such a simplifying way is perhaps the result of the Russian author's own confusion as a former Marxist.[377]

Mandel considers Solzhenitsyn's dealing with communist victims of repression a much more serious problem. He emphasizes the speculative

---

374 Rudi Dutschke, ed. *Sowjetunion, Solschenizyn und die westliche Linke.* Reinbek bei Hamburg: Rowohlt, 1975.

375 Franz Marek. "Unteilbare Solidarität." *Sowjetunion, Solschenizyn und die westliche Linke.* Ed. Rudi Dutschke. Reinbek bei Hamburg: Rowohlt, 1975. 250-260.

376 Ernest Mandel. "'Archipel GULag' oder die unbewältigte Vergangenheit des Stalinismus." *Sowjetunion, Solschenizyn und die westliche Linke* Ed. Rudi Dutschke. Reinbek bei Hamburg: Rowohlt, 1975. 211-225.

377 Mandel, 1975, p. 220-221.

way in which Solzhenitsyn claims that Trotsky would have behaved in a cowardly manner, had he been part of a local show trial. As Trotsky had continued to criticize Stalinism even after he and his family had suffered from persecution, Solzhenitsyn's suggestion that he would not have resisted pressure is ludicrous. Mandel interprets this as an attempt to discredit Trotsky and Trotskyism as political alternatives to Stalinism, something that Stalin himself had fought to do. In this sense, Mandel sees Solzhenitsyn as the product of the Soviet Union's inability to overcome Stalinism. He describes the irony of it all:

> Die Ironie der Geschichte bewirkt jedoch, dass diese eingefleischten Gegner des Stalinismus, die Solschenizyn und Genossen, diese kühnen Kämpfer gegen den Marxismus-Leninismus, als angeblich für den Stalinismus verantwortlich, in einem großen Ausmaß *selbst Gefangene der stalinistische Ideologie bleiben*.[378]

Mandel accuses the "international bourgeoisie" of using *Gulag* to distract from the human rights violations in places like Chile, where—in the name of anti-communism—a violent coup d'état brought about the neo-fascist dictatorship of Augusto Pinochet. He adds that this is precisely the reason why revolutionary socialists *should* support Solzhenitsyn and other Soviet dissidents and fight for their unlimited civil rights.

For those Germans who sided with Brandt's *Ostpolitik*, the discussion surrounding *Gulag* and/or Solzhenitsyn's forced exile was focused on not loosing sight of the past while continuing the dialogue with the East. In January of 1974, Theo Sommer, the editor in chief of the weekly *Die Zeit*, was one of the first liberal leftist authors to address the concrete consequences *Gulag* could have for *Ostpolitik*.[379] In his view, the Soviet Union would do well in publishing *Gulag* within its borders:

---

378 Mandel, 1975, p. 224. "The irony of history has the effect that these die-hard enemies of Stalinism—Solzhenitsyn and his comrades—who bravely fight against Marxism-Leninism and consider it responsible for Stalinism, are *themselves prisoners of Stalinist ideology* to a great extent." (My translation, Mandel's emphasis.)

379 Theo Sommer. "Russische Tragödie: Solschenizyn und die Entspannung." Die Zeit 11 January 1974.

> Ein so großes Land wie die Sowjetunion, das offenbar tatsächlich auf internationale Entspannung aus ist, kann sich auf die Dauer diese innere Spannung der vergangenen und noch nicht vergessenen Angst nicht leisten, die zu artikulieren Solshenizyn [sic] am Werk ist.[380]

According to Sommer, the rapprochement between East and West cannot work as long as the Soviet Union is still hiding from its past, and insulting anyone who raises memories of it. Like other German left-leaning authors, he confronted Soviet criticism of *Gulag* head-on and took sides with the dissident. Sommer went so far as to claim that he would stick to this position even if it meant receiving praise from the "Springer Press" and *Ostpolitik*-opponent Gerhard Löwenthal from the TV channel ZDF.

Sommer, Mandel, Rosenbaum, Augstein, Böll, and Bienek are examples of German writers, critics, and publicists who were part of the left, had varying disagreements with the content of *Gulag*, but nevertheless believed in the importance of taking Solzhenitsyn's side in his conflict with the Soviet Union, be it—as in the case of Mandel—a political avowal in order to avoid losing political legitimacy, or the result of a genuine belief that Solzhenitsyn did share some common ground with the Western left—as Böll did. They did not question the factual accuracy of *Gulag*, and there was little discussion about the work's genre: these authors accepted Solzhenitsyn's claim that this was both a history and a literary experiment in which he presented his interpretation of Soviet history. At the same time, it was understood as a political work. As Theo Sommer put it: "Alexander Solschenizyns Werk „Archipel GULAG"—eine Dokumentation, kein Roman—ist eine Herausforderung an die Obrigkeit."[381]

These authors accept the consensus that to reject *Gulag* and its author would be political self-immolation: the discussion about this work had developed in such a way that criticism, or even a misinterpretation of it, could be redrawn as, say, an attempt to deny the crimes of the Soviet Union or to slander or delegitimize the dissidents. By the mid-70s, for liberal leftists or non-Stalinist

---

380 Sommer, 1974. "A country as large as the Soviet Union, which is obviously serious about international détente, cannot afford to sustain the inner tension of the past and the unforgotten fear that Solzhenitsyn is articulating, for a longer period of time." (My translation.)

381 Sommer, 1974. "'Gulag Archipelago'—a documentation and not a novel—is a challenge to the establishment." (My translation.)

communists it was very important to distance themselves from Soviet communism: Solzhenitsyn's work and the way the Soviet Union treated him for publishing it were seen as a final de-legitimation of Soviet ideology. As Rosenbaum and Mandel suggested, if the left was to survive in the West, it was to be through its independence from the USSR. This does not mean that these authors' rejection of Soviet communism was mere lip service; the variety and depth of the arguments they give in discussing communism's failure to protect civil rights leave little room for doubt as to their sincerity.

As Rosenbaum pointed out, the "Solzhenitsyn Affair" in 1974 became a crisis point for the left, as the tanks of the Warsaw Pact in Prague had been in 1968. In this case, it was not so much the legitimacy of Soviet influence in Eastern Europe as the legitimacy of communism as an ideology that was questioned. By repressing Solzhenitsyn in such a spectacular way—shipping him off, as they had previously done to Joseph Brodsky—the Soviet Union showed its own inability to deal with dissent. Thus, in an unintentional way, the USSR itself bolstered support for Solzhenitsyn and diminished its own partisan base abroad. David Bethea and Siggy Frank, who write about Russian literature in exile, consider that exile itself bolsters the writer's reputation, and even plays an important part in the canonization of such authors.[382]

The exile factor notwithstanding, the speed with which many West German left-leaning authors decided to side with Solzhenitsyn and condemn the state that persecuted him is the reflection of a long process of renunciation of communism. This is very likely the result of Germany's unique status in Europe as a divided country: if a German sincerely believed in "real socialism", he or she could well have moved to the German Democratic Republic. But for many West Germans, most of whom were acquainted with the restrictions of liberty and the weak economy of the GDR it was a great challenge to believe that the GDR was the better country it claimed to be. The dissemination of information in Germany about Soviet prison camps predated the Federal Republic, as this had been part of Nazi propaganda. But even after 1945—and especially after the return of German prisoners of war and

382 David Bethea and Siggy Frank. "Exile and Russian Literature." *The Cambridge Companion to Twentieth-century Russian Literature.* Eds. Evgenij Dobrenko and Marina Balina. Cambridge: Cambridge University Press, 2011. p. 196.

rehabilitated German victims of the Great Purge in the late 1950s—gulag literature, and scholarship on this subject were widely known. It was thus not the informative value that made Solzhenitsyn's *Gulag* so relevant in West Germany, but the status this book acquired in the particular moment of its publication. It enforced a black-and-white form of reception that resulted in a coagulation of underlying opinions.

Shortly before and in the early stages of his exile, Solzhenitsyn intervened directly in German discussions of his work and ideas. In various interviews and essays he warned Germans of *Ostpolitik*, which he considered a failed policy approach based on "political blindness".[383] Additionally, he associated his work with political goals, as part of an effort to bring about a change of mind in his country and the West. However, his understanding of politicized literary activity posed a challenge for his reception. This is most evident in a public spat he had with Rudolf Augstein, the editor in chief of the *Spiegel*.

In late 1974, Solzhenitsyn publicly accused Augstein of defamation and slander for claiming that his participation in Axel Springer's literary magazine *Kontinent* can be understood as political activity.[384] He also considers that the *Spiegel* claim that *Gulag* was part of a project to indict Soviet officials who had committed crimes against the population a serious misinterpretation of his work.[385] He initially had his lawyer, Mr. Heeb, confront Augstein with an open letter, which thus sums up Solzhenitsyn's demand:

> Es liegt Alexander Solschenizyn viel daran, demgegenüber öffentlich zu erklären, dass er seine Mitarbeit bei dieser Zeitschrift [Kontinent] ebenso wie seine gesamte übrige Arbeit als eine literarische und nicht eine politische Arbeit verstanden wissen möchte. Die Empörung von Alexander Solschenizyn über die Art Ihrer Zeitschrift, derartig schwerwiegende Falschmeldungen über ihn zu verbreiten, ist umso größer, als Sie die gleichzeitige Veröffentlichung des Vorabdrucks des zweiten Bandes von

---

383 For example in: G.R. "Antwort Auf Grass." Frankfurter Allgemeine Zeitung 18 November 1974: 19. Galina Berkenkopf (transl). "Das *Le Monde* Interview von Alexander Solschenizyn." Criticon 21. 1974: 33-6. Alexander Solzhenitsyn. *Warning to the Western World.* London: MW Books, 1976.

384 Rudolf Augstein. "Dokumentation einer Korrespondenz." Der Spiegel 18 November 1974: 180-3.

385 Incidentally, Augstein was not the only one to suggest Solzhenitsyn sought to bring Soviet officials to court, cf.: Robert Kaiser. "KGB 'War Crime' Trials Urged by Solzhenitsyn." The Guardian 29 December 1973: 3.

> ‚Archipel GULAG' mißbrauchen, um diesen Unwahrheiten möglichst viel Publizität und einen Anschein von Authentizität zu verleihen.[386]

When Augstein defended his paper's right to interpret Solzhenitsyn's work according to its own sources, Solzhenitsyn answered personally with a further open letter. Again, he accuses Augstein of slander and asks for a public apology.

The quagmire Augstein found himself in becomes more obvious, when one looks at Solzhenitsyn's introduction to the first edition of Springer's dissident magazine *Kontinent*:

> Die Intelligenzija Osteuropas spricht eine einzige Sprache, die des Wissens um das Leiden. Wir werden der Zeitschrift »Kontinent« unsere Hochachtung aussprechen, wenn es ihr gelingt, der Stimme Osteuropas eindringlich Gehör zu verschaffen. Wehe Westeuropa, wenn seine Ohren taub bleiben![387]

In their own foreword to the first edition of the magazine,[388] the chief editors of *Kontinent* define their task as an attempt to create a new social and historical situation. According to internal *Kontinent*-staff memos written by conservative activist and early staff member, Ludek Pachman, opposition to *Ostpolitik* was one of the leading motivations in the genesis of *Kontinent*.[389] *Kontinent* was a literary magazine that presented itself as the voice of Eastern European dissident writers, but at the same time as a catalyst for change and a threat to Western readers who did not listen—it isn't hard to see how it could have been understood as political instead of just literary in an artistic sense.

---

386 Augstein, 1974, "Dokumentation", p. 180. "It means a lot to Alexander Solzhenitsyn to declare publicly that he wants his work in this magazine [Kontinent] as well as the rest of his work to be considered literary and not political work. Alexander Solzhenitsyn's indignation towards the way your magazine has spread such seriously wrongful information is even greater due to the fact that you misused the parallel publication of the serialized preview of 'Gulag Archipelago' in order to publicize these lies to the greatest extent possible, and to provide them with a semblance of authenticity." (My translation, my addition in square brackets.)

387 Alexander Solzhenitsyn. "Geleitwort zur ersten Ausgabe." Kontinent 1. 1974: p. 6. "The Eastern European intelligentsia speaks only one language: that of the knowledge of suffering. We will hold the magazine 'Kontinent' in highest regard if it is successful in making the voice of Eastern Europe heard. Woe to Western Europe if its ears stay deaf!" (My translation.)

388 Die Redaktion. "Unsere Aufgabe." Kontinent 1. 1974: 3-4.

389 Axel Springer Verlag Unternehmensarchiv (ASV UA) Kontinent-Mappe: 8.4.

In the end, Augstein decided to simultaneously print all these open letters together and his answer, and let readers judge for themselves. But the question remained: how was one to read Solzhenitsyn?

The Eastern Europe expert Klaus Mehnert offers his response in an article on *Gulag* "as literature."[390] In it, he writes of the difficulty of separating a political from a literary reading of this book. Although he does indeed achieve an interesting analysis of the metaphors used by Solzhenitsyn in this work, he cannot help but digressing to the political implications of Solzhenitsyn's claims regarding Lenin and World War II. In the end, Solzhenitsyn's work of the mid-1970s remained politically volatile.

In general, the mediating reception of *Gulag* was positive in the sense that it embraced it as an important book containing truthful information on the forms of repression in the USSR. Despite surrounding controversies, overall it was welcomed by both those pertaining to the liberal left and the different conservative movements. As cultural historian Karl Schlögel writes:

> Kaum ein literarisches Werk des Dissens ist trotz inhaltlicher und ästhetischer Kontroversen so einhellig begrüßt worden wie Solschenizyns ‚Archipel'.[391]

Disagreements with the ideological aspects of *Gulag* were largely put on hold in an environment intolerant of ambiguousness.[392]

The reaction of West Germany's left-leaning intellectuals and scholars to *Gulag* was very contingent on the particular situation the country was experiencing and thus quite different to the reaction in the other countries of my study.

Solzhenitsyn in 1970's Britain and the US

When it comes to the Anglo-Saxon reaction to *Gulag*, there is a strong correlation in the way scholars and intellectuals in the US and UK dealt with

---

390 Klaus Mehnert. "Der Archipel GULAG als Literatur." *Osteuropa* 7 (1975): 522-33.

391 Karl Schlögel. "Literatur der Dissenz als Ansatz einer Theorienbildung zur sowjetischen Gesellschaft." *Berichte des Bundesinstituts für ostwissenschaftliche und internationale Studien* 31 (1982) p. 27. "Hardly any other dissident work was as unanimously embraced as Solzhenitsyn's 'Archipelago', despite the controversies regarding its content and aesthetics." (My translation.)

392 German reception of *Gulag* that touched revisionist topics will be analyzed in section 3.3.

the book and with the Solzhenitsyn Affair in general. Therefore, I will present their arguments together.

A salient feature of the Anglo-Saxon reception of Solzhenitsyn in the Cold War that differs from the German case is the urgency with which scholars of Eastern Europe and Russian literature not only commented on ideological issues but also used different forms of media to do so. In West Germany, scholars who wrote about Solzhenitsyn outside academia often expressed their political views more openly than when they wrote their academic studies. In the US and UK political opinions were less opaque even in scholarly works.

According to Solzhenitsyn, and the few scholarly studies of Solzhenitsyn's Anglo-Saxon reception, beginning in the 1970s, he was the victim of extensive attacks by journalists and scholars in the West.[393] Solzhenitsyn complained of not being taken seriously by scholars, and of slander in the press.[394] Literary scholar Edward Ericson writes of decade-long attacks on the Russian dissident in the US and the West in general. In 1985, historian Robert Conquest writes that the liberal British media staged an orchestrated attack on the dissident writer in the 1970s.[395] These studies, like Solzhenitsyn's own claims in articles or interviews, form the impression that liberal leftists in the West, including academics, set out to attack the dissident and his work. It is understandable that no author can please everyone, but is there evidence of such widespread antagonism? If so, what was/is it based upon?

Russianist John Dunlop points out in his study of Solzhenitsyn's reception that the bone of contention in discussions of Solzhenitsyn was the Russian author's assessment of the Soviet threat:

> It will be noted that Solzhenitsyn's supporters put the stress on the reality and danger of Soviet expansionism, while his detractors emphasized the pitfalls of an over-reaction to that threat.[396]

---

393 Cf.: Dunlop, 1985; Conquest, 1985; Edward E. Ericson. *Solzhenitsyn, The Moral Vision.* Grand Rapids: Eerdmans, 1980. p. 120ff. Ericson, 1998; Alexander Solzhenitsyn. "Misconceptions about Russia Are a Threat to America." *Foreign Affairs* 58.4 (1980): 797-834.

394 Smith, 1972, p. 1, 10; Kramer, 1980, p. 3.

395 Conquest, 1985, p. 9.

396 Dunlop, 1985, "Reception", p. 31.

To be sure, in the 1970s the Russian writer campaigned against détente in the US and Britain buttressing his views with his experience as a former gulag inmate. As opposed to West German society, which was praised by the author, the societies of the US and UK were harshly criticized by him. Solzhenitsyn gave numerous interviews and speeches and appeared on television in both countries, expressing his opinions emphatically.

Gulag was published in English in 1974, but already by 1975 Solzhenitsyn was delivering speeches in the US—some of which were published in book form.[397] His BBC interview in London in 1976 was likewise subsequently published.[398] Later articles followed, in which Solzhenitsyn commented on topics ranging from President Gerald Ford's foreign policy to his cabinet decisions.[399] These direct interventions in and comments on US- and British public life eclipsed or delayed somewhat the attention to the works he otherwise published at the same time—*Letter to the Soviet Leaders* (1974), *Lenin in Zurich* (1975), and *The Oak and the Calf* (1975).[400] Probably due to the flood of additional material the Anglo-Saxon observer had to digest when it came to the Solzhenitsyn question, the discussions of his work—literary and publicistic—became panoptical, if somewhat desultory. This does not mean that he did not receive serious scholarly attention—a wide variety of scholarly books solely dedicated to the dissident author were published in the late 1970s alone.[401] However, the discussions surrounding Solzhenitsyn's oeuvre

---

397 Alexander Solzhenitsyn. *Solzhenitsyn: the Voice of Freedom.* Washington: American Federation of Labor and Congress of Industrial Organizations, 1975. Alexander Solzhenitsyn. *Drei Reden an die Amerikaner.* Darmstadt: Luchterhand, 1975.

398 Solzhenitsyn, 1976, "Warning"; Alexander Solschenizyn. "Und die Wahrheit wird uns frei machen: Interview mit der BBC." Kontinent No. 11 1979: 24-46.

399 For example: Alexander Solzhenitsyn. "Schlesinger and Kissinger." The New York Times 1 December 1975: 31. Simon Winchester. "Solzhenitsyn snubs Ford." The Guardian 23 July 1975: 4.

400 *Lenin in Zurich* appeared in Russian in the West in 1975, and in English in 1976. *The Oak and the Calf* was published in Russian and German in 1975, its English translation was delayed due to legal battles concerning slander.

401 Some examples are: Kathryn Feuer, ed. *Solzhenitsyn: A Collection of Critical Essays.* Englewood Cliffs, N. J.: Prentice-Hall, 1976; Vera V. Carpovich. *Solzhenitsyn's Peculiar Vocabulary: Russian-English Glossary.* New York: Technical Dictionaries Co., 1976; Francis Barker. *Solzhenitsyn: Politics and Form.* London: Macmillan, 1977; Stephen Carter. *The Politics of Solzhenitsyn.* London: Macmillan, 1977.

were—as opposed to Germany—less of a dialogue (or quarrel) and more of a cacophony.

Détente as a policy became connected to Solzhenitsyn insofar as the message of *Gulag* and his speeches focused on creating an uncompromising bond between a certain type of morality and politics. It encompassed more than just a discussion of policy and became a questioning of the nature of communism and the moral stance the US and UK should take towards communist countries. Nuance was not part of Solzhenitsyn's message, and this posed a challenge in his interaction with his readers and commentators.

As Solzhenitsyn was a writer, and did not see himself as a political theorist, this raises the question of the relationship between of literature and politics: What gave him authority to speak about politics? Was his work only politically or also aesthetically relevant? These were some of the questions central to the Anglo-Saxon debate on the Solzhenitsyn Affair in the 1970s. But before going into these questions, it is important to understand the historical context in which these debates were taking place.

US- and British forms of détente had strong similarities. As *Ostpolitik*, détente was a rapprochement with the countries east of the Iron Curtain. Détente in Britain had a longer history than in the US, or the Federal Republic. However, as a policy it was similar to that which the US pursued in the 1970s when Richard Nixon launched it. The UK and US sought global instead of local goals with this policy, détente was a dialogue meant to bring forth stronger military security and an understanding over spheres of influence. For Britain it was important to maintain a relationship with the USSR that would avert a war in Europe; however, it remained sceptical of strong disarmament policies. The US sought a certain degree of disarmament together with the USSR, and the signing of the first Strategic Arms Limitation Talks Agreement in 1971 was a part of this.

In the US and UK, détente was detached from clear left-right political paradigms: both conservative and liberal-left politicians were for or against it. Political actors were thus pragmatic when it came to the question of negotiating with the USSR; it is no surprise that the term *realpolitik* gained prominence during this time. In contrast, this was seldom the case when it comes to contemporary scholars or publicists: here anti-détente positions tend to overlap with conservative anti-communism. Nevertheless, the relationship between détente and the dissidents from a scholarly and journalistic point of view was aggravated due to the complexity of interpretations of what détente *should* be.

In Britain détente had a different magnitude and significance than in Germany and the US. Historian Sean Greenwood writes:

> British approach to *détente* was more cautious, even pedestrian, compared to other exponents of the policy during the late 1960s and 1970s.[402]

Additional to its goal of securing peace, Britain saw détente as a way to remain influential in Europe—especially through its role as mediator between East and West.[403] This was particularly important when US President Nixon decided to pursue rapprochement with the communist world in the early seventies. Nixon and his security adviser, Henry Kissinger, relied on British diplomats and the Foreign Office for help during their negotiations.[404] With time, however, scepticism about Soviet meddling in African and Asian countries diminished the British enthusiasm over détente.[405]

In a sense, British commentary and analysis of Solzhenitsyn was less linked to concrete policies than in Germany. Anti-communist promoting of Solzhenitsyn was more abstract and less related to specific policy decisions. The broader, more moralistic view of the relationship with the USSR from a British standpoint was akin to that of many commentators in the US. Because of the cultural ties between the two countries, and the semblance in their political positions of the time, there was a strong interaction between British and US scholars and journalists when it came to Solzhenitsyn and his work: their articles and books were published and read in both countries.

In the UK, *Gulag* was pre-published in three instalments in *The Observer*. The work is presented by an unsigned introduction that describes the work as a product of research done by Solzhenitsyn over the course of several

402 Sean Greenwood. *Britain and the Cold War, 1945-1991*. London: Macmillan, 2000. p. 175.

403 Greenwood, 2000, p. 176.

404 Marie Elise Sarotte. "The Frailties of Grand Strategies: A Comparison of Détente and Ostpolitik." *Nixon in the World: American Foreign Relations, 1969-1977*. Eds. Fredrik Logevall and Andrew Preston. Oxford; New York: Oxford University Press, 2008. 146-163.

405 Greenwood, 2000, p. 181.

years.[406] It also notes that the Soviet Union had accused Solzhenitsyn of hatred of the Soviet people and the state, but that it had not "disputed" its accuracy. By doing so, it suggests that the USSR had implicitly confirmed the facts in the work. The impression of a factual relationship between Solzhenitsyn's work and reality is reinforced by the pictures used in the series. Not only pictures taken from the *Gulag*, but also further photographs were used to illustrate the texts. In the second instalment, a contemporary picture of the US citizen Alexander Dolgun is included.[407] Solzhenitsyn allegedly describes his ordeal in Soviet camps when describing a person denominated "A.D.". With the inclusion of the image and the decoded name, Solzhenitsyn's work is associated with an existing person—a US citizen, and thus someone the readers could more likely relate to. In the third instalment, which describes Solzhenitsyn's own arrest, a picture of Solzhenitsyn with two other men is shown with a caption explaining them to be the real-life characters from Solzhenitsyn's previous novel *First Circle*.[408] With this, a link was created not only between *Gulag* and the experience of existing people, but also with the stories described in *First Circle.* In sum, *The Observer* presents an understanding of *Gulag* as a factual account of goings-on in the USSR.

The Observer, a paper that supported the British version of détente, explicitly mentions that the Soviet press was trying to politicize the publication of *Gulag*:

> Tass also claimed that Western newspapers publishing Solzhenitsyn's book were well-known as enemies of East-West détente and supporters of South African racism and the Greek colonels—a description that few readers of THE OBSERVER will recognise as applicable to this newspaper.[409]

---

406 N.N. "Introduction to 'Victims of Terror' by Alexander Solzhenitsyn." The Observer 6 January 1974: 21.

407 Alexander Solzhenitsyn. "Massacre of the Bolsheviks." The Observer 13 January 1974: 21-2.

408 Alexander Solzhenitsyn. "My Arrest by Smersh." The Observer 20 January 1974: 21-2.

409 N.N., "Introduction to 'Victims of Terror'", 1974, p. 21.

The Observer editorial staff distances itself from the accusation that supporting Solzhenitsyn is tantamount to a disapproval of détente, and reiterates this view in an editorial in the second issue serializing *Gulag*.[410]

As in Germany, *Gulag* cannot be seen as marking the end of the left in the UK, but it did become an important instrument for the anti-communist movement. Although many liberal papers, such as *The Observer*, made an effort to support both détente and Solzhenitsyn, in the eyes of many conservative commentators one had to choose one or the other. As I will later exemplify, the issue at stake was that if a state was as brutal as Solzhenitsyn claimed it to be, there was no reason why Britain should sustain a dialogue with it.

In the US, the publication of *Gulag* and Solzhenitsyn's expulsion took place while the Watergate affair was reaching a crescendo. Richard Nixon was under increasing pressure from the US Congress to release the White House recordings which would prove his involvement in an illegal attempt to wiretap the Democratic National Committee at the Watergate Hotel. Only few weeks before the publication of Solzhenitsyn's work, President Nixon had been pleading to the US public that he was not a crook.[411] Only half a year after Solzhenitsyn's expulsion, in August 1974, Nixon resigned his post as a result of Watergate.

Although the Watergate affair led to a scandal of a magnitude hitherto unknown in US history, press coverage of Solzhenitsyn's work and his struggle with the Soviet authorities was copious. His work was serialized in *The New York Times*, and reviews of the text and comments on the author's fate abounded in all major US news outlets.

Some of the coverage of the Solzhenitsyn Affair considered it having some relation to détente, and thus to President Nixon, who had initiated this policy in the US. However, this direct association of both topics did not last long.

Nixon himself took care to praise Solzhenitsyn's courage publicly.[412] But his critics expected more from him. Cyrus Sulzberger of *The New York Times*

---

410 Samuel Pisar. "An Open Letter to Sakharov." The Observer 13 January 1974: 8.

411 Carroll Kilpatrick. "Nixon Tells Editors 'I'm Not a Crook'." The Washington Post 18 November 1973.

412 Murrey Marder. "Nixon Lauds Solzhenitsyn's 'Courage'." The Washington Post 26 February 1974: 1.

tackles the subject of détente and the dissidents on the day of Solzhenitsyn's exile, and asks for a change of policy.[413] He argues that the current form of détente does not affect repression in the USSR. Solzhenitsyn's example shows there is a clear lack of freedom of speech. His point of view is that détente should be continued in a reformed way, as the dissident Andrei Sakharov suggests. This opinion is thus remarkably similar to that expressed in *The Observer* at the same time:[414] It was not a white-washing of the Soviet human rights record but a desire to forge a relationship that would help overcome these failings.

From a conservative point of view, it was not just the present state of affairs that should influence foreign policy. For example, the prominent political journalist Joseph Alsop advises Nixon to take *Gulag* as reading material on his trip to Moscow in June 1974:

> President Nixon ought to be taking 'Gulag Archipelago' along, and reading it with great care, too, for the simplest of all possible reasons.
>
> In brief, from the President's friend General Secretary Leonid Brezhnev on downward, every single existing leader of the Soviet government actively, enthusiastically collaborated in Stalin's terror and its fearful post-war aftermath. If any one of them had not done so, he would not be at the top today. And all these men have joined to perpetuate the grim police machinery that Stalin used; and they are using it themselves today, albeit on a somewhat lesser scale.[415]

Alsop's argument, that, during his dialogue with him, Nixon should keep in mind that Brezhnev—as all leaders of the USSR until then—was basically a criminal, was complemented by his claim that *Gulag* taught people in the US the dangers of history. For Alsop the message of *Gulag* is crystal clear:

> [N]o humane man can read Solzhenitsyn's heavily documented, totally heart-searing facts and figures without reaching a most unsettling conclusion. The Russian people would be immeasurably better off today if the revolution of 1917 had somehow failed to take place. Tsarist autocracy was a pale, feeble, downright comfortable system compared to the bloodstained Soviet tyranny.[416]

---

413 Cyrus L. Sulzberger. "Détente and Dissidence." The New York Times 13 February 1974: 39. All references to this article are from the same page.

414 I refer to the article by Samuel Pisar, cf. Pisar, 1974.

415 Joseph Alsop. "'Gulag Archipelago': 'must Reading' for Mr. Nixon." The Washington Post 26 June 1974: 19.

416 Alsop, 1974, p. 19.

Alsop's opinion is a good example of the way some Western intellectuals considered détente to be an occasion to pass judgement on the USSR as a whole—and considered *Gulag* to provide them with the necessary arguments. But *Gulag* was also seen as an event in itself and analyzed as such.

Historian Stephen Cohen, a member of the liberal left, reviews *Gulag* for *The New York Times.* He contextualizes *Gulag* in the category of "books about the experience of holocaust".[417] He describes it as both a chronology of the crimes of the Soviet Union, and an explanation of why they took place. When it comes to the ideology of the work, Cohen writes:

> We can [...] honor and share Solzhenitsyn's moral condemnation of what happened without necessarily embracing his explanation.[418]

Again, Cohen tries to separate what he sees as the main meaning of the work, and what he considers to be minor issues, such as Solzhenitsyn's conclusions. Other reviews in the same paper focused on retelling the content of *Gulag*, often reinforcing the impression that it is a history,[419] or on explaining the relationship between *Gulag* and Solzhenitsyn's background as a former camp inmate.[420] These reviews avoided criticism even when mentioning controversial aspects of *Gulag*—such as the passages written in defence of the Vlasov Army.[421]

The reason why it is important to mention the trust with which *Gulag* was received from the onset—in the US, UK, and FRG—, and the way that it was assumed to be true from the moment of its publication is because of the recurring claim by scholars such as historian Anne Applebaum that even as late as the 1980s witness accounts of Soviet prison camps were "dismissed" and "belittled" by Western commentators—even among those who would

---

417 Cohen, 1974, p.1.

418 Cohen, 1974, p. 1.

419 For example: N. N. "Stalin Said to have Planned a Vast Pogrom." The New York Times 29 December 1973: 8. Harrison E. Salisbury. "Solzhenitsyn Assesses Purge Trials." The New York Times 30 December 1973: 17.

420 Harrison E. Salisbury. "The Transformation of Solzhenitsyn." The New York Times 1974: 6.

421 The Vlasov Army, a.k.a. Russian Liberation Army, was an army fighting on the side of the Nazis against the USSR during World War II. Salisbury mentions Solzhenitsyn's defence of this army without commenting on it, in: Salisbury, 1973, p. 17.

condemn similar crimes elsewhere.[422] Applebaum, who has recently written several books on the Soviet camp system, claims that "Soviet pressure on Western academics and journalists helped skew their work"[423] on Solzhenitsyn during the Cold War. Applebaum asserts that gulag memoirs including Solzhenitsyn's were rejected and that this was done under the influence of Soviet pressure and propaganda. An early example of a scholar with an analogous impression is historian Martin Malia. In his review of *Gulag* from 1977, Malia claims that the initial reception of *Gulag* in the US and Western Europe was mainly negative.[424] Malia presents the position of the European Left "on the whole" as considering *Gulag* "an embarrassment" that requires "discrediting".[425] Malia writes that liberals in the US try to present *Gulag* as posing a threat to détente, but unfortunately cites no examples.[426] Russianist John Dunlop later claims in his study of Solzhenitsyn's US reception that a pro-détente sentiment was the reason for the alleged liberal dismissal of the writer, describing this point of view as follows:

> Thus, while liberals see Solzhenitsyn as calling up an *offensive* 'holy war' against the USSR, conservatives see him summoning the West to *defend* itself against ongoing and increasing communist expansionism.[427]

However, his more specific claim goes beyond the question of détente and reaches the realm of worldview:

> For *The [New York] Times* and the liberal establishment for which it presumes to speak, Solzhenitsyn represents an irrational and potentially dangerous man [...] who foolishly dares to criticize the inherent good sense of the American system, a legacy of the Enlightenment. *The Times* rejects Solzhenitsyn and his message *in toto*.[428]

Although Dunlop grossly generalizes that *The New York Times* and the "liberal establishment" that it represents fully reject both the Russian dissident

---

422 Applebaum, 2004, p. xx-xxi.
423 Applebaum, 2004, xxii. The full quote reads: "Finally, Soviet propaganda was not without its effect. Soviet attempts to cast doubt upon Solzhenitsyn's writing, for example, to paint him as a madman or an anti-Semite or a drunk, had some impact. Soviet pressure on Western academics and journalists helped skew their work too."
424 Malia, 1977, p.48.
425 Malia, 1977, p. 49.
426 Malia, 1977, p. 48-49. This accusation is all the more controversial, as the position he attributes to US liberals was the official view of the Soviet press.
427 Dunlop, 1985, "Reception", p. 46.
428 Dunlop, 1985, "Reception", p. 43.

and his message, his examples of such opinions are scarce. He does quote one critical *New York Times* op-ed—written after Solzhenitsyn's *Harvard Address* in June of 1978—, which he describes as the "summa of the liberal indictment against Solzhenitsyn".[429] This unsigned article, *The Obsession of Solzhenitsyn*, criticizes him after praising his courage and expressing its agreement with many of his appraisals.[430] Its objection lies in the absolute terms of Solzhenitsyn's message, in his tendency "to view the world as a conflict between light and darkness, God and the Devil." The author of this article claims that relations with the USSR cannot be forged in such absolute terms without risking a nuclear war:

> Much as we have been instructed and inspired by Mr. Solzhenitsyn, his willingness to set aside all other values in the crusade against Communism bespeaks an obsession that we are happy to forgo in this nation's leaders. A certain amount of self-doubt is a valuable attribute for people who have charge of nuclear weapons.

Reading the article closely, it appears that the disagreement lies not in the assessment of communism, but in Solzhenitsyn's willingness to compromise other values in favor of an all out campaign against it. The dissident's condemnation of the ending of the Vietnam War, as much as his denunciation of US non-involvement in other global hot spots, suggest that peace is not among his top priorities.[431] Because Solzhenitsyn derides the US system of checks and balances that forces the president to justify his decisions,[432] the author of the editorial feels the need to point to the risk of having a president with such resolute views *and* nuclear weapons.

Dunlop openly agrees with Solzhenitsyn's warning about a growing Soviet threat, and he does not hide his disapproval of the writer's critics.[433] Dunlop even accuses "liberals" who doubt Solzhenitsyn's literary talent of taking the

---

429 Dunlop, 1985, "Reception", p. 42.

430 N.N. "The Obsession of Solzhenitsyn." The New York Times 13 June 1978: 18. All the following references to this article refer to the same text and the same page.

431 Berman, ed., 1980, p.15.

432 Solzhenitsyn writes about the US situation: "A statesman who wants to achieve something important and highly constructive for his country has to move cautiously and even timidly; thousands of hasty (and irresponsible) critics cling to him at all times; he is constantly rebuffed by parliament and the press. He has to prove that his every step is well-founded and absolutely flawless." Berman, ed., 1980, p. 8-9.

433 Dunlop, 1985, "Reception", p. 48.

"low road".[434] Perhaps political considerations enhanced Dunlop's sensitivity when discussing the writer's reception, and helped create this apparent need for an all-embracing approval: For Dunlop, Solzhenitsyn as a person, his political message *and* his talent as a writer were all tightly linked and negative or mildly dismissive comments of one aspect of his work or style could be interpreted as all-out aggression. Seen from today's point of view, it is difficult to understand the above plea for a nuanced approach to foreign policy in *The New York Times* as the "indictment" of a writer. Nowadays, when we no longer have to consider a possible threat of Soviet expansionism, it is necessary to look at reception texts in all their subtlety.

Claims by conservative scholars such as Conquest (earlier), Malia, and Dunlop that Solzhenitsyn was the victim of a general attack by liberals in the West due to their allegiance to détente, or their sycophancy to the USSR, or other political reasons are important to look at not just because they lack convincing evidence but also because of the persistency of this idea. As the example from Applebaum's book shows, the view that this was the way Solzhenitsyn was treated by the press and by academics during this period is widespread. Political scientist and author of several books on Solzhenitsyn, Daniel Mahoney, claims in 2001 that in the 1970s and 80s the Russian was criticized and rebuffed by US scholars and journalists because of their alleged standard rejection of anti-communism.[435] In 2003, Mahoney goes so far as to claim that few other authors have "been so systematically misunderstood or have been the subject of as many wilful distortions" as he has.[436] The reception I discuss here is mediating reception (in Grimm's terms) that attempts to divulge concrete opinions of Solzhenitsyn's work. If scholars continue to write that the author's Cold War reception was negative—for whatever reason—they are in turn creating an image that lastingly affects the perception of his work. It is therefore of great consequence to re-examine this early reception. A new assessment of liberal comments on Solzhenitsyn in the 1970s reveals a less acrimonious, and in fact, mainly benevolent

434 Dunlop, 1985, "Reception", p. 44.

435 Daniel J. Mahoney. *Aleksandr Solzhenitsyn: The Ascent from Ideology.* Lanham, MD: Rowman & Littlefield Publishers, 2001. p. 9.

436 Daniel J. Mahoney. "The continuing relevance of Aleksandr Solzhenitsyn." *Society* 41.1 (2003). p. 67.

reception. After all, liberal newspapers were the ones that published *Gulag* in segments—and certainly did not do so as a favor to the Soviet Union.[437]

An overall positive appraisal of Solzhenitsyn and his work at the time is evident in the exchange between columnist and author William Safire and John Leonard, editor of *The New York Times Book Review.*[438] This debate, which put Western political bias in the spotlight, is very instructive about the challenges in dealing with politics in dissident literature. Safire expresses discomfort about the way "Westerners of all persuasions outdo each other to embrace one man as their champion", because, he argues, this leads to the "Schweitzerization" of the author—the creation of an unassailable icon. Safire warns that "the adversary of our adversary is not always our ally"—and that it could turn out that Solzhenitsyn does not agree with Western democracy even if he is an opponent of the USSR. Lastly, he indicates that if the dissident's political vision turns out to differ from that of the US, his literary work would be re-evaluated:

> Then the flip-flopping will begin: His literary works will be judged on merits other than the circumstances in which they were written and he may be re-evaluated more as a Mailer with a cause than a Dostoyevsky with an understanding character.

In the end, he writes, "today's intellectual inspiration may become tomorrow's former hero, the old champ who turns into a bore." Safire advocates a more objective approach to the dissident because the bubble of adulation surrounding the author will someday pop—proving to Moscow the political bias in the appreciation of culture in the US.

Leonard, clearly upset by Safire's article, starts by comparing Safire to the Munchkins from *The Wizard of Oz*, and later to cartoon character "Denis the Menace badmouthing Saint Francis of Assisi".[439] According to Leonard, reviewers of Solzhenitsyn are not "Pavlovian dogs" but are in fact capable of

---

437 The Soviet commentator Yuri Zhukov accused *The New York Times* of carrying out a campaign against détente through their reports on Solzhenitsyn and Sakharov, among other things. Cf.: Hedrick Smith. "Russian Accuses Western Press of Campaign Against Détente." The New York Times 12 October 1974: 6.

438 The Safire quotes that follow are all taken from: William Safire. "Solzhenitsyn without Tears." The New York Times 18 February 1974: 25.

439 The following quotes from Leonard are all from: John Leonard. "The Last Word: Solzhenitsyn as a Media Creature." The New York Times 3 March 1974: 447.

criticism. However, he makes it very clear that Solzhenitsyn's talent should not be questioned, regardless of the quality of his latest works.

> The person who wrote 'One Day in the Life of Ivan Denisovich', 'Cancer Ward' and, especially 'The First Circle' belongs in the first rank of the world's writers, period.

Leonard adds that a similar principle applies to his politics. Whatever ideas Solzhenitsyn may embrace, it is the duty of Western government to protect him.

> At issue is not whether Solzhenitsyn is "always our ally." He is an individual, not a nation-state. At issue is whether we, squeezing on the bagpipes of our "democratic principles," will always be *his* ally, and the ally of individuals like him, be they darlings of the media, novelists of genius, public nuisances, peasants, munchkins or columnists. A West expansive enough to permit the fiction of Spiro Agnew to be published by Ladies Home Journal and Playboy Press is surely permissive enough to swallow the witness of Solzhenitsyn, even if he refuses to sign a loyalty oath.

Leonard writes that he would have the same respect for Safire, if his colleague had been thrown "in a prison camp for 11 years" and later on deported to Albania for having criticized the US government.

The Safire-Leonard exchange poses important questions that often lurked in the background of Solzhenitsyn's reception. Did the dissident enjoy Western recognition because of his persecution or because of his talent? How does one define a "great writer"—especially when the quality of his work changes dramatically from one work to another? Is it adequate to analyze Solzhenitsyn's work primarily by aesthetic/literary criteria or not, and why?

In 1976, russianist George Gibian writes about *Gulag*:

> [*Gulag*] overwhelms us with the sheer amount of human pain which it expresses. An exclusively technical analysis of the book saturated with suffering and bearing witness to a gigantic historical and national tragedy would be an exercise in callousness.[440]

Gibian admits that non-literary factors have played a part in making this book so exceptional: the author's "fame", his "heroic conduct", etc.[441] However, he explains that this work stands out from other books on the Soviet camps through its strength—rendered through the polemicizing style—and its far

---

440 George Gibian. "How Solzhenitsyn Returned His Ticket." *Solzhenitsyn: a Collection of Critical Essays.* Ed. Kathryn Feuer. Englewood Cliffs, N. J.: Prentice-Hall, 1976. p. 113.

441 Gibian, 1976, p. 112.

reaching political message—an "all-out barrage against Soviet ideology and reality".[442] Thus, Gibian's initial warning about the callousness of a technical analysis of this work is soon toned down. He assesses the use of different rhetorical modes, dramatizations, fictionalizations as being very effective in:

> [...] driving home the conclusion that not only since Stalin took power, not merely since 1937 or 1938, not through some aberration of the system, but from the beginning of the Soviet state in 1917, and basically, from root to crown, the Soviet Union has been a perversion of a true human community.[443]

Gibian concludes that the way *Gulag* was written was excellent in putting its political message across. He understands the role of the author to be linked with political or social commentary. In a later article on Solzhenitsyn, Gibian argues that "Solzhenitsyn is so important a figure in world literature and thought that we cannot postpone consideration of his views."[444] Furthermore:

> His views of the illnesses of the Russian national culture and exhortations for the future are more original than we would surmise from most comments about him. They deserve to be understood and taken seriously.[445]

Gibian assumes that there is a general opinion of Solzhenitsyn—which is based mostly on his speeches and articles and not on his novels—that amounts to a misinterpretation of the author. He does not solely blame his readers for this impression, but adds that Solzhenitsyn is in fact, "usually unequivocal, sometimes even simplistic" in his speeches and articles.[446] The critic therefore argues that Solzhenitsyn's fiction is a more reliable source about his ideas.[447]

For Gibian, Solzhenitsyn's status affects the relevance of his political message, and the way he expresses his ideas is, at least in some cases, what substantiates his work's value. Nevertheless, it seems that, in the end, it is the extra-literary aspect of the critic's opinion of current affairs in the Soviet Union which makes the dissident's opinion relevant or not. In such a case, precisely what Safire warned about (a politicization of Solzhenitsyn's

---

442 Gibian, 1976, p. 113, 115, 119.
443 Gibian, 1976, p. 117-8.
444 George Gibian. "The Russian Theme in Solzhenitsyn." *Russian literature and American critics: in honor of Deming B. Brown.* Ed. Kenneth N. Brostrom. 4 Vol. Ann Arbor: Michigan Slavic Publications, 1984. p. 71.
445 Gibian, 1984, p. 72.
446 Gibian, 1984, p. 70.
447 Gibian, 1984, p. 63, 70-73.

reception) could indeed become true. Some critics agree that *Gulag* is a masterpiece because of the way it conveyed a certain message. But is using political criteria the best possible way of dealing with a dissident writer's oeuvre? This could potentially result in the dismissal of a writer's work, if the critic disagrees with his or her political ideas. Alas, this would be reminiscent of the way Soviet critics went about their work. Analyzing a dissident's work on purely literary terms would appear to be a way out of this quagmire. But then, this, as in Solzhenitsyn's case, could be interpreted as "callousness" in view of the suffering the author describes, as Gibian warns.

In 1964, literary critic Victor Erlich proposed to "resist the temptation of proclaiming a nonconformist Soviet story or novel a literary masterpiece simply and largely because we have found it a major political event or a moving human testimony."[448] Solzhenitsyn translator and literary critic Max Hayward, on the other hand, defended the amalgamation of political and aesthetic criteria in the evaluation of Soviet literature precisely because the Soviet government had merged both.[449] Indeed, as I have delineated in the case of the early reception of *Gulag Archipelago*, the political aspects of the work overrun all others. The confiscation of Solzhenitsyn's manuscript by the KGB, the death of his friend who was hiding it, the expulsion of the author from the Soviet Union—all of this in the midst of East-West negotiations—are some of the key extra-literary aspects that played an important part in enhancing the political status of the work. It is understandable that such a voluminous work on the delicate subject of political repression in the world's largest country, combined with all other contingent factors was not easily turned into the object of a purely formalist, aesthetic analysis. But once the *Gulag*'s reviewers made their position towards political repression and the prison camp problem clear, other, more complex political ideas in the book continued to be ignored. It is very likely that, as a result of political restraints, reviewers and critics felt the need to put on the breaks after touching on the subject of Solzhenitsyn's anti-communism, and not go further into his proposals about what Russia should become, or what he thinks about the West and democracy. These latter subjects were trickier to tackle as long as the perceived Soviet threat loomed on the horizon.

---

448 Erlich, 1964, p. 406.
449 Hayward, 1964, p. 432-433. Hayward translated *Ivan Denisovich* into English.

Solzhenitsyn's Late Cold War Reception

In the 1980s, the three countries of my study went through a phase of conservative rule: Margaret Thatcher was the British Prime Minister from 1979 to 1990 and was followed by her fellow party member John Mayor; Ronald Reagan was US president from 1981 to 1989, and was succeeded by his fellow Republican George H. W. Bush Sr.; and Christian-Democrat Helmut Kohl was the German Chancellor from 1982 to 1998.

Thatcher and Kohl were—without a doubt—thoroughly conservative and anti-communist, but their approach to East-West relations was very different from Reagan's. Thatcher's premiership was plagued early on with other pressing needs—economic troubles at home, conflicts in Ireland and the Falklands—hence, her anti-communist rhetoric was not followed by action.[450] In general, Thatcher put economic priorities before ideological ones.[451] Despite his earlier criticism of *Ostpolitik* and rapprochement with East Germany, Kohl became a key player in the interaction that eventually led to German reunification in 1990.[452] West Germany's and the Soviet Union's pragmatic approach to reunification in light of a collapsing East Germany made a peaceful solution to the problem possible. Ideologically, West German anti-communism was thus less focused on the Soviet and German present, but rather on the past. In the 1980s, the right-wing German historian Ernst Nolte sparked what was later dubbed "the Historians' Quarrel": a discussion on the alleged primacy of the gulag over Auschwitz.[453] Some of Solzhenitsyn's work played a background role in the aftermath of this row, and I will discuss it in section 3.3, as it is an essential part of Solzhenitsyn's revisionist reception. In the US of the 1980s, however, anti-communism gained force as a rhetorical, political, and military means. With the beginning of the war in Afghanistan in 1979—in which Soviet forces invaded the country in order to support the local communist government in the confrontation with a variety of opposing forces—US-Soviet relations cooled and the tone became increasingly acrimonious in what was termed the "Second Cold War".

---

450 Greenwood, 2000, p. 183.

451 Greenwood, 2000, p. 183-184.

452 A. James McAdams. "Explaining Inter-German Cooperation in the 1980s." *German Studies Review* 13.DAAD Special Issue (1990): 99-114.

453 Dan Diner and Wolfgang Benz, eds. *Ist der Nationalsozialismus Geschichte? Zu Historisierung und Historikerstreit.* 4391 Vol. Frankfurt Main: Fischer, 1987.

According to the historian Michael Cox, the Reagan candidacy and presidency were regarded as successful because of his convincing way of presenting himself as someone who could rebuild US political and military supremacy and deter the Soviet Union.[454] Cox describes how the Reagan administration not only believed in the Soviet threat, but also knew how to gain political capital from Cold War fears, both in the US and in Europe:

> After all, if the American public could be persuaded that the USSR was growing in international influence (a point disputed by some observers) then it would be much easier for the administration to legitimize its rearmament programme at home and its more assertive role abroad. [...]
>
> According to many American strategists, increased allied fears of the USSR would also undermine Western Europe's perceived drift towards neutralism as well. Finally, by emphasizing the totalitarian nature of the Soviet menace, it was hoped that the United States would regain the moral high ground it had held during the Cold War but had lost as a result of Vietnam, Watergate, and revelations about the subversive anti-democratic role of the CIA in the Third World.[455]

Paradoxically, Reagan sought to regain a certain position in the world by increasing US involvement around the globe—even if it meant the controversial participation in various conflicts.

Reagan relied heavily on the advice of distinguished experts on Eastern Europe (provided they shared his ideological outlook).[456] Most notably, he invited the historian of Russian history Richard Pipes to be the head of the Eastern European Desk on the National Security Council.[457] Political scientist Jeane Kirkpatrick and Richard Pipes played an important role in defining the Reagan Doctrine. Furthermore, Pipes was responsible for writing the National Security Decision Directive nr. 75 which stipulated the goal of "rolling back"

---

454 Michael Cox. "Whatever Happened to the 'Second' Cold War? Soviet-American Relations: 1980-1988." *Review of International Studies* 16.2 (1990). p. 160.

455 Cox, 1990, p. 160.

456 James M. Scott. "Reagan's Doctrine? The Formulation of an American Foreign Policy Strategy." *Presidential Studies Quarterly* 26.4, Intricacies of U.S. Foreign Policy (1996). p. 1047-1048.

457 Chester Pach. "The Reagan Doctrine: Principle, Pragmatism, and Policy." *Presidential Studies Quarterly* 36.1, Presidential Doctrines (2006). p. 81.

the influence of the USSR in the world and support regime change in that country.[458]

The Reagan Doctrine was part of a military and ideological counteroffensive that led to the support of so-called freedom fighters and other anti-communist activists around the world—most famously the Contras in Nicaragua and the Mujjahedin in Afghanistan. Although this policy was not immediately defined by this name—it has also been called the "Kirkpatrick Doctrine"[459]—it was a key part of Reagan's foreign policy from the beginning.[460] Ideologically, it was embedded in the idea that the Soviet Union was "the most dangerous enemy ever known to man"[461] and that negotiating with it amounted to "selling" Eastern Europeans "into slavery."[462] This sense of urgency led to compromise with autocratic or otherwise non-democratic movements over democratic ones in the fight against communism, mainly because they were seen as potentially more successful than the latter.[463] Such a policy was openly advocated in Jeane Kirkpatrick's essay *Dictatorships and Double Standards*, which is widely regarded as the manifesto behind the Reagan Doctrine, but it operated more discreetly during the Reagan presidency: while Kirkpatrick openly speaks of supporting autocracies, Reagan speaks of "exporting Americanism" or supporting "freedom fighters."[464] Here, Kirkpatrick explains why certain autocrats are better than others:

---

458 Cf. Pach, 2006, p. 81-82; Scott, 1996, p. 1048-9; Andrew E. Busch. "Ronald Reagan and the Defeat of the Soviet Empire." *Presidential Studies Quarterly* 27.3, The Presidency in the World (1997). p. 454.

459 As a precursor of the Reagan Doctrine, this policy is defined by Jeane Kirkpatrick in: Jeane J. Kirkpatrick. "Dictatorships and Double Standards." Commentary November 1979.

460 Pach, 2006, p. 79.

461 Reagan quoted in: Pach, 2006, p. 79.

462 Reagan quoted in: Pach, 2006, p. 79. Already here, the rhetorical similarity to Solzhenitsyn's views is apparent, as the dissidents uses the same metaphors in his 1975 speeches.

463 "In Iran and Nicaragua (as previously in Vietnam, Cuba, and China) Washington overestimated the political diversity of the opposition–especially the strength of "moderates" and "democrats" in the opposition movement; underestimated the strength and intransigence of radicals in the movement; and misestimated the nature and extent of American influence on both the government and the opposition." Cf.: Kirkpatrick, 1979.

464 Kirkpatrick, 1979; Pach, 2006, p. 80.

> Generally speaking, traditional autocrats tolerate social inequities, brutality, and poverty while revolutionary autocracies create them.
>
> Traditional autocrats leave in place existing allocations of wealth, power, status, and other resources which in most traditional societies favor an affluent few and maintain masses in poverty. But they worship traditional gods and observe traditional taboos. They do not disturb the habitual rhythms of work and leisure, habitual places of residence, habitual patterns of family and personal relations. Because the miseries of traditional life are familiar, they are bearable to ordinary people who, growing up in the society, learn to cope, as children born to untouchables in India acquire the skills and attitudes necessary for survival in the miserable roles they are destined to fill. Such societies create no refugees.[465]

As this argument shows, a disregard for historical realities as well as a selective view of human rights were a key part of this ideology. After all, the simple example of Franco's Spain shows how much suffering and how many refugees a "traditional" autocratic state can create. The idea of preferring certain types of tyranny over others, or tolerating and even promoting certain human rights violations over others is excusable to some people if it is done in the name of tradition. However, these arguments often lack plausibility, and for those who consider certain rights as inalienable, they remain problematic. However, this problem cannot be simplified as a conflict between conservatives and liberals, as some liberals supported these policies. On the other hand, even some conservatives who advocated tyrants chose their words more carefully when expressing their preference for an "autocrat". Political scientist Clair Apodaca describes the situation:

> The Reagan Administration wanted to legitimize its strategy of creating or maintaining a human rights double standard. With friendly countries that abused the human rights of their citizens, the Reagan strategy was quiet diplomacy and persuasion, while with communist countries it was public denouncements and isolation, if not outright military intervention. When Reagan could not ignore human rights, he attempted to redefine them as anticommunism.[466]

---

465 She continues: "Precisely the opposite is true of revolutionary Communist regimes. They create refugees by the million because they claim jurisdiction over the whole life of the society and make demands for change that so violate internalized values and habits that inhabitants flee by the tens of thousands in the remarkable expectation that their attitudes, values, and goals will "fit" better in a foreign country than in their native land." Kirkpatrick, 1979.

466 Clair Apodaca. *Understanding U.S. Human Rights Policy: A Paradoxical Legacy.* New York: Routledge, 2006. p. 111-112.

To be fair, as tough as Reagan's policies were, he did display enough flexibility when offered the chance to seriously negotiate peace with the Soviet Union in the late 1980s.[467] But the political atmosphere created both by the suasive rhetoric and the concrete policies of the Reagan doctrine affected the way Soviet dissidents were treated in the US, and the way they were discussed. The preference for "traditional"—albeit authoritarian—regimes or dissidents over more modern and Western-leaning activists which was displayed openly in hot spots such as Afghanistan was exercised more discreetly in the case of Soviet dissidents.[468] But the belief that well-established dissidents who rooted their political ideas in a nation's past were more worthy of support than liberal dissidents also applied to them. As I will show, the political culture of the Reagan era influenced the way discussions on Soviet dissidents developed. Under the political circumstances of the 1980s, it was particularly challenging to deal with discordance over some of Solzhenitsyn's ideas while discussing and evaluating his work.

By the 1970s, Solzhenitsyn's status as the most admired contemporary Russian writer had already been established. The extensive media coverage of his plight and his camp-related texts had forged an indelible link between his name and the fight against Soviet injustice. But Solzhenitsyn's desire to influence the fate of his country motivated him to continue writing and outlining what type of country Russia should become. The fact that he was not only against something but for something else, could not be overlooked. However, the controversial nature of some of his ideas remained difficult to address. Even as the Soviet Union began to crumble, it was not easy to admonish works by the world's most famous anti-communist writer. Bitter rows between Western scholars—and even more aggressive fights among Russian émigrés—show that, under certain circumstances, once a writer's status is established, it is not very easy to express more differentiated views on his work—no matter how it evolves. But precisely these conflicts illustrate how even the objectivity of scholarship and freedom of expression came

467 Cf. Cox, 1990, p. 166-167.

468 Incidentally the Reagan administration's type of conservatism displays many similarities to Solzhenitsyn's, especially when it comes to the dissident's benevolent evaluation of Tsarist autocracy, and the belief that—in case of regime change in Russia—a "traditional" authoritarian state was preferable to a "Western-style" democracy. Cf.: Solzhenitsyn, 1976; 1980; and Pach, 2006, p. 79.

under duress in the West—in their own way. A paradigmatic case is a scholarly row between historian and literary critic Sidney Monas and Russianist John Dunlop in 1981.

Sidney Monas published an article on Solzhenitsyn's political views in *Gulag* and other works in *Slavic Review* in 1981.[469] He begins with a detailed description of the different volumes of *Gulag* and then comes to his point:

> The literary weakness of the third volume of *Gulag Archipelago* is its ideological inadequacy.[470]

Monas' view differs from Solzhenitsyn's on various issues and he criticizes his work for several reasons. Monas focuses solely on the author's political message, firstly in *Gulag* and then in several other works.[471] He problematizes the writer's claim that the Soviet prison camp system is an instrument of God used to ultimately destroy communism, and to root its survivors in Christianity and nationalism: Monas disagrees with the metaphysical interpretation of Marxism and the prison camp system.[472] Solzhenitsyn's suggestion that a Christian, nationalist authoritarian regime should replace the current Soviet one awakens Monas' suspicions, as he doubts that non-Christians and/or citizens with dissenting opinions would have enough freedom and security in such a state.[473] Concretely, he fears this might lead to the intolerance seen in Russia's Tsarist past—where pogroms and wars against non-Christians were not uncommon.[474] The critic disagrees with Solzhenitsyn's condemnation of Western liberalism and its rule of law based on a constitution instead of on purely moral principles.[475] Monas confronts Solzhenitsyn's accusation that US scholars of Russia are mainly communists and that Russian Jewish émigrés are trying to "'reconcile Americans with communism in the USSR'" with a reality greatly different to

---

469 Sidney Monas. "GULag and Points West." *Slavic Review* 40.3 (1981): 444-56.

470 Monas, 1981, p. 446.

471 Apart from *Gulag*, he quotes or alludes to: *Nobel Lecture*, *Letter to the Soviet Leaders, From Under the Rubble, Harvard Address, August 1914, Misconceptions about Russia, Warning to the Western World, The Oak and the Calf.*

472 Monas, 1981, p. 446.

473 Monas, 1981, p. 447-452.

474 Monas, 1981, p. 446-8.

475 Monas, 1981, p. 449-450. Solzhenitsyn's scepticism towards the rule of law is founded on his belief that "this creates an atmosphere of spiritual mediocrity that paralyzes man's noblest impulses," as he explained in his *Harvard Address*. Cf.: Berman, ed., 1980, p. 8.

the dissident's claims.[476] Overall, Monas' disputes Solzhenitsyn's political analysis and his generalizations regarding other people's political views. Nevertheless, he finishes his article on a hopeful note:

> Even Solzhenitsyn's powerful prose and great literary imagination will, I suspect, find it difficult to sustain the prospect of a viable peasant-Christian-national Russia of the future. Along with a more receptive eye to the West, one might perhaps hope for a more genuinely polyphonic ear for the music of Russia's past-including an ear for noise.[477]

In an interesting turn, Monas ends by expressing trust that Solzhenitsyn's literary talent will help him realize why his own political vision is unviable. The expectation that a talented writer must possess the ability to perceive subtlety and to review his opinion in view of counterevidence results in a combination of aesthetic and political requirements. As such, these abilities do not have a political nuance, but Monas' expected result is political: in Solzhenitsyn's case, that he may change his mind about what is desirable for Russia's future and tone down his reproval of the West.

John Dunlop wrote an article as a response to Monas' in the same journal.[478] He characterizes Monas' article as an "often diffuse collection of misrepresentations and misconceptions."[479] Dunlop starts by criticizing Monas for not taking into account the entirety of Solzhenitsyn's work—including some rare book chapters printed separately in literary journals—in his analysis, but especially for not engaging in "significant literary criticism".[480] He then accuses Monas of "misrepresentation and simplification of Solzhenitsyn's views" resulting from his inclusion of Solzhenitsyn's "publicistic utterances" in presenting the Russian's views.[481] Because Dunlop claims that the knowledge of the entirety of the work is important, it seems contradictory that the publicistic work of the author should not count. Perhaps Dunlop simply considered, as Gibian does in his article above, that these latter works make the author appear more radical than he sees him. At any rate, Dunlop dismisses Monas' criticism point by point by claiming that it is "incorrect" or

---

476 Quoted in Monas, 1981, p. 452. (The Solzhenitsyn quote is from "Misconceptions about Russia", 1980.)
477 Monas, 1981, p. 456.
478 John B. Dunlop. "Important Points Missed." *Slavic Review* 40.3 (1981): 457-60.
479 Dunlop, 1981, p. 457.
480 Dunlop, 1981, p. 457.
481 Dunlop, 1981, p. 457-8.

"simply wrong".[482] He also negatively compares Monas with what he calls "some of the best Western literary critics" whose appreciation of Solzhenitsyn has only increased, and who were unaffected by the Russian dissidents' illiberal views.[483]

Monas' short response to Dunlop focuses on delineating the considerations behind his original article.[484] Solzhenitsyn's isolation and his "increasingly strident polemical tone" concern Monas; but his greater worry is the fact that the Russian's "great literary gifts and equally impressive moral stature were being mobilized on behalf of an influential political position" that he considers alarming.[485] By making use of negative Jewish stereotypes in his work, by coupling nationality with religious affiliation, by treating those who disagree with him with unfairness, and by declaring his scepticism towards constitutionalism and the rule of law, Solzhenitsyn was moving in a direction that Monas finds troubling.[486] Monas considers these worries legitimate and criticizes Dunlop's "best Western literary critics" precisely for "tending to roll over and play dead" when confronted with Solzhenitsyn's illiberal views.[487]

What at first sight seems to be a disagreement about what Solzhenitsyn's views are can be understood differently when other analyses of Solzhenitsyn's work written by Dunlop are taken into account. In this case, Monas and Dunlop's disagreement is reduced to their possession of opposing views on what Russia's political future should look like. Moreover, the direction this debate took runs parallel to the discussion between Soviet émigrés about how to deal with Solzhenitsyn's nationalism, and freedom of speech, respectively. In two of his books dedicated to the phenomenon of Russian nationalism, Dunlop defends Solzhenitsyn's and other Russian nationalists' political vision as a viable alternative to communism in that country.[488] In *The Faces of Contemporary Russian Nationalism* Dunlop rightly

---

482 Dunlop, 1981, p. 458-9.
483 Dunlop, 1981, p. 457.
484 Sidney Monas. "Sidney Monas Replies." *Slavic Review* 40.3 (1981): 461-3.
485 Monas, 1981, "Replies", p. 461.
486 Monas, 1981, "Replies", p. 462-463.
487 Monas, 1981, "Replies", p. 461.
488 John B. Dunlop. *The Faces of Contemporary Russian Nationalism.* Princeton, N.J.: Princeton University Press, 1983. John B. Dunlop. *The New Russian Nationalism.* New York: publ. with The Center for Strategic and International Studies, Georgetown University by Praeger, 1985.

recognizes that there are many forms of Russian nationalism, and that the Soviet government since Stalin has supported certain types of Russian nationalism.[489] Nevertheless, the goal of this book is to present the much wider phenomena of dissident Russian nationalism as an alternative to communism, worthy of Western support.[490] The analyst's preferential support for nationalist dissidents is based on his scepticism that the pro-democratic, more "Westernized" dissidents would be able to mobilize enough support:

> As for the dissenting nationalists, the evidence suggests that their views have considerably greater appeal for the ethnic Russian intelligentsia than do those of their neo-Westernizer opponents.[491]

The deep ideological rift between the nationalists and "neo-Westernizers" (as Dunlop calls them) was shaped in part by their differences in status and influence, and precisely by the amount of Western support they were able to secure.

Pro-democratic, Western-leaning dissidents were, like their nationalist counterparts, no homogenous group. However, they differed from the nationalists on key issues: they did not consider the adherence to Russian Orthodoxy to be a pre-requisite for being genuinely Russian, they shared a critical stance towards both the Soviet regime and its Imperial predecessor, and they endorsed a pluralistic, democratic form of government. Among such dissidents were reform-socialists—such as historian Roy Medvedev, Orthodox Christians—such as writer Andrey Sinyavsky, human rights activists—such as physicist Andrey Sakharov, and pro-democracy activists—such as journalist Vadim Belotserkovsky.[492] The relationship between these activists and Russian nationalist dissidents—and Solzhenitsyn in particular—was protean, but most pro-democracy, Western-leaning dissidents defended their nationalist counterparts' right to free speech. This also applied to Roy

---

489 Dunlop, 1983, p. 7-28.
490 Dunlop, 1983, p. 286-290.
491 Dunlop, 1983, p. 241.
492 Roy Medvedev. *Let History Judge: the Origins and Consequences of Stalinism.* 1st ed. New York: Knopf, 1971; Andrey Sinyavsky (Abram Tertz). *For Freedom of Imagination.* New York: Holt, Rinehart & Winston, 1971; Andrei Sakharov. *My Country and the World.* 1st ed. New York: Knopf: distributed by Random House, 1975; Vadim Belotserkovsky and Leonid I. Plyushch, eds. *UdSSR: Alternativen der demokratischen Opposition. Sammelband.* Achberg: Achberger Verlagsanstalt, 1978.

Medvedev and Andrey Sakharov, who never left the USSR. They defended Solzhenitsyn's rights when he was persecuted by the Soviet government, despite ideological disagreement.[493]

Andrey Sinyavsky saw himself primarily as a writer and literary critic, and not as a political thinker.[494] His political importance in the dissident movement stems from the fact that he and Yuli Daniel were the first Soviet writers to be indicted for the content of their literature (and not for surrogate charges), and they were the first defendants of a show trial who insisted on a non-guilty plea.[495] This trial sparked outrage in the Soviet Union and abroad.[496] In 1966, Sinyavsky was sentenced to seven years hard labor for "anti-Soviet propaganda". While Solzhenitsyn was being expelled from the Writers Union in 1969, Sinyavsky was already serving his sentence in a forced labor camp as a result of publishing satirical and ironic texts in the West (under the pseudonym Abram Tertz). In 1972, he was given the choice between remaining in camp or leaving the country, and Sinyavsky opted to emigrate to France.[497] Once in France, Sinyavsky originally supported Solzhenitsyn, but later expressed his disappointment at Solzhenitsyn's nationalist claims and his association with famous anti-Semites such as Igor Shafarevich.[498] Although he identified himself as an Orthodox Christian, Sinyavsky disapproved of the anti-Jewish undertone of many of his fellow believers who were part of the Russian nationalist movements.[499] Nevertheless, to the end

---

493 Harvey Fireside. "Dissident Visions of the USSR: Medvedev, Sakharov & Solzhenitsyn." *Polity* 22.2 (1989): 213-229; Associated Press. "Roy Medwedjew verteidigt Solschenizyn." Frankfurter Allgemeine Zeitung 8 February 1974: 6.

494 Brumberg, 1980; Catharine Theimer Nepomnyashchy. "Andrei Donatovich Sinyavsky (1925-1997)." *The Slavic and East European Journal* 42.3 (1998): 367-71.

495 Cf. Chamberlin, 1969; Applebaum, 2003, p. 533-534; Harriet Murav. "Sinyavsky's Trial." *The Slavic and East European Journal* 42.3 (1998): 389-393.

496 William Henry Chamberlin. "The Voice of Silent Russia." *Russian Review* 28.2 (1969): 152-9.

497 Michael Beausang. "Andrey Sinyavsky: Exile and Writer." Mosaic Spring 1975: 15-20.

498 Andrey Sinyavsky. "Russophobia." Partisan Review 57 (1990): 339-44.

499 Abraham Brumberg. "On Cultural Dissidence: A Conversation with Andrei Sinyavsky." The New Republic 9 February 1980: 27-32; Sinyavsky, 1990.

of his days he remained committed to the belief that freedom of conscience and freedom of the press should also apply to those he disagreed with.[500]

Belotserkovsky, a journalist and supporter of Andrei Sakharov's human rights campaign, left the Soviet Union in 1972.[501] He wrote a critical article about Solzhenitsyn's *Letter to the Soviet Leaders* in 1975, rejecting Solzhenitsyn's willingness to compromise with an authoritarian government as long as it adopts Christian principles.[502] Both Sakharov and Belotserkovsky considered such a notion to be contrary to their efforts to democratize the Soviet Union.[503] Sakharov writes:

> Solzhenitsyn writes that perhaps our country has not matured to the point of democratizing the system, and that when accompanied by respect for law and by Orthodoxy the authoritarian system was not all that bad, since under that system Russia preserved its national health until the twentieth century. These opinions are alien to me. I consider the democratic path of development the only possible one for any country.[504]

Belotserkovsky shares this view and explains why Solzhenitsyn's nationalist rhetoric is decidedly inadequate to address the problems of the Soviet Union:

> The ruling class in Russia is monolithically Russian, while Russian society is a heterogeneous conglomeration of different national elements. Hence the propagation of any brand of Russian nationalism not only parallels official propaganda, but also makes it more difficult to create a *social*-democratic movement—the only viable political solution to the major problems.[505]

---

500 Olga Carlisle. "Solzhenitsyn and Russian Nationalism: an Interview with Andrey Sinyavsky." The New York Review of Books 22 November 1979; Kathleen Parthé. "Sinyavsky on His Way to Tomorrow." *The Slavic and East European Journal* 42.3 (1998): 394-8. This also applied specifically to Solzhenitsyn: "Mr. Sinyavsky believes that Mr. Solzhenitsyn should be published and allowed to return to the Soviet Union, which Soviet authorities say is impossible because of Mr. Solzhenitsyn's deep hostility to the Soviet state" Bill Keller. "In the Russian Motherland, Fascination now with those who Chose Exile." The New York Times 8 January 1989.

501 Vadim Belotserkovsky. "The Passing of Yelena Bonner." Russian Life September /October 2011: 64.

502 Cf.: Vadim Belotserkovsky. "Letter to the Future Leaders of the Soviet Union: An Alternative to Solzhenitsyn's Program." *Partisan Review* XLII.2 (1975): 260-71.

503 Belotserkovsky, 1975, p. 260-261; On Sakharov and Medvedev's differences with Solzhenitsyn, cf.: Fireside, 1989.

504 Andrei Sakharov. "In Answer to Solzhenitsyn." New York Review of Books 5 September 1973: 5-6.

505 Belotserkovsy, 1975, p. 269.

Solzhenitsyn's relationship with these dissidents was difficult—even to those who refrained from making programmatic political proposals, like Sinyavsky. As Sidney Monas had originally pointed out, Solzhenitsyn unfairly accused "third wave" émigrés of promoting communism in the West.[506] This already hints at the acrimony in these relationships. Solzhenitsyn refused to protest against Sinyavsky's trial in 1966; and later wrote that as opposed to Sinyavsky—who had spent years in a prison camp for publishing his work abroad—God had led *him* to success.[507] In an article in 1985, Solzhenitsyn suggests that the Soviet government was too lenient towards Sinyavsky for releasing him into exile a few months before the end of his seven-year prison camp sentence, and for not giving him a second sentence.[508] Being a prison-camp survivor himself, Solzhenitsyn had an idea of the harsh conditions Sinyavsky had survived—all the more as Sinyavsky did not serve time in a privileged intellectual-labor camp as Solzhenitsyn had for four years.[509] Belittling Sinyavsky's predicament underlines the bitterness of the author that was most likely the result of the fervency with which he believed in his own views.

In 1985, Belotserkovsky was fired from *Radio Liberty* for criticizing Solzhenitsyn's novel *August 1914*, but difficulties between them went beyond that.[510] Solzhenitsyn's article *Our Pluralists* is presented as an answer to Belotserkovsky's *Democratic Alternatives* and Sinyavsky's journal *Syntax.*[511] Solzhenitsyn begins by claiming that a group of dissidents has focused its attention on slandering him, and he defines this group as those who defend the plurality of opinions.[512] He counters that there is and can only be one truth, and that this truth is God's truth, making diversity of opinions superfluous.[513] This is a scathing article, in which he questions the credentials of the pro-democracy camp of Soviet dissidence and accuses them of "hating

506 Monas, 1981, p. 452. The "Third Wave" of Russian emigration was that of the 1970s, and consisted mainly of forced exiles and a high number of (forced or voluntary) Jewish exiles.

507 Alexander Solzhenitsyn. *The Oak and the Calf: sketches of literary life in the Soviet Union.* New York: Harper & Row, 1980. p. 204, 220. He refused to sign a collective letter by sixty-six Soviet writers condemning the trial or to participate in demonstrations demanding an open trial, cf.: Michael Hanne. *The Power of the Story: Fiction and Political Change.* Oxford: Berghahn, 1994. p. 176.

508 Alexander Solzhenitsyn. "Our Pluralists." *Survey* 29.2 (125) (1985): p. 18.

509 Sinyavsky was sent to the "Potma" prison camp complex in Mordovia.

Russia" and of trying to convince the West that "*Russians* must be destroyed".[514] For example, he writes:

> It is the sincere belief of many pluralists that communism is not an evil. [...]
>
> How one-dimensional it has made itself, this pluralism: it has diminished itself to mere hatred of Russia, and nothing more. [...]
>
> Foolishly, mindlessly, they push the West along Hitler's path: the fight is not against communism, but against the Russian people.
>
> Lies and trickery were the last things we were led to expect in the pluralist spectrum. Surely they could have been left to Soviet propaganda? No, the pluralists have taken them over as their birthright.[515]

Moreover, he singles out those Jewish émigrés, who, in his opinion, are not sufficiently assimilated and wrongly criticize Russia.[516] However, this article's main purpose is allegedly to defend the image of Russia in the West,[517] and the main bulk of the article focuses on what he considers "slander" of Russia. For example, he accuses the "pluralists" of calumny for claiming that the "accursed" Russians had anything to do with communism (p. 3). In contrast, Solzhenitsyn paints the following, historically highly inaccurate, picture of Imperial Russia:

> In old Russia there was no Cheka, no Gulag, no mass rounding-up of the innocent, the population at large were not systematically compelled to swear allegiance to the lie, there was not ritual public criticism, children were not made to disown their parents, no one was punished for having the wrong relations, people chose their occupations freely and were paid for their work, married women in towns did not need to work—a father could feed a family of five or seven children unaided, citizens could move freely from place to place, and—most precious gift of all—anyone who wished could emigrate immediately...[518]

He pleads with his fellow émigrés via different rhetorical means in an apparent dialogue to which he adds sensational quotations that are attributed

---

510 The content of this dispute will be discussed in part 3.3.

511 Solzhenitsyn, 1985, p. 1.

512 Solzhenitsyn, 1985, p. 2.

513 Solzhenitsyn, 1985, p. 2.

514 Solzhenitsyn, 1985, p. 12, 18-19.

515 Solzhenitsyn, 1985, p. 12.

516 Solzhenitsyn, 1985, p. 15. He later compares them with "a troop of mischievious gnomes over the prostrate body" of Russia, p. 19.

517 Alexander Solzhenitsyn. *Meine amerikanischen Jahre.* Munich: Langen Müller, 2007. p. 130-132.

518 Solzhenitsyn, 1985, p. 4.

to no one—while informing the reader that he knows very well whom he means.[519] At the core is his conviction that plurality of opinions is counterproductive:

> But if a hundred mules all pull different ways the result is no movement at all.[520]

This element of his worldview provides the key to understanding the level of animosity between Solzhenitsyn and the pro-democracy camp: Solzhenitsyn's certainty that his vision for Russia was the right one was underpinned by the conviction that other points of view were not only wrong, they were distracting "the people" from striving for the right path.

Sinyavsky's views pose the sharpest contrast to those of Solzhenitsyn precisely because of the similarities they share: both are Orthodox Christians, Russians, gulag survivors, and writers. The fact that their outlook was nonetheless so different surely aggravated the matter. It was not as easy to plead with Sinyavsky that "if you continue to express your thoughts in Russian, at least show the people that created that language some kindness" or accuse him of "hatred of Orthodox Christianity" as it was with non-Christian Soviet émigrés.[521] Sinyavsky was committed to freedom of speech as an inalienable right, and he considered democracy the preferable political system. But Solzhenitsyn considered the focus on "rights" and "democracy" to be absurd as long as the spiritual and physical needs of the population were not met.[522] To further exacerbate the situation, Sinyavsky displayed no reverence towards Russian cultural or political icons of the past. His book *Strolls with Pushkin* (1975)[523]—an attempt to debunk the Pushkin myth in Russian culture—caused an explosion of anger among the nationalist dissident camp. Slavicist Stephanie Sandler explains how several elements of Sinyavsky's worldview sparked the antagonism of other émigrés and resulted in difficulties in finding publishers in the West:

---

519 Solzhenitsyn, 1985, p. 4.
520 Solzhenitsyn, 1985, p. 3.
521 Cf. Solzhenitsyn's clumsy attempt to ridicule Sinyavsky's Christianity and the ease with which he accuses Jewish Russians of criticizing Russia as a result of their "foreigness", in: Solzhenitsyn, 1985, p. 16, 19-23, quotes from pp. 23, 28.
522 Solzhenitsyn, 1985, p. 20-22.
523 *Progulki s Pushkinym* in Russian.

> Siniavskii's conviction that cultural and political tolerance are necessary conditions for free expression, as well as his forthright views of Solzhenitsyn, must be part of the reason for the scandal surrounding *Progulki s Pushkinym* and a reason that he remains one of the least published but most publicized émigré writers in the former Soviet Union.[524]

Sandler adds that the questions "who counts as Russian, who loves Russia, who merits Russia's hatred" are central to this polemic.[525] Solzhenitsyn's success in defining these issues is a result of the weight of his own reputation being put behind the nationalist and traditionalist vision, and the susceptibility of scholars and publishers in the 1980s to champion this in place of the more "Westernized" vision of Russia.[526] Thus, the reason why I have dwelled on the fractious relationship between these different strands of dissent is to clarify why John Dunlop, and indeed others like him, considered cooperation between the two dissident camps to be impossible and why they felt compelled to choose which group the West should support.

Dunlop seems to agree with Solzhenitsyn's view that Russian nationality and Orthodox Christianity belong together, and that Orthodox teachings should play a role in shaping policies.[527] Thus, upon Solzhenitsyn's request, Dunlop calls this dissident and other like-minded people the *vozrozhdentsy* ("resurrectors"), because they strive for a "Russian national and religious renaissance".[528] Solzhenitsyn and the *vozrozhdentsy* are not all exiles. In fact, many of these thinkers continued to work and publish in the USSR. Dunlop supports their ideas, such as "encouraging Russian and Eastern Slavic fertility", paving the way for women to leave the workplace and become child rearers and giving "maximum support for the nuclear family and for revival of traditional morality" because he considers these to be a logical

---

524 Stephanie Sandler. "Sex, Death and Nation in the Strolls with Pushkin Controversy." *Slavic Review* 51.2 (1992). p. 296.

525 Sandler, 1992, p. 296.

526 About Sinyavsky's difficulties to publish, cf.: Carlisle, 1979. Katrina Vanden Heuvel reports of the difficulties that ensued from criticizing Solzhenitsyn at *Radio Liberty* and in the émigré journal *Kontinent* in: Katrina vanden Heuvel. "No Free Speech at Radio Liberty." Nation 7 December 1985: 612-5. Arnold McMillin describes the lack of freedom of opinion and the veneration of Solzhenitsyn in the émigré press, in: Arnold McMillin. "Exiled Russian Writers of the Third Wave and the Émigré Press." *The Modern Language Review* 84.2 (1989): 406-413.

527 Dunlop, 1983, p. 106-108; 242ff.

528 Dunlop, 1983, p. 242.

answer to Soviet population's decline and to the problem of "how to mobilize the populace for a conflict against China".[529] Dunlop presents Solzhenitsyn's rejection of both the current communist government and democratic Western forms of government in favor of an authoritarian state which is "rooted in Russian historical tradition".[530] He argues that Solzhenitsyn and the *vozrozhdentsy* "hold that God and the Orthodox faith are higher than the nation" and many hold "a belief in the necessity of a divinely anointed monarch, a hypostasis of the nation".[531] These thinkers draw much inspiration from Russia's Tsarist past, and react defensively when historians—in the West or in the USSR—reveal the negative sides of Tsarist rule.[532] Solzhenitsyn reacts particularly sensitively when historians point out historical continuities between Imperial Russia and the Soviet Union, and claims that such views amount to "downplaying the ruinous significance of Marxist ideology".[533] Because Dunlop defends the position of these dissidents, it is not surprising that he dedicates part of his last chapter to reprimanding scholars who criticize Solzhenitsyn and other Russian nationalists. He not only rebuffs those émigrés who disagree with Solzhenitsyn—simply because they disagree with him—but he also criticizes scholars who come to different conclusions about Russian history than Solzhenitsyn and like-minded writers. This is not necessarily because he is convinced of the truthfulness of Solzhenitsyn's and his co-thinkers' historical views, but because he considers opposing views among scholars and émigrés to be detrimental to US policy. Dunlop explains that these views "exacerbate anti-Western sentiment" among Russian nationalists, and if the US government were to listen to those views, it would lead to a growing hostility towards the US on the part of these Russians.[534] Here, his train of thought follows the pattern of the Reagan Doctrine: if the main goal is to bring forth a Soviet retreat in the world and a regime change within the USSR, finding a potentially successful partner among the dissidents outweighs ideological affinity with this partner in such "secondary" matters like democracy, equality, freedom of speech, etc.

---

529 Dunlop, 1983, p. 108.
530 Dunlop, 1983, p. 245.
531 Dunlop, 1983, p. 278.
532 Cf.: Dunlop, 1983, p. 279ff; Solzhenitsyn, 1980.
533 As paraphrased in: Dunlop, 1983, p. 282-283.
534 Dunlop, 1983, p. 284.

Moreover, one must do everything possible not to alienate these non-democratic dissidents from the US in order to ensure their loyalty against communist forces.[535]

Notwithstanding his awareness that there are "unattractive and potentially threatening currents" among the Russian nationalists, Dunlop believes that supporting Solzhenitsyn's type of nationalism would lead to a type of isolationism which would have positive effects on the arms race: "an inward-looking non-militaristic Russia could save American taxpayers millions of dollars in armament outlays."[536]

In his later book—*The New Russian Nationalism*—Dunlop reiterates his advice, and belittles the fears some Western scholars and policymakers have expressed about Russian nationalists' authoritarianism by claiming that, in Russia, a "Franco-type government [...] might eventually prepare the way for democracy, as happened in post-Franco Spain."[537] He explains why:

> For the West to allow the problem of authoritarianism to stand in the way of its taking at least a neutral stand toward the Russian nationalists strikes one as foolhardy. The termination of Marxism-Leninism's hegemony in the Soviet Union would be of immediate and immense benefit to the West and indeed to all the countries in the world.[538]

For Dunlop, it is not that authoritarianism is good, but that communism is worse. This is very much in tune with the drastic views held by the Reagan administration.[539] Nevertheless, the ardour with which this scholar sought to iron out contending views seems bewildering from today's viewpoint.

---

535 Cf. Kirkpatrick, 1979.

536 Dunlop, 1983, p. 286.

537 Dunlop, 1985, "Nationalism", p. 40.

538 Dunlop, 1985, "Nationalism", p. 40.

539 Cf. Kirkpatrick's criticism of Carter's lack of action in Iran and Nicaragua: "Yet despite all the variations, the Carter administration brought to the crises in Iran and Nicaragua several common assumptions each of which played a major role in hastening the victory of even more repressive dictatorships than had been in place before. These were, first, the belief that there existed at the moment of crisis a democratic alternative to the incumbent government: second, the belief that the continuation of the status quo was not possible; third, the belief that any change, including the establishment of a government headed by self-styled Marxist revolutionaries, was preferable to the present government. Each of these beliefs was (and is) widely shared in the liberal community generally. Not one of them can withstand close scrutiny." Kirkpatrick, 1979.

By reading these texts, Dunlop's row with Sidney Monas about Solzhenitsyn's political vision acquires nuance. The problem is no longer that Solzhenitsyn's ideology contains illiberal or authoritarian elements, but that Dunlop considers these to be preferable to communism. Solzhenitsyn is, in a sense, the enemy's enemy, and his nationalist views are assessed by Dunlop as a lesser evil. In this respect, Dunlop is adhering to the mainstream ideology of the 1980s.[540]

In an article on Solzhenitsyn, Norman Podhoretz, a well-known neoconservative thinker, defends a similar position.[541] Podhoretz describes the disappointment of many liberals when they realized that Solzhenitsyn was not only no liberal thinker, but, in fact, an anti-liberal and anti-Western one. Nevertheless, he considers Solzhenitsyn's message of prime importance because he sees it as the only way the West can save itself from communism. Unlike Dunlop, whose aim was merely to see the Soviet military threat recoil, Podhoretz considers the danger of communist rule to be transferable. In this sense, he describes Solzhenitsyn's quest as follows:

> Solzhenitsyn's terrible and terrifying question to us is this: is it possible that courage like his own is all that we require to escape from the fate he has come to warn us against? Is it possible that the courage first to see the truth about Communism and then the correlative courage to act upon it can guide our steps to safety as his own courage guided Solzhenitsyn's, that it can make the Soviet leaders back down and ultimately, perhaps, even collapse, just as they did when confronted by Solzhenitsyn himself?

Because of the seriousness of this question, Podhoretz suggests ignoring his anti-democratic views, as they amount to mere decoys:

> Forcing us to face that terrible question, rubbing our noses in it, has been Solzhenitsyn's prophetic mission to the West. To seize upon the anti-democratic Slavophilia of his message to the Russian people as an excuse for continuing to evade the challenge of his life and his work would only confirm the worst of his charges against us—the charge that we are cowards. And it would bring us ever

---

540 It is well documented that in the 1980s, the US turned a blind eye to human rights violations while pursuing the aim of destroying communism. For examples, cf. "International Court of Justice: Case Concerning Military and Paramilitary Activities in and against Nicaragua (Nicaragua v. United States)." *International Legal Materials* 25.5 (1986): 1023-289; Apodaca, 2006.

541 All the following quotes are from: Norman Podhoretz. "The Terrible Question of Aleksandr Solzhenitsyn." Commentary 1 February 1985.

> closer to the day when we too might find ourselves plunged headlong into that pit out of which Solzhenitsyn once clawed his way so that the dead might be remembered and the living might be saved.

Whatever the motivation for criticism of Solzhenitsyn may have been, for Podhoretz it was strategically important to neglect it. This does not mean that the Slavophilic tendencies in Solzhenitsyn's work were ignored. But it is true that the negative reverberations from these tendencies—the ethnocentricity, chauvinism, etc.—did not receive the attention their controversial nature might have otherwise aroused in Western democracies.

As Dunlop's arguments above already hint at, in some respects Solzhenitsyn's Slavophilic worldview was even capable of exerting influence on the way Russian history was perceived and portrayed in the US. In 1989, Ewa Thompson describes the success Solzhenitsyn had in propagating a specific image of Russia and the Russians in the US.[542] He presented Imperial Russia as a as "a gentle and nonaggressive country which has been overrun by external and evil forces", ignoring the role Russians themselves played in the USSR.[543]

> While Russia's military conquests have empowered countless Russians culturally, politically, and economically, Solženicyn writes as if no transfer of benefits had occurred. Not one character in his novels-least of all the narrator himself-tries to foster in other characters a new self-perception, one given less to self-pity and more to a recognition of this fact. It is characteristic that all major characters in Solženicyn's novels consider Russian to be their mother tongue. Solženicyn seems not to realize that in these Russian-speaking camps, prisons, and institutions the non-Russians might feel incomparably more victimized than the Russians.[544]

According to Thompson, if it had not been for Solzhenitsyn's sustained efforts during his exile, and the willingness of academics and journalists to welcome his vision of Russia, the much more critical assessment of Russia's Tsarist past and nationalist present by pro-democracy dissidents might have nuanced the soon-to-be predominant image of Russia in the US. Thompson concludes:

---

542 Ewa M. Thompson. "The Writer in Exile: The Good Years." *The Slavic and East European Journal* 33.4 (1989). p. 503.

543 Thompson, 1989, p. 502. (She refers to: Solzhenitsyn, 1980, "Misconceptions").

544 Thompson, 1989, p. 503.

> This, I contend, is a case of cultural imperialism: an imposition of the Russian perception of Russia onto the foreign perception, owing to the mediation of an exiled writer of great rhetorical gifts. Solženicyn's physical presence on the American scene, enhanced by the media and the academy, has been essential to the dissemination of this view.[545]

Nevertheless, Solzhenitsyn's vision and image of Russia was not forcibly imposed by the author on his host country: it was shared by influential politicians and scholars who were able to defend these views for political reasons. To be sure, the conservative camp was not homogenous: Richard Pipes may have agreed with Solzhenitsyn on the Soviet peril, but he famously disagreed with him when it comes to the Tsarist Empire.[546] However, the atmosphere of the late Cold War allowed for some whitewashing of autocratic governments past and present in the name of opposition to communist oppression.

After the Cold War, David Rowley wrote a study about Western scholars' assessment of Russian nationalism.[547] Rowley came to the conclusion that typically, scholars in the US and UK were benevolent towards Solzhenitsyn and like-minded nationalist dissidents.[548] This was already the case in the 1970s:

> Indeed, no Western scholar in the 1970s attempted to argue that the Communist regime might be preferable to a government based on Russian nationalism.[549]

The view that a traditional form of authoritarianism would be preferable to communism in Russia did not emerge in the 1980s, but it became part of the ideological mainstream in this later decade.[550] This is astonishing in the

---

545 Thompson, 1989, p. 503. She defines cultural imperialism in this case as follows: "In some cases the radical name of 'cultural imperialists' may well be applied to those writers who have benefitted enormously from exile. With their rhetorical brilliance, the intensity of their convictions, and the advantages of the Rahmen afforded by exile, they have imposed on foreign audiences a vision of the world born and bred in conditions very different from those prevailing in the host countries." (p. 501).

546 Richard Pipes. "Solzhenitsyn and the Russian Intellectual Tradition." *Encounter* (1979): 52-5.

547 David G. Rowley. "Review: Russian Nationalism and the Cold War." *The American Historical Review* 99.1 (1994): 155-171.

548 Rowley, 1994, p. 157.

549 Rowley, 1994, p. 158.

550 Historian Adam Ulam and political scientist Leonard Schapiro were early exponents of this view, cf.: Adam Bruno Ulam. *Ideologies and Illusions: Revolutionary Thought from Herzen to Solzhenitsyn.* Cambridge: Harvard University Press, 1976; Leonard

sense that by the 1980s—and especially in the later part of the decade—the Soviet Union was going through a democratization process that was unrivalled in Russian history. There was an increasing contrast between the nationalist, authoritarian rhetoric of some dissidents, and the democratic tendencies both of the state and the bulk of the Soviet people—who embraced their new freedoms. As I have shown, throughout the 1980s certain members of the Third Emigration tried in vain to refer Western scholars and policymakers to the potential dangers of Russian nationalism, even as taken in opposition to communism in its late form.[551] Nevertheless, according to Rowley, Cold War worries prevailed. Only the fall of communism would transform the hitherto abstract problem of Russian nationalism in its more religious and dissident form into a tangible and urgent question.

All these discussions reveal important issues that arose during the Cold War. Sidney Monas is a rare example of a Western critic who did not share Solzhenitsyn's political views and wrote about it. It would hardly be fair to consider his criticism an attack on the writer. Nevertheless, criticism of Solzhenitsyn's work and his views was a difficult matter in an environment rooted in a bipolar vision of the world. The Reagan Doctrine made the politicization and instrumentalization of scholarship of Eastern Europe seem justified and even lofty. Along the way, it proved to be detrimental to the freedom of speech and freedom of scholarship—both for dissenting émigrés and for certain scholars. This is not the place to evaluate the success of Reagan's policies in reaching their goals, or to assess if the sacrifices were worth making. What remains to be seen in this study is how the image of Solzhenitsyn crafted and protected in this era lived on after the Soviet foe was conquered. How did Solzhenitsyn's status change after the collapse of communism? Which aspects of his work made him relevant or irrelevant? Was his work analyzed in a more thorough and wholesome manner, or did the analysis remain selective? What political issues took over once communism was no longer perceived as an imminent threat? A look at the

---

Schapiro. "Some Afterthoughts on Solzhenitsyn." *Russian Review* 33.4 (1974): 416-421.

551 Cf. Rowley, 1994, p. 159ff; and the section about Solzhenitsyn's late Cold War reception in this book.

evolution of Solzhenitsyn's reception after 1991 might help us understand this.

Solzhenitsyn's Reception upon the Collapse of European Communism

1985 brought the greatest shift in Soviet politics since the introduction of Lenin's *New Economic Policy* in 1921. Lenin's liberalization of the economy in the 1920s—hitherto considered the most radical relaxation on Marxist principles in Soviet history—soon paled in comparison with the reforms that the new General Secretary of the Communist Party, Mikhail Gorbachev, was to bring about. Under Gorbachev a severe restructuring of the economy, a thorough democratization of politics and a liberalization of press and religious freedom took place. Under the mottos of *perestroika* (reconstruction) and *glasnost* (openness), the Soviet Union changed radically. Political intervention in culture ceded as the market economy took over the regulation of cultural output. This had profound consequences for Russian culture, as Solomon Volkov put it: "When the Soviet regime fell, the totalitarian stick vanished completely, but so did the carrots."[552] State sponsorship for the arts all but disappeared, and Soviet Russian writers faced competition from popular dissident and foreign writers as never before. This new situation affected not only local cultural mechanisms, but had strong repercussions in the Western study of Russian literature.

After liberalization, and even more so after the collapse of the USSR, political categories in Western criticism of Russian literature changed: a new canon of Russian literature was to emerge and the binary divisions of the Cold War—between Soviet and anti-Soviet, or local and émigré literature—were to become inessential. The witness-bearing role of gulag-related literature could be relegated as Russian (and foreign) historiography caught up with this subject and archives became increasingly accessible.[553] There is a general consensus in Western criticism that the disappearance of Soviet censorship

552 Solomon Volkov. *The Magical Chorus: a History of Russian Culture from Tolstoy to Solzhenitsyn.* Tran. Antonina W. Bouis. 1st ed. New York: Alfred A. Knopf, 2008. p. 278.

553 This was a slow, steady process, cf.: Gert Meyer. "Perestrojka und Geschichtswissenschaft in der Sowjetunion." *Wir brauchen die Wahrheit: Geschichtsdiskussion in der Sowjetunion.* Ed. Gert Meyer. 2. ed. Cologne: Pahl-Rugenstein, 1989; Iurii N. Afanas'ev. "The Phenomenon of Soviet Historiography." *Russian Studies in History* 40.2 (2001): 32-64.

and later on of the Soviet state was a moment of radical change in the study of Russian literature both in Russia and abroad. There were roughly two reasons for this. One was the ascertainment that for the first time in Russian history, there was full freedom of the press and Russian readers and writers possessed the right to read and write as they pleased. The literary historian Reinhard Lauer describes this as the moment when Russian literature won its "totality."[554] This was also seen as a time to re-think the canon, as I will later show.

The second reason why the study of Russian literature had to readjust to this new era is that its perceived *relevance* changed markedly.[555] As the Slavicist Andrew Wachtel rightly points out, until then, Eastern European literature, "whatever the author's style or theme", was marketed as being relevant for *political* reasons.[556] Once Cold War categories became obsolete, the sales of Eastern European literature nosedived: editors, scholars, and publishers needed to find new reasons to justify publishing, reading, or writing about these authors.[557] To do this, they needed to recur to new categories and labels. Both the re-evaluation of the canon and the assessment of authors' relevance were part of an intertwining process, often described as a period of "normalization" of Russian literature.[558] Indeed, several literary critics and literary historians agree that the divisions in Russian literature were an abnormal phenomenon that led to certain peculiarities. Until now, among certain circles within the USSR and among many Western scholars, the assumption that *samizdat* (illegally self-published literature) was *per se* of better quality than officially published literature is very common.[559] Despite its variety, literature in exile was likewise considered to be of a finer quality than local Soviet literature, in part due to its "external" origin alone.[560] Once writers

---

554 Lauer, 2000, p. 898.

555 Andrew Baruch Wachtel. "Writers and Society in Eastern Europe, 1989-2000: The End of the Golden Age." *East European Politics & Societies* 17.4 (2003): 583-621.

556 Wachtel, 2003, p. 587, 614-615.

557 Wachtel, 2003, p. 615.

558 David C. Gillespie. *The Twentieth-Century Russian Novel: an Introduction.* Oxford; Washington, D.C.: Berg, 1996. p. 5.

559 Cf. Wachtel, 2009, p. 240-241.

560 Bethea; Frank, 2011, p. 196. "In an interdependent relationship, exile and creative greatness have come to condition each other. Exile becomes significant because it produces great writers; writers become significant because they have been exiled."

enjoyed widespread freedoms, new expectations and criteria could be introduced. Some critics now wondered if the systemic changes in Russia would lead to a greater involvement of authors in politics, or to an abdication from political commentary.[561] In order to participate in the re-evaluation and re-canonization process of Russian literature in a more efficient manner, and to understand the changing role of its writers, Western critics began to pay more attention to the domestic reception of Russian writers and to take this into account in their studies.

After the eventual disintegration of the USSR, scholars and journalists in the West tried to ascertain which role Solzhenitsyn would play in his country's future. On the one hand, he started dictating concrete suggestions for political and social reform, on the other, he was not in a hurry to return to his country. As I have shown in the previous section, some of his works were read politically and were contextualized in the ideological debates about the Soviet Union and the way the West should relate to it during the Cold War. Now that this state was foe no longer, the question arose about the future of Solzhenitsyn's fervent anti-Soviet literature and the general relevance of his work. The fall of the communist bloc was seen as the right time to retrospectively examine his role in the demise of this ideology.

As much as Solzhenitsyn had suffered from political intervention in literature in the Brezhnev era, shortly before the dissolution of the Soviet Union, he once more enjoyed state sponsorship—as he had at the beginning of his career in the 1960s. He was published with state support in his country from 1989 onwards; Gorbachev dictated a decree restoring his citizenship and invited him to return to his country.[562] But Solzhenitsyn never returned to the Soviet Union. After several conflicts between member republics of the USSR, as well as arcane political intrigues within the Russian SSR, the Soviet Union dissolved in December of 1991. It was not until 1994 that the author resettled in Russia.

---

561 Gillespie, 1996, p. 5; 140-142; Andrew Baruch Wachtel. *Remaining Relevant after Communism: The Role of the Writer in Eastern Europe.* Chicago: University of Chicago Press, 2006.

562 Martin Walker. "The exile comes full circle." The Guardian 8 October 1990.

Nevertheless, already by 1990, Solzhenitsyn had fervently refocused on the future of his country and published a booklet titled *How to Rebuild Russia*.[563] It was published and distributed by the organ of the Union of Communist Youth, the *Komsomolskaia Pravda* newspaper.[564] Although this manifesto was directed at the Russian people, it did draw some attention in the West.[565] However, the assessment of his booklet merged with the general reappraisal of the author's legacy.

How to Rebuild Russia is a relatively thick booklet, or a small book. It was immediately translated and published in English and German. It is a program for restructuring Russia according to principles that Solzhenitsyn devised or borrowed from the Russian Empire, the Bible, Oswald Spengler, Pope John Paul II, and others. It consisted of a two-phase plan to chop up the Soviet Union into a Greater Russia (*Velikorossiia*) and several new independent states (in the Baltics, the Caucasus, and Central Asia). Russia, Belarus, Ukraine, and the north of Kazakhstan were, according to Solzhenitsyn, part of one nation. In his own way, the author attempts to show that he cares for these neighbors, by claiming that he speaks to them not as a foreign people but as if he were one with them and addresses Ukrainians and Belorussians as "brothers".[566] Unfortunately, Solzhenitsyn did not refrain from using the word "malorossy" (little Russians) for the Ukrainian people,[567] which is considered a pejorative term; and from questioning Ukrainians' right to parts of their territory and from belittling the independence of their language.[568] Similarly, the Russian dissident suggested that Kazakhs should give up most of their land and remain in a small portion of their country which he saw as their sole historical homeland.[569] Moreover, land sales should be restricted to certain people he considered worthy of it; he excluded foreigners and

---

563 Alexander Solzhenitsyn. *Kak nam obustroit' Rossiiu?* Paris: YMCA-Press, 1990.

564 Michael Scammell. "To the Finland station?" The New Republic 19 November 1990. p. 18.

565 David Remnick. "Native Son—'Kak Nam Obustroit' Rossiyu?' ('how Shall we Organize Russia?') by Aleksandr Solzhenitsyn." New York Review of Books 14 February 1991. John B. Dunlop. "Russian Reactions to Solzhenitsyn's Brochure." *Report on the USSR* 14 (1990): 3-8. Scammell, 1990.

566 Solzhenitsyn, 1990, p. 8-9.

567 For example, in: Solzhenitsyn, 1990, p. 5, 8.

568 Solzhenitsyn, 1990, p 5-10.

569 Solzhenitsyn, 1990, p. 5.

"speculators" from this right.[570] The education system should no longer be atheistic.[571] A "normal" form of family life should be facilitated—women should stay at home and rear children, men should be the breadwinners.[572] The second part of the plan presents a new system of elections based on the Tsarist system of village councils (*zemstvo*).[573] Legal voting age should be raised to twenty or more, and only people who have lived in a city or village for three consecutive years or more should be allowed to vote.[574] Solzhenitsyn's scepticism towards political parties and election campaigns is visible in his complicated suggestions of how presidential candidates should be chosen and recommended to the people in a single public report.[575] He ends by claiming that "the moral principle should rule over legal principle", because "Justice is the compliance to moral law over judicial law."[576]

Until 1991, Solzhenitsyn was primarily defined by scholars and journalists as an anti-Soviet and anti-communist writer, something his self-fashioned image emphasized.[577] What was his relevance now that communism collapsed?

There are roughly two opposing views on Solzhenitsyn's influence and legacy in the aftermath of the fall of communism. On the one hand, there is the assessment of certain scholars of Russian literature who claim that by the time the Soviet Union fell, Solzhenitsyn had become irrelevant in his country and abroad. On the other, are the scholars who see in Solzhenitsyn a writer with transcendent qualities—be they political or aesthetic—, which played a key role in the fall of communism.

It is undeniable that when *The Gulag Archipelago* was initially published, it became the center of an explosive debate that forced many thinkers in the West to clearly determine their relationship towards the USSR. Nevertheless,

570 Solzhenitsyn, 1990, p. 15-16.

571 Solzhenitsyn, 1990, p. 21.

572 Solzhenitsyn, 1990, p. 21. "Normal" is the term the author used.

573 Solzhenitsyn, 1990, p. 41-50.

574 Solzhenitsyn, 1990, p. 42.

575 Solzhenitsyn, 1990, p. 38-39; 46. The "all-Zemstvo Assembly" would choose the candidates.

576 Solzhenitsyn, 1990, p. 50. "Nravstvennoe nachalo dolzhno stoiat vyshe, chem iuridicheskoe. Spravedlivost'—eto sootvetstvie s nravstvennym pravom prezhde, chem s iuridicheskim." (My translation.)

577 Cf.: Solzhenitsyn, 1980, "Oak"; Walter Laqueur. *Black Hundred: the rise of the extreme right in Russia.* 1st ed. New York: Harper Collins Publishers, 1993. p. 288-289.

Solzhenitsyn's thought went beyond a condemnation of communism, and included aspects of other ideologies. Solzhenitsyn's nationalism and other related aspects of his thought have made him particularly popular among conservative or even right-wing scholars and journalists, who have remained his most faithful readers and have become the most prolific writers on his life and oeuvre. It is for this reason that in the period from 1991 to this day, there is an increasing rightward slant in his reception—which explains why far less liberal or leftist reception will be discussed in the next pages.

Among those who consider that Solzhenitsyn played a decisive role in the collapse of the USSR and/or the end of communism as an ideology is political scientist Daniel J. Mahoney. For example, in a book about Solzhenitsyn's thought, Mahoney portrays the dissident's role in history as follows:

> With *The Gulag*, Solzhenitsyn initiated the final struggle-the decisive blow against communism-that allowed others such as Pope John Paul II, Ronald Reagan, Mikhail Gorbachev, and Václav Havel to play their crucial roles in the denouement of European communism.[578]

In a later article, Mahoney explains how it is that Solzhenitsyn could play such a pivotal role in history:

> More than any other figure in the twentieth century, Solzhenitsyn exposed the ideological 'lie' at the heart of communist totalitarianism, the 'illusion that men and social organizations can be transformed at a stroke' (R. Aron). *The Gulag Archipelago* is one of the masterpieces of the century, *the* book that undermined the moral legitimacy of the entire communist enterprise.[579]

Mahoney claims that after *Gulag* certain ideological beliefs were no longer defensible. He adds that Solzhenitsyn has continuously been under attack in the West, and is the object of "widespread hostility in both Russia and the West" due to critics' refusal "to forgive Solzhenitsyn for his pivotal role in defeating the communist behemoth."[580]

Historian Malia defines Solzhenitsyn's work—and *Gulag* in particular—as the historical turning point when it became "indisputable" that the prison camps were central to communist ideology, but also that "as late as the 1980s" there

---

578 Mahoney, 2001, p. 8.
579 Mahoney, 2003, p. 67.
580 Mahoney, 2003, p. 68. In his text, it remains unclear who the carrier of this hostility is.

was resistance in the West to believing these claims.[581] He bases these doubts on some Western scholars' scepticism about what appears to be an overblown number of victims of Soviet terror—and he even explains a few paragraphs later, that there is no way of obtaining conclusive evidence in relation to this question.[582] Years later, Malia vents his disappointment at the lack of a stronger condemnation of communism.[583] The publication of *Gulag* was significant in turning people in the West away from the Soviet dream, but apparently, for this anti-communist scholar,—even years after the fall of communism—this was not enough. In this sense, a kind of pessimism dampens the achievements of *Gulag*.

Literary critic Ericson similarly considers Solzhenitsyn's work crucial in the fall of communism.[584] In an article about the legacy of *Gulag,* he writes:

> [D]espite the resistance [among intellectuals to Solzhenitsyn's way of viewing the modern world], *The Gulag Archipelago* played a crucial role in bringing about the great watershed moment in world history through which we recently passed. Although many factors of course converged to effect this historical moment, no fair-minded analysis can leave the role of *Gulag* out of account.[585]

His reasons for bequeathing *Gulag* with such importance are that it allegedly delegitimized "Communism among Soviet citizens", and secondly, it tore "away the illusions" many Westerners had about "the Soviet experiment."[586] Ericson is so convinced of the magnitude of Solzhenitsyn's historical influence that he concludes that neglecting to mention the Russian author in histories of the Soviet Union, or those of the fall of communism is the result of "the old negative consensus" on the author which has shifted its focus from criticizing him to considering him irrelevant.[587]

These are only a few examples of authors from different disciplines ascertaining that Solzhenitsyn's work—and especially *Gulag*—changed history. These claims can be summarized as the delegitimization of

---

581 Martin Malia. *The Soviet Tragedy: A History of Socialism in Russia, 1917-1991.* New York: Free Press; Maxwell Macmillan International, 1994. p. 261.

582 Malia, 1994, p. 262.

583 Martin Malia. "Judging Nazism and Communism." *The National Interest* 69 (2002): 63-78.

584 Ericson, 1998, p. 184; Ericson, 2008, p. 514.

585 Ericson, 2002, p. 147.

586 Ericson, 2002, p. 147.

587 Ericson, 2002, p. 158.

communism due to the exposure in *Gulag* of the state's cruelty to its own citizens. At the same time, the idea that worldview criticism of Solzhenitsyn's work and/or the reluctance to acknowledge his historical influence amount to political bias of some kind reflects the continuing effect of Cold War tensions in scholarship. Between 1989 and 1991 all communist governments in Eastern Europe had given up their monopoly of power. But the decade-long environment of suspicion and even the fear of the spread of this ideology did not disappear immediately. For some scholars, anti-communism continues to be important—even if only as an affirmation of a conviction. However, for many other scholars, communism and anti-communism as ideologies are no longer central concerns. In the specific case of Solzhenitsyn, due to the marked politicization of his work, the fall of communism was the cue for some scholars to re-examine his work—all the more now that he was again published in Russian *in* Russia. This also meant that the relevance of Solzhenitsyn would rely on new criteria.

As early as 1991, Russianist Nancy Condee was writing about the dwindling relevance of Solzhenitsyn's work in a country that now enjoyed widespread freedom of expression.[588] Condee elucidates how a "creator cult" previously surrounded Solzhenitsyn, as well as the singer-poet Vladimir Vysotzky in Russia.[589] Both figures were dissidents who served as important points of reference in the 1970s and early 80s and gaining widespread admiration for their courage. Condee explains that the fact that their works became legally available at a time when a) almost anything could be legally published, and b) the Soviet population was suffering economic woes unseen in decades, worked against them.[590] By then, Solzhenitsyn's work—his newest manifesto as much as *The Gulag Archipelago*—"were greeted with a deafening silence by cultural consumers".[591] But it was not only bad timing that made Solzhenitsyn's work seem superfluous, but also the content of his newer texts which revealed how little he was in tune with the "political realities" of his contemporaries.[592] Solzhenitsyn's lengthy[593] and difficult style made his work

---

588 Nancy Condee and Vladimir Padunov. "Perestroika Suicide: Not by 'Bred' Alone." *New Left Review* I.189 (1991): 67-89.
589 Condee, 1991, p. 72.
590 Condee, 1991, p. 73-74.
591 Condee, 1991, p. 74.
592 Condee, 1991, p. 75.

even more inaccessible to readers of the late 20th century. This does not mean that his style or message had changed and become more convoluted; according to Condee, the circumstances of his readers had affected their willingness to read these works.[594] When his books were published abroad and smuggled into the Soviet Union in defiance of government authorities, Solzhenitsyn was able to ignore marketing and publishing norms and defy readers' preferences as to the length and language of a work—and get away with it.[595] However, the continuing neglect of these aspects of the literary milieu in a freer context led to an inability to connect with his readers back home—all these factors lead Condee to warn that Solzhenitsyn's work is "in danger of disappearing into the paper-pulping plants".[596]

In 1989, Solzhenitsyn explains in an interview with David Aikman that the *Red Wheel* was not "designed to be read through easily, for amusement, but to understand our history."[597] He attaches so much importance to this series, that he mentions in the same interview that a precondition of his return to his country was that this series should be sold in every bookstore of the entire Soviet Union.[598] Hence, in the eyes of the author, the relevance of the content justified the difficulty of his texts. Moreover, his desire to be read by all in the Soviet Union shows evidence of his self-image as a kind of teacher, and not, say, as an elitist writer with a select readership.

Some years later, Russianist Rosalind Marsh similarly describes the publication of *Gulag* in Russia as anti-climactic.[599] Solzhenitsyn repeatedly wrote of his belief that his books would cause abrupt change in, or even the demise of, the Soviet Union.[600] In 1976, he told television viewers in the UK:

---

593 This applies to *Red Wheel* which was likewise published at the time in Moscow.

594 Condee, 1991, p.75.

595 Condee, 1991, p. 75.

596 Condee, 1991, p. 74.

597 David Aikman. "Russia's Prophet in Exile." TIME 24 July 1989.

598 Aikman, 1989.

599 Rosalind Marsh. "The Death of Soviet Literature: Can Russian Literature Survive?" *Europe-Asia Studies* 45.1 (1993): 115-139.

600 Solzhenitsyn, 1980, "Oak", p. 291; Solzhenitsyn, 1974, vol. 1, p. 298; Solzhenitsyn, 1995, p. 210.

> If today the three volumes of *Gulag Archipelago* were widely published in the Soviet Union and were freely available to all, then in a very short space of time no Communist ideology would be left.[601]

His Russian fans who shared his views had to face the disappointment of the bland reception the dissident had in his country, once he was finally published there for the first time since the 1960s.[602] This is not to say that his work did not stir passions; *How to Rebuild Russia* sparked angry protests in the Ukraine and Kazakhstan as a result of Solzhenitsyn's dismissive view of their independence.[603] But, on the whole, it seems Solzhenitsyn's Russian reception in the early 1990s was not the bombshell he expected. Marsh argues that *Gulag* and later on the *Red Wheel* series largely fell on deaf ears for two reasons.[604] When *Gulag* was published, it no longer had any novelty value: much had been published on this subject by then in the Soviet Union, and many intellectuals had read it when it was circulating underground. As for *The Red Wheel*, it simply did not seem to spark enough interest for readers to go through thousands of pages on the pre-revolutionary era.

Solomon Volkov, a US-based Russian cultural historian, delineates how different factors led to the general lack of interest in Solzhenitsyn's texts upon the progressive fall of communism in the late 80s and early 90s.[605] According to Volkov, it was not only Solzhenitsyn's mammoth novels on the early 20th century that suffered from his inflexibility towards readers. He writes that Solzhenitsyn's inability to adapt to the audience he was addressing nullified the effect of his political manifestos: the complexity of his demands and his archaic language were inadequate for a mass readership.[606] In certain cases—he mentions his political appeals to Russians both in the 1970s and 1990s—it seems that aesthetics worked against Solzhenitsyn's political reception.[607] He claims that both *Gulag*'s aesthetic quality and the political

601 Solzhenitsyn, 1976, "Warning", p. 16.
602 Marsh, 1993, p. 119.
603 Cf. Volkov, 2008, p. 286; Conor O'Clery. "Back in the USSR." The New Republic 19 November 1990: 22-3. Solzhenitsyn suggested the creation of a Greater Russia consisting of Russia, Belarus, Ukraine and North Kazakhstan, cf.: Solzhenitsyn, 1990, p. 4-13.
604 Both of the following reasons are explained in: Marsh, p. 119-120.
605 Volkov, 2008, p. 285ff.
606 Volkov, 2008, p. 285-6.
607 Volkov, 2008, p. 287-289.

circumstances in which it was published had made it so prominent in the 1970s in the West.[608] But by the time it was published in the USSR, there was nothing more it could do: communist ideology and the Soviet state were already crumbling.[609] Many Russians' disinvolvement with Solzhenitsyn is the result of seeing him exclusively as "a great director and actor who had a successful run in the show called *Struggle Against Communism* playing prophet and ascetic moralist."[610]

Looking closely at reassessments of Solzhenitsyn's work in which his role in the past is emphasized in contrast to his lesser importance upon the collapse of the USSR, these do not seem to be attempts to discard him or deny his importance. In some cases, one can almost sense a whiff of melancholy in the description of the publication of *Gulag* in the USSR and the lack of impact it had.

After 1991, a good number of scholars began to see non-political—even aesthetic aspects—of Solzhenitsyn's work as disadvantageous to his readership and even to its literary quality. His language, which had been formerly highly praised,[611] is seen in a different light once his main readership was recognized as the Russian public. The length of his works is no longer an object of admiration as a matter of course[612] but it is often enough considered to be a flaw. But politics has never really receded from Solzhenitsyn's reception, and this is true both among his admirers and those who see his work in a more critical light.

For certain authors the appraisal of Solzhenitsyn's role in the Cold War became clouded with the publication of his recent dictations: Russian reactions to them seemed to prompt a reconsideration by Western observers of their view of the writer. German critic Fritz J. Raddatz expressed surprise at the tone of Solzhenitsyn's recommendations for his country.[613] The

---

608 Volkov, 2008, p. 229.

609 Volkov, 2008, p. 284.

610 Volkov, p. 295.

611 I have touched this subject when discussing *Ivan Denisovich* in chapter two.

612 As late as 1987, Rudolf Augstein expressed his admiration for the length of the different parts of Solzhenitsyn's *Red Wheel* series: Rudolf Augstein. "'Man lügt über mich wie über einen Toten'." Der Spiegel 26 October 1987: 218-51.

613 Fritz J. Raddatz. "Ayatollah Solschenizyn: Wie Russland neu einrichten?" Die Zeit 16 November 1990.

Russian author's musings on the moral meaning of the earth, his precise commands as to who should be allowed to buy property and who should not, and his warnings against democracy made the German critic wonder if it was Solzhenitsyn's message that had changed, or the West's view of it.[614] He writes candidly:

> Kann es sein, daß dieselben Thesen, in früherem Zusammenhang geäußert, damals sinnvoll und heute unsinnig sind? Daß, was Solschenizyn damals in „Irrtum des Abendlandes" formulierte, sich jetzt verzerrt zu einem peinlichen Ausrufen „russischer Reinheit"?[615]

Raddatz answers by quoting French philosopher Bernard Henri-Levy, who writes that upon the collapse of communism it has simply become clearer that Solzhenitsyn always saw communism as a Western phenomenon and now perseveres in his fight against other forms of "Europeanization" of Russia by dictating Imperial Russian administrative units as the way forward.[616]

The suggestion that the Cold War had obscured the less attractive aspects of Solzhenitsyn's thought is plausible. As I have shown in the previous section, political priorities did eclipse underlying details within the author's work: the anti-communist message was at times considered to be more important in the ideological war against the USSR than the actual political preferences of the author. But while the Cold War was going on, Western literary criticism underwent great changes and brought forth crucial developments: feminist criticism, queer studies, post-colonialism, and other new readings found their way into the mainstream. These new approaches to literature evolved in parallel with Solzhenitsyn's writing career, but their paths did not cross. The study of Russian literature might have been marginalized from these debates while there was still a political divide between East and West, but after 1991 there has been no reason for excluding it from more contemporary trends of criticism. A study of Solzhenitsyn's work from a feminist or a post-colonial point of view can result in completely new understandings of his work. However, it is possible that it may turn out that the world has changed more

---

614 Raddatz, 1990; Solzhenitsyn, 1990, on land: p. 15-19; on democracy: p. 28-39.

615 Raddatz, 1990. "Can it be that the same propositions—spoken in a different, earlier context—were then sensible and now nonsensical? Is what Solzhenitsyn back then phrased as 'the Western Error' now distorted into embarrassing calls for 'Russian purity'?" (My translation.)

616 Raddatz, 1990.

than Solzhenitsyn anticipated—making the ideological and idiosyncratic rift between his work and his readership ever greater.

In the UK, Mike Jarrett was very direct in his claim that Solzhenitsyn's "books date badly".[617] Solzhenitsyn's insistence—despite democratization under Gorbachev—in promoting an old model of authoritarianism rooted in the teachings of the Russian Orthodox Church was seized as an opportunity to note that even his works which are historically important are no longer compatible with modern views: his homophobic and anti-feminist comments as well as his "racial antagonism" towards certain prisoners in *Gulag* make the author's darker side "painfully evident."[618] Cold War politics aside Jarrett did not see much future for the Russian's oeuvre from an aesthetic point of view.

Jarret does not delve into details, but he probably is referring to passages in *Gulag* such as the one in which Solzhenitsyn claims that homosexual love is the lowest form of love, and that platonic marriage with a stranger is the highest.[619] Solzhenitsyn details how he sees these relationships and the people who went into them. First, he describes some of the women who marry men on the other side of the wall that divided the sexes in the camp:

> In that very same Kengir [prison camp], Lithuanian women were *married* across the wall to Lithuanian men whom they had never seen or met[.] In this marriage with an unknown prisoner on the other side of a wall—and for Roman Catholic women such a marriage was irreversible and sacred—I hear a choir of angels. It is like the unselfish, pure contemplation of the heavenly bodies. It is too lofty for this age of self-interested calculation and hopping up-and-down jazz.[620]

He then goes on to explain that women entered lesbian relationships because it was harder for them to be separated from the opposite sex than for men:

> And the women themselves and the doctors who treated them in the divided compounds confirm that the women suffered worse than the men from the separation. They were particularly excited and nervous. Lesbian love developed

617 Mike Jarrett. "A Shrill Prophet." The Guardian 19 January 1991: 23.

618 Jarrett, 1991, p. 23. Examples of homophobia, mysoginy, and racial prejudice in *Gulag* can be found in: Solzhenitsyn, 1974, vol. 1, p. 151, 441; 1975, vol. 2, p. 75 ff., 228-239; 248-249.

619 Solzhenitsyn, 1975, vol. 2, p. 248.

620 Solzhenitsyn, 1975, vol. 2, p. 249. In the Russian version this passage is in: Alexander Solzhenitsyn. *Arkhipelag GULag: 1918-1956: opyt chudozhestvennogo issledovaniia.* 2 Vol. Paris: YMCA-Press, 1973. p. 242-243.

> swiftly. The gentle and the young went about looking sallow, with dark circles under their eyes. The women of a cruder type became the "men." No matter how the jailers tried to break up such pairs they turned up again in the same bunks. They sent one or the other of these "spouses" away from the camp.[621]

Sociologist Adi Kuntsman writes that expressions of disgust and contempt towards homosexuality pervade Russian gulag literature.[622] In her analysis—which does not include Solzhenitsyn—she delineates how the negative description of the psyche and bodies of homosexuals is very common in gulag memoirs.[623] This is a phenomenon visible in this example from Solzhenitsyn's *Gulag*. Solzhenitsyn describes an abnormal psychological state that leads to lesbian relationships and results in physical symptoms such as "sallowness" and "circles under the eyes". According to Kuntsman, the visibility of homosexuality is emphasized with repulsion,[624] and this, together with the underlying expression of disgust towards this behavior can be understood as an affirmation of certain boundaries that mark what is correct and what is perverse, or dirty, and confirms certain social hierarchies.[625] By expressing disgust, the author may be trying to affirm his or her higher standing in a moral hierarchy—a question which was important to many gulag authors, who felt their moral (and physical) survival was under threat.[626] Through his or her revulsion towards homosexuality—which in the case of men was illegal in the USSR—the gulag memoirist tries to humanize him-or herself and gain a sense of respectability.[627] However, Kuntsman does point out that gulag memoirs have had a lasting influence in the way the Russian intelligentsia defines its mores, and that homophobia in this context has had a long-term effect.[628] According to Kuntsman, in the Russian language, the linguistic association of homosexuality with criminality—a topic too vast to go into here—stems from gulag memoirs.[629] The moral authority

---

621 Solzhenitsyn, 1975, vol. 2, p. 249.

622 Adi Kuntsman. "'With a Shade of Disgust': Affective Politics of Sexuality and Class in Memoirs of the Stalinist Gulag." *Slavic Review* 68.2 (2009). p. 310-11.

623 Kuntsman, 2009, p. 312, 320.

624 Kuntsman, 2009, p. 314.

625 Kuntsman, 2009, p. 317.

626 Kuntsman, 2009, p. 321, 323.

627 Kuntsman, 2009, p. 326.

628 Kuntsman, 2009, p. 326.

629 Kuntsman, 2009, p. 308, 312, 315-17, 320. Solzhenitsyn uses some of the terms referred to by Kuntsman, for example "bitches" for homosexual men, and the

that gulag authors possessed through their status as victims gave their views on homosexuality a special legitimacy, in addition to their readers' perception of these texts as the truth:

> And finally, the memoirs were seen as the true history, juxtaposed to the lies, silences, and distortions that had constituted official Soviet historiography. The status of these memoirs as true testimony and as the "real history" metonymically granted them unquestioned authority about the other issues described by the survivors. Among them were same-sex relations, which for the memoirs' authors—and later for their readers—became forever linked to criminality, violence, and monstrosity.[630]

Kuntsman's constructive suggestion in dealing with these texts is to regard them not as truthful historical sources, but literary works, and to evaluate their moral judgements and definitions of humanness with more care.[631]

Solzhenitsyn's condemnation of homosexuality is indeed something that can be seen differently now, when most Western countries have finally decriminalized homosexuality. Anti-feminism in Solzhenitsyn's work, however, was anachronistic even at the time of the publication of *Gulag* and other works containing this tendency.[632] This is an intriguing aspect of Solzhenitsyn's work that has unfortunately been neglected. Feminist criticism is not new, and it has been an important part of contemporary literary criticism for decades—which makes it striking that Solzhenitsyn has been ignored by it. This is, however, part of a wider problem in studies of Solzhenitsyn's work. Literary scholar Lisa Ryoko Wakamiya writes that Solzhenitsyn—despite his continuing canonization as "Russia's last great writer"—has been the object of a type of critical exile, a neglect by modern critics to analyze his work according to current theoretical approaches.[633] She believes that the Russian author's negative view of post-modernism, as well as the apparent

---

general accusation of "pederasty", for example in: Solzhenitsyn, 1975, vol. 2, p. 422.

630 Kuntsman, 2009, p. 326.

631 Kuntsman, 2009, p. 328.

632 Female emancipation was an integral part of Soviet ideology and reality—even if full equality was not achieved. Cf.: Janet S. Schwartz. "Women under Socialism: Role Definitions of Soviet Women." *Social Forces* 58.1 (1979): 67-88; Mary Buckley. "Women in the Soviet Union." *Feminist Review*.8 (1981): 79-106; Jill M. Bystydzienski. "Women and Socialism: A Comparative Study of Women in Poland and the USSR." *Signs* 14.3 (1989): 668-84.

633 Wakamiya, 2009, p. 69.

isolationism of his works written after exile, have contributed to the lack of studies of his work from contemporary critical viewpoints.[634] Speaking of how the Russian author has been "under-researched", Ericson writes in an article on "worldview criticism" that a potential literary critic interested in gender issues would likely avoid studying Solzhenitsyn due to the contrast between such a critic's worldview and Solzhenitsyn's.[635] Ericson finds the greatest difference between such a modern critic and the Russian author to be that the former would believe in "relativistic assumptions" and the latter was "committed to the fundamentally non-arbitrary character of the moral life".[636] Nevertheless, I will sketch why studying Solzhenitsyn's anti-feminism might help understand his thought and morality in its complexity notwithstanding the question of agreement or disagreement with his views on morality.

Solzhenitsyn's view of female desire in *Gulag* contrasts with his moral condemnation of state violence against prison camp inmates. In the text quoted above, he claims that women turn to homosexuality because they suffer more from lack of sexual companionship than men, and he backs this surprising assertion by saying that "the women themselves and the doctors who treated them" confirm this.[637] Here, female desire—as opposed to male desire—is at the root of what he sees as sexual deviation. This condescending attitude towards women, who do not seem to have their bodies and emotions under control, is strengthened by his repeated claims that motherhood and wifely duties are what gives women's lives meaning.[638]

More shocking and even puzzling is an earlier passage about rape in a camp in which security was apparently very low.[639] He explains how attractive women were raped by many men who invaded the camp. He describes how this takes place in front of other men and women: Men become aroused and want to join in. Then Solzhenitsyn describes how unattractive or older women who are not raped observe these gang rapes and become aroused

634 By isolantionism she means the perception that he ignored his readers' interests and preferences. Wakamiya, 2009, p. 70-71.

635 Edward E. Ericson. "Worldview Criticism of Solzhenitsyn." *Put' Solzhenitsyna v Kontekste Bolshogo Vremeni. Sbornik Pamiati 1918 - 2008.* Ed. Liudmila I. Saraskina. Moscow: Russkii Put', 2009. p. 219.

636 Ericson, 2009, "Worldview", p. 219.

637 Solzhenitsyn, 1975, vol. 2, p. 249.

638 Solzhenitsyn, 1975, vol. 2, p. 239, 240, 244-245.

639 Solzhenitsyn, 1975, vol. 2, p. 233.

themselves, envious of the women getting raped, and later violently attack the rape victims out of envy.

> Obvious old age and obvious ugliness were the only defenses for a woman there—nothing else. Attractiveness was a curse. Such a woman had a constant stream of visitors on her bunk and was constantly surrounded. They propositioned her and threatened her with beatings and knives—and she had no hope of being able to stand up against it but only to be smart about whom she gave in to—to pick the kind of man to defend her with his name and his knife from all the rest, from the next in line, from the whole greedy queue, from those crazy juveniles gone berserk, aroused by everything they could see and breathe in there. And it wasn't only men that she had to be defended against either. Nor only the juveniles who were aroused. What about the women next to them, who day after day had to see all that but were not themselves invited by the men? In the end those women, too, would explode in an uncontrollable rage and hurl themselves on their successful neighbors and beat them up.[640]

Solzhenitsyn describes a horrifying scene of violence towards "attractive" women, and then switches to what he sees as the perspective of the "obviously old" or "obviously unattractive" women who were allegedly left untouched, and re-words gang rape as an "invitation" by men, and rape victims as "successful" women. Not only is this depiction of the thoughts of a female witness of rape highly unrealistic—as well as the assumption that in an environment of gang rape physical beauty plays such a key role—, it is also ethically questionable. In a book in which almost every act of violence described is condemned with overflowing pathos, it is bewildering to read such an ambivalent interpretation of rape.

The lack of commentary on such passages from *Gulag* is astonishing. It is true that the second and third volumes of *Gulag* did not sell as well as the first volume.[641] One could think that these passages—which are found in the second volume—were ignored by readers and scholars because they were not read at all; or that critics usually focused on the first volume, but not the rest of the work. This might explain why Australian scholar Boris Frankel

---

640 Solzhenitsyn, 1975, vol. 2, p. 233. In the Russian version: Solzhenitsyn, 1973, vol. 2 p. 228. The translation does not deviate in meaning from the Russian.

641 Simon Bessie from Harper & Row—*Gulag*'s publisher in English—claims they printed 3 million copies of the first volume, less than 900 thousand of the second, and 120 thousand of the third volume. Charles Trueheart. "Solzhenitsyn and his Message of Silence; The Exile, Writing, Warning and Waiting at his Secluded Estate." The Washington Post 24 November 1987.

reproves of Solzhenitsyn's sexist call for women to return to the kitchen and child-rearing as early as 1974,[642] but does not mention the more offensive claims made in *Gulag*.[643] Nonetheless, some critics did write about these later volumes of *Gulag* even back in the 1970s. Lionel Abel, for instance, comments about the second volume of *Gulag* in 1976 in this manner:

> Solzhenitsyn's carefully detailed reports on why such and such an inmate committed suicide, on how the women inmates suffered more than the men, and at what human cost (100,000 lives), and for what peculiar purpose (not industrial use), the White Sea-Baltic Canal was engineered, dug, and celebrated—these facts do more, I think, than document the lamentable story of what men have done to men under the Soviets.[644]

Abel counts these reports about women's suffering in Soviet camps as "facts" and he later praises this work as genuine *littérature engagée* precisely because it allegedly presents facts as they are.[645] In an article on Solzhenitsyn's ideology, Sidney Monas mentions the *Gulag* chapter on women, describing it as "touching."[646] He does not criticize any aspect of the Russian's depiction of women, but he does point out that it is "typical" of him to express his "warmest sympathy" for the "sublimated" form of eros between people who never met.[647]

In Germany, the passages I have quoted on homosexual love and rape were printed in *Der Spiegel* in 1974 as part of their publication of several excerpts of this work.[648] The text is introduced by an article claiming it contains possibly more shocking facts than part one.[649] Its function as a text is seen as helping these cases of state violence to cease by presenting them as repeatable. In the first page of the excerpts about women in prison camp we

---

642 Already in his *Letter to the Soviet Leaders* (1974) Solzhenitsyn makes such a call.

643 Boris Frankel. "The 'Gulag Archipelago' and the Left." *Theory and Society* 1.4 (1974). p. 482. Australia is not part of my study, but I decided to mention Frankel because he published in a US-based journal and is one of the few scholars to mention Solzhenitsyn's attitude towards women at all.

644 Lionel Abel. "A Poem we Need Today: Review of The Gulag Archipelago Two." Commentary March 1976. p. 64.

645 Abel, 1976, p. 67.

646 Monas, 1981, p. 445.

647 Monas, 1981, p. 445.

648 Alexander Solzhenitsyn. "Frauen im Lager." Der Spiegel 28 October 1974. p. 131-132; 146.

649 N.N. "Solschenizyn: 'Morgenröte der Vernichtung'." Der Spiegel 28 October 1974: 121-6.

see a picture of Solzhenitsyn cuddling with his second wife.[650] Later on, in the passage on rape, women who are raped are described as "glücklichere" (happier or luckier instead of "more successful" as in the Russian or in the English translation) and rapists are "Kunden" ("clients" instead of "visitors" as in the Russian or in the English version).[651] The fact that these passages were published in one of the most widely read German news magazines is evidence against the possible assumption that they had remained obscure or unknown to the public.[652]

From our perspective, it is troubling to see these claims by Solzhenitsyn were passed by without serious commentary, or were even considered to be facts. Again, it seems that the trust endowed to the author and his work clouded a critical approach to the text. In a review of this volume of *Gulag*, philosopher Manès Sperber explains that readers accorded Solzhenitsyn with his/her full trust from the start because by the time of his first publication, even most communists were already condemning the crimes of Stalin.[653] However, two further factors enhanced his reputation in such a way that Solzhenitsyn's works were transformed from being "literary truth" to being the "absolute truth": his tenacity upon his persecution by the Soviet state in the 1970s, and his literary talent.[654] Thus, the infallibility of *Gulag* was the result of a combination of literary and extra-textual factors of its time. However, most of these contingent factors should pose no hindrance to a later reassessment of this work. Even if one does not categorize *Gulag* as a history, the question remains: why did the author present female desire and sexual violence in his diegesis in such a way? In this sense, a study of the image of women in his works would be beneficial and indeed indispensable to his future readers.

---

650 Solzhenitsyn, 1974, "Frauen", p. 128.

651 Solzhenitsyn, 1974, "Frauen", p. 131-132.

652 Unfortunately, *Spiegel*-readers' reaction to this odd combination of a romantization of Solzhenitsyn and his negative views on women cannot be part of this study.

653 All following references to Sperber stem from: Manès Sperber. "Stacheldraht und Seele: Der Zweite Band von Alexander Solschenizyns 'Archipel GULag'." Frankfurter Allgemeine Zeitung 28 December 1974.

654 All this notwithstanding, Sperber himself did dare write of his disapproval of Solzhenitsyn's *schadenfreude* about the death of certain people in the prison camps, and his disagreement with Solzhenitsyn's claim that religion precluded tyranny.

After 1991, Solzhenitsyn's name as an author and his main legacy continues to be attached to his testimony of the prison camp experience. In this context, scholars at times differentiate between witness authors whom they consider to be ideologically viable—because of their stance towards communism—and those whom they don't. For example, one current expert in gulag literature in the US, Dariusz Tolczyk, considers ideological distance towards communism to be decisive in assessing the literary quality of gulag literature, which is the main reason he emphasizes Solzhenitsyn's relevance in this genre.[655] Historian Anne Applebaum likewise regards ethical aspects to be essential in evaluating gulag memoirs, including the recognition of the Soviet Union as "evil" or the desire to "set the record straight"—which is something she finds in Solzhenitsyn's work.[656] It is understandable that during the Cold War, when the threats of ideological domination or nuclear war were part of everyday life, scholars would consider disloyalty to the Soviet state so crucial in assessing literature. In this sense, it might even help plausibly explain why they ignored aspects of his work which were controversial or even contrary to Western values. But once these threats were gone, it is high time to ask if such criteria are really sufficient to promote and canonize anti-Soviet literature. As it will become clear in the next two sections, Solzhenitsyn's political relevance today has grown in other ideological niches which exist far from the general interpretation of gulag literature as part of a human rights discourse. Although anti-communism continues to be a common denominator among Solzhenitsyn's admirers and commentators, other ideological currents—such as revisionism and political Christianity—have made their claim on the author. In a way, this cannot come as a surprise, as Solzhenitsyn was never a purely anti-communist writer. As early as 1975, Leonard Schapiro noted:

> We shall understand nothing of Solzhenitsyn and of the Russian tradition to which he belongs if we persist in seeing him as a straightforward anti-communist for whom the destruction of communist rule would be the solution of all Russia's problems.[657]

---

655 Dariusz Tolczyk. *See no Evil: literary cover-ups and discoveries of the Soviet camp experience.* New Haven: Yale University Press, 1999. p. 254ff.

656 Applebaum, 2011, p. xi-xii. This view is criticized in a review by historian M. Dobson: Miriam Dobson. "Stalin's Gulag: Death, Redemption and Memory." *The Slavonic and East European Review* 90.4 (2012): 735-43.

657 Schapiro, [1975], p. 386.

Solzhenitsyn's works have always been embedded in a complex web of thought, which consists of many different elements. Readers sharing an ideological affinity with these other aspects of Solzhenitsyn's thought noted this quite early on. Nevertheless, as communism lost its relevance as an ideology, it is these other aspects of his thought that percolate and are becoming more central to his reception.

3.3 Solzhenitsyn in Revisionist Debates

Introduction

The term revisionism in this subchapter refers specifically to the endeavor to create an image of the (overwhelming) collective responsibility of the Jews for the Russian Revolution, to efforts to revise the history of World War II in order to minimize or deny the crimes of the Germans and the Axis powers, and the demonization of the role of the Allies in World War II. Central to these views is that mainstream historical research does not convey the truth of history; this often includes accusations of programmatic manipulation or conspiracy by the state or outside "powers".

This type of revisionism is an heir to the irredentist movements that appeared after World War I, which did not accept the borders drawn by the Versailles Peace Treaties. Similarly, some post-1945 revisionists are unsatisfied with the borders drawn after the war, and believe to have a rightful claim to territories beyond these borders.

As an ideology, one main goal of revisionism is to justify certain actions. For example, in the post-war years, West German revisionists sought to exonerate the Nazis by claiming either that World War II was necessary to defend Germany from communism, or the Jews, or both; or that the war was incited by the Allies and the Germans were just the victims. This was a reaction to what they saw as the humiliation of occupation and re-education by the Allies, whom they perceived as culturally inferior, and what they saw as a besmirching of German "honor" by assigning them the blame for WWII and for the genocide of innocent people.[658] Some German revisionists

658 Brigitte Bailer-Galanda. "'Revisionismus'-Pseudo-Wissenschaftliche Propaganda des Rechtsextremismus." *Wahrheit und "Auschwitzlüge".* Eds. Brigitte Bailer-Galanda, Wolfgang Benz, and Wolfgang Neugebauer. Vienna: Deuticke, 1995. 16-

emphasize the suffering of the Germans who were expelled from Poland, the Czech Republic, and other Eastern European territories in 1945 as a way to palliate the crimes committed by the Germans against civilians during the war. British revisionists, on the other hand, seek to change the view of history by trying to exonerate the "negative" image of British Nazi sympathizers and early appeasement policies towards the Nazis.

As a rule, revisionist movements are national, and thus have their own—often conflicting—priorities. The term "revisionism" has been used for centuries, to define diverse political movements. There is no sense in explaining all the different meanings the term can have, but it is important to mention one use of revisionism which is close to the subject of my work although I choose not to use in this sense.

In the US, the term revisionism has been used by Sovietologists and scholars of Soviet history since the 1980s. It is no homogenous school of history, which is why historian Steven Merritt Miner suggests understanding this form of revisionism as an attitude more than a school of thought.[659] In general, these scholars have sought a more nuanced approach to the history of the Soviet Union than what they saw was taken by so-called "traditionalist" anti-Communist historians. They contested the indiscriminate use of the term "totalitarian" by "traditionalist" scholars for a state that had changed radically since the purges of the 1930s; they also believed it is justified to study aspects of Soviet history beyond the repression of society by its government.[660] Some of these scholars may believe that socialism with a human face is or was possible, some do not wish to make political pronouncements of this kind. The reason why I do not wish to use this term with this *signifié* is because this term is not used in the same way in Soviet studies in other countries, not even by British scholars in the same field.[661] On the other hand, the term revisionism as applied to the crimes committed in

---

32; Wolfgang Benz. "'Revisionismus' in Deutschland." *Wahrheit und "Auschwitzlüge"*. Eds. Brigitte Bailer-Galanda, Wolfgang Benz, and Wolfgang Neugebauer. Vienna: Deuticke, 1995. 33-45.

659 Steven Merritt Miner. "Revelations, Secrets, Gossip and Lies: Sifting Warily through the Soviet Archives." The New York Times 14 May 1995: 19.

660 One of the most straightforward explanations of the priorities of US "revisionist" scholars is found in: Sheila Fitzpatrick. "New Perspectives on Stalinism." *Russian Review* 45.4 (1986): 357-73.

661 Hopkins, 2008, p. 245.

World War II by the Nazis is used in this way in Great Britain and other European countries and has a more universal application.

Revisionism in Solzhenitsyn's Work and Reception

Discussing Solzhenitsyn's relation to nationalism, Jews, and World War II is a thorny issue. Political scientist Schapiro claimed in 1975 that it was a "slanderous and untrue allegation" that anti-Semitism could be found in Solzhenitsyn's work, and was based on the ignorance of his critics and their tendency to assume "guilt by association".[662] He explains that Solzhenitsyn's intellectual proximity to Slavophile thought, which is quite prone to anti-Semitism, led to confusion. More recently, Thornton makes a similar warning that the fact that Solzhenitsyn is nationalistic should not lead to "guilt by association".[663] Nationalism, as well as liberalism or conservatism, can take many different shapes. Thornton suggests that scholars should go beyond the three possible political categories of "liberal, fascist, communist".[664] Because Thornton does have a point, and because of the pervading narrative that Solzhenitsyn's nationalism or anti-Semitism are rumors or calumny,[665] in this section I will discuss both aspects of his work which are read as nationalistic, anti-Semitic, or otherwise revisionistic, and their reception.

Solzhenitsyn and World War II

When Solzhenitsyn was expelled from the Soviet Union, Soviet journalists and scholars wrote articles and even small books discrediting the dissident. One of these books was written by the historian Nikolay Yakovlev and published in English.[666] With the sensational title *Solzhenitsyn's Archipelago of Lies* it hardly strikes its reader as objective. The book summarizes the claims that "justified" the expulsion of Solzhenitsyn. Firstly, he depicts Solzhenitsyn as someone who insults and hates Russia. He comments on the

---

662 Schapiro, [1975], p. 388.
663 Thornton, 1999.
664 Thornton, 1999.
665 For example, cf.: David Remnick. "The Exile Returns." The New Yorker 14 February 1994: p. 70-74; John Earl Haynes and Harvey Klehr. *In Denial: Historians, Communism and Espionage.* New York: Encounter Books, 2003. p. 17; Daniel Mahoney. "The Moral Witness of Aleksandr Solzhenitsyn." *First Things: A Monthly Journal of Religion and Public Life* 196 (2009): p. 44-48.
666 Nikolai Yakovlev. *Solzhenitsyn's Archipelago of Lies.* Moscow: Novosti, 1974.

books *August 1914* and *The Gulag Archipelago* in order to illustrate that Solzhenitsyn does not appreciate the accomplishments of the Russian people. He criticizes the description of the Battle of Tannenberg in *August 1914* as emphasizing Russian defeat and thus "vilifying all things Russian".[667] Yakovlev describes *Gulag* as follows: "The book is the manifesto of a vicious enemy of the Russian people."[668] In *Gulag,* he finds proof of this in Solzhenitsyn's positive portrayal of the so-called Russian Liberation Army (ROA) under General Andrey Vlasov, which fought for the Nazis. Yakovlev constructs this as a claim that the Russians did not want to win the war against the Nazis: he therefore focuses on proving the courage of the Russian people in the war. Yakovlev's article contains both accurate quotes from Solzhenitsyn's work, as well as statements about the author which smack of slander, such as:

> He saw the destruction of those whom he had always worshiped –the Prussian militarists, and he began spreading slanderous rumours aimed at undermining the morale of Soviet troops.[669]

Lastly, Yakovlev clarifies that there is no justification for Stalinist repression, but he objects to Solzhenitsyn's deprecating depiction of the victims who retained faith in the Party:

> Moreover, the tragedy in the history of our country is for Solzhenitsyn an occasion for jeering and gloating over what people had gone through who had been imprisoned but who have retained their faith in the Party. There is not one word showing respect for such men in the thick book. Only mockery.[670]

In general, Yakovlev's book is paradigmatic of Soviet criticism of Solzhenitsyn, as expressed in different articles and open letters.[671] It also seems to reflect the concerns of the Party leadership. Solzhenitsyn's KGB file, published in 1994, reveals Chairman Brezhnev and the Politburo's contempt towards Solzhenitsyn for ridiculing the Red Army and his praise for

---

667 Yakovlev, 1974, p. 12.
668 Yakovlev, 1974, p. 33.
669 Yakovlev, 1974, p. 23.
670 Yakovlev, 1974, p. 38.
671 For example: TASS. "Statement on Solzhenitsyn." The New York Times 3 January 1974: 10; N.N. "Die Welt ins Gewissen geredet: Neue Angriffe gegen Solschenizyn." Frankfurter Allgemeine Zeitung 7 January 1974: 20. Ernst-Ulrich Fromm. "Moskau führt gegen Solschenizyn eine neue Schlacht am Wolchow." Die Welt 30 January 1974: 2; N.N. "Rache für eine zerstörte Welt: Der Fall Solschenizyn aus Moskauer Sicht." Der Spiegel 4 February 1974: 79-82.

the Vlasov troops; they seemed genuinely concerned that former Vlasovites and other Nazi-collaborators would join forces with Solzhenitsyn.[672] The reason why it is so important to understand the arguments behind the Soviet accusations is because there are certain elements of this criticism which have been mentioned in the West in different contexts and with other intentions. However, because of the similarity in content, this has led to misinterpretations of these criticisms.

In chapter two, I have already described the way Solzhenitsyn deals with communist victims of the gulag—which is indeed lacking in compassion. In that context, I also scrutinized his relativization of the crimes of the Nazis in contrast to Soviet repression. This was done as part of the assessment of *Gulag* as witness literature. But here I will clarify how these topics—as well as the treatment of Nazi collaborators—are embedded in a very specific ideology.

Soviet propaganda may have attempted to portray Solzhenitsyn as an anti-nationalist who loved the Germans, but Solzhenitsyn's portrayal of Nazi collaborators does not fit into this explanation.

In *Gulag*, Solzhenitsyn considers that the Soviet citizens who collaborated with the Nazis were unfairly treated and he tries to make a case for them. In an emotional passage, he tries to demonstrate that they had no evil intentions in collaborating, but were driven to the arms—in every sense of the word—of the Nazis by hunger:

> People who have never starved as our war prisoners did, who have never gnawed on bats that happened to fly into the barracks, who have never had to boil the soles of old shoes, will never understand the irresistible material force exerted by any kind of appeal, any kind of argument whatever, if behind it, on the other side of the camp gates, smoke rises from a field kitchen, and if everyone who signs up is fed a bellyful of kasha right then and there—if only once! Just once more before I die![673]

Solzhenitsyn explains that World War deserters and traitors were not the ones who betrayed their country, their country had betrayed them: "It was not they, the unfortunates, who had betrayed the Motherland, but their calculating Motherland who had betrayed them".[674]

672 Korotkov (ed.), 1994, p. 291-2, p. 345ff.
673 "Kasha" is the Russian word for porridge. Solzhenitsyn, 1974, vol. 1, p. 246.
674 Solzhenitsyn, 1974, vol. 1, p. 240.

General Vlasov defected to the Nazis after he was taken as a prisoner of war in 1942.[675] Initially, he was mainly active in doing propaganda work for the Nazis to recruit new collaborators. In the later part of the war, he fought at the head of the so-called Russian Liberation Army. The Nazis did not have a consistent policy towards Vlasov and the ROA; their trust and support were desultory.[676] From an ideological point of view, the Nazis considered all Russians *Untermenschen* and the war of extermination against the Soviet Union had been claimed to be a "total war", but the idea of collaboration with willing Soviet citizens surged when the Nazis felt weaker.[677] Regarding the motivation of Vlasov and his army, there is scholarly consensus that they were politically motivated, hunger not having played a key role in their defection.[678] Because Vlasov did fight for the Nazis, and knew what they stood for, his political motivation will always remain problematic. There is much speculation about his concrete ideological reasons for this collaboration, but because this is not a historical enquiry, the crucial question is what Vlasov meant to Solzhenitsyn.

In the Soviet Union, Vlasov was executed as a traitor. The whole Vlasov episode was seen as a source of shame for the Soviet Union, and something that was seldom spoken of.[679] The cult of Vlasov began in the early post-war years among second wave Russian émigrés, who claimed that he stood for anti-communism and a certain type of freedom from oppression.[680] Solzhenitsyn was the first Soviet citizen to write apologetically of him.[681] Solzhenitsyn seems to believe in the symbolic Vlasov, who was a Russian

---

675 Mark Elliott. "Andrei Vlasov: Red Army General in Hitler's Service." *Military Affairs* 46.2 (1982): 84-87.

676 Elliot, 1982, p. 84-85.

677 Matthias Schröder. *Deutschbaltische SS-Führer und Andrej Vlasov 1942-1945: "Rußland kann nur von Russen besiegt werden".* Paderborn: Schöningh, 2001. p. 10.

678 Cf.: Elliott, 1982; Schröder, 2001, p. 135ff.

679 This policy of silence about Nazi collaboration began during the war and went on until Perestroika, cf.: Alexander Dallin and Ralph S. Mavrogordato. "The Soviet Reaction to Vlasov." *World Politics* 8.3 (1956). p. 315-316; Thomas Parland. *The Extreme Nationalist Threat in Russia: the Growing Influence of Western Rightist Ideas.* 3 Vol. London: Routledge Curzon, 2005. p. 62-64.

680 George Fischer. "General Vlasov's Official Biography." *Russian Review* 8.4 (1949): 284-301.

681 Parland, 2005, p. 63.

patriot who fought with the Nazis out of love for his homeland. He is a symbolic figure with a specific function: to undermine the only unquestioned accomplishment of the Soviet Union, which was to defeat Hitler. Shifting admiration from the Red Army to the Vlasov Army was an attempt to shatter any legitimacy the Soviet Union might still have in the eyes of its citizens, or the West.

In the West, this attempt was often interpreted within the paradigm of totalitarianism: the Vlasovites were caught between two evils. For example, US diplomat George F. Kennan criticizes the Soviet accusation of apologetics, and writes:

> The reviewer can find in these passages of the book no hint of anything resembling sympathy for the Nazis—only pity for the Russians involved, a reproach to the Western allies for the heartlessness and thoughtlessness of their handling of this problem, and a determination to raise the question: what had to be wrong with a political regime in order that "several hundred thousand young men in the ages of twenty to thirty should take up arms against their fatherland in alliance with its most bitter enemy"?[682]

Kennan is an example of a reviewer who focuses on the compassion Solzhenitsyn shows for the Vlasovites, without looking for an ideological explanation beyond anti-Soviet criticism. Another similar case is that of the German writer Heinrich Böll. He correlates Solzhenitsyn's passage on the Vlasovites with his benevolent description of the Gestapo,[683] but he makes an effort to understand the author.[684] He accepts the idea that the Vlasovites were deceived, and tries to see Solzhenitsyn's Gestapo passages as either rhetorical mistakes or as the result of the Russian author's rage against the Soviets.

> Mag sein, daß Solschenizyn hier im Zorn etwas zu sehr verallgemeinert, zwei nationale Konten zu eröffnen—und aus- oder anzugleichen. [...] *Die* Gestapo war schlimm genug, und daran zweifelt gewiß auch Solschenizyn nicht. [...]

---

682 George F. Kennan. "Between Earth and Hell." The New York Review of Books 21 March 1974.

683 Solzhenitsyn's Gestapo passages are discussed in the subchapter about *Gulag* in chapter 2.1 of this book.

684 Böll, 1974.

> Gewiß ist, und keiner kann nach der Lektüre des *Archipels GULag* daran zweifeln, daß Solschenizyn nicht einen einzigen Greuel der Nazis bagatellisiert.[685]

Nevertheless, Solzhenitsyn's readers did not always remain at this general level. His words were at times instrumentalized in arguments of a more controversial nature. Historian Martin Malia sees in the Vlasov passages in Solzhenitsyn's *Gulag* a proof that communism was worse than Nazism, because Solzhenitsyn describes how Red Army soldiers defected to the Nazis, but not the other way around.[686] Malia ends his argument by saying that these claims have caused Solzhenitsyn "trouble" from the Western Left, but that they have not been able to refute his facts. Historically, it has long been known that not only did some German soldiers defect to the Red Army; the number of Soviet collaborators who returned to the Red Army was so great that the Nazis eventually lost their trust in them.[687]

It is very true that some Western leftists vocally disapproved of these passages. Especially in West Germany, the far left, and "New Left" anti-fascist intellectuals expressed their bewilderment openly. Historian Friedhelm Boll notes in a study of Solzhenitsyn's German reception that allusions to World War II had a particularly emotional response.[688] The polarized reaction was most obvious in the more radical left and right-wing press.

Slavicist and editor of the left-wing magazine *Kürbiskern* Friedrich Hitzer characterizes Solzhenitsyn as a Russian nationalist who yearns for pre-revolutionary Russia.[689] He sees *Gulag* as a propagandistic text which includes both facts and fiction; however, Hitzer considers this to be a strategic mixture of both. Hitzer comments on the political instrumentalization of this book, which would not have received the same reception if it had been written by someone in the West. *Gulag*'s passages on Vlasov and the Gestapo are interpreted as an attempt to demonize the USSR, which is untenable from an anti-fascist point of view:

---

685 Böll, 1974. "Perhaps Solzhenitsyn in his rage has over-generalized here, and opened up two national accounts which he adjusts and balances. [...] *The* Gestapo was bad enough, and surely even Solzhenitsyn does not doubt that.[...] It is certain—and no one can doubt this after reading 'Gulag Archipelago'—that Solzhenitsyn does not trivialize a single Nazi atrocity." (My translation.)

686 Malia, 1977, p. 56. This is, of course, historically inaccurate.

687 Dallin, 1956, p. 320.

688 Boll, 2000, p. 336-337.

689 Friedrich Hitzer. "Solschenizyns Ausverkauf." Kürbiskern 2. 1974: 129-40.

> Die Behandlung deutscher Antifaschisten durch Wlassow-Leute unterschied sich in nichts von der durch die SS—wer hier Solidarität verlangt, verlangt Selbstaufgabe vor einem Todfeind all dessen, wofür das andere Deutschland gekämpft hat.[690]

Hitzer addresses Heinrich Böll directly and elaborates that these problematic parts of *Gulag* were not a mistake or misunderstanding: it is therefore logical that German right-wingers are praising them.[691]

Hitzer's article and those of his other colleagues[692] in *Kürbiskern* were characterized by Meyer as being a regurgitation of Soviet criticism in her study of the reception of Soviet dissidents.[693] It is not surprising how the similarity in focus and language could have led to this conclusion. But a key difference is that Soviet criticism came to the conclusion that Solzhenitsyn was slandering the Russian nation. German anti-fascists, on the other hand, see the dissident as a Russian nationalist who instrumentalizes politically charged historical inaccuracies. The focal similarities to Soviet propaganda clouded the divergence of both arguments.[694]

Nevertheless, it is understandable that German anti-fascists were irked by Solzhenitsyn's defence of the Vlasovites and therefore directed their criticism at this aspect of his work: in a recent study on the Vlasov movement, Matthias Schröder delineates how the "ROA" has been used to support nationalist and revisionist versions of history in West Germany ever since the war ended.[695] This is the case both in popular memory culture—such as TV shows, documentaries, and novels—and in historiography. Central to this

---

690 Hitzer, 1974, p. 135-136. "The way German anti-fascists were treated by Vlasov's people was in no way different from how they were treated by the SS—whoever calls for solidarity in this case, is calling for the renunciation to a mortal enemy of all that the other Germany fought for." (My translation.)

691 Hitzer, 1974, p. 137.

692 Elvira Högemann-Ledwohn. "Solschenizyn - Erfolgsautor der BRD." Kürbiskern 1. 1973: 108-25; Günter Herburger. "Solschenizyns Wiederkehr." Kürbiskern 2. 1974: 140-1.

693 Meyer, 1985, p. 71-72.

694 This was the case not only for this particular magazine; it is also the case in Wolfgang Gutmann's review of *Gulag* in the anti-fascist journal *Die Tat*. He scrutinizes the veracity of *Gulag*, and interprets the aforementioned passages as ideologically motivated distortions of history. He characterizes *Gulag* as an expression of Solzhentisyn's atavistic vision. Wolfgang Gutmann. "Weder Dichtung noch Wahrheit: Solschenizyns Sehnsucht nach Vergangenheit." Die Tat 19 Januar 1974: 9.

695 Schröder, 2001, pp. 116-129.

interpretation of history are the images of the "decent" German soldiers (or "reasonable Nazis") on the side of Vlasov juxtaposed with that of the "crazy Führer" who missed his chance of winning against the Soviets with the help of collaborators.[696] Schröder criticizes the lack of historical foundation of these claims—including the uncritical use of Nazi memoirs—and the political instrumentalization of the "Vlasov myth" by Germans.[697] As early as 1974, Solzhenitsyn was identified in the conservative press as someone who "commemorated" those Soviet citizens who served Hitler.[698] Historian Joachim Hoffmann's well-known book on the Vlasov Army is a further example of a politicized defense of the movement. Incidentally, Solzhenitsyn is quoted throughout the book.[699] This makes it entirely plausible that German anti-fascists felt compelled to discuss the Vlasov passages in *Gulag* because they considered them relevant to their own, local ideological battles and not necessarily because Moscow prompted them to do so.

Solzhenitsyn's reception among strongly conservative or right-wing Germans shows that these passages from his work, as well as others, could easily be instrumentalized to diminish the magnitude of the crimes of the Nazis.[700] This has a certain irony, as Solzhenitsyn recurrently praised the Germans for their alleged repentance for their crimes and willingness to confront the past. Social-democrat journalist Ulrich Rosenbaum makes the point that some of the Germans who gloated at Solzhenitsyn's praise of the German people and their confrontation of the past were precisely those who were not keen on confronting the past.[701] Joachim Fest's relief that finally someone had "dared" say what was always between-the-lines—that Hitler had just been repeating

---

696 Cf.: Schröder, 2001, p. 117; 122.

697 Schröder, 2001, p. 124-129.

698 Henk Ohnesorge. "Stalin trieb sie unter Hitlers Fahnen." Die Welt 19 Februar 1974: 7.

699 Hoffmann quotes Solzhenitsyn to criticize the British as "treacherous" (p. 294). He refers to Solzhenitsyn when he lists sources that defend the deeds of the Vlasovites *vis à vis* the crimes of the Soviets (p. 306; 310; 367). Hoffmann describes Solzhenitsyn as someone who has done much to disseminate this subject (p. 421). He dedicates his book to several Vlasovites and German Nazis (p. 10). Joachim Hoffmann. *Die Geschichte der Wlassow-Armee.* 1st ed. 27 Vol. Freiburg: Rombach, 1984. About Hoffmann's place in the German revisionist movement, cf.: Wippermann, 1997, p. 68-69.

700 Boll, 2000, p. 337.

701 Rosenbaum, 1974.

what Stalin had already done—is one example.[702] In more extreme cases, Hitler's crimes did not even need to be mentioned, as the article by Igor von Glasenapp about Solzhenitsyn's poem *East Prussian Nights* shows.[703] Solzhenitsyn's poem relates his observations during the war, while he was part of the Red Army. In it, he voices his grief over the violence against the Germans.[704] Glasenapp expresses relief that Solzhenitsyn has spoken for the "violated, pillaged, and plundered" Eastern Prussia, where the Red Army allegedly committed crimes "unimaginable in our era".[705] Of course the excesses of the Red Army in Northern Poland were despicable, but here they become the pinnacle of violence of our era, which they were not. The crimes against humanity committed by the Nazis were not only numerically higher, but they were also the result of gruesome ideological policies and military orders. Racist violence by the Nazis was not only focused in exterminating the Jewish people, but also included atrocities against Slavic peoples:

> Slavic groups living in the Soviet Union—Russians, White Russians, and Ukrainians—were subjected to policies of annihilation from the moment German troops crossed the Soviet boundaries in 1941. Among the earliest victims of conquest were Bolshevik commissars, who were summarily executed, and millions of captured troops, who were starved to death.[706]

The Red Army raped and plundered in isolated incidents against their own policy and as a result of lack of discipline.[707] The German discourse of

702 Fest, 1974.

703 Igor von Glasenapp. "Solschenizyns 'Preussische Nächte'." Criticon 24.1974: 175-6.

704 An excerpt of the poem is the following: "A moaning, by the walls half muffled: The mother's wounded, still alive./ The little daughter's on the mattress, Dead./ How many have been on it? A platoon, a company perhaps?/ A girl's been turned into a woman,/ A woman turned into a corpse." Despite its pathos for the victim, the text is written from a very phallocentric point of view. Alfred M. de Zayas. "Prussian Nights." *The Review of Politics* 40.1 (1978): 154-6. p. 154.

705 His words are: „[...] die unbeschreibliche Tragödie eines Landes und eines Volkes. Unbeschreiblich und unfassbar, denn die Vorstellungskraft der Menschen reicht nicht aus, um zu begreifen, dass so etwas noch in unserem Zeitalter geschehen kann." Glasenapp, 1974, p. 175. "[...] the undescribable tragedy of a land and a people. Undescribable and unfathomable because human imagination is not enough to grasp that something like this can happen in our era." (My translation.)

706 Connelly, 1999, p. 6.

707 Contrary to certain German narratives, violence and disorderly conduct towards the civilian population was expressly forbidden in the Red Army, cf.: Aleksandr S. Seniavskii and Elena S. Seniavskaia. "The Historical Memory of Twentieth-Century

victimhood, which portrays the violence towards Germans at the end of the war as equal—or worse—than what had preceded it, is part of a long-standing revisionist narrative.[708]

Over the decades, German revisionists have continued to find inspiration in Solzhenitsyn's later works.[709] The common denominator between Solzhenitsyn and the German right is an ethnocentric, nationalist narrative which is argued for in similar patterns, and in some cases with the same examples. Historians Ian Kershaw and Moshe Lewin explain:

> Not only German nationalists and apologists for Nazism, but also vehemently anti-communist Russian nationalists, emphasise the extent of Stalinist terror, the one tendency in order to point out that Stalin claimed even more victims than Hitler (as if that excused anything in the horrors perpetrated by Nazism), the other to appropriate to Stalinism genocide of a comparable or even worse kind than that of the Nazis in order to stress the evil they see embodied in communism itself.[710]

Solzhenitsyn and Russian Nationalism

In the 1980s, Solzhenitsyn was successful in convincing scholars and members of the Reagan administration of his vision of Russia's oppression. He often described Russia's plight in such terms as its "annihilation" or "mass slavery".[711] If some assessed this as human-rights activism or concern for the lack of democracy, the post-Soviet years were to reveal Solzhenitsyn's priorities in a crude manner. His rhetoric did not soften but rather became more radical and more focused on concrete issues that show his nationalist

---

Wars as an Arena of Ideological, Political, and Psychological Confrontation." *Russian Studies in History* 49.1 (2010): 53-91. pp. 78-81.

708 Bill Niven. "Implicit Equations in Constructions of German Suffering." *A Nation of Victims? Representations of German Wartime Suffering from 1945 to the Present.* Ed. Helmut Schmitz. 67 Vol. Amsterdam: Rodopi, 2007. 105-123.

709 It is important to note that Solzhenitsyn's later work, *Two Hundred Years Together,* was published in Germany by Herbig Verlag, a publisher that has printed the works of other strongly conservative authors such as Ernst Nolte and the revisionist David Irving.

710 Ian Kershaw and Moshe Lewin. "Introduction: The regimes and their dictators: perspectives of comparison." *Stalinism and Nazism: Dictatorships in Comparison.* Eds. Ian Kershaw and Moshe Lewin. Cambridge: Cambridge University Press, 1997. p. 8.

711 For example: "The third and final revolution is irrevocably underway, with Brezhnev's bulldozer bent on scraping Russia from the face of the earth." Solzhenitsyn, 1980, p. 811.

preoccupations.[712] Therefore, it seems unlikely that the hyperbole and ethnocentrism of his earlier pronouncements were merely the result of the perceived communist threat.

Nationalism can be defined as an ideology which considers the "nation" to be the peak of its loyalty and determines the legitimacy of a government by its adherence to nationalist principles.[713] A nationalist ideology defines who belongs to the nation, which are the legitimate geographical borders of this nation, and what type of politics is the most adequate for it.[714] Not all forms of nationalism are revisionist. Nationalism becomes revisionist under certain circumstances, as is the case in some of Solzhenitsyn's work and his reception. Irredentist rhetoric regarding changing borders is typical of revisionist narratives.

In Russia, as in Germany, anti-Semitism has been a recurrent part of nationalism, because the gentile nationalist population has used the image of the Jews as a reference point to define their own nationhood.[715] As I will show, nationalism, revisionism, and anti-Semitism are closely linked with each other as they appear in both Solzhenitsyn's work, and parts of his reception.

Solzhenitsyn can be understood as a nationalist writer because his work gives evidence for the following points which, together, form the core of a nationalist outlook:

a) His belief in the existence of a Russian nation as a unit based on a specific religion, attached to a certain territory and a certain culture.

---

712 Judith Devlin. *Slavophiles and Commissars: Enemies of Democracy in Modern Russia.* Basingstoke: McMillan, 1999. p. 65-70.

713 I work with Yitzhak Brudny's definition of nationalism, as used in his study about Russian nationalism in the second half of the 20th century, cf.: Yitzhak M. Brudny. *Reinventing Russia: Russian Nationalism and the Soviet State, 1953 - 1991.* Cambridge, Mass.: Harvard University Press, 1998.

714 Cf. Brudny, 1998.

715 Vadim Rossman. *Russian Intellectual Antisemitism in the Post-communist Era.* Lincoln and London: Published by the University of Nebraska Press for the Vidal Sassoon International Center for the Study of Antisemitism SICSA, the Hebrew University of Jerusalem, 2002; Klaus Holz. *Nationaler Antisemitismus: Wissenssoziologie einer Weltanschauung.* Hamburg: Hamburger Ed., 2001; Laqueur, 1993.

b) His heightened sense of exclusivity as to who belongs to the nation and who has the right to become involved in its politics.

c) His conviction that the Russian nation comes first and that trespasses against this nation are graver than those against others.

Central to Solzhenitsyn's nationalist claims is his view that the Russian nation has been the main victim of Soviet communism,[716] and that communism was imposed upon it largely by foreign elements.[717] By arguing that no one has suffered more than the Russians since the Bolsheviks came to power, Solzhenitsyn is laying the foundations for the justification of a different type of government that looks primarily after Russians' interests (as he defines them).[718] This is one of the central narratives that make his work ideological, as Eagleton has pointed out: ideas that seek to protect the power interests of certain groups can constitute an ideology.[719] It is not the fact itself that he makes moral or political pronouncements that is ideological, but the function they have in his work.

His idea of nation becomes revisionistic when Solzhenitsyn claims that other countries belong to Russia, as he did repeatedly from 1990 onwards.[720] After his return to Russia in 1994, his advocacy for a so-called "reunification" with Ukraine, Belarus, and North Kazakhstan became even more vocal.[721] Solzhenitsyn's worry for the Russian nation increased and in 1995 he went so far as to claim that Russians were the only people with no right of self-determination—even while Russia was waging war against Chechen independence.[722] In doing this, Solzhenitsyn embeds his narrative in local Russian revisionistic debates. At the same time he interacts with Western audiences: he tries to convince other countries of his position, and his foreign readers can identify his position as similar to or different from their own.

---

716 "Each of the [Soviet] republics was exploited without mercy, but the ultimate degree of exploitation was reached in the RSFSR, and today the most poverty-stricken rural areas of the U.S.S.R. are the Russian villages." in Solzhenitsyn, 1980, p. 813.

717 This is the central thought in: Solzhenitsyn, 2002, vol. 2.

718 Solzhenitsyn, 1974, vol.1; Solzhenitsyn, 1980.

719 Eagleton, 2007, p. 30.

720 I have already mentioned this view as expressed in his political pamphlet *How to Rebuild Russia* in the subchapter "Solzhenitsyn's Reception upon the Collapse of European Communism" in chapter 3.

721 Devlin, 1999, p. 69.

722 Devlin, 1999, p. 69.

In an interview for the US magazine *Forbes*, when asked about Ukrainian independence, Solzhenitsyn explained his position using US-right-wing rhetoric:

> Forbes: Well, what about Ukraine? Hasn't Russia made threats toward several of the former U.S.S.R. member states?
>
> Solzhenitsyn: Imagine that one not-very-fine day, two or three of your states in the Southwest, in the space of 24 hours, declare themselves independent of the U.S. They declare themselves a fully sovereign nation, decreeing that Spanish will be the only language. All English-speaking residents, even if their ancestors have lived there for 200 years, have to take a test in the Spanish language within one or two years and to swear allegiance to the new nation. Otherwise they will not receive citizenship and be deprived of civic, property and employment rights.
>
> What would be the reaction of the United States? I have no doubt that it would be immediate military intervention.
>
> But today Russia faces precisely this scenario. In 24 hours she lost eight to ten purely Russian provinces, 25 million ethnic Russians, who have ended up in this very way— as 'undesirable aliens.'[723]

This shows how Solzhenitsyn has contributed to his own "adoption" by strongly conservative—and even right-wing observers. Until then, a number of right-wing scholars and writers had already noted Solzhenitsyn's conservative worldview, but after 1991, the Russian author was less inhibited with regard to more controversial issues. It does not mean that he became unable to adapt his message to his audience: in a similar interview in 1994 with *Der Spiegel* he uses the division of the two Germanys as a metaphor for the "injustice" of the new borders.[724] By using such an uncontroversial example, Solzhenitsyn could at least expect a positive reaction. In the more

723 Paul Klebnikov. "'Zhirinovsky is an Evil Caricature of a Russian Patriot'." Forbes 9 May 1994.

724 "SOLSCHENIZYN: Die Abtrennung der Ukraine, von Belorußland und Kasachstan weckt in uns genauso ein Gefühl wie bei Ihnen wahrscheinlich damals die Trennung von Ostdeutschland.
SPIEGEL: Die DDR-Bürger wurden nie nach ihrem Einverständnis gefragt." Rudolf Augstein, Fritjof Meyer, and Jörg Mettke. "'Wie ein Sekretär des Volkes'." Der Spiegel 31 October 1994: 139-63. "SOLZHENITSYN: The separation of the Ukraine, of Belarus, and Kazakhstan evokes in us exactly the same feeling that the separation of Eastern Germany probably did in you back then. SPIEGEL: The citizens of the GDR were never asked for their consent." (My translation.)

conservative press, his call for a revision of the borders was likened to the German loss of the Baltics and Eastern Prussia.[725]

Solzhenitsyn's image of Russia is that of a Greater Russia, very much like the Tsarist Empire. His vision of "the Russian" is also adapted from that of pre-revolutionary Russia. For him, Orthodox Christianity, the Russian language, and a certain type of culture define a Russian. He rejects any type of continuity from the Tsarist era to the Soviet one. For example, the ruthless russification campaigns that were carried out during the Soviet era are explained by Solzhenitsyn as an affront to Russians, because the Soviets had decided to "rape" their language by making it the official language of the Union.[726] In practical terms, his definition of a Russian means that the Soviet leadership was not Russian because its members were either foreign or simply did not count as Russians (because they were not believers). In this way, Solzhenitsyn can argue:

> To begin with, the West's vision has been obscured by the false cliché according to which the Russians are the 'ruling nationality' of the U.S.S.R. They are no such thing and never have been at any time since 1917. For the first 15 years of Soviet power it fell to the Russians, Ukrainians and Byelorussians to bear the crippling, devastating blow of communism (the declining birth rates of recent years have their roots in that period), and in the process their upper classes, clergy, cultural tradition and intelligentsia, as well as the main food-producing section of the peasantry, were wiped out almost without trace.[727]

In several of his historical books, Solzhenitsyn has tried to prove how and why the revolutions of February and October 1917 cannot be understood to be the result of Russian revolutionary endeavor. From *the Red Wheel* to *Two Hundred Years Together* Solzhenitsyn has meticulously delineated how foreigners and anti-Russian sons of Russia have "destroyed Russia".[728]

---

725 Wolfgang Kasack. "Solschenizyns Patriotismus." Die politische Meinung 40. 1995: 71-5.

726 "The decision to retain Russian as the official language was purely mechanical; one language after all had to serve in this capacity. The sole effect of this use of Russian has been to defile the language; it has not encouraged Russians to think of themselves as masters: just because a rapist addresses his victim in her own language, this does not make it any less of a rape." Solzhenitsyn, 1980, p. 812.

727 Solzhenitsyn, 1980, p. 812.

728 Yohanan Petrovsky-Shtern. *Lenin's Jewish Question.* New Haven: Yale University Press, 2010. p. 164.

Solzhenitsyn played an important role in the demythologization of Lenin.[729] Unfortunately, he bases some of his arguments on ethnicity. Like many other conservative Russian authors, Solzhenitsyn emphasizes Lenin's murky ethnic origin as proof of his disloyalty.[730] This has earned him praise in the West, for example from conservative literary critic Ericson who writes that, in *Lenin in Zurich*, Solzhenitsyn was able to "fathom Lenin's soul"—a man Ericson also considers to be a "deracinated intellectual".[731]

There is an ethically problematic aspect of a nationalist interpretation of history as performed by Solzhenitsyn and this becomes more evident when he touches the subjects of Jews in Russia.

> One may claim that Russian conservative writers from Menshikov and Shulgin to Kozhinov and Solzhenitsyn failed to think critically, my point is that they failed to think historically. They called themselves Russian historians, implying that they could speak and think about history in a particularly Russian way. As a result they created a xenophobic, anti-Semitic, imperialistic discourse that might very well be Russian but it is hardly historical.[732]

The Western reception of Solzhenitsyn's nationalism is limited to the usefulness of the narrative in a local context. However, the fact that he makes use of topoi that place him in the realm of right-wing debates has served as a basis for the international attention he has received from the right, as I show in the concrete case that follows in the next section.

Solzhenitsyn and "the Jews"

A sociological definition of anti-Semitism is that of Klaus Holz, which consists of the assignment of certain characteristics to "Jews", their perception as foreign or inimical, and the negative judgement of them as a group.[733] Historically, there are recurring characteristics that have been attached to the Jews in order to vilify them.[734] One of the most common anti-Jewish

---

729 Laqueur, 1993, p. 155.

730 Petrovsky-Shtern, 2010, p. 164ff.

731 Ericson, 1980, p. 140.

732 Petrovsky-Shtern, 2010, p. 167-168.

733 Holz, 2001, p. 38.

734 Rudolph Loewenstein. "Anti-Semites in Psychoanalysis." Ed. Werner Bergmann. 2 Vol. Berlin: de Gruyter, 1988. 35-51. Ulrich Herbeck. *Das Feindbild vom 'jüdischen Bolschewiken' zur Geschichte des russischen Antisemitismus vor und während der Russischen Revolution.* Berlin: Metropol-Verlag, 2009.

stereotypes in the 20th century was that of the "Jewish Bolshevik". It is true that some Jews took part in the Bolshevik movement, but the idea of the "Jewish Bolshevik" goes beyond this fact. Historian Jonathan Frankel describes the implications:

> The theory that the Bolshevik seizure of power in Russia was part of a plot by the Jewish people methodically to subvert the social system in order then to take control of the entire world constituted from the first a key element in Nazi ideology. It was thus *a*, perhaps *the*, primary justification, in Nazi thinking and in popular attitudes (in so far as they were involved), which made the Holocaust possible.[735]

Frankel adds that Jews were never majority in the Cheka or the Bolshevik party, and their percentage was similar to their percentage in the population.[736] Still, Solzhenitsyn alleges that Jews were playing a dominant role.

Already in Solzhenitsyn's most famous work—*The Gulag Archipelago*—the reader becomes acquainted with this idea. Although it is true that the central theme of the book is to protocol the longevity of the Soviet prison camp system and therefore condemn communism as a whole, it contains other ideological arguments too. One of them was that the prison camp system was thought up by Naftaly Frenkel, a "Jew" who hated Russia. Because Solzhenitsyn argues that forced labor did not exist in Russia before 1917, it makes the claim all the more sensational.[737] Unfortunately the author keeps silent about the sources of his information, making his characterization even more problematic.

Solzhenitsyn starts by saying that there is a legend that Naftaly Frenkel thought up the camps, and he sets out to clarify this allegation which he sarcastically calls "unpatriotic".[738] Then he tells the story as if he knew the facts. According to Solzhenitsyn, Frenkel was a Turkish Jew born in Constantinople. However, until today, Frenkel's ethnic/religious origin is unknown; what is known is that his prison registration card states that he was born in Haifa, in the Ottoman Empire.[739] But Solzhenitsyn gives us a very

---

735 Frankel, 2010, p. 170.
736 Frankel, 2010, p. 174-5.
737 Cf.: Solzhenitsyn, 1974, vol. 1, p. 456-458; Solzhenitsyn, 1975, vol. 3, p. 95-96.
738 Solzhenitsyn, 1975, vol. 2, p. 75.
739 Applebaum, 2004, p. 32. Being born in Haifa during Ottoman rule does not imply a Jewish background, he may have had German Christian origin, for instance.

detailed account of who this man was—even before he came to Russia. Following a tale of how Frenkel the trader became a millionaire, Solzhenitsyn writes how he published a newspaper to slander his competitors, and how he was a speculative arms dealer in Gallipoli. After 1917, "some fateful force beckoned him to the Red power."[740] Solzhenitsyn goes on with this list of misdeeds, until he comes to tell us of how, after landing in a camp as a convict, he was immediately put in a privileged position there and was even flown to a meeting with Stalin. Solzhenitsyn writes that Frenkel and Stalin talked for three hours but that:

> The stenographic report of this conversation will never become public. There simply was none. But it is clear that Frenkel unfolded before the Father of the Peoples dazzling prospects for constructing socialism through the use of prison labor. Much of the geography of the Archipelago being described in the aftermath by my obedient pen, he sketched in bold strokes on a map of the Soviet Union to the accompaniment of the puffing of his interlocutor's pipe.[741]

Solzhenitsyn claims that Frenkel was the "nerve of the Archipelago",[742] that he planned the use of prison labor to construct socialism, and even suggests that what he writes in the very book we are reading was cooked up by Frenkel in front of Stalin. But, how does he know all this, if there was no record of the meeting, and he was not there?

Solzhenitsyn then points out that he has added a portrait of Naftaly Frenkel to the book we have in our hands. He writes: "It is evident from his face how he brimmed with a vicious human-hating animus."[743] A further disturbing part of what he does is not only that he seems to derive evil from looks, but that he placed Naftaly Frenkel on a page in which we see the picture of five other alleged Gulag administrators (who are not mentioned in the immediate context of the text)—all of whom have Jewish-sounding names.[744] The two names that stand out are that of Frenkel, who has just been introduced to us by Solzhenitsyn, and the infamous Yagoda, who was the chief of the Soviet secret police from 1934-36. Because no further explanation is offered, the

740 Solzhenitsyn, 1975, vol. 2, p. 77.
741 Solzhenitsyn, 1975, vol. 2, p. 78.
742 Solzhenitsyn, 1975, vol. 2, p. 76.
743 Solzhenitsyn, 1975, vol. 2, p. 80.
744 Solzhenitsyn, 1975, vol. 2, p. 79.

layout of the images seems to suggest all these men share something in common. Nathan Larson explains how this is problematic:

> Being that Jews are a minority in this post, and being pictures very scarcely used in this work, it seems hardly a coincidence that Solzhenitsyn puts such an emphasis on Jews – in picture and in the text.[745]

The suggestion that Jews dominated the Soviet secret service is not only discordant with historical evidence, it is precisely an anti-Semitic enemy image related to that of the "Jewish Bolshevik."[746] These stereotypes were exploited to justify the pogroms of the Russian Civil War and violence against Jews during World War II.[747] This makes Solzhenitsyn's allusions seem not only tendentious, but almost incendiary.[748] But Solzhenitsyn does not leave it at that. Later on in the text, Solzhenitsyn, who promises the reader that he will later explain his "hypothesis" about what fateful force drew Frenkel to the Soviet Union (p. 77), continues to tell us about him (pp.138-141). Here, Solzhenitsyn again describes a meeting between Stalin "the evil king" with Frenkel "the evil sorcerer".[749] Frenkel allegedly agreed to help Stalin plan the building of a railroad to Finland, with the condition that he would be freed from the gulag and declared head of a new "empire" of prison laborers.[750] Again, here Solzhenitsyn suggests that Frenkel had a key role in the creation and expansion of the Soviet prison labor system, an unsubstantiated allegation.[751] Solzhenitsyn repeatedly uses further anti-Semitic stereotypes in describing Frenkel: of him being a "speculator", of having a special talent for

---

745 Nathan D. Larson. *Aleksandr Solzhenitsyn and the Modern Russo-Jewish Question.* Ed. Andreas Umland. 14 Vol. Stuttgart: Ibidem-Verlag, 2005. p. 31-32. There are only a handful of pages with pictures in the almost two thousand pages of *Gulag*, and only a couple with pictures of people.

746 Cf.: Herbeck, 2009, p. 442; Jonathan Frankel. "The 'Non-Jewish' Jews Revisited. Solzhenitsyn and the Issue of National Guilt." *Insiders and Outsiders: Dilemmas of East European Jewry.* Eds. Richard I. Cohen, Jonathan Frankel, and Stefani Hoffman. Oxford: The Littman Library of Jewish Civilization, 2010. 166-187. Laqueur, 1993, p. 170.

747 Lustiger, 1998, p. 58.

748 In later works these allusions have factual character, as is the case in: Alexander Solschenizyn, *Zweihundert Jahre zusammen: Die Juden in der Sowjetunion*. Vol. 2. 2. ed. Munich: Herbig, 2004. (For example in p. 378).

749 These are the words he uses. Solzhenitsyn, 1975, vol. 2, p. 139.

750 Solzhenitsyn, 1975, vol. 2, p. 139.

751 Anne Applebaum points out that Solzhenitsyn gives Frenkel too much responsibility and influence in the creation and expansion of the gulag. Applebaum, 2004, p. 32-33.

commerce,[752] of being "[l]ike Trotsky" who "always lived aboard trains".[753] Most important is of course the suggestion that he is part of some Jewish tribe of camp guards. When Solzhenitsyn offers his conclusion that he has "the feeling that he [Frenkel] really hated this country!" it is difficult not to understand it as a result of his "Jewish", and hence (allegedly) foreign, origin.[754]

The description of Naftaly Frenkel's role in the Soviet prison system in *The Gulag Archipelago* is an example of why his lack of source disclosure can become polemical. Solzhenitsyn makes outrageous allegations that fit into the mold of old anti-Semitic stereotypes, but how and why did he come to these claims? There is a tension between the lofty intention of keeping alive the memory of the dead and making chimerical allegations about what brought about this system of oppression. If his sources were known, one could identify to what degree these sources were faulty or if they were propaganda of some sort. But by keeping them secret, Solzhenitsyn becomes the sole author of these allegations and must be considered as responsible for them.

Solzhenitsyn's innuendos that Jews had a special role in creating the Soviet system of terror have played into Russian nationalist conspiracy theories, but they are also part of German revisionist narratives and conspiracy theories. Germans did not need Solzhenitsyn to come up with the images of "Jewish Bolsheviks" or the so-called "Jewish Cheka"—as I mentioned before, these were common stereotypes since the Nazi era. Nevertheless, his claims in *Gulag* and in later works have played to these arguments and, in some cases, have been used to legitimize these claims. Not only the allegation of "Jewish guilt", but also Solzhenitsyn's exaggerations about the scope of repression in the Soviet Union have come in handy for such purposes.

---

752 Solzhenitsyn, 1975, vol. 2, p. 77, 78, 139-141. Already in the first volume of *Gulag*, Solzhenitsyn identifies "primordial commerce" as the "bread and butter" and "pastime" of the Jews: Solzhenitsyn, 1974, vol. 1, p. 441.

753 The only thing that Frenkel could have had in common with Trotsky was that Trotsky was of Jewish origin. By suggesting that "both lived in trains"—which they did not do literally—, Solzhenitsyn creates an image akin to that of a modern "Wandering Jew".

754 Solzhenitsyn, 1975, vol. 2, p. 141. This insinuation becomes more caustic upon reading other texts in which Solzhenitsyn accuses Jews of hating Russia and wanting to harm it: Solzhenitsyn, 1980, especially pp. 808ff; Solzhenitsyn, 1985, especially pp. 21-23. (See also: Toker, 2000, p. 122.)

In *Gulag*, Solzhenitsyn claims that many groups of people were annihilated because of their origin. He particularly emphasizes the fate of rich peasants (*kulaki*), and claims that all of them—young and old—were killed by the Soviets because of their origin, just as Hitler later did with the Jews. He writes:

> This was the *first* such experiment-at least in modern history. It was subsequently repeated by Hitler with the Jews, and again by Stalin with nationalities which were disloyal to him or suspected by him.[755]

It is well-documented that rich peasants were not all killed for their origin, or even sent to the prison camps *in toto*, and that the nationalities repressed by Stalin were not executed like the Jews by the Nazis.[756] The cruel deportation of rich peasants was indeed unprecedented in Russian history, but it is quite different to Solzhenitsyn's picture. Historian Steven Barnes describes the life of *kulaki* in exile thus:

> They came with their family, but children were able to leave once they had their passport (16 years). They had to earn their living, they were allowed to have gardens, but they had to pay a tax for the upkeep of the settlement. Invalids, old people and pregnant women without a husband were given supplies for free.[757]

In 1936, their rights were restored.[758] This is very far from the treatment the Jews received in the Nazi era. The deportation of different nationalities in the Soviet Union during World War II was indeed a harrowing ordeal; unfortunately, many of these nationalities had already suffered mass deportation and forced famine under the Tsars.[759] Therefore, this particular example makes Solzhenitsyn's argument of primacy seem weaker. Another of Solzhenitsyn's examples concerns the Spanish children of the Civil War, who had come to the country as refugees. He claims that they, too, were deported.[760] This group of people was not deported nor interned in prison

---

755 Solzhenitsyn, 1974, vol. 1, p. 55.

756 Cf.: Lynne Viola. "The Other Archipelago: Kulak Deportations to the North in 1930." *Slavic Review* 60.4 (2001): 730-755; Kaznelson, 2007.

757 Barnes, 2011, p. 23.

758 Barnes, 2011, p. 24.

759 On the historical treatment of peoples of the Caucasus, cf.: John B. Dunlop. *Russia confronts Chechnya: Roots of a Separatist Conflict.* Cambridge: Cambridge University Press, 1998; Georgi Chochiev. "On the History of the North Caucasian Diaspora in Turkey." *Iran & the Caucasus* 11.2 (2007): 213-26.

760 Solzhenitsyn, 1974, vol.1, p. 86.

camps.[761] According to the historian Immaculada Colomina Limonero the Spaniards who did go to prison camp were sent there for individual reasons.[762]

Solzhenitsyn's exaggerations regarding the amount of people repressed, or the reasons why they were abused or killed, make the Soviet Union seem incomparably worse than anything before it. When this hyperbole is taken literally and then combined with his claim that Jews were behind this machine of repression, it can become incendiary.

Already by 1987, German historian Ernst Nolte had published an article in which he argued precisely that the Nazis would not have perpetrated genocide against the Jews if they had not been afraid that the communists would do the same to them.[763] This claim sparked the heated debate among German historians and intellectuals known as the "Historians Quarrel". Historians and other intellectuals, such as Dan Diner and Jürgen Habermas, criticized this view for its lack of historical evidence and racist undertones.[764] Others pointed at its ignorance of all evidence that ideologically, Hitler's and other Germans' exterminational anti-Semitism predated the Soviet gulag: the topos of the 'Jewish Bolshevik' was not the trigger of this type of anti-Semitism but it was one propaganda tool among many.[765] Nevertheless, Nolte continues to stick to this argument.

In 2002, Nolte makes use of Solzhenitsyn's reputation and *Gulag* to buttress his claims that Hitler's deeds were "puerile" compared to Stalin's.[766] He also draws from *Gulag* to prove that Hitler and Goebbel's fear of "Jewish Bolsheviks" was justified.[767] Nolte claims that *Gulag* and Stephane Courtois' *Black Book of Communism* make it undeniable that there is a "causal nexus"

---

761 Immaculada Colomina Limonero. *Dos Patrias, Tres Mil Destinos: vida y exilio de los niños de la guerra de España refugiados en la Unión Soviética.* Ed. Alicia Alted Vigil. 1st ed. 3 Vol. Madrid: Cinca, 2010.

762 Those who were imprisoned were charged with stealing or similar crimes, something few disputed, cf.: Colomina Limonero, 2010, p. 86ff.

763 Nolte, 1987.

764 Cf.: Diner, "Aporie", 1987, pp. 62-73; Habermas, 1987; Habermas, 1988.

765 Kershaw and Lewin delineate how initial exterminational anti-Semitic arguments (for example in *Mein Kampf*) did not base their case on "Jewish Bolshevism". Cf.: Kershaw, 1997, p. 6-7.

766 Nolte, 2002, p. 58.

767 Nolte, 2002, p. 230-231.

between the fear of communism and the Shoah.[768] He does not deny that the Shoah took place, or that anti-Semitism was its motivation, but he asks his readers for some sympathy towards the Nazis who allegedly acted out of fear of a "Jewish Bolshevik" threat.[769] The German historian uses the term "Jewish Bolshevism" in quotation marks, but not to distance himself from it:

> Ich bin daher überzeugt, dass der Begriff »jüdischer Bolschewismus« nicht bloss eine bösartige Erfindung zu politischen Zwecken darstellt, sondern dass er geschichtlich gut genug begründet ist, um nicht von der Wissenschaft ausgeschlossen zu werden, wie grauenhaft die nationalsozialistische Konsequenz auch gewesen ist.[770]

Nolte's linkage of Judaism with Bolshevism and his attempt to justify the Nazis' ideological obsession with this idea seem to try to at least lessen—if not exonerate—the guilt of the German genocide against the Jews. Nolte is known to be a part of the German "New Right".[771] However, similar arguments—to different degrees—are made relatively often in Germany, even by scholars who do not identify themselves directly with the Right. The resulting minimization of Nazi crimes is seldom accidental, especially in a scholarly environment. Historian Wolfgang Wippermann has pointed out that, although comparisons between Nazism and communism may have multiple motives, a significant one is the relativization of German guilt and a sign of "putting the past behind".[772] It is precisely the way that the Shoah has been relativized through tendentious comparisons with the gulag that makes claims of "supremacy-in-horror" of the gulag seem suspect.

For example, in several articles the literary critic Wolfgang Kissel has attempted to portray the gulag as an "unprecedented" *Zivilisationsbruch*—a

---

768 Nolte, 2002, p. 231.

769 Nolte, 2002, p. 232.

770 Nolte, 2002, p. 233-234. "I am therefore convinced that the term 'Jewish Bolshevik' is not solely a malicious invention for political purposes but that it has sufficient foundation in historical evidence in order not to be cast out of science [the scientific community], no matter how harrowing the national socialist consequence was." (My translation, my clarification in brackets.)

771 Cf.: Richard Stöss. *Die 'neue Rechte' in der Bundesrepublik.* Berlin: Friedich Ebert Stiftung, 2000.

772 Wolfgang Wippermann. *Wessen Schuld? vom Historikerstreit zur Golhagen-Kontroverse.* Berlin: Elephanten Press, 1997. p. 9.

term coined by historian Dan Diner to describe the Shoah.[773] He bases this statement on Solzhenitsyn's work: „Im *Archipel GULag* wird erstmal das ganze Ausmaß eines präzedenzlosen Zivilisationsbruches sichtbar."[774] He attributes Solzhenitsyn with the uncovering of a series of genocides committed in the Soviet Union which serve as proof of the singularity of this "breach of civilization". However, the fact that he uses *Gulag*'s ahistorical examples—such as the alleged genocide of Russian peasants[775]—, as well as hyperbolic claims—for example, that the Cheka was a historically unique punitive organ—to make his point align his narrative with common revisionist narratives. Moreover, adopting the rhetorical means that are used to define the Nazi extermination of the Jews to describe something that was comparatively less grave can be misleading.[776]

In the case of Kissel, as in Nolte's, it seems that these authors make use of Solzhenitsyn's claims to "confirm" something that they were already convinced of. It is likely that utilizing Solzhenitsyn's untarnished reputation seems a convenient way of expressing these thoughts—despite the dissident's dwindling fame in the West.

Historian Dietrich Beyrau has recently published an article in which he explains why Solzhenitsyn's *Two Hundred Years Together* has had a difficult reception abroad.[777] In his analysis, he divides Eastern and Western Europe as two entities with different types of nationalism and different types of memory. While he sees Western Europe (including Germany) to have an

---

773 Wolfgang S. Kissel. "Der Zivilisationsbruch als Kategorie der russischen Kultur- und Literaturgeschichte." *Literaturforschung heute.* Ed. Wolfgang Klein. Berlin: Akademie Verlag, 1999. 153-164; Kissel, 2000. The term translates as: breach of civilization.

774 Kissel, 2000, p. 98. "For the first time, the entire magnitude of an unprecedented breach of civilization becomes visible in *Gulag Archipelago.*" (My translation.)

775 He also does so in his earlier article, Kissel, 1999, p. 161.

776 Rhetorically, the gulag can be used in a similar way, with similarly confusing results. For example, when Amnesty International criticized the US' Guantánamo detention center in Cuba as the "gulag of our time" both conservatives and liberals in the US not only rejected the metaphor, but refused to engage with the content of its criticism. The difference in magnitude was deemed too great. Cf.: David Bosco. "Gulag Vs Guantanamo." The New Republic 3 June 2005; Cathy Young. "Guantánamo is not the Gulag." The New York Times 10 June 2005.

777 Dietrich Beyrau. "Solschenizyn über die Juden im sowjetischen Experiment." *Put' Solzhenitsyna v kontekste Bolshogo Vremeni. Sbornik Pamiati 1918 - 2008.* Ed. Liudmila I. Saraskina. Russkii Put', 2009. 226-242.

inclusive and malleable type of nationalism which is compatible with liberalism, the East, however, has an organic type of nationalism which personifies the nation and allows it to be perceived as owning a moral quality.[778] Beyrau argues that the memory of the Shoah is part of Western culture and the memory of the Jews as communist perpetrators belongs to the East. Beyrau seems to argue that Eastern Europeans have a right to practice the "memory" of this non-existing phenomenon, because they have an illiberal type of nationalism. He compares the historical fact of the Shoah—which in fact took place *mainly* in Eastern Europe, but which has been recently remembered more strongly in the West—and the anti-Semitic rumors about Jewish communists in Solzhenitsyn's works and in other Eastern European texts.[779] He ignores both the ahistoricity of the latter form of memory, and the fact that the stereotype of the "Jewish Bolshevik" is also part of German history—and is therefore not specifically Eastern European. His leniency towards Eastern European nationalist memory culture may be part of a broader phenomenon of displaying more tolerance towards anti-Semitic claims when they are made by Russians than when they are made at home, in Germany. This may be why precisely Solzhenitsyn's word—as a respected Russian Nobel Prize winner—is used in the West to add special weight to revisionist arguments, albeit with mixed results.

The German scholar of memory studies, Aleida Assmann, argues that the Historians' Quarrel was not the beginning of a type of discourse, but a process in which the decades-long West German narrative of German suffering as a counterweight to the crimes against the Jews was finally polemicized.[780] After the Quarrel, attempts to relativize the crimes of the Nazis in Germany were not as easily accepted by public opinion. If Nolte did not feel the need to buttress his arguments with as prestigious a name as Solzhenitsyn's in 1987, this was no longer the case in 2002, as I have shown.

Another prominent example of this phenomenon is the case of Martin Hohmann. When Hohmann, a politician from the German Christian Democratic Party (CDU), tried to belittle German guilt in World War II by

---

778 Beyrau, 2009, p. 238-239.
779 Beyrau, 2009, p. 226-237.
780 Aleida Assmann. "On the (in)Compatibility of Guilt and Suffering in German Memory." *German Life and Letters* 59.2 (2006): p. 190-191.

pointing to the alleged guilt of the Jews in the Soviet Union in a speech on the German national holiday, a scandal broke out.[781] Strikingly, he defended himself by pointing to Solzhenitsyn's findings in *Two Hundred Years Together.*[782] After a long discussion and increasing public pressure, Hohmann was finally expelled from the CDU.

Nonetheless, Assmann argues that the German tendency to emphasize German suffering in the war and its aftermath, and leave all other aspects of the war in the background, is regaining popularity: "Today perhaps it is German suffering which once again pushes aside memories of the Holocaust and blunts the consciousness of German guilt."[783] This shows an ethnocentric aspect of historical memory, which is analogous to that of Russian conservatives, such as Solzhenitsyn. Solzhenitsyn draws an inflated picture of the suffering Russians, and even when he admits to other peoples being victims of oppression, he continues to place the blame on non-Russians. The similarity in the narratives and their weak historical base show how Russian and German nationalisms are not as different from each other as Dietrich Beyrau argues. The fact that Russian nationalist rhetoric supplements German nationalist (and revisionist) arguments makes it all the more important to understand this as an international phenomenon with similar repercussions.

Because Solzhenitsyn uses methods analogous to those of revisionist Germans—by playing a zero-sum game of guilt and victimhood—it is probable that he will continue to have a favored reception among this group of people. His rhetoric is useful to German nationalists to a certain extent, but beyond certain limits it is only useful to Russian nationalists.

Solzhenitsyn's vision of Russian history goes beyond the time of the Soviet Union. The main bulk of his work focuses on the pre-revolutionary era. His series of historical novels—*The Red Wheel*—is an attempt at explaining how it was that a fully functioning state could end up on the wrong path. In the

---

781 N.N. "Antisemitismus Affäre: 'Dann haben wir ein Problem'." Stern 5 November 2003. Hans Peter Schütz. "Hohmann-Affäre: Lupenreiner Goebbels." Stern 12 November 2003. Bartosz Jalowiecki. "Lies the Germans Tell Themselves." Commentary January 2004: 43-6.

782 Harry Nutt. "Projekt der Entschuldung. Hohmann und das 'Tätervolk'." Frankfurter Rundschau 6 November 2003.

783 Assmann, 2006, p. 193.

mid-1980s, Solzhenitsyn published a re-written version of one of the volumes of this series, called *August 1914.* In this book, he explains in detail the beginning of Russia's woes. Solzhenitsyn dedicates a large portion of the book to the description of Prime Minister Pyotr Stolypin's policies and then his death at the hands of an assassin. With this work, he contributed to a "renaissance" of interest in Stolypin.[784] But, more controversially, he identified Stolypin's murder—Dmitrii Bogrov—as a Jew acting on Jewish motives. In the US, this ignited a series of controversies about anti-Semitic undertones in the volume. The way the debates unfolded is very telling about the difficulties of discussing anti-Semitism in the work of an established literary authority like Solzhenitsyn.

For decades, there had been (often unspecified) allusions to the impression gained by some readers that some of Solzhenitsyn's works are anti-Semitic in nature. However, countless scholars and journalists have defended Solzhenitsyn from what they see as an unfounded accusation.

In 1985, *New York Times* contributor Richard Grenier made an effort to defend Solzhenitsyn from historian Richard Pipes' alleged accusation of anti-Semitism made at a conference in the US that year.[785] Pipes is quoted as saying that Solzhenitsyn's portrayal of political assassin Dmitrii Bogrov as a Jew acting on behalf of Jewish interests is historically inaccurate, as he was a renegade who was differently motivated.[786] He places this idea in the context of other Russian nationalists' thought, which see the revolutionary movement in Russia as a Jewish enterprise. Without going into Pipes' arguments, Grenier quotes a large number of scholars and people he identifies as Jews who claim that it is "ludicrous" and "unfair" to say Solzhenitsyn is anti-Semitic. Among others, he presents historian Adam Ulam's opinion, whom he paraphrases as saying that the depiction of Bogrov (Premier Minister Pyotr Stolypin's murderer) could "lend itself" to an anti-Semitic interpretation—probably because of his demonizing description—but that one should look at the Russian author's work as "a whole".[787] Ulam concludes that Solzhenitsyn

---

784 Laqueur, 1993, p. 121.

785 Richard Grenier. "Solzhenitsyn and Anti-Semitism: A New Debate." The New York Times 13 November 1985: 21.

786 Quoted in: Grenier, 1985.

787 Quoted in: Grenier, 1985.

resents "foreign influence" in Russia—meaning that of the Jews—but that this is not anti-Semitic. Slavicist Seth Wolitz responded to this article with a letter in which he decried Grenier's method of not discussing the content of the criticism he was trying to rebuke, but simply presenting the opinion of prestigious scholars and famous Jewish personalities in order to clear Solzhenitsyn's name.[788] Wolitz contends that being Jewish does not "guarantee necessarily superior interpretative competence based on genetics or ethnicity". Wolitz maintains that what Ulam describes—the image of the Jews as outsiders—does in fact "sound like classical cultural political anti-Semitism".

But this was not the first time Solzhenitsyn's view was defended. In the early 1980s, when Solzhenitsyn's fellow prison mate Lev Kopelev wrote in his memoirs how Solzhenitsyn claimed that Jews were not real Russians, Schapiro defended this view, saying that the refusal to see assimilated Jews as Russians was not anti-Semitism.[789] He added that it was unlikely that Solzhenitsyn would make folksy anti-Semitic claims.

These discussions are a good example of how different definitions of anti-Semitism and different perceptions of history can affect how we categorize texts. Solzhenitsyn's own views and newer studies on his anti-Semitism further illustrate this problem.

Solzhenitsyn was aware that some of his readers believed him to be anti-Semitic, and was reminded of this by several journalists in the United States. When Richard Grenier published the above-mentioned article, he also quoted from a letter he received from Solzhenitsyn on the subject of anti-Semitism in his work. Solzhenitsyn complained that he was writing the true and tragic history of Russia but that "in my face is flung the base accusation of 'anti-Semitism' (cynically used as a club by some), and a string of false arguments is basely ascribed to me."[790] The Russian author continues by noting that the term has lost its precise meaning, and gives his own definition:

---

788 Seth Wolitz. "Solzhenitsyn and anti-Semitism: A Test." The New York Times 4 December 1985, sec. Letters: 30. All the following quotations from Wolitz are from this same source.

789 Leonard Schapiro. "Soviet Heroes." New York Review of Books 13 October 1983.

790 Solzhenitsyn as quoted in: Grenier, 1989.

> "If a biased and unjustified attitude towards the Jewish nation is understood by this term—then I tell you assuredly: not only is there no—nor could there be—'anti-Semitism' in my work, nor for that matter in any book worthy of being called *literature*. To approach a literary work with the measuring stick of 'anti-Semitism' is vulgar, an under-developed understanding of the nature of a literary work. By this measuring stick Shakespeare could be proclaimed 'anti-Semite,' and his creative work struck out."[791]

Solzhenitsyn makes *tabula rasa* by offering a highly questionable definition of anti-Semitism, clearing his past work from this reproach and exonerating any literary work by claiming that it would be vulgar to use "the measuring stick of 'anti-Semitism'" on it—thus smothering any debate on the matter altogether. These arguments lack in content, as they are purely claims which rely on the credibility of the author. But this same circumstance was repeated in a later interview in the US. David Aikman asked him in 1989 what he thought of the accusation of anti-Semitism made as a result of his depiction of the revolutionary Dmitrii Bogrov.[792] Solzhenitsyn alleges that his critics in the West condemned his novel before it was published and compared this to Soviet methods of slander. He repeated the above definition of anti-Semitism and the claim "it would be impossible to have anti-Semitism in any genuinely artistic work." He ended his statement by assuring that his novel contained no generalizations about the Jews, and added the following:

> In writing a book one cannot always ask, How will this be interpreted? You have to think, what actually happened? My duty was to describe things as they happened.[793]

In his statement, Solzhenitsyn tries to discredit his critics by claiming that they had commented on an unread and even unpublished novel, and again precludes fiction from being capable of being anti-Semitic. To further secure his position, he professes to be writing history as it happened and defines this as his task as a novelist.

It is indeed odd for a novelist to consider a description of "what actually happened" as his duty: being a novelist includes the freedom and the ability to create a diegesis, a plot and compelling characters. There is no obligation for historical truth in fiction. However, if we take Solzhenitsyn at his word and

---

791 Solzhenitsyn as quoted in: Grenier, 1989.
792 Aikman, 1989.
793 Aikman, 1989.

accept his definition of his work, a devaluation of his texts is likely to occur: if historical accuracy is to be the parameter, he has little chance of passing the test.

Solzhenitsyn's claim that critics were accusing him of anti-Semitism in *August 1914* before its publication is unlikely, but not entirely impossible; nevertheless, there are scholars who have considered this novel to contain anti-Semitism *after* reading the novel. Solzhenitsyn's definition of anti-Semitism is unfeasible because of the subjectivity in determining what a "prejudicial and unjust attitude" is. If a person who firmly believes that "Jews control the media" is asked if he possesses a prejudicial and unjust attitude towards the Jews, he might say "no" because he really believes this claim to be true. Nevertheless, it is not Solzhenitsyn's amateurish definition that would make him an anti-Semite. This simply underlines the writer's lack of awareness of what anti-Semitism amounts to. Anti-Semitism in his work must be defined by objective measures.

In a review of *Red Wheel,* literary critic and poet Tomas Venclova discusses the satanization of Lenin in *Lenin in Zürich* and of Bogrov in *August 1914* as the main culprits of the revolution.[794] He reflects on the effect the latter might have, being that Solzhenitsyn assigns Bogrov's motivation as arising from his Jewish origin. Venclova also points at the difficulty of criticizing Solzhenitsyn since immediate accusations of being a communist or a KGB agent ensue. Venclova's fears were not unfounded. In 1985, journalist and Soviet dissident Vadim Belotserkovsky was discharged from *Radio Liberty* after criticizing Solzhenitsyn's *August 1914* for alleged anti-Western and anti-Semitic content.[795] Initially, Belotserkovsky's criticism was expressed in an article in the US magazine *The Nation* and focused mainly on Solzhenitsyn and his peers' negative view of democracy and the US.[796] His argument was that by propagating Solzhenitsyn's unfounded claims that the US wishes to destroy Russia, and that democratic endeavours in Russia lead to chaos, *Radio*

794 Tomas Venclova. "War and Pieces." The New Republic 28 August 1989: 33-7. Venclova is a Lithuanian-born literary critic and poet who immigrated to the US in the 1970s and works at Yale University.

795 Ulrich Schiller. "Seltsame Töne aus dem Äther." Die Zeit 7 February 1986.

796 Vadim Belotserkovsky. "Undoing the West in the Soviet Union." Nation 16 March 1985: 289-308.

Liberty is reinforcing the claims made by Soviet propaganda.[797] He bemoans the uncritical way that Solzhenitsyn's ideas are repeated by others and is particularly concerned that the authority of this author is making anti-democratic and anti-Semitic views popular among dissidents in the Soviet Union.[798] As a result of this article, Belotserkovsky was fired from *Radio Liberty* in what was seen as unfair treatment by US journalist Katrina vanden Heuvel from *The Nation*. Vanden Heuvel argues that firing Belotserkovsky for criticizing the station was a false pretence because a) other members of staff had expressed criticism on other issues without even getting a reprimand, and b) there has been a long history of intolerance towards Western-leaning Jewish dissidents at *Radio Liberty*.[799] Christopher Reed from *The Guardian* confirms this bleak picture.[800] Reed adds that the Russian nationalist influence at *Radio Liberty* used not only Solzhenitsyn to back its anti-democratic and anti-Semitic views but even the infamous *Protocols of the Elders of Zion*. It is clear that *Radio Liberty* had serious political problems. But, unfortunately, the short-lived media attention given to both Solzhenitsyn's possible anti-Semitism and the controversial nature of Russian nationalism did not focus on the content of Solzhenitsyn's work and why it can be seen as problematic. It was therefore very easy for *Washington Post* correspondent Charles Trueheart to re-fashion this controversy into one of "the harshest attacks against" Solzhenitsyn.[801] Trueheart defends Solzhenitsyn from the claim that *August 1914* contains anti-Semitism by claiming that Solzhenitsyn's wife is "half-Jewish" and that Jews have defended Solzhenitsyn from the charge of anti-Semitism. Only in recent years has a more thorough approach to this question taken place.

In the past decade, Russianists Norman Pereira and Noah Shneidman took it upon themselves to analyze the question of Solzhenitsyn's anti-Semitism.[802]

---

797 Belotserkovsky refers to Solzhenitsyn's publicistic articles, as well as *August 1914*, cf. Belotserkovsky, 1985, p. 306-308.

798 Belotserkovsky, 1985, p. 308.

799 Vanden Heuvel, 1985, p. 614-615.

800 Christopher Reed. "The Media: Taking Liberties on the Air / Anti-Western Propaganda on US-Backed Radio Liberty." The Guardian 19 August 1985.

801 Trueheart, 1987. All future Trueheart references refer to this article.

802 Norman Pereira. "Alexander Solzhenitsyn and Anti-Semitism." *Varieties of Antisemitism: History, Ideology, Discourse.* Eds. Murray Baumgarten, Peter Kenez, and Bruce A. Thompson. Newark: University of Delaware Press, 2009. 264-274.

Pereira defines anti-Semitism as a "systematic portrayal of Jewish people as evil, despicable, contemptible—thereby inciting hatred towards all Jews."[803] According to this definition, and believing Solzhenitsyn's own claim that he is not anti-Semitic, Pereira clears Solzhenitsyn of this accusation. Shneidman has a similar definition of this phenomenon, and comes to a comparable conclusion.[804] However, both scholars do delineate in great detail how Jewish anti-heroes are prominent in Solzhenitsyn's work. For example, Pereira writes that—even if seen as mere historical fiction and taking into account artistic license—Solzhenitsyn's portrayal of Dmitrii Bogrov in *August 1914* is "tendentious."[805] Shneidman finds that "the most loathsome Jewish character in Solzhenitsyn's prose" is Izrail' Helph'and a.k.a. "Parvus" from *Lenin in Zurich.*[806] The Russian author presents "Parvus" as a highly influential character whose support of Lenin basically decided the outcome of the Russian Revolution.

In the latter part of his article, Pereira shifts his focus on Solzhenitsyn's two-volume work *Two Hundred Years Together* (2001-2002)[807], which the Russian author describes as a history of the relationship between Russians and Jews. Pereira explains why this work is highly problematic:

> The author draws heavily from old Jewish histories and encyclopedias, 'balanced' by citations from notoriously anti-Semitic publications that simply reiterate a litany of alleged Jewish perfidy. The word *zhid* ("Yid") appears on many, many pages of the first volume, undoubtedly because if was so widely used at the time, but even with quotation marks it jars the modern reader, and its endless repetition—presumably for the sake of full historical authenticity—seems gratuitous.[808]

Pereira is a US-educated, Canadian scholar, who publishes in both countries. Noah N. Shneidman. *Double Vision: the Jew in Post-Soviet Russian Literature (1991-2006).* Niagara Falls, NY: Mosaic Press, 2007.

803 Pereira, 2009, p. 264.

804 "Classical anti-Semitism presuposes a hostile attitude toward Jews, but there is no apparent expression of direct hostility toward Jews neither in Solzhenitsyn's works, nor in his behaviour and actions." Shneidman, 2007, p. 197.

805 Pereira, 2009, p. 266.

806 Shneidman, 2007, p. 180.

807 Alexander Solzhenitsyn. *Dvesti let vmeste: 1795-1995.* 1 Vol. Moscow: Russkii put', 2001. Alexander Solzhenitsyn. *Dvesti let vmeste: 1795-1995.* 2 Vol. Moscow: Russkii put', 2002.

808 Pereira, 2009, p. 267. *Zhid* is a pejorative for Jew, *evrei* being the Russian neutral term.

Further aggravation stems from Solzhenitsyn's euphemistic descriptions of repression against Jews in Imperial Russia, his minimization of the severity of pogroms in the Tsarist era, and his indignation that Jews who were involved in the revolutionary movement continued to be so after they were granted equal rights in 1917.[809] Solzhenitsyn uses his allegation that Jews played an exaggerated role in the Civil War to justify the anti-Semitic pogroms between 1919 and 1922.[810] In sum, Pereira writes that—despite the use of "unfortunate stereotypes" in some cases—it is not a general contempt towards Jews as a religious or ethnic minority that can be found in Solzhenitsyn's work, but rather towards those Jews the Russian author sees as "apostates".[811] He admits that Solzhenitsyn's views are likely to "give offense" to many "or even most Jews",[812] but he believes that Solzhenitsyn is "entitled" to his views.[813]

Pereira's article raises many important points: firstly, he confirms that Solzhenitsyn does show tendentiousness in presenting certain Jews, that he uses dubious sources in his work, and that he considers collective violence against Jews to be justified because of the "transgressions" of certain Jews. But Pereira's definition of anti-Semitism is so narrow that all of these obviously offensive aspects in the Russian author's work can be dismissed as "views" that he is entitled to. This underlines the importance of finding a workable definition of anti-Semitism in literature—one that can make the distinction between opinions and offensive ethnic generalizations more obvious. Analyzing the historical accuracy of the claims helps determine if the author is referring to unfortunate historical circumstances, but it is not enough to explain what the author's intentions are with regard to his narrative.

Many historians who have reviewed Solzhenitsyn's *Two Hundred Years Together* come to the conclusion that the Russian author exaggerates the number of Jews in the Soviet secret service, Jews' role in Bolshevism, their role in the assassination of the Tsar, and that he minimizes the gravity of their oppression in Imperial Russia and the Soviet Union, and justifies pogroms

---

809 Pereira, 2009, p. 267-270; Shneidman, 2007, p. 188-191.
810 Pereira, 2009, p. 270-271; Shneidman, 2007, p. 187.
811 Pereira, 2009, p. 273.
812 Pereira, 2009, p. 273.
813 Pereira, 2009, p. 274.

throughout Russian history.[814] Solzhenitsyn's selection of tendentious works, ignorance of primary sources, misuse of outdated secondary sources, and biased historical interpretation are the main reasons why this work is not considered a work of history by reputed representatives of this profession.[815]

When it comes to Solzhenitsyn's fiction, one is prone to be more generous when it comes to facts—despite the author's own fervent claims of historical accuracy. Nevertheless, Russianist Theodor Friedgut is right in pointing out that *the way* that Solzhenitsyn made some of his characters seem demonic by using old anti-Semitic stereotypes makes his work problematic.[816] This is the case both in the depiction of the supernaturally evil "Parvus" who helps Lenin acquire the necessary money for the revolution, but even more so in the case of Dmitrii Bogrov, Stolypin's assassin.[817]

> Perhaps even more revealing for understanding Solzhenitsyn is the contrast Solzhenitsyn creates between Peter Stolypin and his assassin, Bogrov. Stolypin lives to serve Russia and its peasants. Bogrov thinks only that Stolypin wants a more Russian character for Russia, and that this will be "uncomfortable" for the Jews. Every one of Bogrov's thoughts as depicted by Solzhenitsyn is what will be good for the Jews, without consideration of Russia. Solzhenitsyn's depiction in *August 1914*, despite considerable contrary historical debate, makes the clear claim that Stolypin was killed by an anti-Russian Jew, not by an anarchist revolutionary or a double agent of the secret police[.][818]

Friedgut concludes that in order to understand Solzhenitsyn's concepts of nation and Russianness one must recognize that for him, a Jew can only be Russian if he is no longer a Jew.[819] In Solzhenitsyn's worldview, Jews are

---

814 John Klier. "No Prize for History." *History Today* 52.11 (2002): 60. Vadim Rossman. "Review of 'Dvesti Let Vmeste'." *The Slavic and East European Journal* 46.2 (2002): 390-2. Arno Lustiger. "Der erste Kreis des Antisemitismus, Anmerkungen zu Alexander Solschenizyns Werk über Russen und Juden 'Zweihundert Jahre Gemeinsam'." Frankfurter Allgemeine Zeitung 8 June 2002: 51. Leonid Luks. "Rezension: Zweihundert Jahre Zusammen. Bd. 2: Die Juden in der Sowjetunion." *Jahrbücher für Geschichte Osteuropas* 56.4 (2008): 609-11.

815 Cf. previous footnote. One author who defended him was Nolte, cf.: Ernst Nolte. "Vieldeutige Ko-Existenz." Junge Freiheit 22 November 2002. This journal, however, is affiliated to the radical right.

816 Theodore H. Friedgut. "Aleksandr Solzhenitsyn and the Modern Russo-Jewish Question." *Shofar* 26.3 (2008): 205-208.

817 Friedgut, 2008, p. 206-207.

818 Friedgut, 2008, p. 207.

819 Friedgut, 2008, p. 207.

deemed foreigners and thus have no right to participate in Russian politics—which explains his antagonism towards people like Bogrov and other revolutionaries.[820]

So what does Solzhenitsyn's narrative on Dmitrii Bogrov actually look like, and why is this so controversial?

Dmitrii Bogrov was the grandson of the writer Grigorii Bogrov, who was of Jewish origin but converted to Christianity and wrote in Russian (instead of Yiddish) about Jewish themes.[821] Grigorii was part of the radically critical intelligentsia who blamed the Jews of Petersburg for communal problems.[822] Dmitrii was an anarchist double agent who murdered Stolypin with the unknowing aid of the Tsarist secret police, apparently in order to prove his loyalty to his anarchist comrades.[823] Even historian Michel Heller, who describes Solzhenitsyn's passages on Bogrov as "marvellously written", admits that according to available sources Bogrov acted as an anarchist and not on behalf of Jewish interests.[824] Solzhenitsyn reduces Bogrov's complex personality, his political beliefs, and his criminal deed to his Jewish origin in *August 1914* and *Two Hundred Years Together*. Because in this latter work the author claims to be writing history in a non-fictionalized form,[825] I will first show what this looks like in *Two Hundred Years Together.* In the first volume, while discussing Russian-Jewish relations from 1795 to 1916, Solzhenitsyn describes how several attempts had been made to kill Stolypin, but only

820 Friedgut, 2008, p. 207.

821 Gabriella Safran. "Bogrov, Grigorii Isaakovich." *The YIVO encyclopedia of Jews in Eastern Europe* 2010. (http://www.yivoencyclopedia.org/article.aspx/Bogrov_Grigorii_Isaakovich) (as of 20 February 2013).

822 "The writer Grigorii Bogrov, echoing earlier criticisms of the way Petersburg Jewry handled its own communal affairs in the imperial capital, reported that 'because of the intrigues and lack of consensus on the part of Petersburg Jews, provincial Jews are forced to remain chained to places where their enemies' fists continue to pound them.'" Benjamin Nathans. *Beyond the Pale: the Jewish Encounter with Late Imperial Russia.* 45 Vol. Berkeley: University of California Press, 2002. p. 190.

823 Richard Bach Jensen. "The International Campaign Against Anarchist Terrorism, 1880–1930s." *Terrorism and Political Violence* 21.1 (2009): 89-109. p. 97.

824 Michel Heller. "Yesterday and Today in Solzhenitsyn's *The Red Wheel.*" *Survey* 29.2 (125) (1985): p. 43-44.

825 For example in his foreword, cf: Alexander Solzhenitsyn. *Zweihundert Jahre zusammen: Die russisch-jüdische Geschichte 1795-1916*. Vol. 1. Munich: Herbig, 2002. p. 7-10.

Bogrov was capable of ingeniously achieving this goal.[826] He describes Bogrov as a naive young man, lacking a capacity to understand politics, who derives his motivation from his Jewish surroundings:

> Noch jung und unreif, wie er war, konnte Bogrow selbst die Bedeutung Stolypins für den Staat nicht in ihrer Gesamheit erfassen. Dafür hatte er seit seiner Kindheit die tagtäglichen und erniedrigenden Seiten der politischen Ungleichberechtigung gesehen und war von seiner Familie, seiner Umgebung und durch sich selbst angeheizt worden zu glühendem Hass gegen die zaristische Obrigkeit. Offenbar konnte sich in diesen Kiewer jüdischen Kreisen, die doch so ideologisch beweglich schienen, keine mildere Haltung gegen Stolypin für dessen Bemühungen, die antijüdischen Beschränkungen aufzuheben, herausbilden, und wenn doch, so wurde diese mildere Haltung bei manchen der Wohlhabenderen durch die Erinnerung an seine energische Niederschlagung der Revolution von 1905/06 und die Verärgerung über seine Bemühungen um eine »Verstaatlichung des russischen Kreditwesens«, den offenen Wettstreit mit privatem Kapital, doch überwogen. In den Kreisen der Kiewer (und der Petersburger, wo der heranwachsender Mörder sich ebenfalls aufhielt) Juden wirkte dieses allradikale Feld, in dem sich der junge Bogrow im Recht und sogar verpflichtet fühlte, Stolypin zu töten.[827]

Solzhenitsyn describes Bogrov's desire to kill the Prime Minister as a direct result of his Jewish surroundings, even if he mentions that he lived in places where Jews were an exceptional minority. Kiev had a special status within the Pale of Settlement, so that only certain (wealthy) Jews were allowed to live there, and Saint Petersburg was beyond the Pale for all but selected Jewish

826 Solzhenitsyn, 2002, "Zweihundert Jahre", vol. 1, p. 431.

827 Solzhenitsyn, 2002, "Zweihundert Jahre", vol. 1, p. 431. Only parts of this work have been translated into English, so I quote from the German translation. The corresponding Russian text is in p. 440 (vol. 1); there are no semantic differences between the German and the original. "Still young and immature, even Bogrov himself was unable to grasp Stolypin's significance for the state. But ever since his childhood he had seen the daily humiliating aspects of political inequality, and was fuelled up by his family, his surroundings and himself with smoldering hatred towards Tsarist rule. Evidently, these Kievite Jewish circles, which appeared to be so ideologically versatile, could not develop a milder stance towards Stolypin and his attempts to abolish anti-Jewish restrictions. If they did develop this milder stance, it was among the rich, among whom the memory of his energic crushing of the Revolution of 1905-1906 and the anger towards his attempts at 'nationalizing the Russian credit system', direct competition against private capital, overcame it after all. The radical environment of these Kievite Jewish circles (and those of Petersburg, where the maturing murderer also spent time) had its effect on Bogrov, who felt he was right and even obligated to kill Stolypin." (My translation from the Russian.)

citizens.[828] Nevertheless, he assumes that Bogrov, the assimilated anarchist, drew his inspiration precisely from these few Jews to commit his act of violence and that he did this for their sake.[829] He then explains that deeds have long-term consequences and that salvation can only come if one always allows God to direct one's "moral compass".[830] Later, he goes straight to the point and writes:

> Erster Schritt: Stolypin ermordet, im Krieg die Nerven verloren—und Russland lag unter den Stiefeln der Bolschewiken.
>
> Zweiter Schritt: Die Bolschewiken waren bei all ihrer Barberei viel unbegabter als die zaristische Regierung, und nach einem Vierteljahrhundert gaben sie in kurzer Zeit halb Russland an die Deutschen ab, darunter auch Kiew.
>
> Dritter Schritt: Die Hitlertruppen kamen leicht nach Kiew hinein—und vernichteten das Kiewer Judentum.
>
> Wieder Kiew, wieder September, nur eben 30 Jahre nach Bogrows Schuss.[831]

Apparently, in Solzhenitsyn's understanding of history, because a man of Jewish origin killed a minister in Kiev, some supernatural force made sure that Kiev's Jewish population would be annihilated thirty years later. Russia was an autocratic Empire at the time, Stolypin's political influence was limited and he was replaceable.[832] But Solzhenitsyn not only vastly exaggerates the importance of Stolypin's position by claiming that, had Stolypin survived, the Bolsheviks would have never come to power and the Nazis would have never invaded Russia. He completely neglects the Nazis' responsibility for their own deeds, instead shifting the blame on Bogrov and the Jews of Kiev. If fate

---

828 Nathans, 2002, p. 88, 190ff.

829 He repeats this thought in: Solzhenitsyn, 2002, "Zweihundert Jahre", vol. 1, p. 435.

830 Solzhenitsyn, 2002, "Zweihundert Jahre" vol. 1, p. 435.

831 Solzhenitsyn, 2002, "Zweihundert Jahre" vol. 1, p. 435. (Russian version, vol. 1, p. 444). "First step: Stolypin is killed—nerves are lost at war, and Russia lies under the boots of the Bolsheviks. Second step: despite all gruesomeness, the Bolsheviks end up being much less talented than the Tsarist government, within a quarter of a century they quickly hand over half of Russia to the Germans, including Kiev. Third step: Hitler's troops easily reach Kiev and destroy Kievite Jewry. The same Kiev, also in September, only thirty years after Bogrov's shot." (My translation from the Russian.)

832 Although he was able to suggest certain political reforms, Prime Minister Stolypin's time in office depended fully on the Tsar's will, who would have likely sacked him if he had lived, cf.: Peter Scheibert. *Russland.* Eds. Carsten Goehrke, Peter Scheibert and Manfred Hellmann. 31 Vol. Frankfurt Main: Fischer Taschenbuch Verlag, 1992. p. 258ff; Geoffrey A. Hosking. *Russland: Nation und Imperium: 1552 - 1917.* Berlin: Siedler Verlag, 2000. p. 464-470.

ensures that the murder of one man by one Jew leads to the death of thousands, by the same standards would it not have followed that the murder of thousands of Kievite Jews by the Nazis leads to the punishment of even more Germans?

Solzhenitsyn's treatment of Bogrov in *August 1914* is similar in nature, but it takes up more than 200 pages of a 994-page text. Because the central plot of the novel is the World War I Battle of Tannenberg and other minor battles between the Imperial Russian Army and the Germans in what was then Königsberg (now Kaliningrad), it is surprising how much attention the author pays to the assassination of Prime Minister Stolypin, an event seemingly unrelated to the war. Having read Solzhenitsyn's later work mentioned above, it becomes clear that he sees Stolypin's death as leading to Russia's downfall and thus as somewhat connected to his overall concept of protocolling Russia's troubles. In *August 1914*, Solzhenitsyn describes Bogrov as a rich young man with a weak physique, who avoided all forms of physical strain.[833] The narrative voice switches from a descriptive, omniscient narrator to internal focalizers: at times it is Bogrov's perspective narrated as a third person, or Stolypin's, etc. The omniscient narrator denies that Bogrov was an anarchist,[834] and both the omniscient narrator and Bogrov's narrative remind the reader that Bogrov's main priority were the Jews.[835] In a particularly disturbing inner monologue, Bogrov considers the possibility of killing Tsar Nicholas II, but decides not to:

> Den Zaren irgendwo anders umzubringen (nur nicht in Kiew)—das wäre gegangen. Aber wenn in Kiew und wenn durch seine, Bogrows, Hand—dann würde es zu einem schrecklichen Judenpogrom kommen, das dumpfe rasende Volk würde sich erheben. Das lebendige, ihm innig verbundene jüdische Blut Kiews! Das Letzte, was Bogrow in seinem Leben herbeiführen möchte: das Kiew jemals der Ort einer Massenvernichtung von Juden werden würde, weder in diesem September noch in einem späteren!
>
> Die dreitausendjährige unfehlbar leise Stimme.[836]

833 Alexander Solzhenitsyn. *August Vierzehn.* Tran. Swetlana Geier. Munich: Piper, 1987. p. 581-583.

834 Solzhenitsyn, 1987, p. 754-755.

835 Solzhenitsyn, 1987, p. 755, 780, 788.

836 Solzhenitsyn, 1987, p. 617. (Russian version: 1983, vol. 2, p. 152) "To kill the Tsar anywhere but in Kiev would work. But if in Kiev, and then by him—Bogrov—it would cause a terrible Jewish pogrom; the dark, mad crowd would rise. Kievite Jewry,

Solzhenitsyn "judaizes" Bogrov by emphasizing his links to the Jewish people and creating an impression of unwavering loyalty to them. In an almost perverse manner, he also makes an implicit reference to the annihilation of Kiev's Jews in September 1941 by the Germans by making Bogrov "think" about what could happen in "other" Septembers due to his possible deeds in September 1911. In this sense, Solzhenitsyn's *August 1914* and the text about Bogrov in *Two Hundred Years Together* are ideologically related.

At the end of *August 1914*, the author informs the reader of how he had started writing this book in 1937, and why he re-wrote it so many times since then, and then he points out that the historical characters and events described in the book—explicitly mentioning Stolypin's assassination by Bogrov—are written according to the historical facts.[837] Within the text of the novel, he at times interrupts the narrative with pages of small print in which he gives further historical details. He explains this practice by claiming that, had not Russian history and memory been attacked and Russian historians annihilated, he would not have had to include these pages.[838] Solzhenitsyn's constant suggestions that he is describing historically accurate events are a form of *Leserlenkung*, of guiding the reader to a certain type of interpretation. Solzhenitsyn does not stick to the facts as they are represented by mainstream historians, and instead of allowing his historical appreciation to be guided by reputed representatives of this profession, he repeatedly creates an image that he is telling the truth, that the "real" historians were either killed or somehow silenced,[839] and that attempts were made to force him into silence about certain facts, etc.[840] By cherry-picking certain historical characters or events to prove certain ideas about history—such as the idea that Bogrov's crime was a fateful justification of the later extermination of

---

which was so alive and kindred to him! The thing that Bogrov wanted to avoid above all things was that Kiev would one day become the location of a mass killing of Jews—not this September or any other September! The three-thousand-year-old unfailingly quiet call." (My translation from the Russian.)

837 Solzhenitsyn, 1987, p. 998.

838 Solzhenitsyn, 1987, p. 634.

839 Solzhenitsyn, 1987, p. 634, Augstein, 1987, p. 251.

840 For example, he claims he was allegedly under pressure by unnamed Russian Jews about not mentioning Dmitrii Bogrov's Jewish origin, in Solzhenitsyn, 2001, vol. 1, p. 442-443. Similar claims were made in his essay "Our Pluralists", cf.: Solzhenitsyn, 1985, p. 6-8; 27-28.

Kiev's Jews—Solzhenitsyn is using methods common to right-wing revisionist propaganda. In an article about the methodology of right-wing "historiography" and propaganda, Austrian historian Gustav Spann describes how authors of such works reject mainstream historiography, and filter information according to their pre-conceived ideological prism.[841] Selecting events and characters to fit a certain concept of history is one of the main methods used by such authors, "dabei werden entscheidende Tatsachen und Zusammenhänge ausgeblendet, fälsche Kausalzusammenhänge hergestellt, Ursache und Wirkung vertauscht."[842] Solzhenitsyn uses such methods in his portrayal of certain events, as in the case of Bogrov and the murder of Stolypin. It is highly unlikely that Bogrov acted as a Jew, and there is no evidence that points to the probability that Stolypin would have changed the course of history, had he lived; furthermore, the crime of one man of Jewish origin will never amount to a justification of the murder of thousands of Jewish men, women, and children. Nevertheless, this is what the Russian dissident has consistently claimed.

Solzhenitsyn's tendency to blame Jews for catastrophes is not only based on cases in which he overemphasizes the importance of their Jewish origin, he also re-constructs history in order to be able to blame them. A salient example is his claim that a "Jew" ordered the execution of Tsar Nicolas II and his family. He accuses the revolutionary Yakov Sverdlov of ordering the executions.[843] Sverdlov is the descendant of a cantonist, that is, a Jew taken from his home to serve in the Russian military outside the Pale of Settlement for at least 25 years.[844] Solzhenitsyn expresses his indignation that Sverdlov was so unthankful to the Russian monarchy that he allegedly committed this crime.[845] Historically, it was Lenin who ordered the execution of the Tsar and

---

841 Gustav Spann. "Methoden der Rechtsextremer Tendenz-Geschichtsschreibung und Propaganda." *Wahrheit und "Auschwitzlüge".* Eds. Brigitte Bailer-Galanda, Wolfgang Benz, and Wolfgang Neugebauer. Vienna: Deuticke, 1995. p. 49-50.

842 Spann, 1995, p. 50, "in such cases, decisive facts and contexts are left out, false causal links created, and cause and effect turned around." (My translation.)

843 Solzhenitsyn, 2002, vol. 1, p. 137.

844 Cantonists were forceably assimilated in Russian culture, which often meant that they were also baptized. Cf. Nathans, 2002.

845 Solzhenitsyn, 2002, vol. 1, p. 137.

his family.[846] Solzhenitsyn not only blames someone else for this, he gives this other person a Jewish identity, and suggests he should have been somehow indebted to the Tsar. The accusation of regicide levelled at the Jews has been popular among Russian nationalists for years.[847] Patriarch Alexei II even suggested that the execution of the Tsar and his family might have been "ritual murder."[848] But even if Solzhenitsyn's claims are not the most extreme, they play to the narrative of the Jews as aliens who have used their power to damage Russia.

Walter Laqueur underlines the absurdity of Solzhenitsyn's narrative that emphasizes the origin of revolutionaries as "foreign", when one takes into account his loyalty towards the Tsars—who were often of foreign origin.[849] Tsar Nicholas II was the son of Danish Princess Dagmar, and his wife was Princess Alexandra from Hesse (Germany). This shows how the exclusion of Russian Jews from the "nation" is rooted in ideological double standards. If we look back at Klaus Holz' definition of anti-Semitism—the assignment of certain characteristics to "Jews", their perception as foreign and/or inimical, and a negative judgement of them as a group[850]—it is not easy to defend Solzhenitsyn from the claim that his works contain an anti-Semitic bias. Solzhenitsyn's definition of nation excludes Jews, whom he portrays as "foreign" to Russia—despite their two-hundred year history on the territory. As I have shown, he uses the acts of individual Jews to justify violence against Jews as a group, and disproportionally blames them for Russia's troubles. Solzhenitsyn also resorts to common stereotypes to characterize Jews, be they physical, temperamental, or ideological. Whatever his intention might be, there is textual evidence of anti-Semitism in his work. The fact that anti-Semitic scholars and journalists in different countries have quoted his work and praised it is not an abuse of Solzhenitsyn's work: he has contributed to this trend.

---

846 Cf.: John D. Klier. "The Dog that Didn't Bark: Anti-Semitism in Post-Communist Russia." *Russian Nationalism, Past and Present.* Ed. Geoffrey A. Hosking. Basingstoke: Macmillan, 1998. 129-147.

847 "Right-wing anti-Semites have resorted to the equation of Jews and revolution, exemplified by their claim that 'the Jews killed the Tsar.'" Klier, 1998, p. 140.

848 Klier, 1998, p. 142.

849 Laqueur, 1993, p. 98.

850 Holz, 2001, p. 38.

Solzhenitsyn was a courageous individual, who believed in certain principles and stuck to them despite a tremendous outside pressure. He helped a generation of people in the West to question their indifference towards—or even their support of—Soviet human rights violations. Unfortunately, he also believed in things that are prejudiced and insulting to certain people groups. It is only fair towards Solzhenitsyn for us as scholars to take him seriously as an author in his entirety and not only when we agree with him. Literary scholar Gary Saul Morson wrote a movingly honest essay on his confrontation with Fyodor Dostoevsky's anti-Semitism:

> When I first became aware of Dostoevskij's political messianism, Russian Orthodox chauvinism, intellectual obscurantism, and anti-Semitism, I tried to ignore or excuse these disturbing facts, because to convict Dostoevskij was to convict myself. Besides, I wrote a dissertation, several articles, and a book on Dostoevskij, and it would have been difficult for me to devote so much energy to studying a writer of whom I thought ill. For both personal and professional reasons, then, I needed to love Dostoevskij, and so I did.[851]

After many years, Morson finally summons up the courage to confront the fact that Dostoevsky wrote many things that he finds despicable. Not only in the West, but also in the Soviet Union, Dostoevsky's anti-Semitic texts were swept under the rug and literary critics devised different ways of protecting his reputation.[852] Morson points out that denying this aspect of his work just because it was considered to be no longer appropriate or politically correct was not the fairest or most honest way of dealing with the problem.[853]

We do writers like Dostoevsky or Solzhenitsyn no favor by claiming them to be unfailing authors of canonical works of literature. Is it not more befitting of scholarly standards and more consistent with reality to understand that these authors may have been very talented, but also very complex and at times even highly controversial figures? Solzhenitsyn's revisionist reception will live on for many years, and it is crucial that we as literary critics acknowledge the reasons for this phenomenon and find a way of dealing with them.

---

851 Gary Saul Morson. "Dostoevsky's Anti-Semitism and the Critics: A Review Article." *The Slavic and East European Journal* 27.3 (1983). p. 316.

852 Morson, 1983, p. 312-313.

853 Morson, 1983, p. 314.

3.4 Political Christianity

Alexander Solzhenitsyn was a Russian Orthodox Christian and his Christian worldview has had a protean reception in the West. When Michael Charlton from the BBC asked Solzhenitsyn if he desired to return to a "patriarchal kind of Russia, [...] to Orthodoxy", Solzhenitsyn scoffed:

> It is quite easy to imagine that some journalists writing mostly about women's fashions thought up this headline, and so the story gets around that I am calling for a patriarchal way of life.[854]

There is considerable confusion surrounding Solzhenitsyn's relationship to Orthodoxy and a patriarchal way of life. However, Christian scholars and publicists have long appreciated Solzhenitsyn's religious ideas.

There are two key issues regarding Christianity in Solzhenitsyn's Western reception: one is the view that he is a Christian and has prophetic powers, and the other is that his work shows evidence of an ideological form of Christianity. The opinion that Solzhenitsyn is prophetic is not very scientific, prophecy not being a scientific category. However, the persistence of this image makes it necessary to at least sketch its form and arguments. The second aspect of his Christian reception is based on the way both Solzhenitsyn and some of his readers consider it necessary for Christianity to influence social and political life. This inevitably leads to ideological premises. Although I am aware that Solzhenitsyn and those who agree with him see these as moral and not ideological or political premises, much speaks for the latter interpretation.

Although most of those who use the term "prophetic" for Solzhenitsyn's work do not delve into details of what they mean, it seems to be that they identify two aspects in his work: a critical analysis of the present which is then used to make predictions or recommendations about the future.

Stephen Carter describes the prophetic aspect of Solzhenitsyn's works as his ability to explain why, ever since the Renaissance, humanity has been on a failed path towards progress.[855] Atheistic humanism has led to moral decay, to communism and materialism—Solzhenitsyn sees the solution in a moral

---

854 Solzhenitsyn, 1976, "Warning", p. 11-12.
855 Carter, 1977, p. 139.

revolution.[856] Oskar Gruenwald points out that the Christian worldview and the rejection of the Enlightenment in Solzhenitsyn's message make his "prophetic" tone seem "out of step" among those who are embedded in a secular, atheistic worldview.[857] Although Gruenwald sees this critically, he has rightly identified why not all of Solzhenitsyn's readers can embrace his message; the specificity of it makes it impossible to achieve a universal acceptance.

John Dunlop explains that many of Solzhenitsyn's fans in the US saw him as someone whose prophetic voice called for a moral renewal:

> A number of Solzhenitsyn's supporters, on the other hand, see him as a prophet rallying a demoralized and dispirited America to meet a growing Soviet challenge.[858]

Like a Biblical prophet, Solzhenitsyn's challenge would have an effect on international relations. According to Dunlop, his ability to predict the future was also part of his prophetic gift.[859] The idea that Solzhenitsyn has the prophetic ability to predict the future has often been used to legitimize the author as someone with a special gift. This topos was used most often directly after his return to Russia, but it continues to appear in articles or books about him. Journalist David Remnick from *The New Yorker* has been one of the proponents of this idea. In his article 'The Exile Returns' he dwells on the different historical events he suggests that Solzhenitsyn was able to predict.[860] This may add little more than an exotic flair to the author. But for Christian scholars such as Ericson or Mahoney, Solzhenitsyn's prophetic predictions are part of what legitimizes his overall message—which is probably why they criticize those who do not agree that the author is prophetic.[861]

Michael Hanne interprets Solzhenitsyn's condemnation of Western decadence and "moral collapse" as a repetition of Soviet propaganda which was buttressed by his unwillingness to acquire an informed position on the

---

856 Carter, 1977, p. 139.
857 Gruenwald, 1980, p. 138.
858 Dunlop, 1985, "Reception", p. 48.
859 Dunlop, 1985, "Reception", p. 27.
860 He mentions Solzhenitsyn's claim that one day he would return to Russia, and that one day his books would be legally published there. Remnick, 1994.
861 Ericson, 1980, p. 122; Mahoney, 2001, p. 33.

West.[862] His "apocalyptic vision of relations between the West and the Soviet Union" failed to materialize, revealing the inadequacy of his vision of the future.[863]

Solzhenitsyn made so many different claims about the future of Russia and the West that it is not surprising that not all of them became reality—and in some cases we may be glad they did not. But the discussion of his ability to prophesize is rather unfruitful outside a theological environment. However, Solzhenitsyn's "prophetic tone" in his criticism of contemporary lifestyles has political repercussions because he argues that morality should define public life, even more than the law.[864] This form of "prophecy" leads to what I consider a politicized view of Christianity, which can be interpreted as positive or negative, depending on the reader's worldview and understanding of history.

Political scientist Gerhart Niemeyer considers Solzhenitsyn to be a moral authority because he dared to tell us the truth about "totalitarianism": about how people in totalitarian countries live—willingly or unwillingly—in "sin before God".[865] A different opinion is that of David Wilson, who rejects Solzhenitsyn's prophetic claims that the West is on the brink due to its lack of piety and its abundance of hedonism.[866] Wilson expresses scepticism that things are as dangerous as Solzhenitsyn makes them seem: after all, spiritual belief and a sense of mission are no deterrents from state violence against its citizens or others, as many examples show.

The relationship between morality and politics is central to Solzhenitsyn's Christian reception. Carter argues that Solzhenitsyn "elevates moral and aesthetic considerations above political ones."[867] He considers this his most extreme demand:

---

862 Hanne, 1994, p. 183.
863 Hanne, 1994, p. 184.
864 Cf. the *Harvard Address* (1978) and *How to Rebuild Russia* (1990).
865 Gerhart Niemeyer. "Alexander Solschenizyn." *Konservative Köpfe: von Machiavelli bis Solschenizyn.* Ed. Caspar v. Schrenck-Notzing. Munich: Criticon Verlag, 1978. p. 197.
866 David B. Wilson. "The West is Flabby, but..." The Boston Globe 16 July 1978: 7. All following references to Wilson allude to this article.
867 Carter, 1977, p. 94.

> Solzhenitsyn is clearly making some very radical demands, the most radical being that morality must begin to dictate the external and internal politics of nations.[868]

Solzhenitsyn's view that morality should rule over people's behavior and over political decisions is sometimes seen as taking the opposite path to political action, as Emmet Kennedy argues.[869] He delineates how "morality and religion were not an issue" for people in the US or for Soviet dissident Andrey Sakharov, but for Solzhenitsyn "they were the only issue": "a purely political solution would be to 'take part in the lie.'"[870] This view that morality can be a form of opposition to politics itself is analogous to Solzhenitsyn's claim that a "point of view" is an antidote to ideology.[871] Dunlop explains this thought:

> A point of view is the ultimate and perhaps only enemy of ideology, for not only does it provide a reasoned critique of the ideology and the system it spawns but it offers an *alternative world-view* which prompts its adherents to do spiritual battle with the ideology.[872]

These authors argue with the premise that morality is an alternative to ideology; but its socio-political consequences are evident in the following example.

Solzhenitsyn argues in his *Harvard Address* that morality should precede laws, because laws cannot protect people from evil.[873] He considers freedom to be a right that should be coupled with religious piety (as it was in the past), and the West's "harsh spiritual crisis and political impasse" to be the result of granting rights without pre-conditions.[874] His conviction that faith is more important than rights results in an analogous assessment of political leaders—faith is more important than deeds. For example, in an article about the importance of repentance, Solzhenitsyn listed Tsar Ivan IV "the Terrible"

---

868 Carter, 1977, p. 92.

869 Emmet Kennedy. *Secularism and its Opponents from Augustine to Solzhenitsyn.* Basingstoke: Palgrave Macmillan, 2006.

870 Kennedy, 2006, p. 217.

871 Solzhenitsyn, 1974, vol. 1, p. 131.

872 John B. Dunlop. "The Gulag Archipelago: Alternative to Ideology." *Solzhenitsyn in Exile: Critical Essays and Documentary Materials.* Eds. John B. Dunlop, Richard S. Haugh, and Michael Nicholson. Stanford: Hoover Institution, 1985. p. 169.

873 "Life organized legalistically has thus shown its inability to defend itself against the corrosion of evil." Berman, ed., 1980, p. 9.

874 "And yet in early democracies, as in American democracy at the time of its birth, all individual human rights were granted on the ground that man is God's creature. That is, freedom was given to the individual conditionally, in the assumption of his constant religious responsibility." in: Berman, ed., 1980, p. 18.

among those Russians who had created a better world because he was a Christian who repeatedly repented of his deeds.[875] Solzhenitsyn's benevolent views on Franco's Spain are similarly based on the fact that this dictatorship was a Christian one, and thus better than an atheist one.[876] The way he applies moral criteria to evaluate societies and politicians is not based on the humanist understanding of the universality of human rights.[877] It is based on Christian values which are not necessarily compatible with the latter understanding of human rights: for a humanist, if a Christian dictator kills someone, it's a crime regardless of the dictator's faith. For Solzhenitsyn, the dictator's faith matters. This aspect of his thought allowed him to befriend current Russian President Vladimir Putin, who is a former KGB agent. His faith recommended him to the author, who had nothing to say about Putin's dire human rights record. Solzhenitsyn's Christian worldview operates ideologically.

Solzhenitsyn's concrete recommendations of what social and political life should look like were briefly mentioned in section 3.2—they include restoring women to the role of child-rearers, returning to a rural life-style, and having schools and entertainment that reflect Christian values.[878] Solzhenitsyn's vision for a better future may seem prophetic for some readers—as something they agree is necessary—but for many others it seems atavistic and patriarchal.

Some Western scholars who operate with a Christian worldview will continue to agree with Solzhenitsyn on these issues, but for those with a secular scientific point of view these ideas will remain alienating. The lack of universality of political Christianity means that this type of reception will remain marginal.

---

875 Alexander Solzhenitsyn. "Reue und Selbstbeschränkung als Kategorien des nationalen Lebens." *Stimmen aus dem Untergrund. Zur geistigen Situation in der UdSSR.* Ed. Alexander Solschenizyn. Darmstadt: Luchterhand, 1975. 117-156. p. 128.

876 Alexander Solzhenitsyn. "Ispanskoe Interv'iu." Kontinent 44. 1975: 429-40.

877 Solzhentisyn on humanism and human rights, cf: Solzhenitsyn, 1990.

878 He makes these and more programmatic recommendations in: Solzhenitsyn, 1990.

3.5 Comparative Chapter Conclusion

In this chapter I have analyzed the reception of Solzhenitsyn's work from a political point of view over several decades. Solzhenitsyn never received as much attention in the West as when he published *The Gulag Archipelago* in the 1970s. The readers of this era were Solzhenitsyn's target audience and the reception of this work in this historical context often took the form of "mediating reception." The way he was read then became a defining moment for future generations of readers. However, the political constraints of this era affected his reception by making it less nuanced than it could have been under different circumstances. *Gulag* was read in a specific political mode. In the three countries of my study, it was interpreted as a significant contribution to the debate about the meaning of communism. The discussions revolving around the interpretation of *Gulag* and the assessment of the Solzhenitsyn Affair remained largely on a superficial level and focused on general questions: how should one react towards Solzhenitsyn's ordeal? What should be the Western political consequences with respect to Soviet human rights violations? The three countries of my study were democratic, and it is therefore not surprising that the overall scholarly and journalistic reaction was that of solidarity towards Solzhenitsyn as a human being, and condemnation of the way the state treated him. At the time, it was already part of Western intellectuals' self-image to side with the oppressed. The second question however, caused considerable conflict: is the Soviet Union hopelessly criminal, or is it a reformable state? It is here that a polarization took place both in the media and academia, promoting a black and white image of the USSR and its culture. In the end, history showed both the Soviet state's capability of evolving but also the vulnerability that led to its collapse.

One of the greatest challenges in dealing with dissident literature is the fact that it often has a political program, which might not be what foreign readers otherwise expect or approve of. Literary critic Michael Hanne counts Solzhenitsyn among the many creative authors who are very good at being opposed to the "status quo" but are "infinitely less persuasive at proposing political arrangements for the future".[879]

---

879 Hanne, 1994, p. 184.

The problem with Solzhenitsyn's more extremist views may be seen today as a mishap, a misunderstanding, or an unforeseen development by some of his commentators. However, the fact that he emerged as a dissident—and one of the most tenacious at that—already comprised the risk of extremism. Before exile he rejected Soviet scholarship for its bias, but after 1974 Solzhenitsyn alleged that both Soviet and Western scholars were concealing the truth about Russian history.[880] His claim to historical truth beyond any attainable evidence or facts was enough to warn his readers that he was not operating within mainstream scientific methods, and that his literature may contain some sort of ideological program. To be sure, not every dissident is an extremist, but the courage needed to oppose one state is not exclusive to those who embrace human rights and democracy. Right-wing extremists and other non-democratic dissidents in East and West share this type of determination and stubbornness as well.[881]

During the Cold War, the radical nature of Solzhenitsyn's message was not a hindrance to his canonization but an advantage. A great number of his admirers in the scholarly world did not only believe in a need to emphasize the evilness of the Soviet Union, they contributed to the artificial polarization of Western opinion on communism and dissent. Supporters of Solzhenitsyn's worldview were very sensitive to criticism of the writer. The narrative of Solzhenitsyn being under attack in the West was an attempt to strengthen the view that the "enemy is among us", that is to say, that many among the elite were pro-communist, thus making the threat of communist takeover seem even greater.

The purposeful support of dissidents with anti-Western ideas was part of a Cold War mentality that an "enemy's enemy is a friend", and the belief that countries like Russia do not necessarily need a democratic government. In the conflict between Westernized and nationalist Russian dissidents, Western institutions such as *Radio Liberty* or the German-funded magazine *Kontinent* consciously took sides with the nationalist branch, a decision mirrored by some experts on Russian history and culture. This tendency caused

---

880 For example in: Solzhenitsyn, 1980, "Misconceptions".
881 Cf.: Spahn, 1995; Michael Shermer and Alex Grobman. *Denying History: who says the Holocaust never happened and why do they say it?* Berkeley: University of California Press, 2000.

disappointment among pro-Western dissidents, like Andrey Sinyavsky, who once wrote:

> It is curious, however, that some Western groups speak out at times on behalf of Russian nationalists and authoritarians, even though it would seem that Russian democrats should be psychologically closer to them. The logic seems to be that freedom and democracy are good for the West, but Russia requires something a bit more simple and brutal. Something suitable for savages.[882]

At the time, the idea that nationalism would be a successful movement to replace communism seemed rational, but ethnic violence fueled by nationalism in former communist countries has shown the downside of such policies. A thorough discussion about the effects of such mechanisms in culture and scholarship would be very fruitful.

The focus on these very general political ideas, instead of allowing for political readings more in tune with the literary theories of the time—feminism, cultural criticism, etc.—left a deep void in Solzhenitsyn's reception. The tension of the Cold War conflict in scholarship meant that a more critical, or more nuanced approach to the study of a politically explosive text by one of the Soviet Union's most famous victims would have been too controversial—as the few attempts at a differentiated approach to Solzhenitsyn in the 70s and 80s show. But it is also the result of the general shyness of Russianists to apply these contemporary methods during the Cold War. The fact that many new critical approaches were embedded in leftist ideas surely contributed to this neglect.

This black hole of criticism was not immediately addressed after 1991, because the overwhelming changes in the Russian literary scene moved other, very general questions to the foreground: Who belonged in the canon now, and how could scholars integrate Russian émigré writers in the corpus of Russian literature as a whole? Solzhenitsyn's reassessment was part of these discussions.

During the Cold War, Solzhenitsyn's literary talent was widely regarded as unquestionable; his work was often hailed as a series of masterpieces. But the appreciation of the aesthetic qualities of his work remained murky. Those who defended the literary quality of the work often lacked aesthetic

---

882 In: Andrey Sinyavsky. "Russian Nationalism." *Massachusetts Review*. Winter 31.4 (1990). p. 475-494.

arguments for their view, and resorted to political ones. After 1991, aesthetic evaluations of his work gave protean results. For many critics, the length of Solzhenitsyn's books, the overpopulation of their diegesis, the difficulty of his language, and the tiring historical details in most of his novels were now considered disadvantageous.

After 1991, Solzhenitsyn was again a part of Russian society and his political message was seen from a decidedly distant point of view, as a mere curiosity. He was no longer politically relevant to the bulk of the Western readership. This allowed scholars a new aesthetic appreciation of his work, while continuing to ignore the richness and complexity of Solzhenitsyn's political ideas. This is very unfortunate, because it has left many controversial issues unresolved. For instance, critical confusion or even silence regarding Solzhenitsyn's illiberal views and the increasing anti-Semitism of his works calls for a reassessment of his work. Only a direct confrontation with these aspects of works such as *August 1914* or *Two Hundred Years Together* can explain their popularity among right-wing scholars and activists in Russia and the West.

Solzhenitsyn's case shows us how a politically charged environment forced a selected number of political readings to dominate a reception that could have been very multifaceted. In chapter four of this book, I will exemplify how the emphasis of one aspect of a dissident's work is often part of an instrumentalization for different socio-political and historical priorities.

4. Solzhenitsyn in History

In the last two chapters I analyzed Solzhenitsyn's reception from the point of view of witness literature and from political perspectives. The aesthetics of Solzhenitsyn's work is evaluated mostly as either camp literature or political literature. Nevertheless, there is a third aspect which I have already alluded to and will now make my focus: Solzhenitsyn's relationship to history. Both his persona and his corpus have a close link to history. Western celebrity culture in the mid-20th century had evolved in such a way that it allowed for a person like him—a man whose media profile was based on his victim status—to become a widely admired luminary.[883] His publications became sensational and secured his place in the cultural history of Russia and abroad. His life-writing—memoirs and autobiographically inspired texts—and his historical fiction and non-fiction all use history for diverse purposes: ideological, contextual, informative, etc. His reception shows different ways of dealing with the historical aspect of his work and the historization of his persona. In part one of this chapter, I will comment on the advantages and disadvantages of reading Solzhenitsyn's work as historiography, and discuss controversies surrounding questions of truth and factual accuracy. In part two of this short chapter I will illustrate the advantages of approaching his work and his agency with the theoretical tools of memory studies. This allows an assessment of his contribution to history that acknowledges his subjectivity, political proclivity, and loose handling of facts. In the area of memory studies, history, and personal experience cross paths with historiography and literature.

---

883 Daniel J. Boorstin. *The Image or What happened to the American Dream*. London: Weidenfeld and Nicolson, 1961. p. 53-60.

4.1 Solzhenitsyn and Historiography

> A people which no longer remembers has lost its history and its soul. Yes, the main thing is to recreate. When I sit down to write these books, my only task is to recreate everything as it happened. That's my main aim.[884]

The relationship between history and literature, and literature and truth, is a complex one. In Solzhenitsyn's case, the perception of truth in his work was closely related to common assumptions about Russian literature and the particular condition of Soviet literature and historiography. But it is also a result of the type of self-image he created. As the quote above shows, he spoke of himself as someone who "recreated" history. In his *Nobel Lecture*, he also spoke of the artist's task of "conquering falsehood";[885] and he wrote a famous plea to his fellow citizens to *Live not by Lies.*[886] He was successful in presenting his work as revealing the truth about Russian history. As I have shown throughout this study, his work—especially his texts about the camps—are often described as history. This reading of Solzhenitsyn's camp literature was influenced by his image as truth-teller, and directly affected by the Soviet Union's own dismal record in discussing its own problems, including its human rights record. In the Khrushchev era, sensitive subjects of recent history which had hitherto been ignored in Soviet historiography were discussed, yet a historian's duty consisted mainly in finding an ideological explanation for them.[887] Many different topics remained taboo, however, and the Brezhnev era brought additional political restraints. Historian Iurii Afanas'ev writes that, in the 1970s, "even admitting that there could be two viewpoints on a single problem was tantamount to a voluntary departure from the Academy of Sciences system."[888] As a result, journalists and writers were quicker than historians in grabbing opportunities to discuss delicate subjects

884 Solzhenitsyn, 1976, "Warning", p. 16.

885 "But writers and artists can achieve more: they can CONQUER FALSEHOOD! In the struggle with falsehood art always did win and it always does win! Openly, irrefutably for everyone! Falsehood can hold out against much in this world, but not against art." Solzhenitsyn, 1970.

886 Alexander Solzhenitsyn. "Live Not By Lies." The Washington Post 18 February 1974: A1.

887 Afanas'ev, 2001, p. 56.

888 Afanas'ev, 2001, p. 60.

openly.[889] This was the context in which Solzhenitsyn and other critical authors were published.

Western historians working on Soviet history had their share of difficulties. Access to archives was highly restricted, and they couldn't rely on their Soviet colleagues' objectivity. Unsurprisingly, when certain authors in the USSR began writing about prison camps or other taboo topics, and claimed to speak the truth, this caught the historians' attention. In many cases, the fact that these works were not scholarly did not hinder their use as sources in Western histories of Russia. This led to a series of complications.

During the Cold War, one of the most prominent Western historians of Stalinist repression was Robert Conquest. He describes Solzhenitsyn as a "witness of the dead" and a "witness for the truth" confronting Soviet lies.[890] He considers his testimony to be "totally authoritative", because it is "quite obviously true" and is enhanced by his witness status.[891] In his influential book, *The Great Terror*, he draws liberally from *Ivan Denisovich* in his descriptions of prison camps in his chapter titled "In the Labour Camps".[892] He writes that he is aware that *Ivan Denisovich* refers to a different period than the one he writes about, but he decides to use it because it confirms what was already known in the West.[893] In his later book, *Stalin and the Kirov Murder*, Conquest relies on a claim in Solzhenitsyn's literary memoir to confirm that Khrushchev "knew" that Stalin had ordered the murder of the Leningrad Party Leader Sergei Kirov.[894] In the referenced passage, taken from one of his memoirs, Solzhenitsyn writes:

> Khrushchev was quite sure that Stalin had murdered Kirov, but realized that Kirov was not a person of any importance in his own right.[895]

Conquest's statement that Khrushchev said he was certain that Stalin murdered Kirov is based on a memoir, written years later by a person—

---

889 Cf.: Meyer, 1989, "Perestrojka", p. 12.

890 Conquest, 1985, p. 3.

891 Conquest, 1985, p. 11.

892 For example, in endnotes number: 49, 51, 54, 59, 60, 62, 64-69, 71, 74, 75, 81-83, 89, 90, 95-97, 126, etc. For a full list of all references to Solzhenitsyn, see Conquest, 1969, pp. 601-604.

893 Conquest, 1969, pp. 565-571. He skips this note in the later edition (cf. Conquest, 1992).

894 Robert Conquest. *Stalin and the Kirov Murder.* London: Hutchinson, 1989. p. 117.

895 Solzhenitsyn, 1980, "Oak" p. 43 (this is the page quoted by Conquest.)

Solzhenitsyn—who claims to have heard a similar allegation was made in a "two- or three hour conversation" between two other people—Khrushchev and Tvardovsky—a month after it happened.[896] J. Arch Getty reproached Conquest's uncritical use of novels and memoirs in *Stalin and the Kirov Murder* in a review essay in 1989.[897] But already in 1986 historian Robert Thurston had confronted Conquest's biased use of Soviet dissident material—including Solzhenitsyn's.[898] This criticism has been repeated more recently in an article by Matt Lenoe who accuses Conquest of adopting the narrative that Stalin had killed Kirov—despite lack of reliable evidence—in order to underline the brutality of the Soviet leader.[899] However, Lenoe also describes earlier criticism of Conquest's work as ideologically motivated.[900] He places the past discussion about sources in the context of the trench wars between US historians who adhere to the "totalitarianism" theory and those who pleaded for a differentiated appreciation of Soviet history.

Contemporary historians have, of course, a much wider range of sources available to them than Conquest and Getty did in the past. Nevertheless, Soviet dissident material seems to have been used not only as a source of information but as a form of authoritative confirmation. Conquest writes that Solzhenitsyn's claims related to facts that non-communists in the West already knew and that they were "obviously" true. However, in a review of *Gulag* he lists claims that were not based on historical facts, for example that the Spanish refugee children of the Civil War were all sent to camps in the USSR.[901] Historian Martin Malia displays a similar attitude. He defines the purpose of *Gulag* as being to "spread The Truth" in East and West.[902] Malia sees this book as a confirmation of what he had believed about communism:

---

896 Solzhenitsyn, 1980, "Oak", p. 41; in p.vii, he states that he started writing this text when he was 49 (i.e. 1967).

897 J. Arch Getty. "Review: [untitled]." *Russian Review* 48.3, Gorbachev Reforms: Special Issue (1989): 348-51.

898 Robert W. Thurston. "On Desk-Bound Parochialism, Commonsense Perspectives, and Lousy Evidence: A Reply to Robert Conquest." *Slavic Review* 45.2 (1986): p. 240.

899 Matt Lenoe. "Did Stalin Kill Kirov and Does It Matter?" *The Journal of Modern History* 74.2 (2002): 352-80. p. 366-367.

900 Lenoe, 2002, p. 367.

901 Conquest, 1976, p. 91; Conquest, 1985, p. 3. For more on the fate of the Spanish refugees see: Colomina Limonero, 2010.

902 Malia, 1977, p. 47.

> For those without illusions about the Soviet system, *The Gulag* comes as the supreme, overwhelming confirmation of facts that the soft-headed in the West all too readily tend to forget[.][903]

As much as Malia has criticized Getty and other scholars over the years for ignoring Solzhenitsyn's claims,[904] his pre-emptive assumption that Solzhenitsyn was right does not help in making his stance credible. Although Solzhenitsyn is a prestigious writer and a prison camp witness, Getty's and Thurston's criticism does have its validity. Solzhenitsyn produced very important literary works and very compelling memoirs, but he was not a historian. It is true that he wrote about many truthful things that Soviet historians long kept silent—or even lied—about but that does not automatically make all he says factually accurate.

After 1991, many expected a change in the politicized atmosphere of Russian history writing, but Stephen Kotkin describes a different picture:

> But the writing of Soviet history continues to be more deeply conditioned not by the availability or unavailability of sources but by researchers' worldviews and agendas, and the times in which they live, not to mention the tenure process and patterns of patronage. [905]

According to Kotkin, this is not an anomaly, as he considers that good history writing should be political.[906] In this context, Kotkin underlines the importance of Soviet memoirs that express disillusionment with the Soviet state as particularly useful for historians.[907] Recent works on the gulag display a similar position to his.[908] As much as he and other anti-communist historians may defend the use of memoirs or even fictional works as sources to further their political cause, one could also argue that reliance on more solid sources would make their work more unassailable and, indeed, more objective. It is, after all, very likely that the politicized memoirs that Kotkin defends are less accurate precisely because of their ideological slant. As I have shown in sections 3.2 and 3.3 of this book, Solzhenitsyn's own ideology leads in some cases to ahistorical claims which bring forth controversies of their own.

---

903 Malia, 1977, p. 48.
904 Cf. Malia, 1994, 261-262; Malia, 2002, p. 73.
905 Stephen Kotkin. "The State-Is It Us? Memoirs, Archives, and Kremlinologists." *Russian Review* 61.1 (2002): 35-51. p. 36
906 Kotkin, 2002, p. 38.
907 Kotkin, 2002, p. 49-50.
908 This was briefly discussed in section 2.3 of this book.

In the 1980s, certain scholars in the US defended Solzhenitsyn's obviously euphemistic version of Tsarist Russia as to avoid alienating him and other nationalist dissidents from the West.[909] This ideological move had its repercussions. According to Ewa Thompson, Solzhenitsyn was successful in introducing his view into the mainstream.[910] However, his image of Imperial Russia as a "gentle" country, free of repression, and viciously destroyed by communism; and the Russian people as underdogs victimized for decades, is inconsistent with the simultaneous "successful territorial and political expansion" of the country.[911] This view of Russia may appear to be useful in a political argument, but at the same time it compromises historical objectivity and relativizes the long history of repression in pre-revolutionary Russia. Furthermore, as a result of its inaccuracy, the use of politically motivated hyperbole can have an opposite effect. When Solzhenitsyn tries to explain why the USSR is worse than what preceded it, and writes that in Tsarist Russia "camps there were none, the very concept was unknown" and that Western scholars who write about camps in Imperial Russia are "echoing" Soviet propaganda,[912] he is making his argument more vulnerable. This narrative is not only problematic when used by Solzhenitsyn, or during the Cold War. Even today, the image of a benevolent version of the Tsarist forced labor system is ineffectively used, for example by Anne Applebaum, to underline the cruelty of the Soviet camps.[913] She delineates the development of the Soviet camp system and its adoption of the Tsarist term *katorga* for the political prison camps, describing with horror how the prisoners of the Soviet *katorga* had to wear numbered uniforms.[914] As inhumane as wearing a number on clothing was, the Tsarist practice of maiming or branding the faces of *katorga* prisoners[915]—which she fails to mention—is much more terrifying. These examples illustrate how political bias in historical arguments can have

---

909 A prominent example is that of John Dunlop, a case discussed in the subchapter "Solzhenitsyn's Late Cold War Reception" in section 3.2 of this book.

910 Thompson, 1989, p. 502.

911 Thompson, 1989, p. 502-503.

912 Solzhenitsyn, 1980, "Misconceptions", p. 804.

913 Applebaum, 2004, p. xxxiff, 438ff.

914 Applebaum, 2004, p. 439.

915 Markus Ackeret. *In der Welt der Katorga: die Zwangsarbeitsstrafe für politische Delinquenten im ausgehenden Zarenreich (Ostsibirien und Sachalin)*. Munich: Osteuropa-Institut, 2007. p. 36.

an opposite effect. An uncritical use of anti-communist dissident texts for such purposes is not the most commendable—or even convenient—strategy.

Beyond the paradigm of Cold War hostilities in Western academia, some literary critics and historians explain the ambiguous relationship between Russian literature and history by referring to the particular nature of Russian literature. Literary scholar Barbara Walker writes that Russian memoirs have been read by Western historians as accurate and objective descriptions of history because these historians were unaware that Russian memoirs contain gossip and biased exaggerations—something she says Russian readers were conscious of.[916] She therefore suggests reading them precisely as sources revealing social relations defined by gossip, partisanship, and social struggles.[917] This proposal is very attractive, for it offers a good way to understand, for example, Solzhenitsyn's literary memoir *The Oak and the Calf* without focusing on all the details he "got wrong".[918] However, it is very likely that Solzhenitsyn would reject a reading that doubts the truth value of his claims.[919] But other Western literary critics offer different interpretations of the relationship between history and Russian literature, and Solzhenitsyn's work specifically.

Historian Geoffrey Hosking places Solzhenitsyn's work within a specific Russian tradition:

> [...] a kind of moral chronicle or 'literary investigation', uncovering the truth about the history of Soviet society and using the material thus brought forth to illuminate man's moral and spiritual nature.[920]

Richard Freeborn and Alexis Klimoff likewise consider the dedication with which Solzhenitsyn worked to "uncover" Soviet history as part of the

---

916 Barbara Walker. "On Reading Soviet Memoirs: A History of the 'Contemporaries' Genre as an Institution of Russian Intelligentsia Culture from the 1790s to the 1970s." *Russian Review* 59.3 (2000): p. 328-331.

917 Walker, 2000, p. 330, 351-352.

918 Walker analyzes this work in: Walker, 2000, p. 350ff.

919 Cf. his claims about the relationship between his work and truth quoted at the beginning of this section. Regarding *The Oak and the Calf*, Solzhenitsyn tried to defend some of his controversial claims in court, cf.: N.N. "Rechtsstreit um Solschenizyns Buch 'die Eiche und das Kalb'." Frankfurter Allgemeine Zeitung 19 September 1975: 25; Wallace Turner. "Couple Who Helped Solzhenitsyn Publish in U.S Charge Him with Libel." The New York Times 25 October 1980: 11.

920 Hosking, 1980, p. 101. (He refers to an approach to the novel as literary form, not a specific work.)

perceived duty of a Russian writer.[921] This view is rooted in the knowledge that, throughout the centuries, Russian literature and scholarship have been subjected to diverse forms of censorship. Therefore, it was not implausible to interpret the inclusion of political topics or dissenting versions of history in literature as a form of defiance.

Wachtel and Klimoff consider the way Russian writers appropriated history testifies to a different understanding of history and fiction: according to them, as opposed to Western readers, Russians did not perceive a division between literature and history.[922] This view hardly simplifies the question of how to deal with Russian literature and its versions of history. The fact that readers take historical claims in literature seriously creates its own problems: Laqueur's study of political extremism in Russia warns not to underestimate the propaganda power of historical novels, since they play an important role in disseminating conspiracy theories.[923]

Russian literature has evolved differently than literature in countries with less censorship. It has developed creative ways to deal with censorship,[924] and touched upon subjects that scholars were not able to discuss. However, the types of truth found in Russian literature may not be too dissimilar to those of other countries. In literature, there are many different forms of truth, which are independent of historical accuracy.[925] As Peter Lamarque points out, to judge a work by its factual accuracy is only sensible in certain genres—for instance, the historical novel—but even then only to a certain extent.[926] Invented dialogue can work very well, or not, depending on the craftiness of the author—but certain historical inaccuracies might result in unintended effects that make the work fail.[927] The truth value of Solzhenitsyn's historical novels

921 Freeborn, 1976, p. 1; Klimoff, 1996, p. 6.

922 Andrew Baruch Wachtel. *An Obsession with History: Russian Writers Confront the Past.* Stanford: Stanford University Press, 1994.

923 Laqueur, 1993, p. 171.

924 Lev Loseff. *On the Beneficence of Censorship: Aesopian Language in Modern Russian Literature.* Ed. Wolfgang Kasack. 31 Vol. Munich: Otto Sagner, 1984.

925 Peter Lamarque. "Literature and Truth." *A Companion to the Philosophy of Literature.* Eds. Garry Hagberg and Walter Jost. 44 Vol. Chichester: Wiley-Blackwell, 2010. 367-385.

926 Lamarque, 2010, p. 375.

927 Lamarque, 2010, p. 375.

can be analyzed with the same parameters as non-Russian works of the same genre, and lose less of their worth than if treated as historiography.

But there are further modern approaches to texts that could yield fruit in this case. Stephen Greenblatt's new historicist understanding of history and literature could very well help comprehend the subversive nature of some of Solzhenitsyn's works, without recurring to their factual informative value.[928] By analyzing the type of reality they present and the discourses they try to break, one can assess if they constitute counter-histories or attempts to restore an elitist, pre-revolutionary understanding of historiography.

Furthermore, when it comes to Solzhenitsyn's memoirs, studying them with the same scholarly methodology as their non-Russian counterpart has great potential. If Soviet dissident memoirs were interpreted with the same analytical skills that are often applied to other memoirs, the reader might profit more from the experience and scholars would be less vulnerable to accusations of political bias or sloppy research. After all, a critical view of autobiographies and memoirs is not exactly new in the West.[929] Historian Jörg Engelbrecht emphasizes that autobiographies and memoirs are most useful as sources relating to the author's mentality and cultural background, not as "objective" testimonies of the past.[930]

Maurice Halbwachs' ground-breaking works about the influence of our socio-cultural environment on memory and his concept of semiotization of history—remembering history only in so far as it is useful and meaningful—have influenced Western scholarship in the fields of history and autobiography for decades.[931] More recently, Astrid Erll pointed out that memory is only one among many modes of remembering: myth, religious memory, political

---

928 Catherine Gallagher, and Stephen Greenblatt. *Practicing New Historicism*. Chicago: University of Chicago Press, 2000.

929 Already in the nineteenth century autobiographies were studied as *literary* and not historical texts, cf.: Georg Misch. *Geschichte der Autobiographie*. Berlin: Teubner, 1907. p. 36.

930 Jörg Engelbrecht. "Autobiographien, Memoiren." *Einführung in die Interpretation historischer Quellen*. Ed. Bernd-A Rusinek. Paderborn: Schoningh, 1992. p. 61; Saunders shares a similar position, in: Saunders, 2008, p. 322.

931 Maurice Halbwachs. *Les Cadres Sociaux de la Mémoire*. Paris: Nouv. éd., 1935. Maurice Halbwachs. *La Mémoire Collective*. Paris: Presses Universitaires de France, 1950.

history, generational memory, etc. are all modes of referring to the past.[932] Historiography is the medium of one of those modes, namely, of history.[933] Memoirs and autobiographical accounts have been especially important sources in memory studies, micro-history, and oral history precisely because their subjectivity makes them valuable testimonies of human experience.[934] And it is precisely in this area that Solzhenitsyn's memoirs can be read most fruitfully.

4.2 Solzhenitsyn and Memory Culture in East and West

In the West, Solzhenitsyn became a historian-like figure because of the way his work was read in the 1960s-70s. But precisely because works such as *Gulag* were so often read as history, some conservative scholars ignore its massive role in memory culture and decry a lack of memory culture surrounding the Soviet prison camp experience.[935] In doing that, not only is the long-term resonance of Solzhenitsyn's work ignored, but also the ambivalent nature of memory culture which does not guarantee a specific political outcome.

Solzhenitsyn's obituaries and recent histories of Russian literature reveal the way that the author is remembered today, and how his relevance is perceived. In all major news sources in the US, UK, and Germany, Solzhenitsyn's death in 2008 was reported as a major event.[936] His obituaries reveal the extent to which his persona has been associated with the memory of Soviet prison camps—all of them emphasize the importance of *Ivan Denisovich* and *Gulag* not only in Solzhenitsyn's oeuvre, but in 20th century

---

932 Astrid Erll. "Cultural Memory Studies: an Introduction." *Cultural Memory Studies: An International and Interdisciplinary Handbook.* Ed. Ansgar Nünning. Berlin: Walter de Gruyter; 2008. p. 7.

933 Erll, 2008, "Introduction", p. 7.

934 Cf.: Georg G. Iggers. "Allgemein westlich oder spezifisch modern?" *Westliches Geschichtsdenken, eine interkulturelle Debatte.* Ed. Jörn Rüsen. Göttingen: Vandenhoeck & Ruprecht, 1999. pp. 101-117; Neumann, 2008, p. 333-343.

935 Cf.: Mahoney, 2001, p. 7; Haynes, 2003; Applebaum, 2004, p. xviii-xxii.

936 Robert Conquest. "Solzhenitsyn Was a Russian Patriot." Wall Street Journal 8 August 2008; N. N. "Alexander Solzhenitsyn. Obituary." The Telegraph 5 August 2008; Viktor Jerofejew. "Archipel Gulag zerstörte die Sowjetunion." Welt Online 4 August 2008 (http://www.welt.de/ kultur/article2273669/Archipel-Gulag-zerstoerte-die-Sowjetunion.html) (as of 3 September 2010); Lev Grossman. "Remembering Aleksandr Solzhenitsyn." TIME 4 August 2008.

history.[937] In this context, Solzhenitsyn is misleadingly described as an "icon of freedom"[938] and a "tireless champion of human rights and the dignity of man", who fought against "censorship and tyranny".[939] Moreover, his relevance is relegated to decades past. Indeed, the image of Solzhenitsyn as a person who combated Soviet injustice is so strong that several journalists express bewilderment at Russian president (and ex-KGB agent) Putin's patronage of and friendship with the author. Kerstin Holm decries Putin-driven memory culture surrounding Solzhenitsyn as an ideological usurpation.[940] Like Holm, Karl Grobe expresses doubts that the canonization of the author is part of dealing with the Soviet past.[941]

Solzhenitsyn's *Two Hundred Years Together* was similarly considered to be out of keeping with his image.[942] Jens Hartmann, who underlines the historical relevance of *Gulag*, cannot hide his disappointment with Solzhenitsyn's late work, which makes him resemble a "decrepit anti-Semite".[943] Gerd Koenen similarly considers this work a mistake that harmed the author's reputation, but he is optimistic that:

---

937 Jörg Mettke. "Mit Ruhm bestraft." Der Spiegel 11 August 2008: 148-149. Rita Anna Tüpper-Fotiadis. "'Nicht mit der Lüge leben'." Die politische Meinung September 2008: 64-68. Anne Applebaum. "Erinnerung an Alexander Solschenizyns Gulag." Welt Online 6 August 2008 (http://www.welt.de/debatte/ kommentare/article6072665 /Erinnerung-an-Alexander-Solschenizyns-Gulag.html) (as of 3 September 2010).

938 Cf.: Grossman, 2008.

939 Cf. Ralph Dutli. "Volksfreund Russlands, Staatsfeind der Sowjets." Frankfurter Allgemeine Zeitung 5 August 2008: 35.

940 Kerstin Holm. "Wem gehört Solschenizyn?" Frankfurter Allgemeine Zeitung 18 August 2008: 33. A similar view is expressed by Tüpper-Fotiadis, 2008, p. 68.

941 Karl Grobe. "Die gestohlenen Leben." Frankfurter Rundschau 4 August 2008.

942 Jens Hartmann. "Solschenizyn, der Heilige der russischen Seele." Welt Online 4 August 2008. (http://www.welt.de/kultur/article2271702/Solschenizyn-der-Heilige-der-russischen-Seele.html) (as of 12 June 2012); Gerd Koenen. "Europas Linke und Solschenizyns Zorn." Welt Online 4 August 2008 (http://www.welt.de/ kultur/article2271702/Solschenizyn-der-Heilige-der-russischen-Seele.html) (as of 5 September 2010); Friedemann Kohler. "Mit seinem Spätwerk konnte der Westen wenig anfangen." Der Spiegel Online 4 August 2008. (http://www.spiegel.de/ kultur/literatur/0,1518,druck-569808,00.html) (as of 4 April 2011).

943 „Mit diesem Alterswerk tat er sich jedoch keinen Gefallen. Sätze wie die Juden seien die „Hefe der Revolution" gewesen, das Auflisten von Juden in der Umgebung Lenins und Stalins, um den Beitrag der Juden am kommunistischen Terror zu untermauern, aber auch die Verharmlosung von Pogromen ließen Solschenizyn wie einen altersschwachen Antisemiten aussehen." Hartmann, 2008. "He did not do himself a favor with his late work. Phrases such as: Jews are the 'yeast of the

> [D]ie unvergängliche historische Leistung des Autors des „Archipel GULag" bleibt, wie immer sein Alterswerk im historischen Rückblick einmal bewertet werden wird, in jedem Fall unvergänglich.[944]

Beyond the narrative of a writer who committed a few *faux-pas* in his late years, some journalists take the opportunity to point out that the Solzhenitsyn "we all know and love" in the West is not quite the same writer that Russians know. For example, Jörg Mettke writes that the West fashioned for itself a false image of Solzhenitsyn as a pro-Western dissident, which made it unable to perceive his Orthodox Christian, backward-looking visions of Russia.[945] Lev Grossman juxtaposes the meaning Solzhenitsyn had for many people in the West, and Solzhenitsyn's foul opinion of Western politics and lifestyle.[946]

Recent Western histories of Russian literature honor Solzhenitsyn's role in bringing the subject of the prison camp experience onto the radar of Western readers.[947] However, in today's, much more expanded canon he plays only a minor role. In contrast, from a Russian perspective, Solzhenitsyn's relevance in the cultural canon has grown in the last decade.[948] In Russia, his political relevance has also prospered. A quick look at the Russian memory culture surrounding the author exposes the depth of the rift between the Western and the local perception of Solzhenitsyn's significance.

In his country, Solzhenitsyn's own agency as memory-maker and the *remediation* of his work and persona in the media produced a contrasting image of the author. On the one hand, he is remembered in his role as victim of the gulag, but also as a prestigious legitimizer of the current government. *Remediation* is Astrid Erll's term, which she defines as follows:

---

revolution'; or the listing of Jews in Lenin and Stalins milieu in order to buttress the Jews' contribution to communist terror, or triviliazing pogroms, made Solzhenitsyn appear like a decrepit anti-Semite." (My translation.)

944 Koenen, 2008. "The everlasting historical achievement of the author of *Gulag Archipelago* remains by all means everlasting no matter how his late work may later be evaluated." (My translation.)

945 Mettke, 2008, p. 148.

946 Grossman, 2008.

947 Wachtel, 2009, p. 244-247; Malcolm V. Jones and Robin Feuer Miller, eds. *The Cambridge Companion to the Classic Russian Novel.* Cambridge: Cambridge University Press, 1998; Dobrenko, 2011.

948 Ben A. McVicker. "The Creation and Transformation of a Cultural Icon: Aleksandr Solzhenitsyn in Post-Soviet Russia, 1994-2008." *Canadian Slavonic Papers* 53.2-4 (2011): 305-336.

> With the term 'remediation' I refer to the fact that memorable events are usually represented again and again, over decades and centuries, in different media: in newspaper articles, photography, diaries, historiography, novels, films, etc. What is known about a war, a revolution, or any other event which has been turned into a site of memory, therefore, seems to refer not so much to what one might cautiously call the 'actual events', but instead to a canon of existent medial constructions, to the narratives and images circulating in a media culture. [...] Paradoxically, even despite antagonistic and reflexive forms of representation, remediation tends to solidify cultural memory, creating and stabilizing certain narratives and icons of the past.[949]

Solzhenitsyn's work has been *at its core* "memory-making" material. Alexander Etkind identifies two types of cultural memory: "*soft*" and "*hard*".[950] By *soft memory* he means texts: historical, literary, guidebooks etc. In contrast, *hard memory* consists of (physical) monuments, memorials, state laws, court decisions, etc. Solzhenitsyn has actively created both forms of memory. First of all, he dedicated some of his books to the memory of other Soviet citizens who had shared his experiences. Most of his works—from his first novel to his final work on Russian Jewish history—were intended as descriptions of historical events and processes he believed to be forgotten, distorted or neglected in public memory. The desire to "set the record straight" through a book on historical events is just as much memory-shaping as the setting up of a memorial site. Solzhenitsyn's involvement in creating *hard memory* of Russian history and of himself took different forms. In 1974, with his royalties from *The Gulag Archipelago* Solzhenitsyn created a fund named after himself. One of its aims was to offer financial aid to former gulag inmates. This preserves a symbolic connection between the author's name and the gulag experience. In 1997, he created a literary prize that carries his name. The award includes the prize sum of $25,000 provided by the Solzhenitsyn Fund. Its goal is to preserve the literary traditions of the Fatherland, and to immortalize the memory of the prize-winner in case the

---

949 Astrid Erll. "Literature, Film, and the Mediality of Cultural Memory." *Cultural Memory Studies: An International and Interdisciplinary Handbook*. Ed. Ansgar Nünning. Berlin: Walter de Gruyter; 2008. Cf. especially p. 393-394.

950 Alexander Etkind. "Hard and Soft Cultural Memory: Political Mourning in Russia and Germany." *Grey Room*, 16, (Summer 2004). p. 39-40.

winning author is deceased.[951] A third and more sophisticated form of *hard memory* created by the Russian author is the library he founded in Moscow.[952] Since 2005, the "Russia Abroad Library and Foundation" has been based at the "House of Russian Abroad". It stores documents from Russians who lived in exile, and specializes in memoirs and life-writing. Some of the material was collected by Solzhenitsyn during his own time in exile. The purpose of this library, which was funded by the Solzhenitsyn Foundation and the city of Moscow under Mayor Yuri Luzhkov, is to preserve the cultural heritage of the Russian Diaspora and the memory of Russian exiles. In 2009, the whole library complex was renamed after Solzhenitsyn, following a decree by the governing authorities of Moscow underlining the role of the author in its creation.[953] With this impressive library, the largest of its kind in Moscow, Solzhenitsyn created a very palpable reminder of the importance of the Russian experience in exile, and was elevated to a symbol of the Russian Diaspora.[954]

Solzhenitsyn's presence in the media and in collective memory has further been boosted by his friendship with Putin. Precisely since Putin has been the *de facto* ruler of Russia since the end of 1999, great efforts have been undertaken by the state to canonize Solzhenitsyn's work and to establish forms of *hard memory* for this symbolic author.[955] In this process, the memory of the gulag has not been neglected. Solzhenitsyn's work is now part of the federal school curriculum in Russia and is thus a part of a pedagogical canon. In addition to *The Gulag Archipelago*, school children in Russia are to read *Ivan Denisovich* and *Matryona's Home* in history, literature, and Russian

---

951 This information was taken from the official website: http://www.rp-net.ru/book/premia/ index.php, (last accessed April 2011).

952 Its Russian name is: *Biblioteka-Fond Russkoe Zarubezh'ia*. Information on the library can be found on http://www.bfrz.ru/?mod=static&id=1, (last accessed June 2011).

953 *Dom Russkogo Zarubezh'ia imeni Aleksandra Solzhenitsyna* (The Alexander Solzhenitsyn House of Russian Abroad).

954 Sof'ia Krynskaia. "Solzhenitsyn osnoval biblioteku rosskogo zarubezh'ia." Izvestiia 20 January 2003: 2; N.N. "Größte Bibliothek von Moskau, 'Russen im Ausland', wird eröffnet." RIA Novosti Deutsch 1 September 2005.

955 I speak of Solzhenitsyn's oeuvre as part of the canon in the sense that his work is "understood to be of central importance in a culture." Earl R. Anderson and Gianfrancesco Zanetti. "Comparative Semantic Approaches to the Idea of a Literary Canon." *The Journal of Aesthetics and Art Criticism* 58.4 (2000): 341-360.

classes.[956] Putin's visits to Solzhenitsyn's estate were widely reported in the local media. When Solzhenitsyn was awarded the State Prize, *Rossiiskaia Gazeta* emphasized that Putin would personally hand him the Prize.[957] The article indicated that Solzhenitsyn was the author of the greatest work of the 20th century—*The Gulag Archipelago*. Other forms of *soft memory* of Solzhenitsyn as a *lieu de mémoire* of the Soviet labor camp experience have been theater shows created from adaptations of his works. A show called *Sharashka*, inspired by Solzhenitsyn's book on forced intellectual labor, *The First Circle*, was premiered in a Moscow theater on his birthday in 1999.[958] Since then, a TV series and an opera based on his work have found their way to Russian audiences.[959] In 2009, the opera *Ivan Denisovich* premiered in the superb opera house of Perm.[960] Since the author's death many forms of *hard memory* have been established. Following the author's demise, President Dmitrii Medvedev proclaimed in a decree that a street in Moscow would be named after him, and that the cities of Kislovodsk and Rostov-on-Don would establish memorials to the writer.[961] Soon after that, a street was named after the author—despite a law stating that one must wait for ten years after a person's death in order to do so. Preparations for museums in both Southern Russian cities are under way.[962] A museum in honor of Solzhenitsyn has been established in Moscow.[963]

These modes of *hard memory* have received significant press coverage, making the interaction between *hard* and *soft memory* more obvious.[964] By

---

956 Cf.: N.N. "'Arkhipelag GULAG' budut izuchat' v shkolakh." Vesti 9 September 2009.

957 Cf. Elena Novoselova. "V Kruge - Pervyi." Rossiiskaia Gazeta 6 June 2007.

958 N.N. "Solzhenitsyn snova na Taganke." Nezavisimaia Gazeta 7 December 1999.

959 A TV series based on *First Circle,* directed by Gleb Panfilov, was broadcasted in 2006.

960 Natal'ia Emel'ianova. "Natal'ia Solzhenitsyna priekhala v Perm' na prem'eru opery "Odin den' Ivana Denisovicha." Rossiiskaia Gazeta 15 May 2009.

961 Dmitrii Medvedev. "Ukaz Prezidenta Rossiiskoi Federatsii ot 6 avgusta 2008g. i 1187 'Ob uvekovechenii pamiati A.I. Solzhenitsyna.'" Rossiiskaia Gazeta 6 August 2008.

962 Cf.: Alena Larina. "Pamyat' v sobstvennosti." Rossiskaya Gazeta 20 August 2008.

963 N.N. "V stolichnoi kvartire Solzhenitsyna otkroiut muzei." Moskovskii Komsomolets 1 June 2010.

964 For example: Olg'a Masyukevich. "Ulitsa Solzhenitsyna." Rossiiskaya Gazeta 15 August 2008; Ol'ga Nesterova. "Krasnoe Koleso Zakatilos." Rossiiskaya Gazeta 12 April 2008; Ekaterina Pichugina. "Deputaty otmeniaiut 10-letnii tsenz na

reporting on Solzhenitsyn and repeating certain narratives, the media establishes the author and his work as Russian *lieux de mémoire* (Pierre Nora). However, this does not mean that a static image is being created: I agree with Assmann, who points out that *lieux de mémoire* are dynamic and can change over the years.[965] Memory of a certain event can become stronger or weaker, according to contemporary needs. Assmann gives the example of how the memory of the Holocaust was suppressed for decades in the United States due to the Cold War, as it was considered inconvenient to remember World War II atrocities when the victory over them was achieved through an alliance with the USSR, the new arch-enemy.[966] In a similar manner, memory in today's Russia can tell us more about the present than the past. For instance, in post-Soviet Russia the memory of World War II has been instrumentalized to comfort contemporary generations by boosting their patriotism in the face of the challenges posed by the recent wars in Chechnya and other woes.[967] Russian author Zinovy Zinik explains how Solzhenitsyn's gulag experience plays to current political interests:

> I am old enough to remember how, as Soviet schoolboys, we were from time to time given a talk by a guest lecturer, an Old Bolshevik, on the horrors of the tsarist regime. The aim was to demonstrate how happy and bright our days in the Soviet paradise were. It is alarming to see that Solzhenitsyn's legacy is now being used by the new governors of Russia in a similar way.[968]

Solzhenitsyn's harrowing experience under Stalin may make current human rights violations seem insignificant in comparison. Moreover, some observers note the role Solzhenitsyn plays in creating suspicion of democracy and strengthening Putin's authoritarian rule in Russia. Boris Kolonitskii and Robert Horvath describe this phenomenon in recent articles.[969] Horvath examines

---

memorial'nye nazvaniia ulits i stantsii metro." Moskovskii Komsomolets 19 September 2010.

965 Aleida Assmann. *Der lange Schatten der Vergangenheit: Erinnerungskultur und Geschichtspolitik.* Munich: C. H. Beck, 2006. p. 166-167.

966 Assmann, 2006, p.167-168.

967 Cf.: Serguei Oushakine. *Patriotism of Despair.* Ithaca: Cornell University Press. 2009. p. 191ff.

968 Zinovy Zinik. "Blue-collar Solzhenitsyn." The Times Literary Supplement 6 August 2008.

969 Boris Kolonitskii. "Russian Historiography of the 1917 Revolution: New Challenges to Old Paradigms?" *History & Memory* 21.2 (2009): 34-59. Robert Horvath.

how Solzhenitsyn fits snugly into Putin's crackdown against political opposition:

> In 2005, when the Kremlin was shaken by Ukraine's Orange Revolution and mass protests at home, Solzhenitsyn appeared on state television for an interview that was widely perceived as part of the regime's effort to neutralize the threat of a domestic "velvet revolution." In 2007, as the authorities prepared to orchestrate the presidential succession and brutally suppressed opposition demonstrations, Solzhenitsyn was again deployed as part of the Kremlin's counterrevolutionary strategy. The government broadsheet *Rossiiskaia Gazeta* instigated a national debate around the anti-revolutionary insights contained in Solzhenitsyn's essay, "Reflections on the February Revolution." Later that year, Solzhenitsyn received a state prize from Putin, who boasted that several steps undertaken by his government accorded with Solzhenitsyn's recommendations.[970]

Kolonitskii describes how the current ideological rejection of liberalism and democratization is underpinned by Solzhenitsyn's arguments against the February Revolution of 1917 (as an attempt to dissolve the monarchy and become a democracy).[971] In this sense, Solzhenitsyn in Russia differs from the image of him prevalent in the West, but it does not contrast with the image he created and the message he disseminated. Those in Russia who oppose democracy instrumentalize his message but they are not misinterpreting it. Solzhenitsyn's decade-long battle against pluralism, his scathing criticism of the West, and his support for Putin's government are as much part of his legacy as anti-communism is.

4.3 Chapter Conclusion

In 1987, the Soviet émigré and satirist Vladimir Voinovich published a picaresque novel about an irreverent Russian émigré and his collision with a lionized fellow émigré writer, Sim Symich Karnavalov, whom he meets again in Moscow 2042.[972] Karnavalov can be easily read as a parody of

---

"Apologist of Putinism? Solzhenitsyn, the Oligarchs, and the Specter of Orange Revolution." *The Russian Review* 70.2 (2011): 300-18.

970 Horvath, 2011, p. 300.

971 Kolonitskii, 2009, p. 51-52.

972 Vladimir Voinovich. *Moskva 2042.* Ann Arbor: Ardis, 1987.

Solzhenitsyn.[973] Lesley Milne interprets this novel as an exploration of what Voinovich considers to be an uncritical devotion to Russian dissident writers:

> Voinovich's satire of Solzhenitsyn subjects this idea to critical examination: just because a major writer is in opposition to the State does not necessarily mean that his ideas should be uncritically embraced.[974]

In Voinovich's dystopia, the Moscow of the future becomes as repressive as its Soviet ancestor; however, the symbols of oppression have changed and Karnavalov is able to establish a Christian authoritarian state.[975] Ironically, in the 21st century, Solzhenitsyn did play a prominent role supporting Russia's undemocratic regime. Fortunately, nevertheless, he did not become a Karnavalov. Still, Voinovich made a valid point, in his own satirical way, about writers' fallibility and readers' gullibility.

After analyzing his reception and the way he is remembered, perhaps it is fair to say that Solzhenitsyn has become a literary hero in his own right. He has crafted his image just as he created his literary characters; it is not without reason that one of his character's lines—that a writer is like a second government—is so often used to describe him. But perhaps we can understand him better if we see him similarly to his literary hero Ivan Denisovich. Ivan was devised as an uncouth and maybe even dirty peasant in order to challenge the pristine intelligentsia to feel empathy even for the least significant of Stalin's victims. With his very particular ideas about nationalism, Christianity, women, and the West, Solzhenitsyn is daring us to despise the way he was repressed even in the face of our possible disapproval of his ideology. At the same time, we can be sure that there will always be someone who does agree with precisely such an ideology and for whom Solzhenitsyn will have a different meaning. Despite changes in meaning, his role in memory culture will continue to be relevant, as long as his readers and memory-makers consider him to be so.

---

973 Lesley Milne. "Satire." *The Cambridge Companion to the Classic Russian Novel.* Eds. Malcolm V. Jones and Robin Feuer Miller. Cambridge: Cambridge University Press, 1998. 86-103. Karen L. Ryan-Hayes. "Vojnovič's Moskva 2042 as Literary Parody." *Russian Literature* 36.4 (1994): 453-79.

974 Milne, 1998, p. 100-101.

975 For a description of the novel, see: Erika Gottlieb. *Dystopian Fiction East and West: Universe of Terror and Trial.* Montreal: McGill-Queen's University Press, 2001. p. 249-257.

Conclusions

Analyzing Solzhenitsyn's reception in the West has proved to be a fruitful academic endeavor for several reasons. Despite the singularity of this writer and the historical context of his rise to fame, numerous aspects of his case possess a more global applicability.

It would be almost axiomatic to conclude this study of Solzhenitsyn's reception in the US, UK, and the Federal Republic of Germany by simply pointing at the importance of its ideological and historical context. The previous chapters show in detail the enormous influence of these aspects not only on Solzhenitsyn's creative work, but also on his Western reception. However, given the relatively high level of academic and press freedom in these countries, the effect of politics on literary reception is not self-evident. To conclude, I will sum up some of the key results of my study and discuss the consequences of the interaction between reception and historical context in this particular case, and its significance on a more general scale. The results presented in this book may initially look like a list of interrelated paradoxes. My duty has not only been to show their complexity but to disentangle them from each other and to present the mechanisms that led to these paradoxes.

It was not only the socio-historical context that defined the type of reception Solzhenitsyn received. Solzhenitsyn's works contain specific elements that trigger a different kind of response than other types of literary works do. As a result of their genres, ideology, and topics, the reader (and the critic) is confronted by a triangular challenge in evaluating their aesthetics, ethics, and politics—three elements that are also interconnected. The direction the critic takes, the emphasis s/he makes, is further influenced by external and internal factors: such as her and the author's political environment, its relation to the topic, and the critic's personal motivation. Furthermore, the impulse to find the highest possible relevance—be it aesthetic, ethical, or political—of a particular work for the highest number of readers, is a process that invariably leads to the neglect of other aspects. This need to justify fame is partly the result of modern authors' celebrity status, which makes critics feel compelled to argue not only why this author is famous but also why he is relevant. This is a phenomenon Graeme Turner calls the "myth of success" in celebrity culture, and while it does not mean that the luminary in question is a phony, it denotes the narrative emphasis on the greatness or special quality of a famous person as a result of his or her fame.[976] The creation of a "myth of success" invariably leads to brushing aside the finer detail, and to certain opaqueness. In my study, I have been able to pinpoint some of the areas that were emphasized by critics, as well as other important areas that were ignored in the process.

The Ethic

In the West, Solzhenitsyn is widely perceived as a victim of the gulag who carried out the important ethical task of reminding the world of the plight of the oppressed. Michael Scammell paradigmatically wrote upon his death: "He was a moral and spiritual leader, whose books were noted as much for their ethical dimension as for their aesthetic qualities."[977] But do such widely reproduced descriptions of the author and his reception stand the test of a closer analysis of his work and reception?

First of all, it is important to understand how the image of Solzhenitsyn as a moral icon and ethical writer came about. This image is the result of a combination of factors that include the author's biography, the types of books he wrote, and the way critics react to such works. Furthermore, the historical circumstances in which Solzhenitsyn rose to fame constrained debates about the specifics of his ideology, thus consolidating a hazy image of the author and his political goals.

Several works by Solzhenitsyn have an autobiographical element: in some he draws on his experiences in Soviet prison camps, but also his life in the Russian provinces, in Moscow, and later on in exile in the US. However, the texts that relate to his life in prison camps are by far those which have marked his place in literary history. Three of his most prominent works—*One Day in the Life of Ivan Denisovich*, *First Circle*, and *The Gulag Archipelago*—are inspired by his camp experience. Although the first two are entirely

---

976 Graeme Turner. *Understanding Celebrity*. London: Sage, 2004. p. 96.

977 Michael Scammell. "Russia's Literary Light Who Illuminated Dark World of Soviet Regime" The Guardian 4 August 2008.

fictionalized, their reception shows that they have partly been read as life-writing. Some reviewers retell details from these works and frame them as Solzhenitsyn's experience. This tendency is even stronger in the case of *Gulag Archipelago*, a book that begins with a prologue telling us that nothing in it is fictitious.

The reception of Solzhenitsyn's prison camp related works reveals that in all three countries of my study, his experience as a former inmate was essential to their impact. He further gained authority from Nikita Khrushchev's early approval and Leonid Brezhnev's later censorship. Khrushchev singled out Solzhenitsyn's work *One Day in the Life of Ivan Denisovich* as a milestone in confronting the crimes of the Stalin era. Brezhnev's relentless persecution of the author when he published *The Gulag Archipelago*—a much broader indictment of the Soviet Union's political system—proved how far this state still had to go in the protection of basic individual freedoms. Both these events were central to the attention Western countries paid Solzhenitsyn, and helped to define his image there. The expulsion of the witness in 1974 made it very difficult for Western critics to express anything but full solidarity with him.

Nevertheless, the emphasis on biography did not always work to Solzhenitsyn's advantage. In contrast to most of his Western critics, the Russian author valued his work on the history of pre-revolutionary Russia as his most important contribution. The missing link between these books and his prison ordeal affected critics' interest in them: the impact of the work relating to his imprisonment had defined the expectations of his readers, making his other texts seem almost superfluous.

The paradigm of witness literature helps us understand why readers have ethical expectations from testimonial texts, and why Solzhenitsyn's biography affects their appreciation of these works. Theoreticians agree that these texts are the description of the author's own suffering, that the author has the desire to speak the truth about injustice and to commemorate others who died. There is a widespread view that these texts should possess an ethical function and should not be ideological. The term "witness literature" often includes camp literature, that is, testimonies of the prison camp experience in communist states. This inclusion has some advantages but also poses several challenges.

To understand Solzhenitsyn's camp literature as witness literature is enlightening in the interpretation of certain aspects of its reception. The global resonance of these texts testifies of a universal appeal of such topics. Moreover, researchers of witness and camp literature have noted that critics tend to avoid analyzing such works from a purely aesthetic point of view. This apprehension to focus on aesthetics in a work that speaks of deep human suffering is a result of the fear of appearing insensitive, or that criticism of poor aesthetic quality in such a work may be interpreted as a political reaction. A lack of detailed aesthetic criticism was widespread in Solzhenitsyn's case. However, quite paradoxically, certain critics declared it both out of bounds to discuss the aesthetic aspects of Solzhenitsyn's camp literature and also declared it an aesthetic masterpiece.[978]

But the overbearing effect of Solzhenitsyn's primary identification as a witness also affected critics' willingness to criticize those aspects of his ideology they disagreed with. Some critics would make a short mention of a point in Solzhenitsyn's work that caused them discomfort, but then would wash down their criticism by adding: "who are we (am I) to judge?"[979] Most critics of these works endeavored to see them as a general condemnation of tyranny, thus emphasizing the overall ethical message above more narrowly ideological aspects.

The study of Solzhenitsyn's reception underlines certain limitations in theoretical ponderings regarding witness literature. It is thoroughly understandable that critics attach ethical value to these texts, because authors do so as well. But the expectation of many theorists of witness literature that these texts adhere to humanists values and yet remain somehow politically neutral is difficult to fulfil and is contrary to the expressed wishes of many such authors. Solzhenitsyn did not only seek to bear witness, but also to cause a political catharsis. Scholars of camp literature tend to acknowledge this political activism more easily than their colleagues in the area of witness literature. This is likely the result of the historical development

978 Or, like Scammell, they write that Solzhenitsyn was widely appreciated for both the ethic *and* aesthetic value of his work, but give no examples of the latter. Cf. Scammell, 2008.

979 For example: Leonard Schapiro. "Alexander Solzhenitsyn: Conscience of Western Civilization." *Russian Studies*. Ed. Ellen Dahrendorf. New York: Viking, 1987 [1975]. 376-390; Augstein, "Ehre", 1974.

of camp literature. Camp memoirs and camp fiction were first published while these forms of repression continued to exist, whereas other forms of witness literature, such as Shoah literature, only received attention when the violence described was over. This made the political goals of camp literature more concrete and contingent. The reception of *Ivan Denisovich* and *Gulag* shows the widespread view that these testimonial texts could result in political changes in the Soviet Union. For Solzhenitsyn, the focus on a particular type of oppression was a conscious choice.

Solzhenitsyn condemned the Soviet camp system and political repression in some cases, but not in others. Moreover, his Christian worldview allowed him to downplay the state violence of Tsarist Russia and Christian dictatorships of the 20th century. The ethical quagmire that resulted from these aspects of his ideology was seldom directly confronted. The political environment of the Cold War hardly tolerated a half-hearted embrace of the author and his works. This had lasting consequences: his celebrity status would not have likely been established if an image of him as a conservative rebel with patriarchal and revisionist leanings had spread early on. However, acknowledging the fact that a witness may not adhere to a universal human rights agenda would help critics achieve more nuanced appreciations of this person's literary output. This is especially important when one considers that problematic aspects of the witness' worldview do not necessarily remain "under the rug". As Solzhenitsyn's revisionist reception shows, people with peripheral (and sometimes extremist) political views try to profit from his reputation in order to buttress their less than humanistic narratives.

The Political

The bulk of Solzhenitsyn's political reception focused on very broad questions that made him relevant to a global readership. In the 1970s, Nicholas Anning observed that when the political content in Solzhenitsyn's work increased, so did his authority.[980] This trend reached its zenith with the dramatic publication of *Gulag*, when it became the center of debates about Western attitudes towards communism. However, his prominence did not continue to grow as

---

980 This claim was discussed in chapter three of this book. Cf. also: Anning, 1976, p. 127.

his political activism increased: it remained tied to local historical factors. A political reading that emphasizes the condemnation of Soviet repression concludes that the significance of this work became a thing of the past, once the Soviet Union collapsed. While it is true that in the 1970s he was often in the news and there was wide-spread scholarly interest in his work and his thought, one must recognize that his much greater political and literary activity in the 1990s in Russia was mostly perceived as a mere curiosity in the West. This neglect is one of the reasons why the halcyonic image of Solzhenitsyn as a champion of freedom established in the 1970s endured in the West despite all his illiberal and anti-democratic texts. Once the threat of communism was gone and the possibility arose of adjusting the author's image to the content of his texts, there was little interest in doing so.

Solzhenitsyn's most memorable work is *The Gulag Archipelago.* It contains both factual and more imaginative (literary) elements, and—most importantly—a strong ideological background. This last feature cannot be ignored and needs to be problematized. The fact that a good deal of the content in *Gulag* is based on hearsay and speculation already undermines its status—and authority—as witness literature. The manifest ideological proclivity of *Gulag* is the main reason why I propose to define it as a work of political witness literature, rather than witness literature as such. Although the stated goal of *Gulag* is to keep the memory of those who died in the prison camps—and would thus fit into the classical paradigm of witness literature—I give examples of how the author plays down the suffering of some of the victims of the camps, and shows outright contempt towards other victims. Moreover, instead of focusing on giving an accurate account of the oppression in a particular context, Solzhenitsyn greatly exaggerates certain details of the suffering in Soviet prison camps and does this repeatedly by negatively comparing these camps with those in Nazi Germany or Tsarist Russia—belittling the ordeal suffered by the victims of these other regimes. Last but not least, in *Gulag* Solzhenitsyn unfairly blames Jews for their alleged role in creating the Soviet forced labor system. These aspects of his work are the result of a specific political worldview that defies the works' alleged intentions of keeping alive the memory of the dead and telling the truth about the camps. In this sense, *Gulag* is a combination of testimony about one man's experience in Soviet prison camps and his ideological ponderings about the origins and the meaning of these camps.

As the multifariousness of the political content in his work was overlooked while he was being canonized, his image as a moral paragon was cemented in the West. Those few critics who wished to discuss anti-Semitism in his work often faced accusations that they were repeating Soviet propaganda. On the other hand, revisionist writers who agreed with precisely the problematic aspects of Solzhenitsyn's work profited from the moral halo over him and his work. This is an issue that I address in this book with deliberate care on the basis of the textual evidence in both Solzhenitsyn's texts and his reception. Enunciating the presence of controversial aspects in Solzhenitsyn's works is not an attack on his person but an acknowledgement of the complexity of his work. Articles about the author that merely repeat the rather worn-out narrative of Solzhenitsyn as the conscience of Russia or a human rights activist fail to explain the phenomenon of an author revered by both human rights advocates *and* right-wing extremists.

More needs to be done with regard to criticism of this author's work. In Russia, and among marginal groups of readers in the West, Solzhenitsyn continues to be read as an important political author and his conservative views are appreciated for what they are. Nevertheless, other contemporary political and non-political critical approaches to Solzhenitsyn's work are rare. Although there may be many reasons for this "critical exile", a lack of richness in the material is not one of them. There are plenty of yet unexplored forms of political interpretation of literature which can help us understand this author and his context in new ways. Moreover, as I have discussed in different chapters of this book, studying Solzhenitsyn's work with contemporary theories—such as feminist and queer theory, or memory studies—is very likely to lead to promising results.

The Aesthetic

Redefining an author is also a way of updating and refreshing interest in him. In some cases, such as those of Dostoevsky or Solzhenitsyn, critics long felt compelled to hide or ignore the parts of their ideology that dated badly. For decades, the fact that Dostoevsky was anti-Semitic came into conflict with widespread admiration of him as an author. Some critics responded to this dilemma by ignoring the negative aspects of his works. A more wholesome approach to his work invariably leaves a dent in his reputation and even affects his celebrity worth, but it also proves more adequate to the modern reader, who tends to have increasingly sophisticated political expectations. Today's reader is more likely to assume that mentalities of previous centuries allowed for more bigotry than the 21st century, thus adopting a more distanced position to the text. Critics' negation of the author's anti-Semitism, however, would most likely cause readers' surprise at the critics' blindness, or convey the impression that these views are condoned. Solzhenitsyn's case is similar to Dostoevsky's in many ways, which is why it is so important to keep criticism of him up to date. The main difference between the two authors is, however, that Dostoevsky's aesthetic achievements are much more broadly appreciated than Solzhenitsyn's. The aesthetic features of the latter's oeuvre lack a wider appeal. This is the case even if his translators have indeed contributed to a more global appreciation of his work by using contemporary language and refraining from using the archaisms, slang, or regionalisms that make Solzhenitsyn's Russian ideological and difficult to understand. Solzhenitsyn's interweaving of archival material into some of his later books has had a mixed response at best. The didactic style in works such as *First Circle*, *August 1914*, and *Gulag* leads to discrete aesthetic flaws. For example, it gives some of Solzhenitsyn´s characters a schematic profile, which makes a perception of them as nuanced human beings less likely.

Alas, it is not easy to separate aesthetic assessments from politics. Terry Eagleton recently pointed out that all too often critics consider didactical literature flawed when they disagree with it, but not when they agree.[981] To be sure, developing aesthetic criteria that cope with this dilemma will remain a continuous, at times controversial process.

The one-sided and at times even perfunctory way that Solzhenitsyn was read in the Cold War is perhaps symptomatic of political readings of literature, a problem John Brenkman has poignantly criticized.[982] Much too often, political readings remain at a superficial level that ignores the composite nature of literature, the interplay between formal and semantic levels, and—more paradoxically—neglects the role of the author and the work's socio-political

981 Terry Eagleton. *The Event of Literature*. New Haven: Yale University Press, 2012. pp. 68-69.

982 John Brenkman. "Extreme Criticism." *What's Left of Theory? New Work on the Politics of Literary Theory*. Eds. Judith Butler, John Guillory, and Kendall Thomas. New York: Routledge, 2000. 114-136.

context. To further complicate matters, the very possibility of extricating aesthetic judgement from the social or the political is questionable. In Brenkman's words, "Aesthetic 'judgement' is enabled by a material, institutionalized space of expression and criticism."[983] Universality of aesthetic judgement is conditioned by external factors.[984] To say this is not a denial of the formal in art and literature—the part that can be considered to be primarily aesthetic. Brenkman reminds us that even the aesthetic is interlocked with the political—and that it is important to look at precisely these formal aspects of art in order to better understand its politics. In my work, I have pointed not only at the political aspects on the semantic level of Solzhenitsyn's work, but also to the form he chose to present them. His style, language, and even choice of metaphors may be aesthetic, but their political effect is undeniable. By noting the gender and race issues in Solzhenitsyn's work that have not sufficiently been discussed, I am also exhorting for a *thorough* analysis of the aesthetics of these aspects. As I have argued throughout this book, including questions of form in an analysis of these works' politics enhances the acuteness of these issues.

Concluding Thoughts

Solzhenitsyn was certainly an icon of the Cold War. His place in the cultural canon seems to be so dependent on his political relevance that his slot on the shelf of world literature does not always seem secure. He will always remain attached to the memory of the gulag and will therefore possess an enduring relevance in that arena. His work as a whole took part in a remediation of memory of many different events, making it interesting in multiple ways. If we study his activism as an author and his texts as agents of memory, it can at times seem that he is a literary hero—a protagonist from one of his novels, and perhaps this is one of the best ways that we can understand him in all his complexity.

The West played an important role in building the Russian literary canon by promoting and selecting dissident and émigré writers it considered important. The role of politics in building a "foreign" literary canon as revealed in this

983 Brenkman, 2000, p. 119.
984 Brenkman, 2000, p. 119.

case is that while the focus on a very general political interpretation can boost an author's perceived importance, it can also lead to a complete loss of relevance in changed circumstances. In this sense, what made Solzhenitsyn immensely famous is also what makes him seem all the more extraneous to today's global readership.

A focus on the aesthetic criteria in lieu of the political in canonizing an author's work is often a way of avoiding the vacillations of ideological priorities. However, as the example of the recent Chinese Nobel Prize laureate Mo Yan shows, this position sparks controversies of its own. In this case, Mo Yan's perceived political conformity was criticized by some despite his aesthetic achievements.[985] However, other commentators defended the Nobel committee's choice because, after all, if Western authors are not chosen for their criticism of their states, why should this only apply to others? Rejecting double standards is a valid point. However, it is true that Western authors who become a part of world literature are also subjected to closer inspection depending on the circumstances. For instance, a novel about racial relations in the US South would likely go under careful ethical scrutiny before it becomes part of world literature.

The historical and political context of the writer, the reader, and the work affect the critical prioritization of its aesthetic, ethic, or political content. But all three aspects play an important role, and fully ignoring one of them raises the probability that the work would undergo serious reevaluation in the future. In the case of Solzhenitsyn, the application of too generalized political criteria to assess his work has led to the neglect of specific political aspects of his work, which in fact affect their ethical worth. Due to the political bipolarity of his time he became a moral icon while representing views about women and minorities, which were anachronistic even at the time he expressed them. On the other hand, a text like *Ivan Denisovich* is likely to remain part of world literature. The reasons are both aesthetic, ethic, and political: the choice of writing from the point of view of a peasant allows touches of a personal idiosyncrasy without forcing them upon the reader. The lack of a thorough political program and the elevation of the debate on prison camps to a

---

985 Alison Flood. "Mo Yan wins Nobel prize in literature 2012." The Guardian 11 October 2012. Austin Ramzy. "China's Nobel Laureate Mo Yan Defends Censorship." TIME 7 December 2012.

universal ethical level ensure that readers in different times and places can engage with the text in diverse ways without losing sight of the issue of the injustice of jailing people on false charges. Yet, as critics, we must not forget that it is our duty and challenge not to ignore the more difficult parts of the literary corpus Solzhenitsyn has left behind.

The question of who is worthy of canonization and why remains polemical—but relevant. Perhaps the greatest difficulty in this process is a result of the expectation that the author should not only be talented but also hold morally, ethically or politically defensible views. Refraining from identifying the author as a hero can certainly ease some of the pressure from this question. However, our celebrity culture is unlikely to allow us this easy exit. The best we can do as literary critics and scholars is to defy external pressure and reflect the nuance and complexity of the author and his work in a manner befitting academic standards.

Bibliography

Among the numerous libraries and online archives I had access to during my research I was also allowed access to the files concerning the dissident magazine *Kontinent* at the archive of the Axel Springer Verlag (Axel Springer Unternehmensarchiv) in Berlin. Information from these files is listed in the appropriate footnotes with the abbreviation ASV UA and the file number. All other sources are in print and listed below. I thank the ASV UA for allowing me to use their files, and the Bundestag Library for giving me access to their sources on Solzhenitsyn.

Abel, Lionel. "A Poem we Need Today: Review of The Gulag Archipelago Two." Commentary March 1976.

Ackeret, Markus. *In der Welt der Katorga: Die Zwangsarbeitsstrafe für Politische Delinquenten im ausgehenden Zarenreich (Ostsibirien Und Sachalin).* 56 Vol. Munich: Osteuropa-Institut, 2007. Mitteilungen / Osteuropa-Institut Munich.

Afanas'ev, Iurii N. "The Phenomenon of Soviet Historiography." *Russian Studies in History* 40.2 (2001): 32-64.

Aikman, David. "Russia's Prophet in Exile." TIME 24 July 1989.

—. *Great Souls. Six who Changed the Century.* Lanham: Lexington Books, 2002.

Allen, Brooke. "Politics Parading as Fiction." New Leader 82.3 (1999): 12.

Alsop, Joseph. "'Gulag Archipelago': 'must Reading' for Mr. Nixon." The Washington Post 26 June 1974: 19.

Anderson, Earl R., and Gianfrancesco Zanetti. "Comparative Semantic Approaches to the Idea of a Literary Canon." *The Journal of Aesthetics and Art Criticism* 58.4 (2000): 341-360.

Anning, Nicholas J. "Solzhenitsyn." *Russian Literary Attitudes from Pushkin to Solzhenitsyn.* Ed. Richard Freeborn. London: Macmillan, 1976. 120-140.

Apodaca, Clair. *Understanding U.S. Human Rights Policy: A Paradoxical Legacy.* New York: Routledge, 2006.

Applebaum, Anne. "Erinnerung an Alexander Solschenizyns Gulag." Welt Online 6 August 2008. (http://www.welt.de/debatte/kommentare/article 6072665/Erinnerung-an-Alexander-Solschenizyns-Gulag.html) (as of 3 September 2010).

—. *Gulag: A History.* New York: Anchor Books, 2004.

—. *Gulag Voices: An Anthology.* New Haven: Yale University Press, 2011.

Assmann, Aleida. *Der Lange Schatten der Vergangenheit: Erinnerungskultur und Geschichtspolitik.* Munich: C. H. Beck, 2006.

—. "On the (in)Compatibility of Guilt and Suffering in German Memory." *German Life and Letters* 59.2 (2006): 187.

Associated Press. "Roy Medwedjew verteidigt Solschenizyn." Frankfurter Allgemeine Zeitung 8 February 1974: 6.

Augstein, Rudolf, Fritjof Meyer, and Jörg Mettke. "'Wie ein Sekretär des Volkes'." Der Spiegel 31 October 1994: 139-63.

Augstein, Rudolf. "Solschenizyn oder die Ehre Gottes." Der Spiegel 7 January 1974: 4-5.

—. "Ein Betriebsunfall Namens Stalin." Der Spiegel 11 Februar 1974: 89-91.

—. "Dokumentation einer Korrespondenz." Der Spiegel 18 November 1974: 180-3.

—. "'Man lügt über mich wie über einen Toten'." Der Spiegel 26 October 1987: 218-51.

Bailer-Galanda, Brigitte. "'Revisionismus'-Pseudo-Wissenschaftliche Propaganda des Rechtsextremismus." *Wahrheit und "Auschwitzlüge".* Eds. Brigitte Bailer-Galanda, Wolfgang Benz, and Wolfgang Neugebauer. Vienna: Deuticke, 1995. 16-32.

Barnes, Steven A. *Death and Redemption: The Gulag and the Shaping of Soviet Society.* Princeton: Princeton University Press, 2011.

Beausang, Michael. "Andrey Sinyavsky: Exile and Writer." Mosaic Spring 1975: 15-20.

Belotserkovsky, Vadim, and Leonid I. Plyushch, eds. *UdSSR: Alternativen der demokratischen Opposition. Sammelband.* Achberg: Achberger Verlagsanstalt, 1978.

Belotserkovsky, Vadim. "Letter to the Future Leaders of the Soviet Union: An Alternative to Solzhenitsyn's Program." *Partisan Review* XLII.2 (1975): 260-71.

—. "Undoing the West in the Soviet Union." Nation 16 March 1985: 289-308.

—. "The Passing of Yelena Bonner." *Russian Life* September/October 2011: 64.

Benz, Wolfgang. "'Revisionismus' in Deutschland." *Wahrheit und "Auschwitzlüge".* Eds. Brigitte Bailer-Galanda, Wolfgang Benz, and Wolfgang Neugebauer. Vienna: Deuticke, 1995. 33-45.

Bergman, Jay. "Soviet Dissidents on the Holocaust, Hitler and Nazism: A Study of the Preservation of Historical Memory." *The Slavonic and East European Review* 70.3 (1992): 477-504.

Berkenkopf, Galina (transl). "Das *Le Monde* Interview von Alexander Solschenizyn." Criticon 21. 1974: 33-6.

Berman, Ronald, ed. *Solzhenitsyn at Harvard: The Address, Twelve Early Responses, and Six Later Reflections.* 2nd ed. Washington: Ethics and Public Policy Center, 1980. Ethics and Public Policy Reprints.

Bethea, David, and Siggy Frank. "Exile and Russian Literature." *The Cambridge Companion to Twentieth-Century Russian Literature.* Eds. Evgenij Dobrenko and Marina Balina. Cambridge: Cambridge University Press, 2011. 195-213.

Beyrau, Dietrich. "Solschenizyn über die Juden im Sowjetischen Experiment." *Put' Solzhenitsyna v Kontekste Bolshogo Vremeni. Sbornik Pamiati 1918 - 2008.* Ed. Liudmila I. Saraskina. Moscow: Russkii Put', 2009. 226-242.

Bienek, Horst. "Blutige Farce." Die Zeit 25 Januar 1974.

—. "Ein Rigoroser Moralist." Frankfurter Allgemeine Zeitung 25 December 1988: 10.

Blackburn, Robin. "The First Circle." *New Left Review* I.63 (1970): 56-64.

Bode, Barbara. "Die Diskussion um Solshenizyn als Zentrum der Auseinandersetzungen in der Sowjetliteratur." *Osteuropa* 10 (1965): 679-94.

Böll, Heinrich. "Heinrich Böll Interview: 'Es ist Zeit, öffentlich energisch zu werden'." Der Spiegel 16 July 1973: 100-101.

—. "The Imprisoned World of Solzhenitsyn's *The First Circle.*" *Aleksandr Solzhenitsyn: Critical Essays and Documentary Materials.* Eds. John B. Dunlop, Richard S. Haugh, and Alexis Klimoff. Belmont: Nordland Publishing Company, 1973. 219-230.

—. "Solzhenitsyn and New Realism." *Aleksandr Solzhenitsyn: Critical Essays and Documentary Materials.* Eds. John B. Dunlop, Richard S. Haugh, and Alexis Klimoff. Belmont: Nordland Publishing Company, 1973. 185-187.

—. "Die Himmlische Bitterkeit des Alexander Solschenizyns." Frankfurter Allgemeine Zeitung 9 February 1974.

Boll, Friedhelm, and Stephane Sirot. "Deutsche und französische Intellektuelle und der Fall Solschenizyn." *Deutschland - Frankreich - Rußland Begegnungen und Konfrontationen.* Ed. Ilja Mieck. Munich: Oldenbourg, 2000. 321-344.

Bosco, David. "Gulag Vs Guantanamo." The New Republic 3 June 2005.

Brenkman, John. "Extreme Criticism." *What's Left of Theory? New Work on the Politics of Literary Theory.* Eds. Judith Butler, John Guillory, and Kendall Thomas. New York: Routledge, 2000. 114-136.

Brown , Deming. "Cancer Ward and The First Circle." *Slavic Review* 28.2 (1969): 304-313.

Brudny, Yitzhak M. *Reinventing Russia: Russian Nationalism and the Soviet State, 1953 - 1991.* Cambridge, Mass.: Harvard University Press, 1998.

Brumberg, Abraham. "Dissent in Russia." *Foreign Affairs* 52.4 (1974): 781-98.

—. "On Cultural Dissidence: A Conversation with Andrei Sinyavsky." The New Republic 9 February 1980: 27-32.

Buckley, Mary. "Women in the Soviet Union." *Feminist Review.*8 (1981): 79-106.

Busch, Andrew E. "Ronald Reagan and the Defeat of the Soviet Empire." *Presidential Studies Quarterly* 27.3, The Presidency in the World (1997): 451-66.

Bystydzienski, Jill M. "Women and Socialism: A Comparative Study of Women in Poland and the USSR." *Signs* 14.3 (1989): 668-84.

Carlisle, Olga. "Solzhenitsyn and Russian Nationalism: An Interview with Andrey Sinyavsky." The New York Review of Books 22 November 1979.

Chamberlin, William Henry. "The Voice of Silent Russia." *Russian Review* 28.2 (1969): 152-9.

Chartier, Roger, and Guglielmo Cavallo. "Einleitung." *Die Welt des Lesens von der Schriftrolle zum Bildschirm.* Eds. Roger Chartier and Guglielmo Cavallo. Frankfurt Main: Campus-Verlag, 1999. 9-59.

Chochiev, Georgi. "On the History of the North Caucasian Diaspora in Turkey." *Iran & the Caucasus* 11.2 (2007): 213-26.

Christie, Ian. "Introduction." *Eisenstein Rediscovered.* Eds. Ian Christie and Richard Taylor. London: Routledge, 1993. 30.

Clark, Katerina. "Russian Epic Novels of the Soviet Period." *The Cambridge Companion to Twentieth-Century Russian Literature.* Eds. Evgenij Dobrenko and Marina Balina. Cambridge: Cambridge University Press, 2011. 135-151. Cambridge Companions to Literature.

—. *The Soviet Novel: History as Ritual.* Chicago: University of Chicago Press, 1981.

Cohen, Stephen F. "The Gulag Archipelago." The New York Times June 16 1974: 1.

—. *Rethinking the Soviet Experience: Politics and History since 1917.* New York: Oxford University Press, 1986.

Colomina Limonero, Immaculada. *Dos Patrias, Tres Mil Destinos: Vida y Exilio de los Niños de la Guerra de España Refugiados en la Unión Soviética.* Ed. Alicia Alted Vigil. 1st ed. 3 Vol. Madrid: Cinca, 2010. Biblioteca de Historia Social.

Condee, Nancy, and Vladimir Padunov. "Perestroika Suicide: Not by 'Bred' Alone." *New Left Review* I.189 (1991): 67-89.

Confino, Michael. "Solzhenitsyn, the West and the New Russian Nationalism." *Journal of Contemporary History* 26.3-4 (1991): 611-636.

—. "Present Events and the Representation of the Past: Some Current Problems in Russian Historical Writing." *Cahiers Du Monde Russe* 35.4 (1994): 839-868.

Connelly, John. "Nazis and Slavs: From Racial Theory to Racist Practice." *Central European History* 32.1 (1999): 1-33.

Conquest, Robert. *The Great Terror: Stalin's Purge of the Thirties.* London: Macmillan, 1969.

—. "Evolution of an Exile: Gulag Archipelago." *Solzhenitsyn: A Collection of Critical Essays*, Ed. Kathryn Feuer. Englewood Cliffs, N. J.: Prentice-Hall, 1976. 90-95.

—. "Solzhenitsyn in the British Media." *Solzhenitsyn in Exile: Critical Essays and Documentary Materials.* Eds. John B. Dunlop, Richard S. Haugh, and Michael Nicholson. Stanford: Hoover Institution, 1985. 3-23.

—. *Stalin and the Kirov Murder.* London: Hutchinson, 1989.

—. "Solzhenitsyn was a Russian Patriot." Wall Street Journal 08 August 2008: 15.

Cox, Michael. "Whatever Happened to the 'Second' Cold War? Soviet-American Relations: 1980-1988." *Review of International Studies* 16.2 (1990): 155-72.

Crankshaw, Edward. “A Masterpiece from Russia: Review of *First Circle*.” The Observer 10 November 1968: 26.

Cycon, Dieter. “Der Dichter in der Schlinge.” Die Welt 11 February 1974: 4.

D.W. “Solschenizyn über Norwegen: Wundervoll viel Schnee.” Die Welt 25 February 1974: 3.

Dallin, Alexander, and Ralph S. Mavrogordato. “The Soviet Reaction to Vlasov.” *World Politics* 8.3 (1956): 307-22.

Daniloff, Nicholas. “Red Reveals Torture in Stalin Prison Camps.” The Washington Post 22 November 1962: B5.

Danilov, V. P. “Bukharin and the Countryside.” *The Ideas of Nikolai Bukharin.* Ed. Anthony Kemp-Welch. Oxford England: Clarendon Press, 1992. 69-81.

Devlin, Judith. *Slavophiles and Commissars: Enemies of Democracy in Modern Russia.* Basingstoke: McMillan, 1999.

Die Redaktion. “Unsere Aufgabe.” Kontinent 1. 1974: 3-4.

Diner, Dan, and Wolfgang Benz, eds. *Ist der Nationalsozialismus Geschichte? Zu Historisierung und Historikerstreit.* 4391 Vol. Frankfurt Main: Fischer, 1987. Fischer-Taschenbücher.

Diner, Dan. “Zwischen Aporie und Apologie: Über Grenzen und Historisierbarkeit des Nationalsozialismus.” *Ist der Nationalsozialismus Geschichte? Zu Historisierung und Historikerstreit.* Eds. Dan Diner and Wolfgang Benz. 4391 Vol. Frankfurt Main: Fischer, 1987. 62-73.

Dobrenko, Evgenij, and Marina Balina, eds. *The Cambridge Companion to Twentieth-Century Russian Literature.* Cambridge: Cambridge University Press, 2011. Cambridge Companions to Literature.

Dobrenko, Evgenij. “Socialist Realism.” *The Cambridge Companion to Twentieth-Century Russian Literature.* Eds. Evgenij Dobrenko and Marina Balina. Cambridge: Cambridge University Press, 2011. 97-113.

Dobson, Miriam. “Contesting the Paradigms of De-Stalinization: Readers’ Responses to ‘One Day in the Life of Ivan Denisovich’.” *Slavic Review* 64.3 (2005): 580-600.

—. “Stalin’s Gulag: Death, Redemption and Memory.” *The Slavonic and East European Review* 90.4 (2012): 735-43.

Duncan, Martha Grace. “‘Cradled on the Sea’ Positive Images of Prison and Theories of Punishment.” *California Law Review* 76.6 (1988): 1201-47.

—. *Romantic Outlaws, Beloved Prisons: The Unconscious Meanings of Crime and Punishment.* New York; London: New York University Press, 1996.

Dunlop, John B. *The Faces of Contemporary Russian Nationalism.* Princeton: Princeton University Press, 1983.

—. "The Gulag Archipelago: Alternative to Ideology." *Solzhenitsyn in Exile: Critical Essays and Documentary Materials.* Eds. John B. Dunlop, Richard S. Haugh, and Michael Nicholson. Stanford: Hoover Institution, 1985. 164-175.

—. "Important Points Missed." *Slavic Review* 40.3 (1981): 457-60.

—. *The New Russian Nationalism.* New York: publ. with The Center for Strategic and International Studies, Georgetown University by Praeger, 1985. The Washington Papers.

—. *Russia Confronts Chechnya: Roots of a Separatist Conflict.* Cambridge: Cambridge University Press, 1998.

—. "Russian Reactions to Solzhenitsyn's Brochure." *Report on the USSR* 14. (1990): 3-8.

—. "Solzhenitsyn's Reception in the United States." *Solzhenitsyn in Exile: Critical Essays and Documentary Materials.* Eds. John B. Dunlop, Richard S. Haugh, and Michael Nicholson. Stanford: Hoover Institution, 1985. 24-55.

Dutli, Ralph. "Volksfreund Russlands, Staatsfeind der Sowjets." Frankfurter Allgemeine Zeitung 5 August 2008: 35.

Dutschke, Rudi, ed. *Sowjetunion, Solschenizyn und die westliche Linke.* Reinbek bei Hamburg: Rowohlt, 1975.

Eagleton, Terry. *The Event of Literature.* New Haven: Yale University Press, 2012.

—. *Ideology: An Introduction.* New ed. London: Verso, 2007.

Eley, Geoff. *Forging Democracy: The History of the Left in Europe, 1850-2000.* New York: Oxford University Press, Incorporated, 2002.

Elliott, Mark. "Andrei Vlasov: Red Army General in Hitler's Service." *Military Affairs* 46.2 (1982): 84-87.

Emel'ianova, Natal'ia. "Natal'ia Solzhenitsyna priekhala v Perm' na prem'eru opery "Odin den' Ivana Denisovicha." Rossiiskaia Gazeta 15 May 2009.

Engdahl, Horace. "Philomela's Tongue." *Witness Literature: Proceedings of the Nobel Centennial Symposium.* Ed. Horace Engdahl. Singapore: World Scientific Publishing Co Pte Ltd, 2002. 1-14.

Engelbrecht, Jörg. "Autobiographien, Memoiren." *Einführung in Die Interpretation Historischer Quellen.* Ed. Bernd-A Rusinek. 1674 Vol. Paderborn u. a.: Schoningh, 1992. 61-80. UTB Für Wissenschaft.

Engerman, David C. "The Ironies of the Iron Curtain: The Cold War and the Rise of Russian Studies in the United States." *Cahiers du Monde russe* 45.3/4 (2004): 465-96.

—. *Know Your Enemy: The Rise and Fall of America's Soviet Experts.* Oxford; New York: Oxford University Press, 2009.

Ericson, Edward E. *Solzhenitsyn, the Moral Vision.* Grand Rapids: Eerdmans, 1980.

—. "Solzhenitsyn's Western Reception since 1991." *Transactions of the Association of Russian-American Scholars* 29 (1998): 183-213.

—. "For the Love of Russia: November 1916: The Red Wheel." *Modern Age* (2000): 205-9.

—. "The Gulag Archipelago a Generation Later." *Modern Age* 44.2 (2002): 147-161.

—. and Alexis Klimoff. *The Soul and Barbed Wire: An Introduction to Solzhenitsyn*. 1st ed. Wilmington: ISI Books, 2008.

—. "Worldview Criticism of Solzhenitsyn." *Put' Solzhenitsyna v Kontekste Bolshogo Vremeni. Sbornik Pamiati 1918 - 2008.* Ed. Liudmila I. Saraskina. Moscow: Russkii Put', 2009. 215-220.

—. Ed. *Solzhenitsyn: Myslitel', Istorik, Khudozhnik: Zapadnaia Kritika 1974-2008*. Moscow: Russkii Put', 2010.

Erlich, Victor. "Post-Stalin Trends in Russian Literature." *Slavic Review* 23.3 (1964): 405-419.

—. *Russischer Formalismus*. Munich: Suhrkamp, 1973.

Erll, Astrid, and Ansgar Nünning. *Medien des Kollektiven Gedachtnisses*. 1 Vol. New York: Walter De Gruyter, 2004.

Erll, Astrid. "Cultural Memory Studies: an Introduction." *Cultural Memory Studies: An International and Interdisciplinary Handbook*. Ed. Ansgar Nünning. Berlin: Walter de Gruyter, 2008.

—."Literature, Film, and the Mediality of Cultural Memory." *Cultural Memory Studies: An International and Interdisciplinary Handbook.* Ed. Ansgar Nünning. Berlin: Walter de Gruyter, 2008. 389-398.

Feuer, Kathryn, ed. *Solzhenitsyn: A Collection of Critical Essays*. Englewood Cliffs, N. J.: Prentice-Hall, 1976.

Fest, Joachim. "Das Beispiel Solschenizyn." Frankfurter Allgemeine Zeitung 9 January 1974: 1.

Fireside, Harvey. "Dissident Visions of the USSR: Medvedev, Sakharov & Solzhenitsyn." *Polity* 22.2 (1989): 213-229.

Fischer, George. "General Vlasov's Official Biography." *Russian Review* 8.4 (1949): 284-301.

Fitzpatrick, Sheila. "New Perspectives on Stalinism." *Russian Review* 45.4 (1986): 357-73.

Flood, Alison. "Mo Yan wins Nobel prize in literature 2012." The Guardian 11 October 2012.

Frankel, Boris. "The 'Gulag Archipelago' and the Left." *Theory and Society* 1.4 (1974): 477-495.

Frankel, Jonathan. "The 'Non-Jewish' Jews Revisited. Solzhenitsyn and the Issue of National Guilt." *Insiders and Outsiders: Dilemmas of East European Jewry.* Eds. Richard I. Cohen, Jonathan Frankel, and Stefani Hoffman. Oxford: The Littman Library of Jewish Civilization, 2010. 166-187.

Freeborn, Richard. "Russian Literary Attitudes from Pushkin to Solzhenitsyn." *Russian Literary Attitudes from Pushkin to Solzhenitsyn.* Eds. Richard Freeborn, Georgette Donchin, and Nicholas J. Anning. London: Macmillan, 1976. 1-18.

Frei, Norbert. "Coping with the Burdens of the Past: German Politics and Society in the 1950s." *The Postwar Challenge: Cultural, Social, and Political Change in Western Europe, 1945-58.* Ed. Dominik Geppert. German Historical Institute London; Oxford: Oxford University Press, 2003.

Freidin, Gregory. "By the Walls of Church and State: Literature's Authority in Russia's Modern Tradition." *Russian Review* 52.2 (1993): 149-65

Freundlich, Elisabeth. "Solschenizyns Weg." Frankfurter Hefte: Zeitschrift für Kultur und Politik 31.6 (1976): 51-61.

Friedgut, Theodore H. "Aleksandr Solzhenitsyn and the Modern Russo-Jewish Question." *Shofar* 26.3 (2008): 205-8.

Friedländer, Saul. *Die Jahre der Vernichtung: Das Dritte Reich und die Juden: Zweiter Band 1939-1945.* Munich: Verlag C. H. Beck, 2006.

Fromm, Ernst-Ulrich. "Moskau führt gegen Solschenizyn eine neue Schlacht am Wolchow." Die Welt 30 January 1974: 2.

G.R. "Antwort Auf Grass." Frankfurter Allgemeine Zeitung 18 November 1974: 19.

Galloway, David J. "Polemical Allusions in Russian Gulag Prose." *The Slavic and East European Journal* 51.3 (2007): 535-552.

Getty, J. Arch. *The Origins of the Great Purges: The Soviet Communist Party Reconsidered, 1933-1938.* Cambridge: Cambridge Universtity Press, 1987. Soviet and East European Studies.

—. "Review: [Untitled]." *Russian Review* 48.3, Gorbachev Reforms: Special Issue (1989): 348-51.

Gibian, George. "How Solzhenitsyn Returned His Ticket." *Solzhenitsyn: A Collection of Critical Essays.* Ed. Kathryn Feuer. Englewood Cliffs, N. J.: Prentice-Hall, 1976. 112-119.

—. "The Russian Theme in Solzhenitsyn." *Russian Literature and American Critics: In Honor of Deming B. Brown.* Ed. Kenneth N. Brostrom. 4 Vol. Ann Arbor: Michigan Slavic Publications, 1984. 55-73. Papers in Slavic Philology.

Gillespie, David C. *The Twentieth-Century Russian Novel: An Introduction.* Washington, D.C.: Berg, 1996.

Gitelman, Zvi Y., Musya Glants, and Marshall I. Goldman. *Jewish Life after the USSR.* Bloomington: Indiana University Press, 2003.

Glasenapp, Igor von. "Solschenizyns 'Preussische Nächte'." Criticon 24. 1974: 175-6.

Golczewski, Frank. "Gulag - Die Geschichte der Erinnerung als politischer Konflikt." *Erlebnis - Gedächtnis - Sinn: Authentische und Konstruierte Erinnerung.* Eds. Hanno Loewy and Bernhard Moltmann. 3 Vol. Frankfurt: Campus Verlag, 1996. 265-275.

Goldovskaya, Marina Evseevna, dir. *Vlast' Solovetskaia: Svidetel'stva i Dokumenty.* Prod. Mosfilm. Moscow: Mosfilm, 1988. Film.

Gorham, Michael S. "Mastering the Perverse: State Building and Language 'Purification' in Early Soviet Russia." *Slavic Review* 59.1 (2000): 133-153.

—. "Natsiia ili Snikerizatsiia? Identity and Perversion in the Language Debates of Late- and Post-Soviet Russia." *Russian Review* 59.4 (2000): 614-629.

Gosse, Van. *Rethinking the New Left: An Interpretative History.* New York: Palgrave Macmillan, 2005.

Gottlieb, Erika. *Dystopian Fiction East and West: Universe of Terror and Trial.* Montreal: McGill-Queen's University Press, 2001.

Greenwood, Sean. *Britain and the Cold War, 1945-1991.* London: Macmillan, 2000. British History in Perspective.

Grenier, Richard. "Solzhenitsyn and Anti-Semitism: A New Debate." The New York Times 13 November 1985: 21.

Grimm, Gunter. *Rezeptionsgeschichte: Grundlegung einer Theorie mit Analysen und Bibliographie.* 691 Vol. Munich: Wilhelm Fink, 1977. Uni - Taschenbücher.

Grobe, Karl. "Die gestohlenen Leben." Frankfurter Rundschau 4 August 2008.

Grossman, Lev. "Remembering Aleksandr Solzhenitsyn." TIME 4 August 2008.

Grossman, Vasily, and Ilya Ehrenburg, eds. *The Complete Black Book of Russian Jewry.* Tran. David Patterson. New Brunswick, NJ: Transaction Publishers, 2002.

Grüner, Frank, Urs Heftrich, and Heinz-Dietrich Löwe, eds. *'Zerstörer des Schweigens': Formen künstlerischer Erinnerung an die Nationalsozialistische Rassen- und Vernichtungspolitik in Osteuropa.* Köln: Böhlau, 2006.

Gruenwald, Oskar. "The Essential Solzhenitsyn: The Political Nexus or the Russian Connection." *Thought* 55.217 (1980): 137-52.

—. "Yugoslav Camp Literature: Rediscovering the Ghost of a Nation's Past- Present-Future." *Slavic Review* 46.3/4 (1987): 513-528.

—. "Response: Camp Literature: Archetype for Dissent." *Slavic Review* 48.2 (1989): 280-283.

Günzel, Walter. "Die bösen Friedensstörer." Die Welt 1 January 1974: 4.

—. "Zittern vor leerem Schrecken: Warum einige Linke Solschenizyn vor 'falschen Freunden' warnen." Die Welt 18 February 1974: 4.

Gutmann, Wolfgang. "Weder Dichtung noch Wahrheit: Solschenizyns Sehnsucht nach Vergangenheit." Die Tat 19 Januar 1974: 9.

Habermas, Jürgen. "Apologetische Tendenzen." *Eine Art Schadensabwicklung. Kleine Politische Schriften.* Ed. Jürgen Habermas. 1st ed. 1453 Vol. Frankfurt Main: Suhrkamp, 1987. 120-136.

—. and Jeremy Leaman. "Concerning the Public use of History." *New German Critique* 44 Special Issue on the Historikerstreit (1988): 40-50.

Halbwachs, Maurice. *Les Cadres Sociaux de la Mémoire*. Paris: Nouv. éd., 1935.

—. *La Mémoire Collective*. Paris: Presses Universitaires de France, 1950. Bibliotheque De Sociologie Contemporaine.

Halperin, David M. "Solzhenitsyn, Epicurus, and the Ethics of Stalinism." *Critical Inquiry* 7.3 (1981): 475-497.

Hammond, Andrew. *Cold War Literature: Writing the Global Conflict.* London: Routledge, 2006.

Hanne, Michael. *The Power of the Story: Fiction and Political Change*. Providence; Oxford: Berghahn, 1994.

Hartmann, Jens. "Solschenizyn, der Heilige der russischen Seele." Die Welt Online 4 August 2008. (http://www.welt.de/kultur/article2271702/ Solschenizyn-der-Heilige-der-russischen-Seele.html) (as of 12 June 2012).

Hauschild, Sonja. "Propheten oder Störenfriede? Sowjetische Dissidenten in der Bundesrepublik Deutschland und Frankreich und ihre Rezeption bei den Intellektuellen (1974—1977)." *Digitale Osteuropa-Bibliothek: Reihe Geschichte* 13 (2006). (http://epub.ub.uni-muenchen.de/1359/1/hauschild-dissidenten.pdf) (as of 15 December 2013).

Hayden, Robert M. "Using a Microscope to Scan the Horizon." *Slavic Review* 48.2 (1989): 275-279.

Haynes, John Earl, and Harvey Klehr. *In Denial: Historians, Communism and Espionage*. New York: Encounter Books, 2003.

Hayward, Max. "Solzhenitsyn's Place in Contemporary Soviet Literature." *Slavic Review* 23.3 (1964): 432-436.

Hazzard, Shirley. "'Gulag' and the Men of Peace." The New York Times 25 August 1974.

Heil, Alan L. *Voice of America: A History*. New York: Columbia University Press, 2003.

Heimrich, Bernhard. "Solschenizyn in dritter Instanz." Frankfurter Allgemeine Zeitung 5 May 1976: 1.

Heldt, Barbara. "Gender." *The Cambridge Companion to the Classic Russian Novel.* Eds. Malcolm V. Jones and Robin Feuer Miller. Cambridge: Cambridge University Press, 1998. 251-270.

Heller, Michel. "Yesterday and Today in Solzhenitsyn's *The Red Wheel*." *Survey* 29.2 (125) (1985): 29-45.

Herbeck, Ulrich. *Das Feindbild vom 'Jüdischen Bolschewiken'. Zur Geschichte des Russischen Antisemitismus vor und während der Russischen Revolution.* Berlin: Metropol-Verlag, 2009.

Herburger, Günter. "Solschenizyns Wiederkehr." Kürbiskern 2. 1974: 140-1.

Hingley, Ronald. *Russian Writers and Soviet Society: 1917-1978.* London: Weidenfeld and Nicolson, 1979.

—. "'Works of Protest' Not quite a Breakthrough." The Washington Post 9 December 1962: E1.

Hitzer, Friedrich. "Solschenizyns Ausverkauf." Kürbiskern 2. 1974: 129-40.

Hoffmann, Joachim. *Die Geschichte der Wlassow-Armee.* 1st ed. 27 Vol. Freiburg: Rombach, 1984. Einzelschriften zur Militärischen Geschichte des Zweiten Weltkrieges.

Hofmann, Michael. *Literaturgeschichte der Shoah.* Münster: Aschendorff, 2003.

Högemann-Ledwohn, Elvira. "Solschenizyn - Erfolgsautor der BRD." Kürbiskern 1. 1973: 108-25.

Holm, Kerstin. "Wem Gehört Solschenizyn?" Frankfurter Allgemeine Zeitung 18 August 2008: 33.

Holz, Klaus. *Nationaler Antisemitismus: Wissenssoziologie einer Weltanschauung.* Hamburg: Hamburger Ed., 2001.

Hopkins, Michael F. "Teaching and Research on the Cold War in the United Kingdom." *Cold War History* 8.2 (2008): 241-58.

Horvath, Robert. "Apologist of Putinism? Solzhenitsyn, the Oligarchs, and the Specter of Orange Revolution." *The Russian Review* 70.2 (2011): 300-18.

Hosking, Geoffrey A. "The Russian Peasant Rediscovered: 'Village Prose' of the 1960s." *Slavic Review* 32.4 (1973): 705-24.

—."Review: Solzhenitsyn on Lenin." *Soviet Studies* 28.2 (1976): 276-9.

—. *Beyond Socialist Realism: Soviet Fiction since Ivan Denisovich.* New York: Holmes & Meier, 1980.

—. *Russland: Nation und Imperium: 1552 - 1917.* Tran. Kurt Baudisch. Berlin: Siedler Verlag, 2000.

—. "Love-Hate Relationship: Solzhenitsyn's Revision of the Traditional Version." The Times Literary Supplement 1 March 2002: 3.

—. *Rulers and Victims: The Russians in the Soviet Union.* Cambridge, Mass.: Harvard University Press, 2006.

Howe, Irving. "Predicaments of Soviet Writing." The New Republic 11 May 1963: 19-21.

Hull, David Stewart. "[Untitled]." *Russian Review* 22.3 (1963): 336-337.

Huyn, Hans Graf. *Weder Frieden noch Freiheit: Bilanz der Ostpolitik in Dokumenten.* Informationen über die DDR. No. 6. Bonn: CDU-Bundesgeschäftsstelle, 1974.

Iggers, Georg G. "Allgemein Westlich Oder Spezifisch Modern?" *Westliches Geschichtsdenken Eine Interkulturelle Debatte.* Ed. Jörn Rüsen. Göttingen: Vandenhoeck & Ruprecht, 1999. 169-177. Sammlung Vandenhoeck.

Ingold, Felix P. "Diktatur als Volksherrschaft? Hinweise und Überlegungen zur Restauration des Stalin-Kults in Russland." Neue Zürcher Zeitung 7 April 2007.

"International Court of Justice: Case Concerning Military and Paramilitary Activities in and Against Nicaragua (Nicaragua v. United States)." *International Legal Materials* 25.5 (1986): 1023-289.

Jackson, Robert Louis. "The Mask of Solzhenitsyn: Ivan Denisovich." *One Day in the Life of Ivan Denisovich: A Critical Companion.* Ed. Alexis Klimoff. Evanston, Ill.: Northwestern University Press, 1997. 41-53. Northwestern/AATSEEL Critical Companions to Russian Literature.

Jalowiecki, Bartosz. "Lies the Germans Tell Themselves." Commentary January 2004: 43-46.

Jarrett, Mike. "A Shrill Prophet." The Guardian 19 January 1991: 23.

Jauss, Hans Robert. *Literaturgeschichte Als Provokation der Literaturwissenschaft.* 2nd ed. Konstanz: Universitätsverlag, 1969.

Jenkner, Siegfried. *Erinnerungen Politische Haeftlinge an Den GULAG: Eine Kommentierte Bibliografie.* 2nd ed. Dresden: MEMORIAL, 2005.

Jensen, Richard Bach. "The International Campaign Against Anarchist Terrorism, 1880–1930s." *Terrorism and Political Violence* 21.1 (2009): 89-109.

Jerofejew, Viktor. "Archipel Gulag zerstörte die Sowjetunion." Welt Online 4 Aug 2008. (http://www.welt.de/kultur/article2273669/Archipel-Gulag-zerstoerte-die-Sowjetunion.html) (as of 3 September 2010).

Jin, Ha. *The Writer as Migrant.* Chicago: University of Chicago Press, 2008.

John, Eileen. "Literature and the Idea of Morality." *A Companion to the Philosophy of Literature.* Eds. Garry Hagberg and Walter Jost. 44 Vol. Chichester: Wiley-Blackwell, 2010. 285-300.

Johnson, Sarah L. *Historical Fiction: A Guide to the Genre.* Westport: Libraries Unlimited, 2005.

Johnstone, Diana. "How the French Left Learned to Love the Bomb." New Left Review I.146 (1984): 5-36.

Jones, Malcolm V., and Robin Feuer Miller, eds. *The Cambridge Companion to the Classic Russian Novel.* Cambridge: Cambridge University Press, 1998.

Junge, Marc. *Bucharins Rehabilitierung: Historisches Gedächtnis in der Sowjetunion 1953 - 1991.* Berlin: BasisDruck, 1999.

Kaiser, Robert. "KGB 'War Crime' Trials Urged by Solzhenitsyn." The Guardian 29 December 1973: 3.

—."The Giant of Russian Literature." The Washington Post 5 August 2008: CO1.

Kakutani, Michiko. "Books of the Times; How Stalin's Victims Remember his Rule." The New York Times 15 March 1994: 21.

Kaminer, Wladimir. "Bauarbeiter auf der Baustelle Russland." Die Tageszeitung 1 August 2001: 15.

Kaplan, Fred. "Laureate Assails Russian State Solzhenitsyn Lashes Assembly." Boston Globe 29 October 1994: 2.

—. "Moscow Homecoming Greeted by 5,000. Solzhenitsyn Ends Trip with Renewed Attack." Boston Globe 22 July 1994: 2.

—. "Solzhenitsyn has Taste of New Russia He Finds High Prices and a Political Pitch." Boston Globe 29 May 1994: 2.

—. "Solzhenitsyn's Journey Back Writer Ends 20-Year Exile, but His Reception is in Doubt." Boston Globe 22 May 1994: 1.

Kaplan, Jane. "The Historiography of National Socialism." *Companion to Historiography.* Ed. Michael Bentley. London: Routledge, 1997. 545-590.

Karlinsky, Simon, and Alfred Appel. *The Bitter Air of Exile: Russian Writers in the West, 1922-1972.* Rev ed. Berkeley: University of California Press, 1977.

Kasack, Wolfgang. "Die epische und dramatische Struktur im Werk Solschenizyns." *Über Solschenizyn Aufsätze, Berichte, Materialien.* Eds. Elisabeth Markstein and Felix Philipp Ingold. Darmstadt: Luchterhand, 1973. 184-202.

—. *Die Russische Schriftsteller-Emigration im 20. Jahrhundert Beiträge zur Geschichte, den Autoren und ihren Werken.* 62 Vol. Munich: Sagner, 1996. Arbeiten und Texte zur Slavistik.

—. "Solschenizyns Patriotismus." Die politische Meinung 40 (1995): 71-5.

Kaznelson, Michael. "Remembering the Soviet State: Kulak Children and Dekulakisation." *Europe-Asia Studies* 59.7 (2007): 1163.

Keller, Bill. "In the Russian Motherland, Fascination Now with those Who Chose Exile." The New York Times 8 January 1989.

Kemp-Welch, Anthony, ed. *The Ideas of Nikolai Bukharin.* Oxford England: Clarendon Press, 1992.

Kennan, George F. "Between Earth and Hell." The New York Review of Books 21 March 1974.

Kennedy, Emmet. *Secularism and its Opponents from Augustine to Solzhenitsyn.* Basingstoke: Palgrave Macmillan, 2006.

Kern, Gary. "Solzhenitsyn's Portrait of Stalin." *Slavic Review* 33.1 (1974): 1-22.

—. "Solženicyn's Self-Censorship: The Canonical Text of Odin Den' Ivana Denisoviča." *The Slavic and East European Journal* 20.4 (1976): 421-436.

Kershaw, Ian, and Moshe Lewin. "Introduction: The Regimes and their Dictators: Perspectives of Comparison." *Stalinism and Nazism: Dictatorships in Comparison.* Eds. Ian Kershaw and Moshe Lewin. Cambridge: Cambridge University Press, 1997. 1-25.

Kilpatrick, Carroll. "Nixon Tells Editors 'I'm Not a Crook'." The Washington Post 18 November 1973.

Kirkpatrick, Jeane J. "Dictatorships and Double Standards." Commentary November 1979.

Kissel, Wolfgang S. "Der Zivilisationsbruch als Kategorie der russischen Kultur- und Literaturgeschichte." *Literaturforschung Heute.* Ed. Wolfgang Klein. Berlin: Akademie Verlag, 1999. 153-164.

—. "Samizdat als kulturelles Gedächtnis: Terror und GULag in der russischen Erinnerungsliteratur der Sechziger Jahre." *Samizdat – Alternative Kultur in Zentral- und Osteuropa; Die 60er bis 80er Jahre.* Ed. Wolfgang Eichwede. Bremen: Edition Temmen, 2000. 94-104.

Klebnikov, Paul. "'Zhirinovsky is an Evil Caricature of a Russian Patriot'." Forbes 9 May 1994: 118-22.

Klier, John D. "'Zhid': Biography of a Russian Epithet." *The Slavonic and East European Review* 60.1 (1982): 1-15.

—. "The Dog that Didn't Bark: Anti-Semitism in Post-Communist Russia." *Russian Nationalism, Past and Present.* Ed. Geoffrey A. Hosking. Basingstoke: Macmillan, 1998. 129-147.

—. "No Prize for History." *History Today* 52.11 (2002): 60.

Klimoff, Alexis. "The Sober Eye: Ivan Denisovich and the Peasant Perspective." *One Day in the Life of Ivan Denisovich: A Critical Companion.* Evanston, Ill.: Northwestern University Press, 1997. 3-31. Northwestern/AATSEEL Critical Companions to Russian Literature.

Koehler, Ludmila. "Alexander Solzhenitsyn and Russian Literary Tradition." *Russian Review* 26.2 (1967): 176-184.

Koenen, Gerd. "Europas Linke und Solschenizyns Zorn." Welt Online 4 August 2008. (http://www.welt.de/kultur/article2271702/Solschenizyn-der-Heilige-der-russischen-Seele.html) (as of 5 September 2010).

Kohler, Friedemann. "Mit Seinem Spätwerk Konnte der Westen Wenig Anfangen." Der Spiegel Online 4 August 2008. (http://www.spiegel.de/ kultur/literatur/0,1518,druck-569808,00.html) (as of 4 April 2011).

Kolonitskii, Boris. "Russian Historiography of the 1917 Revolution: New Challenges to Old Paradigms?" *History & Memory* 21.2 (2009): 34-59.

König, Helmut. "Ostforschung - Bilanz und Ausblick." *Osteuropa* 8-9 (1975): 786-814.

Korotkov, Andrej V. *Akte Solschenizyn 1965 - 1977; Geheime Dokumente des Politbüros der KPdSU und des KGB.* Berlin: Ed. q, 1994.

Kotkin, Stephen. "The State-is it Us? Memoirs, Archives, and Kremlinologists." *Russian Review* 61.1 (2002): 35-51.

Kramer, Hilton. "A Talk with Solzhenitsyn." The New York Times 11 May 1980: 3.

Kuntsman, Adi. "'With a Shade of Disgust': Affective Politics of Sexuality and Class in Memoirs of the Stalinist Gulag." *Slavic Review* 68.2 (2009): 308-328.

Kuromiya, Hiroaki. "Review Article: Communism and Terror." *Journal of Contemporary History* 36.1 (2001): 191-201.

Labedz, Leopold. "Introduction." *Solzhenitsyn: A Documentary Record.* New York: Harper & Row, 1971. xvi-xxiv.

Lamarque, Peter. "Literature and Truth." *A Companion to the Philosophy of Literature.* Eds. Garry Hagberg and Walter Jost. 44 Vol. Chichester: Wiley-Blackwell, 2010. 367-385.

Larina, Alena. "Pamiat' v sobstvennosti" Rossiskaia Gazeta 20 August 2008.

Laqueur, Walter. *Black Hundred: The Rise of the Extreme Right in Russia*. 1st ed. New York: Harper Collins Publishers, 1993.

Larson, Nathan D. *Aleksandr Solzhenitsyn and the Modern Russo-Jewish Question*. Ed. Andreas Umland. 14 Vol. Stuttgart: Ibidem-Verlag, 2005. Soviet and Post-Soviet Politics and Society.

Lassner, Phyllis. "Life Writing and the Holocaust." *The Cambridge Companion to the Literature of World War II.* Ed. Marina MacKay. Cambridge: Cambridge University Press, 2009.

Lauer, Reinhard. *Geschichte der Russischen Literatur.* Munich: C.H. Beck, 2000.

Lenoe, Matt. "Did Stalin Kill Kirov and does it Matter?" *The Journal of Modern History* 74.2 (2002): 352-80.

Leonard, John. "The Last Word: Solzhenitsyn as a Media Creature." The New York Times 3 March 1974: 447.

Lewin, Moshe. *The Soviet Century.* London: Verso, 2005.

Leyda, Jay. "Two-Thirds of a Trilogy." *Film Quarterly* 12.3 (1959): 16-22.

Loewenstein, Rudolph. "Anti-Semites in Psychoanalysis." *Error without a Trial* Ed. Werner Bergmann. 2 Vol. Berlin: de Gruyter, 1988. 35-51.

Loseff, Lev. *On the Beneficence of Censorship: Aesopian Language in Modern Russian Literature*. Ed. Wolfgang Kasack. 31 Vol. Munich: Otto Sagner, 1984. Arbeiten und Texte zur Slavistik.

Lukács, Georg. *Der Russische Realismus in der Weltliteratur.* Berlin: Aufbau, 1952.

—. *Solschenizyn*. 28 Vol. Neuwied und Berlin: Luchterhand, 1970.

Luks, Leonid. "Rezension: Zweihundert Jahre Zusammen. Bd. 2: Die Juden in der Sowjetunion." *Jahrbücher für Geschichte Osteuropas* 56.4 (2008): 609-11.

Lustiger, Arno. "Der erste Kreis des Antisemitismus, Anmerkungen zu Alexander Solschenizyns Werk über Russen und Juden 'Zweihundert Jahre Gemeinsam'." Frankfurter Allgemeine Zeitung 8 June 2002: 51.

—. *Rotbuch: Stalin und die Juden: Die Tragische Geschichte des Jüdischen Antifaschistischen Komitees und der Sowjetischen Juden*. Berlin: Aufbau-Verlag, 1998.

Mahoney, Daniel J. *Aleksandr Solzhenitsyn: The Ascent from Ideology*. Lanham, MD: Rowman & Littlefield Publishers, 2001.

—. "The Continuing Relevance of Aleksandr Solzhenitsyn." *Society* 41.1 (2003): 67-71.

—. "The Moral Witness of Aleksandr Solzhenitsyn." *First Things: A Monthly Journal of Religion and Public Life* 196 (2009): p. 44-48.

Malia, Martin. "Review: A War on Two Fronts: Solzhenitsyn and *The Gulag Archipelago.*" *Russian Review* 36.1 (1977): 46-63.

—. *The Soviet Tragedy: A History of Socialism in Russia, 1917-1991.* New York; Oxford: Free Press; Maxwell Macmillan International, 1994.

—. "Judging Nazism and Communism." *The National Interest* 69 (2002): 63-78.

Mandel, Ernest. "'Archipel GULag' oder die unbewältigte Vergangenheit des Stalinismus." *Sowjetunion, Solschenizyn und die westliche Linke* Ed. Rudi Dutschke. Reinbek bei Hamburg: Rowohlt, 1975. 211-225.

Marder, Murrey. "Nixon Lauds Solzhenitsyn's 'Courage'." The Washington Post 26 February 1974: 1.

Marek, Franz. "Unteilbare Solidarität." *Sowjetunion, Solschenizyn und die westliche Linke.* Ed. Rudi Dutschke. Reinbek bei Hamburg: Rowohlt, 1975. 250-260.

Margalit, Avishai. *The Ethics of Memory.* Cambridge, Mass.; London: Harvard University Press, 2002.

Markstein, Elisabeth, and Felix Philipp Ingold, eds. *Über Solschenizyn Aufsätze, Berichte, Materialien.* Darmstadt: Luchterhand, 1973.

Markstein, Elisabeth. *Moskau ist viel schöner als Paris. Leben zwischen zwei Welten.* Vienna: Milena, 2010.

Marsh, Rosalind. "The Death of Soviet Literature: Can Russian Literature Survive?" *Europe-Asia Studies* 45.1 (1993): 115-139.

Masiukevich, Olg'a. "Ulitsa Solzhenitsyna." Rossiiskaia Gazeta 15 August 2008.

Mathewson, Rufus, W. *The Positive Hero in Russian Literature.* 2nd ed. Stanford: Stanford University Press, 1975.

—.and Robert L. Belknap. *Russianness: Studies on a Nation's Identity: In Honor of Rufus Mathewson, 1918-1978.* Ann Arbor: Ardis, 1990. Studies of the Harriman Institute.

May, Rachel. *The Translator in the Text: On Reading Russian Literature in English.* Evanston, Ill.: Northwestern University Press, 1994. Studies in Russian Literature and Theory.

McAdams, A. James. "Explaining Inter-German Cooperation in the 1980s." *German Studies Review* 13. DAAD Special Issue (1990): 99-114.

McMillin, Arnold. "Exiled Russian Writers of the Third Wave and the Émigré Press." *The Modern Language Review* 84.2 (1989): 406-413.

McVicker, Ben A. "The Creation and Transformation of a Cultural Icon: Aleksandr Solzhenitsyn in Post-Soviet Russia, 1994-2008." *Canadian Slavonic Papers* 53.2-4 (2011): 305-336.

Medvedev, Dmitrii. "Ukaz Prezidenta Rossiiskoi Federatsii ot 6 avgusta 2008g. i 1187 "Ob uvekovechenii pamiati A.I. Solzhenitsyna." Rossiiskaia Gazeta 6 August 2008.

Medvedev, Roy. *Let History Judge: The Origins and Consequences of Stalinism.* 1st ed. New York: Knopf, 1971.

Mehnert, Klaus. "Der Archipel GULAG als Literatur." *Osteuropa* 7 (1975): 522-33.

Mendelson, Sarah E., and Theodore P. Gerber. "Failing the Stalin Test: Russians and their Dictator." *Foreign Affairs* 85.1 (2006): 2-8.

Mettke, Jörg. "Mit Ruhm Bestraft." Der Spiegel 11 August 2008: 148-9.

Meyer, Birgit. "Solzhenitsyn in the West German Press since 1974." *Solzhenitsyn in Exile: Critical Essays and Documentary Materials.* Eds. John B. Dunlop, Richard S. Haugh, and Michael Nicholson. Stanford: Hoover Institution, 1985. 56-79.

Meyer, Gert. "Perestrojka und Geschichtswissenschaft in der Sowjetunion." *Wir Brauchen die Wahrheit: Geschichtsdiskussion in der Sowjetunion.* Ed. Gert Meyer. 2. ed. Cologne: Pahl-Rugenstein, 1989. Politik und Zeitgeschichte.

Milne, Lesley. "Satire." *The Cambridge Companion to the Classic Russian Novel.* Eds. Malcolm V. Jones and Robin Feuer Miller. Cambridge: Cambridge University Press, 1998. 86-103.

Miner, Steven M. "Revelations, Secrets, Gossip and Lies: Sifting Warily through the Soviet Archives." The New York Times 14 May 1995: 19.

Misch, Georg. *Geschichte der Autobiographie*. Berlin: Teubner, 1907.

Monas, Sidney. "GULag and Points West." *Slavic Review* 40.3 (1981): 444-56.

—. "Sidney Monas Replies." *Slavic Review* 40.3 (1981): 461-3.

Morson, Gary Saul. "Dostoevsky's Anti-Semitism and the Critics: A Review Article." *The Slavic and East European Journal* 27.3 (1983): 302-17.

Muchnic, Helen. "Solzhenitsyn's 'The First Circle'." *Russian Review* 29.2 (1970): 154-166.

Murav, Harriet. "Sinyavsky's Trial." *The Slavic and East European Journal* 42.3 (1998): 389-393.

N.N. "Special to the New York Times: Russian Defends Labor-Camp Life." The New York Times 13 October 1963: 5.

—. "Special to the New York Times: Solzhenitsyn Links a Suicide to His Work." The New York Times 7 September 1973: 3.

—. "Stalin Said to have Planned a Vast Pogrom." The New York Times: 8. 29 December 1973.

—. "Introduction to 'Victims of Terror' by Alexander Solzhenitsyn." The Observer 6 January 1974: 21.

—. "Bereit, den Tod auf mich zu nehmen." Der Spiegel 7 Januar 1974: 46-51.

—. "Die Welt ins Gewissen geredet: Neue Angriffe gegen Solschenizyn." Frankfurter Allgemeine Zeitung 7 January 1974: 20.

—. "Rache für eine zerstörte Welt: Der Fall Solschenizyn aus Moskauer Sicht." Der Spiegel 4 February 1974: 79-82.

—. "Solschenizyn: 'Morgenröte der Vernichtung'." Der Spiegel 28 October 1974: 121-6.

—. "Rechtsstreit um Solschenizyns Buch 'Die Eiche Und Das Kalb'." Frankfurter Allgemeine Zeitung 19 September 1975: 25.

—. "The Obsession of Solzhenitsyn." The New York Times 13 June 1978: 18.

—. "Antisemitismus Affäre: 'Dann haben wir ein Problem'." Stern 5 November 2003.

—. "Alexander Solzhenitsyn. Obituary." The Telegraph 5 August 2008.

—. "V stolichnoi kvartire Solzhenitsyna otkroiut muzei" Moskovskii Komsomolets 1 June 2010.

Nathans, Benjamin. *Beyond the Pale: The Jewish Encounter with Late Imperial Russia*. 45 Vol. Berkeley: University of California Press, 2002. Studies on the History of Society and Culture.

Nepomnyashchy, Catharine Theimer. "Andrei Donatovich Sinyavsky (1925-1997)." *The Slavic and East European Journal* 42.3 (1998): 367-71.

Nesterova, Ol'ga. "Krasnoe Koleso Zakatilos'." Rossiiskaia Gazeta 12 April 2008.

Niemeyer, Gerhart. "Alexander Solschenizyn." *Konservative Köpfe: Von Machiavelli bis Solschenizyn.* Ed. Caspar von Schrenck-Notzing. Munich: Criticon Verlag, 1978. 189-198.

Niven, Bill. "Implicit Equations in Constructions of German Suffering." *A Nation of Victims? Representations of German Wartime Suffering from 1945 to the Present.* Ed. Helmut Schmitz. 67 Vol. Amsterdam: Rodopi, 2007. 105-123.

Nolte, Ernst. "Vergangenheit, die nicht vergehen will." Frankfurter Allgemeine Zeitung 6 June 1986: 25.

—. *Der Kausale Nexus: Über Revisionen und Revisionismen in der Geschichtswissenschaft*; Studien, Artikel und Vorträge 1990 - 2000. Munich: Herbig, 2002.

—. "Vieldeutige Ko-Existenz." Junge Freiheit 22 November 2002.

Novoselova, Elena. "V Kruge - Pervyi." Rossiiskaia Gazeta 6 June 2007.

Nutt, Harry. "Projekt der Entschuldung. Hohmann und das »Tätervolk«." Frankfurter Rundschau 6 November 2003: 17.

O'Clery, Conor. "Back in the USSR." The New Republic 19 November 1990: 22-3.

Ohnesorge, Henk. "Stalin trieb sie unter Hitlers Fahnen." Die Welt 19 Februar 1974: 7.

Oja, Matt F. "Toward a Definition of Camp Literature." *Slavic Review* 48.2 (1989): 272-4.

Pach, Chester. "The Reagan Doctrine: Principle, Pragmatism, and Policy." *Presidential Studies Quarterly* 36.1, Presidential Doctrines (2006): 75-88.

Parker, David. "Ethics, Value and the Politics of Recognition." *Critical Ethics* Eds. Dominic Rainsford and Tim Woods. Basingstoke: Macmillan, 1999. 152-168.

Parland, Thomas. *The Extreme Nationalist Threat in Russia: The Growing Influence of Western Rightist Ideas*. 3 Vol. London: Routledge Curzon, 2005. Routledge Curzon Contemporary Russia and Eastern Europe Series.

Parthé, Kathleen F. *Russia's Dangerous Texts: Politics between the Lines*. New Haven: Yale University Press, 2004.

—. "Sinyavsky on His Way to Tomorrow." *The Slavic and East European Journal* 42.3 (1998): 394-8.

Pearce, Joseph: *Solzhenitsyn, a Soul in Exile*. San Francisco: Ignatius Press, 2011.

Pereira, Norman. "Alexander Solzhenitsyn and Anti-Semitism." *Varieties of Antisemitism: History, Ideology, Discourse.* Eds. Murray Baumgarten, Peter Kenez, and Bruce A. Thompson. Newark: University of Delaware Press, 2009. 264-274.

Petrovsky-Shtern, Yohanan. *Lenin's Jewish Question*. New Haven: Yale University Press, 2010.

Peturnig, Anna. "Einige Gedanken zur Übersetzungsarbeit an Solschenizyns Archipel GULAG." *Osteuropa* 3 (1975): 151-61.

Pichugina, Ekaterina. "Deputaty otmeniaiut 10-letnii tsenz na memorial'nye nazvaniia ulits i stantsii metro." Moskovskii Komsomolets 19 September 2010.

Pipes, Richard. "Solzhenitsyn and the Russian Intellectual Tradition." Encounter (1979): 52-5.

—. *Russia under the Old Regime*. 1st ed. London: Penguin Books, 1979.

—. "Alone Together." The New Republic 25 November 2002: 26-28.

Pisar, Samuel. "An Open Letter to Sakharov." The Observer 13 January 1974: 8.

Podhoretz, Norman. "The Terrible Question of Aleksandr Solzhenitsyn." Commentary 1 February 1985.

Porter, Robert. *Solzhenitsyn's One Day in the Life of Ivan Denisovich*. Bristol: Bristol Classics Press, 1997.

Raddatz, Fritz J. "Ayatollah Solschenizyn: Wie Russland neu einrichten?" Die Zeit16 November 1990.

Ramzy, Austin. "China's Nobel Laureate Mo Yan Defends Censorship." TIME 7 December 2012.

Rancour-Laferriere, Daniel. "Solzhenitsyn and the Jews: A Psychoanalytic View." *Soviet Jewish Affairs* 15.3 (1985): 29-54.

Reed, Christopher. "The Media: Taking Liberties on the Air / Anti-Western Propaganda on US-Backed Radio Liberty." The Guardian 19 August 1985.

Reiter, Andrea. *Narrating the Holocaust*. Tran. Patrick Camiller. London: Continuum International Publishing Group, Limited, 2005.

Remnick, David. "Native Son—'Kak Nam Obustroit' Rossiyu?' ('how Shall we Organize Russia?') by Aleksandr Solzhenitsyn." The New Yorker 14 February 1991.

—. "The Exile Returns." The New Yorker 14 February 1994: 64-83.

Roberts, Neil. "Solzhenitsyn's Art and Propaganda." *The Cambridge Quarterly* VI.3 (1974): 278-93.

Rosenbaum, Ulrich. "Ist der Wurm Nun aus dem Apfel Gefallen?" Vorwärts 21 February 1974: 3.

Rosenfeld, Alvin H. *The End of the Holocaust*. Bloomington: Indiana University Press, 2011.

Rossman, Vadim. "Review of 'Dvesti Let Vmeste'." *The Slavic and East European Journal* 46.2 (2002): 390-2.

—. *Russian Intellectual Antisemitism in the Post-Communist Era*. Lincoln and London: Published by the University of Nebraska Press for the Vidal Sassoon International Center for the Study of Antisemitism SICSA, the Hebrew University of Jerusalem, 2002.

Rothberg, Abraham. *Aleksandr Solzhenitsyn: The Major Novels*. Ithaca: Cornell University Press, 1971.

Rowley, David G. "Review: Russian Nationalism and the Cold War." *The American Historical Review* 99.1 (1994): 155-171.

Rubenstein, Joshua. "Bookshelf: A One-Man Soviet Nemesis." Wall Street Journal 14 December 1995: A13.

Rückerl, Adalbert. *NS-Verbrechen vor Gericht: Versuch einer Vergangenheitsbewältigung*. 2nd ed. 36 Vol. Heidelberg: Müller, 1984. Recht, Justiz, Zeitgeschehen.

Rus, Vladimir. "One Day in the Life of Ivan Denisovich: A Point of View Analysis." *Canadian Slavonic Papers* 13.2/3 (1971): 165-78.

Ryan-Hayes, Karen L. "Vojnovič's Moskva 2042 as Literary Parody." *Russian Literature* 36.4 (1994): 453-79.

Ryan, Karen L. *Stalin in Russian Satire, 1917-1991*. Madison: University of Wisconsin Press, 2009.

Safire, William. "Solzhenitsyn without Tears." The New York Times 18 February 1974: 25.

Safran, Gabriella. "Bogrov, Grigorii Isaakovich." *The YIVO encyclopedia of Jews in Eastern Europe* (2010). (http://www.yivoencyclopedia.org/article.aspx/Bogrov_Grigorii_Isaakovich) (as of 20 February 2013).

Sakharov, Andrei. "In Answer to Solzhenitsyn." New York Review of Books 5 September 1973: 5-6.

—. *My Country and the World*. 1st ed. New York: Knopf: distributed by Random House, 1975.

Salisbury, Harrison E. "Solzhenitsyn Assesses Purge Trials." The New York Times 30 December 1973: 17.

—. "The Transformation of Solzhenitsyn." The New York Times 31 December 1974: 6.

Sandler, Stephanie. "Sex, Death and Nation in the Strolls with Pushkin Controversy." *Slavic Review* 51.2 (1992): 294-308.

Saraskina, Liudmila: *Aleksandr Solzhenitsyn*. Moscow: Molodaia Gvardiia, 2009.

Sarotte, Marie Elise. "The Frailties of Grand Strategies: A Comparison of Détente and Ostpolitik." *Nixon in the World: American Foreign Relations, 1969-1977.* Eds. Fredrik Logevall and Andrew Preston. New York: Oxford University Press, 2008. 146-163.

Saunders, Max. "Life-Writing, Cultural Memory and Literary Studies." *Cultural Memory Studies: An International and Interdisciplinary Handbook.* Eds. Astrid Erll, Ansgar Nuenning, and Sara B. Young. 8 Vol. Berlin: Walter de Gruyter, 2008. 321-332.

Scammell, Michael, *Solzhenitsyn: A Biography*. 1st ed. London: Norton, 1984.

—. "To the Finland Station?" The New Republic 19 November 1990: 18-23.

—. ed. *The Solzhenitsyn Files: Secret Soviet Documents Reveal One Man's Fight Against the Monolith.* Trans. Catherine Fitzpatrick. Chicago: Edition Q, 1995.

—. "Russia's Literary Light who Illuminated Dark World of Soviet Regime." The Guardian 4 August 2008.

Schapiro, Leonard. "Bukharin's Way." The New York Review of Books 7 February 1974.

—. "Some Afterthoughts on Solzhenitsyn." *Russian Review* 33.4 (1974): 416-21.

—. "Soviet Heroes." New York Review of Books 13 October 1983.

—. "Alexander Solzhenitsyn: Conscience of Western Civilization." *Russian Studies*. Ed. Ellen Dahrendorf. New York: Viking, 1987 [1975]. 376-390.

Scheibert, Peter. *Russland*. Eds. Carsten Goehrke, Peter Scheibert, and Manfred Hellmann. 31 Vol. Frankfurt Main: Fischer Taschenbuch Verlag, 1992. Fischer Weltgeschichte.

Scherrer, Jutta. "Russlands Alt-Neue Erinnerungsorte." *Aus Politik und Zeitgeschichte* 13 March 2006: 24-8.

Schiller, Ulrich. "Seltsame Töne aus dem Äther." Die Zeit 7 February 1986.

Schlögel, Karl. "Literatur der Dissenz als Ansatz einer Theorienbildung zur Sowjetischen Gesellschaft." *Berichte des Bundesinstituts für ostwissenschaftliche und internationale Studien* 31 Vol. (1982).

Schooneveldt, Léon van. "The Moral Witness in the Field of Cultural Remembrance." *Literature and Memory: Theoretical Paradigms - Genres - Functions.* Eds. Ansgar Nünning and Marion Gymnich. Tübingen: Francke Verlag, 2006. 235-247.

Schröder, Matthias. *Deutschbaltische SS-Führer und Andrej Vlasov 1942-1945: "Rußland kann nur von Russen besiegt werden"*. Paderborn: Schöningh, 2001.

Schütz, Hans Peter. "Hohmann-Affäre: Lupenreiner Goebbels." Stern 12 November 2003.

Schwartz, Janet S. "Women under Socialism: Role Definitions of Soviet Women." *Social Forces* 58.1 (1979): 67-88.

Scott, James M. "Reagan's Doctrine? The Formulation of an American Foreign Policy Strategy." *Presidential Studies Quarterly* 26.4, Intricacies of U.S. Foreign Policy (1996): 1047-61.

Shabad, Theodore. "Life is too closely Imitating Art." The New York Times 9 September 1973: 206.

Shannon, William V. "The Russian Visitor." The New York Times 16 July 1975: 33.

Shapiro, Irina H. "Review: [Untitled]." *Slavic Review* 22.2 (1963): 375-377.

Shermer, Michael; Grobman, Alex. *Denying History: who says the Holocaust never happened and why do they say it?* Berkeley: University of California Press, 2000.

Shneidman, Noah N. *Double Vision: The Jew in Post-Soviet Russian Literature (1991-2006)*. Oakville; Niagara Falls, NY: Mosaic Press, 2007.

Sinyavsky, Andrey, (Abram Tertz). *For Freedom of Imagination*. New York: Holt, Rinehart & Winston, 1971.

Sinyavsky, Andrey. "Russophobia." Partisan Review 57 (1990): 339-44.

—. "Russian Nationalism." *Massachusetts Review*. Winter 31.4 (1990). p. 475-494.

Slonim, Marc. "The Challenge was the Need to Stay Alive." The New York Times 7 April 1963: BR4.

Smith, Hedrick. "Russian Accuses Western Press of Campaign Against Detente." The New York Times 12 October 1974: 6.

—. "Solzhenitsyn Puts Back Parts of Self-Censored Works." The New York Times 4 December 1974: 32.

—. "Solzhenitsyn Tells of Struggle to Write Despite Soviet Pressures." The New York Times 3 April 1972: 1.

Solzhenitsyn, Alexander. "Odin Den' Ivana Denisovicha, Povest'." *Novyi Mir*.11 (1962): 9-74.

—. *One Day in the Life of Ivan Denisovich*. Tran. Ralph Parker. 1st ed. New York: Dutton, 1963.

—. *Nobel Lecture* 1970; (http://www.nobelprize.org/nobel_prizes/literature/laureates/1970/solzhenitsyn-lecture.html) (as of 5 October 2012).

—. "Interview with Two Western Correspondents." *Index on Censorship* 2.31 (1973): 31-45.

—. *Arkhipelag GULag: 1918-1956: Opyt Chudozhestvennogo Issledovaniia*. 2 Vol. Paris: YMCA-Press, 1973.

—. *The Gulag Archipelago, 1918-1956. An Experiment in Literary Investigation*. Tran. Thomas P. Whitney. 1 Vol. New York: Harper & Row, 1974.

—. "Massacre of the Bolsheviks." The Observer 13 January 1974: 21-2.

—. "My Arrest by Smersh." The Observer 20 January 1974: 21-2.

—. "Live Not by Lies." The Washington Post 18 February 1974: A1.

—. "Frauen Im Lager." Der Spiegel 28 October 1974: 128-46.

—. "Geleitwort zur ersten Ausgabe." Kontinent 1. 1974: p. 6.

—. *The Gulag Archipelago, 1918-1956: An Experiment in Literary Investigation*. Tran. Thomas P. Whitney. 2 Vol. London: Collins & Harvill, 1975.

—. "Ispanskoe Interv'lu." Kontinent 44 (1975): 429-40.

—. *Drei Reden an die Amerikaner*. 215 Vol. Darmstadt: Luchterhand, 1975. Sammlung Luchterhand.

—. "Intelligenzler." *Stimmen aus dem Untergrund. Zur geistigen Situation in der UdSSR.* Ed. Alexander Solschenizyn. Darmstadt: Luchterhand, 1975. 225-272.

—. "Reue und Selbstbeschraenkung als Kategorien des Nationalen Lebens." *Stimmen aus dem Untergrund. Zur geistigen Situation in der UdSSR.* Ed. Alexander Solschenizyn. Darmstadt: Luchterhand, 1975. 117-156.

—. "Schlesinger and Kissinger." The New York Times 1 December 1975: 31.

—. *Solzhenitsyn: The Voice of Freedom*. Washington: American Federation of Labor and Congress of Industrial Organizations, 1975.

—. *Warning to the Western World*. London: MW Books, 1976.

—. "Und die Wahrheit wird uns frei machen: Interview mit der BBC." Kontinent.11 (1979): 24-46.

—. "Misconceptions about Russia are a Threat to America." *Foreign Affairs* 58.4 (1980): 797-834.

—. *The Oak and the Calf: Sketches of Literary Life in the Soviet Union*. New York: Harper & Row, 1980.

—. "Wider die Pluralisten." Criticon Feburar 1984: 11-6.

—. "Our Pluralists." *Survey* 29.2 (125) (1985): 1-28.

—. *August Vierzehn*. Tran. Swetlana Geier. Munich: Piper, 1987.

—. *Kak Nam Obustroit' Rossiiu?* Paris: YMCA-Press, 1990.

—. *Invisible Allies*. Trans. Alexis Klimoff and Michael Nicholson. Washington, D.C.: Counterpoint, 1995.

—. *Rossiia v Obvale*. Moscow: Russkii put', 1998.

—. *Rußland im Absturz*. Vienna: Böhlau, 1999.

—. *Dvesti Let Vmeste: 1795-1995*. 1 Vol. Moscow: Russkii put', 2001.

—. *Dvesti Let Vmeste: 1795-1995*. 2 Vol. Moscow: Russkii put', 2002.

—. *Zweihundert Jahre zusammen: Die russisch-jüdische Geschichte 1795-1916*. Vol. 1. Munich: Herbig, 2002.

—. *Zweihundert Jahre zusammen: Die Juden in der Sowjetunion*. 2. ed. Vol. 2. Munich: Herbig, 2004.

—. *Meine Amerikanischen Jahre*. Munich: Langen Müller, 2007.

Sommer, Theo. "Russische Tragödie: Solschenizyn und die Entspannung." Die Zeit 11 January 1974.

Spann, Gustav. "Methoden der Rechtsextremer Tendenz-Geschichtsschreibung und Propaganda." *Wahrheit und "Auschwitzlüge".* Eds. Brigitte Bailer-Galanda, Wolfgang Benz, and Wolfgang Neugebauer. Vienna: Deuticke, 1995. 46-67.

Sperber, Manès. "Stacheldraht und Seele: Der Zweite Band von Alexander Solschenizyns 'Archipel GULag'." Frankfurter Allgemeine Zeitung 28 December 1974.

Spoerer, Mark, and Jochen Fleischhacker. "Forced Laborers in Nazi Germany: Categories, Numbers, and Survivors." *The Journal of Interdisciplinary History* 33.2 (2002): 169-204.

Staadt, Jochen; Tobias Voigt; Stefan Wolle. *Feindbild Springer.* Göttingen: Vandenhoeck & Ruprecht, 2009.

Städtke, Klaus. "Zwischenzeit. Anmerkung zu Solženicyns Roman *Der Erste Kreis der Hölle.*" *Eine Andere Welt? Kultur und Politik in Osteuropa 1945 bis heute: Festschrift für Wolfgang Eichwede.* Eds. Wolfgang Eichwede, et al. Stuttgart: ibidem-Verlag, 2007. 97-105.

Stanley, Alessandra. "Now on Moscow TV, Heeere's Aleksandr!" The New York Times 14 April 1995: 1.

Stein, Günter. "Nach Der Belagerung." Vorwärts 21 February 1974: 16.

Steiner, Dieter. "»Eine Familie von Flegeln...« Krach um Alexander Solschenizyns Roman »August 1914«." Stern 18 November 1971: 104-110.

Steele, Jonathan. "Solzhenitsyn's Advice to Kremlin." The Guardian 4 March 1974: 4.

—. "From the USSR: Solzhenitsyn Off the Press, Trotsky Under Wraps." The Guardian 6 May 1991: 11.

—. "Solzhenitsyn Slides into His Place in Russia's Pantheon." The Guardian 31 May 1994: 9.

Stöss, Richard. *Die „neue Rechte" in der Bundesrepublik.* Berlin: Friedich Ebert Stiftung, 2000.

Ströhm, Carl Gustav. "Im Visier der Deutschen Linken: Solschenizyn." Deutschland Magazin February, March 1974: 42-3.

Sulzberger, Cyrus L. "Détente and Dissidence." The New York Times 13 February 1974: 39.

Swayze, Harold. "Review: [Untitled]." *Slavic Review* 34.4 (1975): 825-827.

TASS. "Statement on Solzhenitsyn." The New York Times 3 January 1974.

Timmermann, Heinz. *Der 'Fall Solschenizyn' als Herausforderung and die Westkommunisten.* Cologne: Berichte des Bundesinstituts für Ostwissenschaftliche und Internationale Studien, 1974.

Thompson, Ewa M. "The Writer in Exile: The Good Years." *The Slavic and East European Journal* 33.4 (1989): 499-515.

—. Imperial Knowledge: Russian Literature and Colonialism. 99 Vol. Westport, Conn.: Greenwood Press, 2000.

Thornton, William H. "A Post-Modern Solzhenitsyn?" *Comparative Literature and Culture* 1.3 (1999).

Thurston, Robert W. "On Desk-Bound Parochialism, Commonsense Perspectives, and Lousy Evidence: A Reply to Robert Conquest." *Slavic Review* 45.2 (1986): 238-44.

Toker, Leona. "Toward a Poetics of Documentary Prose--from the Perspective of Gulag Testimonies." *Poetics Today* 18.2 (1997): 187-222.

—. *Return from the Archipelago: Narratives of Gulag Survivors*. Bloomington: Indiana University Press, 2000.

—. "Target Audience, Hurdle Audience, and the General Reader: Varlam Shalamov's Art of Testimony." *Poetics Today* 26.2 (2005): 281-303.

Tolczyk, Dariusz "Who is Ivan Denisovich? Ethical Challenge and Narrative Ambiguity in Solzhenitsyn's Text." *One Day in the Life of Ivan Denisovich: a Critical Companion*. Ed. Alexis Klimoff. Evanston: Northwestern University Press. 1997. pp. 70-84. Northwestern/AATSEEL Critical Companions to Russian Literature.

—. *See no Evil: Literary Cover-Ups and Discoveries of the Soviet Camp Experience*. New Haven: Yale University Press, 1999. Russian Literature and Thought.

Topping, Seymour. "Easing of Curbs on Soviet Literature is Attributed to Order by Khrushchev." The New York Times 29 November 1962.

Trueheart, Charles. "Solzhenitsyn and His Message of Silence; the Exile, Writing, Warning and Waiting at His Secluded Estate." The Washington Post 24 November 1987.

Tüpper-Fotiadis, Rita Anna. "'Nicht mit der Lüge leben'." Die politische Meinung September 2008: 64-8.

Turner, Graeme. *Understanding Celebrity*. London; Thousand Oaks: Sage, 2004.

Turner, Wallace. "Couple Who Helped Solzhentisyn Publish in U.S Charge Him with Libel." The New York Times 25 October 1980: 11.

Tvardovsky, Alexander. "Vmesto Predisloviia." *Novyi Mir.*11 (1962): 8-9.

Ulam, Adam Bruno. *Ideologies and Illusions: Revolutionary Thought from Herzen to Solzhenitsyn*. Cambridge: Harvard University Press, 1976.

vanden Heuvel, Katrina. "No Free Speech at Radio Liberty." Nation 7 December 1985: 612-615.

Venclova, Tomas. "War and Pieces." The New Republic 28 August 1989: 33-7.

Vice, Sue. *Holocaust Fiction*. London: Routledge, 2000.

Viola, Lynne. "The Other Archipelago: Kulak Deportations to the North in 1930." *Slavic Review* 60.4 (2001): 730-755.

Voinovich, Vladimir. *Moskva 2042*. Ann Arbor: Ardis, 1987.

Volkov, Solomon. *The Magical Chorus: A History of Russian Culture from Tolstoy to Solzhenitsyn*. Tran. Antonina W. Bouis. 1. ed. ed. New York: Alfred A. Knopf, 2008.

Wachtel, Andrew Baruch. *An Obsession with History: Russian Writers Confront the Past*. Stanford: Stanford University Press, 1994.

—. "Writers and Society in Eastern Europe, 1989-2000: The End of the Golden Age." *East European Politics & Societies* 17.4 (2003): 583-621.

—. *Remaining Relevant After Communism: The Role of the Writer in Eastern Europe*. Chicago: University of Chicago Press, 2006.

Wachtel, Andrew, and Ilya Vinitsky. *Russian Literature*. Cambridge England; Malden, MA: Polity, 2009. Cultural History of Literature.

Wakamiya, Lisa Ryoko. *Locating Exiled Writers in Contemporary Russian Literature*. Basingstoke: Palgrave Macmillan, 2009.

Walker, Barbara. "On Reading Soviet Memoirs: A History of the 'Contemporaries' Genre as an Institution of Russian Intelligentsia Culture from the 1790s to the 1970s." *Russian Review* 59.3 (2000): 327-352.

Walker, Martin. "The Exile Comes Full Circle." The Guardian 8 October 1990.

Weiner, Amir. "Nature, Nurture, and Memory in a Socialist Utopia: Delineating the Soviet Socio-Ethnic Body in the Age of Socialism." *The American Historical Review* 104.4 (1999): 1114-55.

Wheatcroft, Stephen G. "The Scale and Nature of German and Soviet Repression and Mass Killings, 1930-45." *Europe-Asia Studies* 48 .8 (1996): 1319-1353.

—. "Victims of Stalinism and the Soviet Secret Police: The Comparability and Reliability of the Archival Data. Not the Last Word." *Europe-Asia Studies* 51.2 (1999): 315-345.

Wheatcroft, Stephen G. *Challenging Traditional Views of Russian History. Studies in Russian and East European History and Society*. Basingstoke: Palgrave Macmillan, 2002.

White, Brian. "The Concept of Detente." *Review of International Studies* 7.3 (1981): 165-171.

White, Hayden. "Figural Realism in Witness Literature." *Parallax* 10.1 (2004): 113-24.

Wiesel, Elie. "Art and Culture After the Holocaust." *Cross Currents* 26.3 (1976): 258-69.

Wilson, David B. "The West is Flabby, but..." The Boston Globe 16 July 1978: 7.

Winchester, Simon. "Solzhenitsyn Snubs Ford." The Guardian 23 July 1975: 4.

Wippermann, Wolfgang. *Wessen Schuld? Vom Historikerstreit zur Golhagen-Kontroverse*. Berlin: Elephanten Press, 1997.

—. *Heilige Hetzjagd eine Ideologiegeschichte des Antikommunismus*. 1st ed. Berlin: Rotbuch-Verlag, 2012.

Witte, Georg. *Appell, Spiel, Ritual Textpraktiken in der russischen Literatur der sechziger bis achtziger Jahre*. Wiesbaden: Harrassowitz, 1989. Opera Slavica.

Wolitz, Seth. "Solzhenitsyn and Anti-Semitism: A Test." The New York Times, sec. Letters: 30. 4 December 1985.

Yakovlev, Nikolai. *Solzhenitsyn's Archipelago of Lies*. Moscow: Novosti, 1974.

Young, Cathy. "Guantánamo is not the Gulag." The New York Times 10 June 2005.

Zayas, Alfred M. de. "Prussian Nights." *The Review of Politics* 40.1 (1978): 154-6.

Zehm, Günter. "Was nach der Brautnacht kommt: Die Diskussion um Solschenizyn spaltet Deutschlands Literaten." Die Welt 6 February 1974: 4.

Zinik, Zinovy. "Blue-Collar Solzhenitsyn." The Times Literary Supplement 6 August 2008.

Zorza, Victor. "Story of the Stalinist Terror." The Guardian 31 January 1963: 8.

SOVIET AND POST-SOVIET POLITICS AND SOCIETY

Edited by Dr. Andreas Umland

ISSN 1614-3515

1 *Андреас Умланд (ред.)*
Воплощение Европейской конвенции по правам человека в России
Философские, юридические и эмпирические исследования
ISBN 3-89821-387-0

2 *Christian Wipperfürth*
Russland – ein vertrauenswürdiger Partner?
Grundlagen, Hintergründe und Praxis gegenwärtiger russischer Außenpolitik
Mit einem Vorwort von Heinz Timmermann
ISBN 3-89821-401-X

3 *Manja Hussner*
Die Übernahme internationalen Rechts in die russische und deutsche Rechtsordnung
Eine vergleichende Analyse zur Völkerrechtsfreundlichkeit der Verfassungen der Russländischen Föderation und der Bundesrepublik Deutschland
Mit einem Vorwort von Rainer Arnold
ISBN 3-89821-438-9

4 *Matthew Tejada*
Bulgaria's Democratic Consolidation and the Kozloduy Nuclear Power Plant (KNPP)
The Unattainability of Closure
With a foreword by Richard J. Crampton
ISBN 3-89821-439-7

5 *Марк Григорьевич Меерович*
Квадратные метры, определяющие сознание
Государственная жилищная политика в СССР. 1921 – 1941 гг
ISBN 3-89821-474-5

6 *Andrei P. Tsygankov, Pavel A.Tsygankov (Eds.)*
New Directions in Russian International Studies
ISBN 3-89821-422-2

7 *Марк Григорьевич Меерович*
Как власть народ к труду приучала
Жилище в СССР – средство управления людьми. 1917 – 1941 гг.
С предисловием Елены Осокиной
ISBN 3-89821-495-8

8 *David J. Galbreath*
Nation-Building and Minority Politics in Post-Socialist States
Interests, Influence and Identities in Estonia and Latvia
With a foreword by David J. Smith
ISBN 3-89821-467-2

9 *Алексей Юрьевич Безугольный*
Народы Кавказа в Вооруженных силах СССР в годы Великой Отечественной войны 1941-1945 гг.
С предисловием Николая Бугая
ISBN 3-89821-475-3

10 *Вячеслав Лихачев и Владимир Прибыловский (ред.)*
Русское Национальное Единство, 1990-2000. В 2-х томах
ISBN 3-89821-523-7

11 *Николай Бугай (ред.)*
Народы стран Балтии в условиях сталинизма (1940-е – 1950-е годы)
Документированная история
ISBN 3-89821-525-3

12 *Ingmar Bredies (Hrsg.)*
Zur Anatomie der Orange Revolution in der Ukraine
Wechsel des Elitenregimes oder Triumph des Parlamentarismus?
ISBN 3-89821-524-5

13 *Anastasia V. Mitrofanova*
The Politicization of Russian Orthodoxy
Actors and Ideas
With a foreword by William C. Gay
ISBN 3-89821-481-8

14 *Nathan D. Larson*
Alexander Solzhenitsyn and the Russo-Jewish Question
ISBN 3-89821-483-4

15 *Guido Houben*
Kulturpolitik und Ethnizität
Staatliche Kunstförderung im Russland der neunziger Jahre
Mit einem Vorwort von Gert Weisskirchen
ISBN 3-89821-542-3

16 *Leonid Luks*
Der russische „Sonderweg"?
Aufsätze zur neuesten Geschichte Russlands im europäischen Kontext
ISBN 3-89821-496-6

17 *Евгений Мороз*
История «Мёртвой воды» – от страшной сказки к большой политике
Политическое неоязычество в постсоветской России
ISBN 3-89821-551-2

18 *Александр Верховский и Галина Кожевникова (ред.)*
Этническая и религиозная интолерантность в российских СМИ
Результаты мониторинга 2001-2004 гг.
ISBN 3-89821-569-5

19 *Christian Ganzer*
Sowjetisches Erbe und ukrainische Nation
Das Museum der Geschichte des Zaporoger Kosakentums auf der Insel Chortycja
Mit einem Vorwort von Frank Golczewski
ISBN 3-89821-504-0

20 *Эльза-Баир Гучинова*
Помнить нельзя забыть
Антропология депортационной травмы калмыков
С предисловием Кэролайн Хамфри
ISBN 3-89821-506-7

21 *Юлия Лидерман*
Мотивы «проверки» и «испытания» в постсоветской культуре
Советское прошлое в российском кинематографе 1990-х годов
С предисловием Евгения Марголита
ISBN 3-89821-511-3

22 *Tanya Lokshina, Ray Thomas, Mary Mayer (Eds.)*
The Imposition of a Fake Political Settlement in the Northern Caucasus
The 2003 Chechen Presidential Election
ISBN 3-89821-436-2

23 *Timothy McCajor Hall, Rosie Read (Eds.)*
Changes in the Heart of Europe
Recent Ethnographies of Czechs, Slovaks, Roma, and Sorbs
With an afterword by Zdeněk Salzmann
ISBN 3-89821-606-3

24 *Christian Autengruber*
Die politischen Parteien in Bulgarien und Rumänien
Eine vergleichende Analyse seit Beginn der 90er Jahre
Mit einem Vorwort von Dorothée de Nève
ISBN 3-89821-476-1

25 *Annette Freyberg-Inan with Radu Cristescu*
The Ghosts in Our Classrooms, or: John Dewey Meets Ceauşescu
The Promise and the Failures of Civic Education in Romania
ISBN 3-89821-416-8

26 *John B. Dunlop*
The 2002 Dubrovka and 2004 Beslan Hostage Crises
A Critique of Russian Counter-Terrorism
With a foreword by Donald N. Jensen
ISBN 3-89821-608-X

27 *Peter Koller*
Das touristische Potenzial von Kam''janec'–Podil's'kyj
Eine fremdenverkehrsgeographische Untersuchung der Zukunftsperspektiven und Maßnahmenplanung zur Destinationsentwicklung des „ukrainischen Rothenburg"
Mit einem Vorwort von Kristiane Klemm
ISBN 3-89821-640-3

28 *Françoise Daucé, Elisabeth Sieca-Kozlowski (Eds.)*
Dedovshchina in the Post-Soviet Military
Hazing of Russian Army Conscripts in a Comparative Perspective
With a foreword by Dale Herspring
ISBN 3-89821-616-0

29 *Florian Strasser*
Zivilgesellschaftliche Einflüsse auf die Orange Revolution
Die gewaltlose Massenbewegung und die ukrainische Wahlkrise 2004
Mit einem Vorwort von Egbert Jahn
ISBN 3-89821-648-9

30 *Rebecca S. Katz*
The Georgian Regime Crisis of 2003-2004
A Case Study in Post-Soviet Media Representation of Politics, Crime and Corruption
ISBN 3-89821-413-3

31 *Vladimir Kantor*
Willkür oder Freiheit
Beiträge zur russischen Geschichtsphilosophie
Ediert von Dagmar Herrmann sowie mit einem Vorwort versehen von Leonid Luks
ISBN 3-89821-589-X

32 *Laura A. Victoir*
The Russian Land Estate Today
A Case Study of Cultural Politics in Post-Soviet Russia
With a foreword by Priscilla Roosevelt
ISBN 3-89821-426-5

33 *Ivan Katchanovski*
Cleft Countries
Regional Political Divisions and Cultures in Post-Soviet Ukraine and Moldova
With a foreword by Francis Fukuyama
ISBN 3-89821-558-X

34 *Florian Mühlfried*
Postsowjetische Feiern
Das Georgische Bankett im Wandel
Mit einem Vorwort von Kevin Tuite
ISBN 3-89821-601-2

35 *Roger Griffin, Werner Loh, Andreas Umland (Eds.)*
Fascism Past and Present, West and East
An International Debate on Concepts and Cases in the Comparative Study of the Extreme Right
With an afterword by Walter Laqueur
ISBN 3-89821-674-8

36 *Sebastian Schlegel*
Der „Weiße Archipel"
Sowjetische Atomstädte 1945-1991
Mit einem Geleitwort von Thomas Bohn
ISBN 3-89821-679-9

37 *Vyacheslav Likhachev*
Political Anti-Semitism in Post-Soviet Russia
Actors and Ideas in 1991-2003
Edited and translated from Russian by Eugene Veklerov
ISBN 3-89821-529-6

38 *Josette Baer (Ed.)*
Preparing Liberty in Central Europe
Political Texts from the Spring of Nations 1848 to the Spring of Prague 1968
With a foreword by Zdeněk V. David
ISBN 3-89821-546-6

39 *Михаил Лукьянов*
Российский консерватизм и реформа, 1907-1914
С предисловием Марка Д. Стейнберга
ISBN 3-89821-503-2

40 *Nicola Melloni*
Market Without Economy
The 1998 Russian Financial Crisis
With a foreword by Eiji Furukawa
ISBN 3-89821-407-9

41 *Dmitrij Chmelnizki*
Die Architektur Stalins
Bd. 1: Studien zu Ideologie und Stil
Bd. 2: Bilddokumentation
Mit einem Vorwort von Bruno Flierl
ISBN 3-89821-515-6

42 *Katja Yafimava*
Post-Soviet Russian-Belarussian Relationships
The Role of Gas Transit Pipelines
With a foreword by Jonathan P. Stern
ISBN 3-89821-655-1

43 *Boris Chavkin*
Verflechtungen der deutschen und russischen Zeitgeschichte
Aufsätze und Archivfunde zu den Beziehungen Deutschlands und der Sowjetunion von 1917 bis 1991
Ediert von Markus Edlinger sowie mit einem Vorwort versehen von Leonid Luks
ISBN 3-89821-756-6

44 *Anastasija Grynenko in Zusammenarbeit mit Claudia Dathe*
Die Terminologie des Gerichtswesens der Ukraine und Deutschlands im Vergleich
Eine übersetzungswissenschaftliche Analyse juristischer Fachbegriffe im Deutschen, Ukrainischen und Russischen
Mit einem Vorwort von Ulrich Hartmann
ISBN 3-89821-691-8

45 *Anton Burkov*
The Impact of the European Convention on Human Rights on Russian Law
Legislation and Application in 1996-2006
With a foreword by Françoise Hampson
ISBN 978-3-89821-639-5

46 *Stina Torjesen, Indra Overland (Eds.)*
International Election Observers in Post-Soviet Azerbaijan
Geopolitical Pawns or Agents of Change?
ISBN 978-3-89821-743-9

47 *Taras Kuzio*
Ukraine – Crimea – Russia
Triangle of Conflict
ISBN 978-3-89821-761-3

48 *Claudia Šabić*
"Ich erinnere mich nicht, aber L'viv!"
Zur Funktion kultureller Faktoren für die Institutionalisierung und Entwicklung einer ukrainischen Region
Mit einem Vorwort von Melanie Tatur
ISBN 978-3-89821-752-1

49 *Marlies Bilz*
Tatarstan in der Transformation
Nationaler Diskurs und Politische Praxis 1988-1994
Mit einem Vorwort von Frank Golczewski
ISBN 978-3-89821-722-4

50 *Марлен Ларюэль (ред.)*
Современные интерпретации русского национализма
ISBN 978-3-89821-795-8

51 *Sonja Schüler*
Die ethnische Dimension der Armut
Roma im postsozialistischen Rumänien
Mit einem Vorwort von Anton Sterbling
ISBN 978-3-89821-776-7

52 *Галина Кожевникова*
Радикальный национализм в России и противодействие ему
Сборник докладов Центра «Сова» за 2004-2007 гг.
С предисловием Александра Верховского
ISBN 978-3-89821-721-7

53 *Галина Кожевникова и Владимир Прибыловский*
Российская власть в биографиях I
Высшие должностные лица РФ в 2004 г.
ISBN 978-3-89821-796-5

54 *Галина Кожевникова и Владимир Прибыловский*
Российская власть в биографиях II
Члены Правительства РФ в 2004 г.
ISBN 978-3-89821-797-2

55 *Галина Кожевникова и Владимир Прибыловский*
Российская власть в биографиях III
Руководители федеральных служб и агентств РФ в 2004 г.
ISBN 978-3-89821-798-9

56 *Ileana Petroniu*
Privatisierung in Transformationsökonomien
Determinanten der Restrukturierungs-Bereitschaft am Beispiel Polens, Rumäniens und der Ukraine
Mit einem Vorwort von Rainer W. Schäfer
ISBN 978-3-89821-790-3

57 *Christian Wipperfürth*
Russland und seine GUS-Nachbarn
Hintergründe, aktuelle Entwicklungen und Konflikte in einer ressourcenreichen Region
ISBN 978-3-89821-801-6

58 *Togzhan Kassenova*
From Antagonism to Partnership
The Uneasy Path of the U.S.-Russian Cooperative Threat Reduction
With a foreword by Christoph Bluth
ISBN 978-3-89821-707-1

59 *Alexander Höllwerth*
Das sakrale eurasische Imperium des Aleksandr Dugin
Eine Diskursanalyse zum postsowjetischen russischen Rechtsextremismus
Mit einem Vorwort von Dirk Uffelmann
ISBN 978-3-89821-813-9

60 *Олег Рябов*
«Россия-Матушка»
Национализм, гендер и война в России XX века
С предисловием Елены Гощило
ISBN 978-3-89821-487-2

61 *Ivan Maistrenko*
Borot'bism
A Chapter in the History of the Ukrainian Revolution
With a new introduction by Chris Ford
Translated by George S. N. Luckyj with the assistance of Ivan L. Rudnytsky
ISBN 978-3-89821-697-5

62 *Maryna Romanets*
Anamorphosic Texts and Reconfigured Visions
Improvised Traditions in Contemporary Ukrainian and Irish Literature
ISBN 978-3-89821-576-3

63 *Paul D'Anieri and Taras Kuzio (Eds.)*
Aspects of the Orange Revolution I
Democratization and Elections in Post-Communist Ukraine
ISBN 978-3-89821-698-2

64 *Bohdan Harasymiw in collaboration with Oleh S. Ilnytzkyj (Eds.)*
Aspects of the Orange Revolution II
Information and Manipulation Strategies in the 2004 Ukrainian Presidential Elections
ISBN 978-3-89821-699-9

65 *Ingmar Bredies, Andreas Umland and Valentin Yakushik (Eds.)*
Aspects of the Orange Revolution III
The Context and Dynamics of the 2004 Ukrainian Presidential Elections
ISBN 978-3-89821-803-0

66 *Ingmar Bredies, Andreas Umland and Valentin Yakushik (Eds.)*
Aspects of the Orange Revolution IV
Foreign Assistance and Civic Action in the 2004 Ukrainian Presidential Elections
ISBN 978-3-89821-808-5

67 *Ingmar Bredies, Andreas Umland and Valentin Yakushik (Eds.)*
Aspects of the Orange Revolution V
Institutional Observation Reports on the 2004 Ukrainian Presidential Elections
ISBN 978-3-89821-809-2

68 *Taras Kuzio (Ed.)*
Aspects of the Orange Revolution VI
Post-Communist Democratic Revolutions in Comparative Perspective
ISBN 978-3-89821-820-7

69 *Tim Bohse*
Autoritarismus statt Selbstverwaltung
Die Transformation der kommunalen Politik in der Stadt Kaliningrad 1990-2005
Mit einem Geleitwort von Stefan Troebst
ISBN 978-3-89821-782-8

70 *David Rupp*
Die Rußländische Föderation und die russischsprachige Minderheit in Lettland
Eine Fallstudie zur Anwaltspolitik Moskaus gegenüber den russophonen Minderheiten im „Nahen Ausland“ von 1991 bis 2002
Mit einem Vorwort von Helmut Wagner
ISBN 978-3-89821-778-1

71 *Taras Kuzio*
Theoretical and Comparative Perspectives on Nationalism
New Directions in Cross-Cultural and Post-Communist Studies
With a foreword by Paul Robert Magocsi
ISBN 978-3-89821-815-3

72 *Christine Teichmann*
Die Hochschultransformation im heutigen Osteuropa
Kontinuität und Wandel bei der Entwicklung des postkommunistischen Universitätswesens
Mit einem Vorwort von Oskar Anweiler
ISBN 978-3-89821-842-9

73 *Julia Kusznir*
Der politische Einfluss von Wirtschaftseliten in russischen Regionen
Eine Analyse am Beispiel der Erdöl- und Erdgasindustrie, 1992-2005
Mit einem Vorwort von Wolfgang Eichwede
ISBN 978-3-89821-821-4

74 *Alena Vysotskaya*
Russland, Belarus und die EU-Osterweiterung
Zur Minderheitenfrage und zum Problem der Freizügigkeit des Personenverkehrs
Mit einem Vorwort von Katlijn Malfliet
ISBN 978-3-89821-822-1

75 *Heiko Pleines (Hrsg.)*
Corporate Governance in post-sozialistischen Volkswirtschaften
ISBN 978-3-89821-766-8

76 *Stefan Ihrig*
Wer sind die Moldawier?
Rumänismus versus Moldowanismus in Historiographie und Schulbüchern der Republik Moldova, 1991-2006
Mit einem Vorwort von Holm Sundhaussen
ISBN 978-3-89821-466-7

77 *Galina Kozhevnikova in collaboration with Alexander Verkhovsky and Eugene Veklerov*
Ultra-Nationalism and Hate Crimes in Contemporary Russia
The 2004-2006 Annual Reports of Moscow's SOVA Center
With a foreword by Stephen D. Shenfield
ISBN 978-3-89821-868-9

78 *Florian Küchler*
The Role of the European Union in Moldova's Transnistria Conflict
With a foreword by Christopher Hill
ISBN 978-3-89821-850-4

79 *Bernd Rechel*
The Long Way Back to Europe
Minority Protection in Bulgaria
With a foreword by Richard Crampton
ISBN 978-3-89821-863-4

80 *Peter W. Rodgers*
Nation, Region and History in Post-Communist Transitions
Identity Politics in Ukraine, 1991-2006
With a foreword by Vera Tolz
ISBN 978-3-89821-903-7

81 *Stephanie Solywoda*
The Life and Work of Semen L. Frank
A Study of Russian Religious Philosophy
With a foreword by Philip Walters
ISBN 978-3-89821-457-5

82 *Vera Sokolova*
Cultural Politics of Ethnicity
Discourses on Roma in Communist Czechoslovakia
ISBN 978-3-89821-864-1

83 *Natalya Shevchik Ketenci*
Kazakhstani Enterprises in Transition
The Role of Historical Regional Development in Kazakhstan's Post-Soviet Economic Transformation
ISBN 978-3-89821-831-3

84 *Martin Malek, Anna Schor-Tschudnowskaja (Hrsg.)*
Europa im Tschetschenienkrieg
Zwischen politischer Ohnmacht und Gleichgültigkeit
Mit einem Vorwort von Lipchan Basajewa
ISBN 978-3-89821-676-0

85 *Stefan Meister*
Das postsowjetische Universitätswesen zwischen nationalem und internationalem Wandel
Die Entwicklung der regionalen Hochschule in Russland als Gradmesser der Systemtransformation
Mit einem Vorwort von Joan DeBardeleben
ISBN 978-3-89821-891-7

86 *Konstantin Sheiko in collaboration with Stephen Brown*
Nationalist Imaginings of the Russian Past
Anatolii Fomenko and the Rise of Alternative History in Post-Communist Russia
With a foreword by Donald Ostrowski
ISBN 978-3-89821-915-0

87 *Sabine Jenni*
Wie stark ist das „Einige Russland"?
Zur Parteibindung der Eliten und zum Wahlerfolg der Machtpartei im Dezember 2007
Mit einem Vorwort von Klaus Armingeon
ISBN 978-3-89821-961-7

88 *Thomas Borén*
Meeting-Places of Transformation
Urban Identity, Spatial Representations and Local Politics in Post-Soviet St Petersburg
ISBN 978-3-89821-739-2

89 *Aygul Ashirova*
Stalinismus und Stalin-Kult in Zentralasien
Turkmenistan 1924-1953
Mit einem Vorwort von Leonid Luks
ISBN 978-3-89821-987-7

90 *Leonid Luks*
Freiheit oder imperiale Größe?
Essays zu einem russischen Dilemma
ISBN 978-3-8382-0011-8

91 *Christopher Gilley*
The 'Change of Signposts' in the Ukrainian Emigration
A Contribution to the History of Sovietophilism in the 1920s
With a foreword by Frank Golczewski
ISBN 978-3-89821-965-5

92 *Philipp Casula, Jeronim Perovic (Eds.)*
Identities and Politics During the Putin Presidency
The Discursive Foundations of Russia's Stability
With a foreword by Heiko Haumann
ISBN 978-3-8382-0015-6

93 *Marcel Viëtor*
Europa und die Frage nach seinen Grenzen im Osten
Zur Konstruktion ‚europäischer Identität' in Geschichte und Gegenwart
Mit einem Vorwort von Albrecht Lehmann
ISBN 978-3-8382-0045-3

94 *Ben Hellman, Andrei Rogachevskii*
Filming the Unfilmable
Casper Wrede's 'One Day in the Life of Ivan Denisovich'
Second, Revised and Expanded Edition
ISBN 978-3-8382-0594-6

95 *Eva Fuchslocher*
Vaterland, Sprache, Glaube
Orthodoxie und Nationenbildung am Beispiel Georgiens
Mit einem Vorwort von Christina von Braun
ISBN 978-3-89821-884-9

96 *Vladimir Kantor*
Das Westlertum und der Weg Russlands
Zur Entwicklung der russischen Literatur und Philosophie
Ediert von Dagmar Herrmann
Mit einem Beitrag von Nikolaus Lobkowicz
ISBN 978-3-8382-0102-3

97 *Kamran Musayev*
Die postsowjetische Transformation im Baltikum und Südkaukasus
Eine vergleichende Untersuchung der politischen Entwicklung Lettlands und Aserbaidschans 1985-2009
Mit einem Vorwort von Leonid Luks
Ediert von Sandro Henschel
ISBN 978-3-8382-0103-0

98 *Tatiana Zhurzhenko*
Borderlands into Bordered Lands
Geopolitics of Identity in Post-Soviet Ukraine
With a foreword by Dieter Segert
ISBN 978-3-8382-0042-2

99 *Кирилл Галушко, Лидия Смола (ред.)*
Пределы падения – варианты украинского будущего
Аналитико-прогностические исследования
ISBN 978-3-8382-0148-1

100 *Michael Minkenberg (ed.)*
Historical Legacies and the Radical Right in Post-Cold War Central and Eastern Europe
With an afterword by Sabrina P. Ramet
ISBN 978-3-8382-0124-5

101 *David-Emil Wickström*
Rocking St. Petersburg
Transcultural Flows and Identity Politics in Post-Soviet Popular Music
With a foreword by Yngvar B. Steinholt
Second, Revised and Expanded Edition
ISBN 978-3-8382-0600-4

102 *Eva Zabka*
Eine neue „Zeit der Wirren"?
Der spät- und postsowjetische Systemwandel 1985-2000 im Spiegel russischer gesellschaftspolitischer Diskurse
Mit einem Vorwort von Margareta Mommsen
ISBN 978-3-8382-0161-0

103 *Ulrike Ziemer*
Ethnic Belonging, Gender and Cultural Practices
Youth Identitites in Contemporary Russia
With a foreword by Anoop Nayak
ISBN 978-3-8382-0152-8

104 *Ksenia Chepikova*
‚Einiges Russland' - eine zweite KPdSU?
Aspekte der Identitätskonstruktion einer postsowjetischen „Partei der Macht"
Mit einem Vorwort von Torsten Oppelland
ISBN 978-3-8382-0311-9

105 *Леонид Люкс*
Западничество или евразийство? Демократия или идеократия?
Сборник статей об исторических дилеммах России
С предисловием Владимира Кантора
ISBN 978-3-8382-0211-2

106 *Anna Dost*
Das russische Verfassungsrecht auf dem Weg zum Föderalismus und zurück
Zum Konflikt von Rechtsnormen und -wirklichkeit in der Russländischen Föderation von 1991 bis 2009
Mit einem Vorwort von Alexander Blankenagel
ISBN 978-3-8382-0292-1

107 *Philipp Herzog*
Sozialistische Völkerfreundschaft, nationaler Widerstand oder harmloser Zeitvertreib?
Zur politischen Funktion der Volkskunst im sowjetischen Estland
Mit einem Vorwort von Andreas Kappeler
ISBN 978-3-8382-0216-7

108 *Marlène Laruelle (ed.)*
Russian Nationalism, Foreign Policy, and Identity Debates in Putin's Russia
New Ideological Patterns after the Orange Revolution
ISBN 978-3-8382-0325-6

109 *Michail Logvinov*
Russlands Kampf gegen den internationalen Terrorismus
Eine kritische Bestandsaufnahme des Bekämpfungsansatzes
Mit einem Geleitwort von Hans-Henning Schröder und einem Vorwort von Eckhard Jesse
ISBN 978-3-8382-0329-4

110 *John B. Dunlop*
The Moscow Bombings of September 1999
Examinations of Russian Terrorist Attacks at the Onset of Vladimir Putin's Rule
Second, Revised and Expanded Edition
ISBN 978-3-8382-0608-0

111 *Андрей А. Ковалёв*
Свидетельство из-за кулис российской политики I
Можно ли делать добро из зла? (Воспоминания и размышления о последних советских и первых послесоветских годах)
With a foreword by Peter Reddaway
ISBN 978-3-8382-0302-7

112 *Андрей А. Ковалёв*
Свидетельство из-за кулис российской политики II
Угроза для себя и окружающих (Наблюдения и предостережения относительно происходящего после 2000 г.)
ISBN 978-3-8382-0303-4

113 *Bernd Kappenberg*
Zeichen setzen für Europa
Der Gebrauch europäischer lateinischer Sonderzeichen in der deutschen Öffentlichkeit
Mit einem Vorwort von Peter Schlobinski
ISBN 978-3-89821-749-1

114 *Ivo Mijnssen*
The Quest for an Ideal Youth in Putin's Russia I
Back to Our Future! History, Modernity, and Patriotism according to *Nashi,* 2005-2013
With a foreword by Jeronim Perović
Second, Revised and Expanded Edition
ISBN 978-3-8382-0578-6

115 *Jussi Lassila*
The Quest for an Ideal Youth in Putin's Russia II
The Search for Distinctive Conformism in the Political Communication of *Nashi,* 2005-2009
With a foreword by Kirill Postoutenko
Second, Revised and Expanded Edition
ISBN 978-3-8382-0585-4

116 *Valerio Trabandt*
Neue Nachbarn, gute Nachbarschaft?
Die EU als internationaler Akteur am Beispiel ihrer Demokratieförderung in Belarus und der Ukraine 2004-2009
Mit einem Vorwort von Jutta Joachim
ISBN 978-3-8382-0437-6

117 *Fabian Pfeiffer*
Estlands Außen- und Sicherheitspolitik I
Der estnische Atlantizismus nach der wiedererlangten Unabhängigkeit 1991-2004
Mit einem Vorwort von Helmut Hubel
ISBN 978-3-8382-0127-6

118 *Jana Podßuweit*
Estlands Außen- und Sicherheitspolitik II
Handlungsoptionen eines Kleinstaates im Rahmen seiner EU-Mitgliedschaft (2004-2008)
Mit einem Vorwort von Helmut Hubel
ISBN 978-3-8382-0440-6

119 *Karin Pointner*
Estlands Außen- und Sicherheitspolitik III
Eine gedächtnispolitische Analyse estnischer Entwicklungskooperation 2006-2010
Mit einem Vorwort von Karin Liebhart
ISBN 978-3-8382-0435-2

120 *Ruslana Vovk*
Die Offenheit der ukrainischen Verfassung für das Völkerrecht und die europäische Integration
Mit einem Vorwort von Alexander Blankenagel
ISBN 978-3-8382-0481-9

121 *Mykhaylo Banakh*
Die Relevanz der Zivilgesellschaft bei den postkommunistischen Transformationsprozessen in mittel- und osteuropäischen Ländern
Das Beispiel der spät- und postsowjetischen Ukraine 1986-2009
Mit einem Vorwort von Gerhard Simon
ISBN 978-3-8382-0499-4

122 *Michael Moser*
Language Policy and the Discourse on Languages in Ukraine under President Viktor Yanukovych (25 February 2010–28 October 2012)
ISBN 978-3-8382-0497-0 (Paperback edition)
ISBN 978-3-8382-0507-6 (Hardcover edition)

123 *Nicole Krome*
Russischer Netzwerkkapitalismus
Restrukturierungsprozesse in der Russischen Föderation am Beispiel des Luftfahrtunternehmens "Aviastar"
Mit einem Vorwort von Petra Stykow
ISBN 978-3-8382-0534-2

124 *David R. Marples*
'Our Glorious Past'
Lukashenka's Belarus and the Great Patriotic War
ISBN 978-3-8382-0674-5 (Paperback edition)
ISBN 978-3-8382-0675-2 (Hardcover edition)

125 *Ulf Walther*
Russlands "neuer Adel"
Die Macht des Geheimdienstes von Gorbatschow bis Putin
Mit einem Vorwort von Hans-Georg Wieck
ISBN 978-3-8382-0584-7

126 *Simon Geissbühler (Hrsg.)*
Kiew – Revolution 3.0
Der Euromaidan 2013/14 und die Zukunftsperspektiven der Ukraine
ISBN 978-3-8382-0581-6 (Paperback edition)
ISBN 978-3-8382-0681-3 (Hardcover edition)

127 *Andrey Makarychev*
Russia and the EU in a Multipolar World
Discourses, Identities, Norms
ISBN 978-3-8382-0529-8

128 *Roland Scharff*
Kasachstan als postsowjetischer Wohlfahrtsstaat
Die Transformation des sozialen Schutzsystems
Mit einem Vorwort von Joachim Ahrens
ISBN 978-3-8382-0622-6

129 *Katja Grupp*
Bild Lücke Deutschland
Kaliningrader Studierende sprechen über Deutschland
Mit einem Vorwort von Martin Schulz
ISBN 978-3-8382-0552-6

130 *Konstantin Sheiko, Stephen Brown*
History as Therapy
Alternative History and Nationalist Imaginings in Russia, 1991-2014
ISBN 978-3-8382-0565-6

131 *Elisa Kriza*
Alexander Solzhenitsyn: Cold War Icon, Gulag Author, Russian Nationalist?
A Study of the Western Reception of his Literary Writings, Historical Interpretations, and Political Ideas
With a foreword by Andrei Rogatchevski
ISBN 978-3-8382-0689-9 (Paperback edition)
ISBN 978-3-8382-0690-5 (Hardcover edition)

132 *Serghei Golunov*
Elephant in the Room
Corruption and Cheating in Russian Universities
ISBN 978-3-8382-0670-7

133 *Manja Hussner, Rainer Arnold (Hrsg.)*
Verfassungsgerichtsbarkeit in Zentralasien I
Sammlung von Verfassungstexten
ISBN 978-3-8382-0595-3

ibidem-Verlag / *ibidem* Press
Melchiorstr. 15
70439 Stuttgart
Germany

ibidem@ibidem.eu
www.ibidem-verlag.com
www.ibidem.eu